A Divided Republic: Nation, S
in Contemporary France

This book is an original and sophisticated historical interpretation of contemporary French political culture. Until now, there have been few attempts to understand the political consequences of the profound geopolitical, intellectual and economic changes that France has undergone since the 1970s. However, Emile Chabal's detailed study shows how passionate debates over citizenship, immigration, colonial memory, the reform of the state and the historiography of modern France have galvanised the French elite and created new spaces for discussion and disagreement. Many of these debates have coalesced around two political languages – republicanism and liberalism – both of which structure the historical imagination and the symbolic vocabulary of French political actors. The tension between these two political languages has become the central battleground of contemporary French politics. It is around these two poles that politicians, intellectuals and members of France's vast civil society have tried to negotiate the formidable challenges of ideological uncertainty and a renewed sense of global insecurity.

EMILE CHABAL is a Chancellor's Fellow in History at the University of Edinburgh.

A Divided Republic:
Nation, State and Citizenship
in Contemporary France

Emile Chabal

CAMBRIDGE
UNIVERSITY PRESS

CAMBRIDGE
UNIVERSITY PRESS

University Printing House, Cambridge CB2 8BS, United Kingdom

Cambridge University Press is part of the University of Cambridge.

It furthers the University's mission by disseminating knowledge in the pursuit of education, learning and research at the highest international levels of excellence.

www.cambridge.org
Information on this title: www.cambridge.org/9781107692879

First published 2015
First paperback edition 2016

A catalogue record for this publication is available from the British Library

Library of Congress Cataloguing in Publication data
Chabal, Emile.
A divided republic: nation, state and citizenship in contemporary France / Emile Chabal.
    pages cm
ISBN 978-1-107-06151-4 (Hardback) – ISBN 978-1-107-69287-9
(Paperback) 1. Republicanism–France.   2. Liberalism–France.
3. France–Politics and government–1958–   I. Title.
JA84.F8C45 2015
306.20944–dc23   2014042749

ISBN 978-1-107-06151-4 Hardback
ISBN 978-1-107-69287-9 Paperback

Pour mon père, avec un peu de retard.

Contents

Acknowledgements

I have incurred innumerable debts since I began working on France. In particular, I have benefited from the patience and assistance of a number of individuals. Three of them deserve a special mention. John Lonsdale first taught me to write properly and persuaded me to continue my academic journey; his encouragement at the very earliest stages of my career was priceless. Robert Tombs should be rewarded for his willingness to take on a student whose project was as contemporary as it was politically provocative; I cannot thank him enough for his support and his attention. And Samuel Moyn commented on an earlier draft of this book simply on the basis of intellectual curiosity; I could not have asked for a more attentive reader.

The various institutions at which I have discussed and presented my work all played a role in its elaboration. As a doctoral student and research fellow, Cambridge, Harvard and the Ecole Normale Supérieure provided me with wonderful forums for the development of my ideas. Among those at Cambridge who read or listened to parts of my doctoral thesis in its early stages, I am particularly grateful to David Todd, Richard Drayton, William O'Reilly, Michael O'Brien, Tim Blanning, Sarah Howard and Adam Tooze for their comments. At Oxford, I discovered possibly the most vibrant community of French scholars in the United Kingdom. I still remember many thought-provoking conversations with Robert Gildea, Ruth Harris, Martin Conway, James McDougall, Anne Simonin, Kalypso Nicolaidis and especially Sudhir Hazareesingh, who has been an invaluable critical voice. I thank them all for their patience. Most recently, I have found a new home at the University of Edinburgh. Almost everyone has been extremely welcoming, but I owe a special debt of gratitude to Stephan Malinowski, with whom I have discussed many things Franco-French.

Elsewhere, I have learnt a great deal from Claire Eldridge, Michael Behrent, David Armitage, Michael Herzfeld, Christophe Prochasson, Julian Jackson, David Priestland, Selina Todd, Jane Caplan, Christian

Amalvi, Jonathan Judaken, Kate Marsh, Brian Sudlow, Yann Scioldo-Zürcher, Jim Shields, Cécile Laborde, Daniel Gordon, Camille Robcis, Iain Stewart, Nick Hewlett, Chloe Jeffries, Andrea Smith, Michael Scott Christofferson, Serge Audier, Gwendal Châton and Nicolas Delalande. Without realising it, the students I taught at Cambridge, Oxford and Edinburgh were the first to hear many of my arguments; I hope they will forgive me for testing my ideas on them. I must also thank those French public figures who agreed to be interviewed; their names are included in the bibliography.

No less important are those who made my research possible. A special word of thanks is reserved for Trinity College, Cambridge. It was Trinity that contributed to almost all of my research costs as a postgraduate student, awarded me two one-year scholarships to study in Texas and in Paris, and provided remarkable administrative support. My debt to Trinity is, quite literally, incalculable. The Arts and Humanities Research Council, the Kennedy Memorial Trust, the Student Aid Foundation in Houston, the Centre for History and Economics in Cambridge and the Society for the Study of French History all contributed, to varying degrees, to my financial wellbeing. I received additional support from St John's College (Cambridge), the John Fell Fund (Oxford), the University of Oxford Faculty of History, the Prince Consort and Thirlwall Prize (Cambridge) and the School of History, Classics and Archaeology at the University of Edinburgh. I also benefited from all sorts of in-kind assistance – from offices to sofa beds – that made my research more pleasant or simply more affordable. Those institutions that deserve a particular mention are the Center for European Studies at Harvard University and the Maison Française d'Oxford, both of which provided me with outstanding spaces in which to work. Likewise, I have taken full advantage of the selfless generosity of several Parisian hosts. In my first years of research, the Herlem family offered me exceptional hospitality in Fontenay-sous-Bois, providing the vital human kindness that makes lonely research palatable. And, in the last few years, I have imposed myself (and my ideas) on the long-suffering Pia Torreton: I am sure she knows far too much about my research. As for all those who have been unwise enough simply to offer their friendship and time over the past few years, I offer my sincerest thanks.

This book has been immeasurably improved by my wife, Akhila, and my two dear parents. Akhila will know that she is present on every page. It is because of her that I have emerged more or less sane from this journey. So much of my research has been inspired by conversations with my parents that they hardly need acknowledgement: their inspiration and stimulation have made me who I am. Sadly, my father died as I was preparing the final manuscript. It is hard to think that he will not be here to celebrate the publication of a book that is a result of his love, cajoling, critical engagement and careful attention. But he knew I would dedicate this book to him and I hope he will still be proud of it.

Note on translation

This is a book about language – and, above all, the language the French elites use to talk about politics. Inevitably, this raises the difficult problem of translation. The high drama of much French political rhetoric often sounds odd or mildly amusing in English. Phrases such as 'la République rentre dans l'Histoire' or 'l'avènement d'une fracture coloniale' are virtually impossible to translate adequately. For the sake of consistency, all translations from French in the main text are my own, even where existing English translations exist; I have not translated French text in the footnotes. I also provide explanations in the main text where a term seems to me of particular importance (such as *communautarisme* or *fracture sociale*). I nevertheless urge readers to treat my translations as provisional and imperfect. Obviously, I take full responsibility for any major errors.

Introduction: French politics after the deluge

Almost every observer of French politics agrees that something very significant happened between 1975 and 1985. For those focused on economics, it was the end of the 'Trente Glorieuses' – a period of uninterrupted economic growth since the end of the Second World War that saw France fully enter the industrial, consumer and nuclear age.[1] The closing of this cycle, punctuated by the oil shocks of the 1970s, marked a profound rupture in the country's perception of its economic and political certainties. For those interested in the development of France's intellectual life, it was the sudden collapse of a Marxist consensus that had developed alongside the Trente Glorieuses. With the emergence of the *nouveaux philosophes* and the subsequent success of a wide-ranging 'anti-totalitarian' critique of Marxism in 1977–8, the French intelligentsia rapidly became more fragmented and less ideological than at any point in the previous half-century. For those who looked to party politics, it was the implosion of Gaullism and the election in 1981 of the first Socialist and Communist coalition since the Popular Front that signalled the arrival of a new era. When, a few years later, the new government abandoned its commitment to an orthodox socialism *à la française* and ushered in a new form of consensus politics, complete with periods of 'cohabitation' between right-wing governments and a left-wing president, there was further bemusement. What little certainty that remained in French politics was finally put to rest as the Parti communiste français (PCF) – one of the largest parties in post-war France – entered terminal decline and, in 1984, a resurgent extreme-right made unexpected electoral gains. By 1985, French politics was in a profound state of flux that resembled neither the messy politics of the Third and Fourth Republics nor the convulsions and *grandeur* of the early Fifth Republic.

---

[1] Jean Fourastié, *Les Trente Glorieuses ou la Révolution invisible de 1946 à 1975* (Paris: Fayard, 1979).

For the most part, the realisation that French politics had changed beyond all recognition led to a wave of nostalgia in the 1980s. The apparent irrelevance of right and left meant that politicians struggled to manufacture 'causes' with which to galvanise disaffected voters, while France's intellectual classes yearned for 1968 or the days of Sartrean engagement, when they were beholden to higher principles rather than struggling to make themselves heard in the mass media. Even those who might otherwise have been sympathetic to the appeasement of France's fractious political battles bemoaned the rise of a 'centrist Republic' that seemed to be little more than an apolitical struggle for better 'management' of the country.[2] Of course, this did not mean that pressing social problems disappeared along with partisan disagreement. On the contrary, almost everyone could agree that France faced rising unemployment, difficulties in integrating ethnic minorities, the resurgence of colonial memory, a reinvigorated extreme-right, voter apathy... It was simply that there seemed now to be no framework within which to understand these problems and no principles that could be used to offer solutions. Indeed, for a political culture that had, for so long, chosen ideology over pragmatism, the prospect of consensus was positively frightening: could France still be France without its *guerres franco-françaises*?

It is this concern that provides the backdrop for this study. Throughout the next ten chapters, I shall examine how it is possible to make sense of French political life in a new age of uncertainty. I shall show, on the one hand, how French politics reclaimed a grand ideology and mobilised nostalgia in order to rewrite its national narrative in firmly republican terms; and, on the other, how this new narrative was challenged by an increasingly present liberal critique that sought to embrace the positive consequences of France's more peaceful political life. The aim will not be to provide a comprehensive narrative of French political life since the late 1970s.[3] Rather, I shall suggest a new interpretation that can be used to understand the ways in which a wide range of actors in French politics have conceptualised politics and the political.[4] For this, it will be

---

[2] François Furet, Jacques Julliard and Pierre Rosanvallon, *La République du Centre: la fin de l'exception française* (Paris: Calmann-Lévy, 1988).

[3] This has already been attempted successfully by a wide range of historians and political scientists. See for instance David Howarth and Giorgios Varouxakis, *Contemporary France* (London: Arnold, 2003); Serge Berstein and Pierre Milza, *Histoire du XXe siècle: Tome 3, de 1973 à nos jours: vers la mondialisation et le XXIe siècle* (Paris: Hatier, 2006); Jean-François Sirinelli, *Comprendre le XXe siècle français* (Paris: Fayard, 2005); and John Ardagh, *France in the New Century: Portrait of a Changing Society* (London: Viking, 1999).

[4] On the difference between 'politics' (*la politique*) and 'the political' (*le politique*), see the discussion in Pierre Rosanvallon, *Pour une histoire conceptuelle du politique. Leçon inaugurale au Collège de France faite le jeudi 28 mars 2002* (Paris: Seuil, 2004).

necessary to go beyond traditional categories of 'right' and 'left' – not because these are irrelevant, but because they alone cannot capture the complexity of contemporary politics. It will also be necessary to look at a much wider range of actors than is customary in many studies of politics. Again, the reason for this is to restore to French political life its many layers, particularly given that the development of mass democracy and new communications has made it possible for an ever greater number of people to participate in political discussion. Finally, it will be necessary to emphasise themes over chronology; it is only by asking new questions that we can begin to re-examine a period of recent history that is still open.

The boundaries of politics: actors, sources and methods

This is, first and foremost, a study in political history. It looks at three decades of French history and attempts to build an analysis based on credible sources and multiple voices. It takes into account the importance of specific historical 'moments' and personalities, as well as the deep contexts of French politics. Its purpose is to offer a new interpretation that satisfies the most basic criteria of plausibility and fairly reflects the reasons political actors did or said particular things at a given time. However, this kind of study also raises a number of methodological questions that are specific to the study of the recent past. Of these, three are of particular importance: the range of actors involved; the nature of the sources used; and the importance of related disciplines. I discuss each one in turn.

The question of *who* features in the following chapters is also a question about the conceptual limits of this study. My criteria are (at least in theory) relatively simple: this study confines itself to those actors who form part of a broad consensual middle ground in French politics. This means that I have deliberately left aside those who have mostly been involved in the politics of the extreme left or extreme right. Inevitably there are frequent references to these extremes, since many of those I deal with began their careers as activists, militants or fellow-travellers of radical movements; but these movements are only dealt with insofar as they are relevant to the search for political consensus in France. Thus, while there are some chapters that look at the 'conversion' away from communism or the journey from extreme right to neo-liberal, there are no chapters that deal with these extremes in detail. In the same way, I have mostly chosen to look at the mainstream print and audiovisual media (such as *Le Monde*, *L'Express* or France Télévision) rather than more obviously partisan or radical publications and broadcasts.

Of course, the limits of this consensual space are open for debate: in the conclusion I examine briefly what the notion of consensus in the French context might mean, but I recognise that there can be no easy definition. Nevertheless, my emphasis on the tension between the writing of the national narrative – perhaps the most perfect embodiment of the search for consensus – and a liberal critique of contemporary France should give a fairly clear idea of what I believe has constituted a consensual space in contemporary French politics.

Inside this space, I concentrate above all on four sets of elite actors: political and civil society activists, career politicians, intellectuals and academics, and journalists. Again, the distinction between these different groups is rarely clear-cut: indeed, it is a peculiarity of French politics that there is a great deal of movement between each one. Many of the intellectuals who appear in the following pages have been 'political advisers' and the division between journalist and academic is often virtually non-existent. But, if the reality is that all these actors can easily change their identities, there is still a useful conceptual distinction to be made between them. It is for this reason that, in the majority of my chapters, the focus is on only one set of actors at a time. In some cases, I shine a spotlight on academic historians and the development of historiography; in other cases, I examine networks of intellectuals in think tanks; elsewhere, I turn my attention to party politics and policy decisions. All these spheres are intimately linked, but treating them separately allows us to do justice to the rather different exigencies of each profession.

At the same time, a discussion of different political actors necessarily entails a discussion about the nature of the source material. One unusual aspect of this study is that it often makes use of texts that are very widely available, such as popular essays, government reports or newspaper articles. In part, this is a result of the subject matter: any analysis of the search for political consensus in contemporary France must rest on documents that are freely accessible and can therefore contribute to the formation of this consensus. Moreover, with the exception of personal interviews and short biographical introductions, I am less concerned with the private lives of political actors than their public pronouncements and, most importantly, the ways in which the latter have been interpreted. This is a study of the importance of ideas and language in contemporary politics, but also an investigation into reception and (mis)interpretation. I look at the instrumentalisation of texts, ideas, words, concepts and languages. This automatically means creating what we might call an 'impure' genealogy that acknowledges the source of particular ideas while simultaneously recognising that these can be transformed as they circulate around the political space. It is for this reason that I have made extensive use of audiovisual sources in an attempt to reconstruct debates that otherwise risk appearing rather one-sided on paper. By confronting different sources – textual, audiovisual, spoken – the aim is to give a much wider account of French political history than would be possible using the methods of intellectual or cultural history alone.

This is not to say that this study ignores the relevance of methodological insights from related disciplines. Quite the opposite: although it is a political history of contemporary France, it has been strongly influenced by developments in political thought, anthropology and political sociology. In common with other imaginative and original approaches to contemporary political history – such as Daniel Rodgers's *Age of Fracture* or David Priestland's *Merchant, Soldier, Sage* – the aim is to juxtapose ideas and individuals with their contexts in order to capture a wider range of political participation.[5] This is apparent especially in my focus on meaning and language.[6] Rather than talk about political ideologies or traditions I have mostly made reference to political 'languages'.[7] This reflects the fragmentation and fluidity of contemporary political life in France.[8] Many political actors today resist being defined according to 'ideological' criteria – particularly if these are stigmatised (as in the case of the term 'liberal'). By contrast the concept of language suggests a repertoire of words, concepts, ideas and symbols on which actors can draw in order to justify their opinions.[9] In addition, the concept of language makes it possible for actors to speak several languages

---

[5] Daniel T. Rodgers, *Age of Fracture* (London: Harvard University Press, 2011). David Priestland, *Merchant, Soldier, Sage: A New History of Power* (London: Penguin, 2013)

[6] I have been particularly influenced by the anthropological work of scholars such as Clifford Geertz, Charles Taylor and Michael Herzfeld, and by attempts to conceptualise the 'linguistic turn' in the social sciences. See for instance Clifford Geertz, *The Interpretation of Cultures* (London: Hutchinson, 1975); Charles Taylor, *Philosophy and the Human Sciences*, Philosophical Papers 2 (Cambridge University Press, 1985); Michael Herzfeld, *Cultural Intimacy: Social Poetics in the Nation-State* (London: Routledge, 2005); Malcolm Crick, *Explorations in Language and Meaning: Towards a Semantic Anthropology* (New York: Wiley, 1976); Marshall Sahlins, *Culture in Practice* (New York: Zone Books, 2000); and Manuel Cabrera, *Postsocial History: An Introduction* (Oxford: Lexington, 2004).

[7] In this sense, I differ from Hazareesingh's attempts to document France's 'political traditions' in Sudhir Hazareesingh, *Political Traditions in Modern France* (Oxford University Press, 1994).

[8] This fluidity – and the age of uncertainty more generally – has been theorised in Zygmunt Bauman, *Liquid Times: Living in an Age of Uncertainty* (London: Polity, 2007).

[9] On the use of 'language' as a concept in the study of class, see for instance Gareth Stedman Jones, *Languages of Class: Studies in English Working Class History, 1932–1982* (Cambridge University Press, 1983); and D. Wahrman, *Imagining the Middle Class: The Political Representation of Class in Britain, c. 1780–1840* (Cambridge University Press, 1995).

simultaneously. Thus, despite making a sustained conceptual distinction between a 'republican' and 'liberal' language of politics in France, I show that it is perfectly possible for political actors to use both languages at different times or for different audiences. Finally, the emphasis on language raises the issue of translation.[10] It is well known that modern French politics bequeathed to the world a vast political vocabulary – starting with the words 'right' and 'left' – but this legacy has often obscured the ways in which this vocabulary was originally used in France. The same is true today. I argue that there is an inadequate attempt to understand and translate the meaning of specific French words in their French context. In order to rectify this, I examine the use of common words in contemporary French politics such as 'integration', 'crisis', 'liberalism' or *fracture sociale*. In so doing, I hope to give a clearer account of their multiple meanings, as well as assess the varied circumstances in which they have been deployed.

Taken together, this eclectic methodology has the potential to offer many new insights. It allows us to see how the French have conceptualised and engaged with politics in the past three decades. It exposes the multi-layered intellectual, institutional and political networks that have developed in the same period. And it makes possible the incorporation of France's post-colonial narrative into its recent political history; as I shall show, this post-colonial story belongs not at the margins of French politics but at its very heart. Most of all, a diverse methodology makes it possible to answer the question at the centre of this study: namely, how French politics has coped with the disappearance or transformation of its most important reference points. In the brief prologues to each part, I outline the historiographical context and exactly how this study is structured, but it is enough to say here that this new age of uncertainty demands closer examination, for it has represented the unavoidable horizon of contemporary French politics. I recognise that any conclusions must necessarily be tentative, given that many of the actors who appear in the following chapters have many years of their careers ahead of them. But I nonetheless contend that it is possible to write an original history of the contexts from which they emerged – and that any such history can make an important contribution to our understanding of contemporary French politics.

---

[10] Paula G. Rubel and Abraham Rosman (eds.), *Translating Cultures: Perspective on Translation and Anthropology* (Oxford: Berg, 2003); and Keith Basso and Henry A. Selby (eds.), *Meaning in Anthropology* (Albuquerque, NM: University of New Mexico Press, 1977).

Part I

Writing the national narrative in contemporary France

The return of republicanism

Since the eighteenth century, the French have been deeply concerned with the problem of the nation.[1] The writing of France's national narrative has been a source of impassioned – and sometimes violent – disagreement. One's interpretation of the nation has usually determined one's political orientation, conception of history and view of human progress. The French Revolution, which, for many in the nineteenth and twentieth centuries, was seen to have given birth to the nation and restarted human history, divided France's political establishment.[2] These divisions remained embedded in French politics at least until the end of the Second World War but, even as they withered away under the Fifth Republic, the questions raised by the Revolution remained at the heart of French political life. When did the nation truly take shape? How? Who should it represent and who should remain excluded? What does it mean to 'be' French? What sort of national history can (and should) be written?

These questions – and the answers given to them – lie at the heart of my investigation into the writing of the French national narrative since the late 1970s. It is certainly true that, as France has put aside its so-called *guerres franco-françaises*, many traditional fault lines of French politics have lost their potency.[3] Nonetheless, the question of the national narrative and the nation has retained all its potential for controversy. The resurgence of republicanism since the 1980s – often described as a neo-republican revival – has brought with it a widespread and public

[1] David A. Bell, *The Cult of the Nation in France: Inventing Nationalism, 1680–1900* (London: Harvard University Press, 2001).

[2] On this see the overview in R. Gildea, *Children of the Revolution: The French, 1799–1914* (London: Harvard University Press, 2008).

[3] For instance, it was traditionally the case that the more Catholic a constituency, the greater the strength of the right. For an overview of some of these disputes, see J. Hayward, *Fragmented France: Two Centuries of Disputed Identity* (Oxford University Press, 2007).

interrogation of France's history and values. These debates have frequently been articulated around key moments such as the *affaire du foulard* or the debate surrounding 'ethnic' statistics. But behind these specific events lie other contexts: namely, a wide range of (sometimes colourful) personalities, sociological questions, party-political affiliations, historiographies, and philosophical *prises de positions*. Put simply, neo-republicanism has become one of France's most significant languages of politics, replete with evocative and highly charged words and vivid political symbolism. It has built on a rich French political tradition, and has contributed to the reinterpretation of French history in a variety of imaginative ways.

This should not lead us to believe that neo-republicanism is a unified political philosophy. Over the past three decades, the Republic and republicanism have meant different things to different people, and, while most public figures have been determined to demonstrate their 'republican' credentials, few of them have agreed on what these are. This eclecticism makes it hard to isolate a single 'type' of neo-republicanism. Instead, I want to understand the emergence of a new language of republicanism in its intellectual and political context in order to demonstrate its wide effect on French politics. So, for example, this first part of the book will examine the roots of the republican revival in French philosophy, history, political thought and party politics. It will look at how republicanism has influenced the writing of modern French history, and how it has affected the French state's response to immigration from outside Europe. Finally, it will suggest that neo-republicanism has been intimately tied up with France's post-colonial identities. This juxtaposition of contexts makes it possible to explore in more detail neo-republicanism's multi-faceted language and symbolic repertoire. By examining the issues and ideas that have been at the heart of the republican revival, we gain a better appreciation, not simply of the many meanings of republicanism, but also of the ways in which it has been deployed. This makes it possible to connect the immediate political and socio-economic contexts of French politics with the language of republicanism, which itself has a long history. Inevitably, this multi-layered analysis requires a diverse approach. Hence some chapters deal with political events, while others look at political thought and philosophy or historiography and academic discourse. Ultimately, however, the aim is the same: to explore how, why and with what consequences France's national narrative has been rewritten since the 1970s.

1   Writing histories: two republican narratives

La République se confond pratiquement avec sa mémoire, elle est comme le sujet dans le sujet.   Pierre Nora in *Les lieux de mémoire* (1984)[1]

For a long time it was not at all clear that republicanism would become France's dominant political ideal. Indeed, it was not until the beginning of our period – the 1970s – that republican institutions and ideas truly triumphed. With the decline of the Communist Party and the disappearance of a virulently anti-republican extreme right, the Republic could finally spread its wings, even if the calamitous loss of the French colonial empire cast a long shadow. Seen in retrospect, it makes sense that a period of relative security for the republican political system should have been accompanied by a concomitant resurgence of interest in republican ideas. This had also been the case a century earlier in the 1880s, when the Third Republic looked for myths, symbols and histories that it could use to buttress its new-found strength. The problem for historians is that, during both of these periods of ideological reorientation in the 1880s and the 1970s, new narratives of republicanism were created that sought to fix and unify its meaning. Over time, these have made it difficult to disentangle history from mythology. We must therefore begin by identifying the underlying teleologies and narratives of French republicanism so that we can build a nuanced picture of the neo-republicanism that emerged in the 1980s and 1990s.

As I shall suggest in this chapter, what has often appeared to be a unified neo-republican consensus has in fact contained within it two overlapping but distinct narratives. I have called these the 'transformative' and 'institutional' narratives of republicanism. The former emphasises republican 'values' and how they can be used to transform French politics. It is a critical teleology usually (though not always) deployed by the left to ensure that the state continues to uphold 'republican' values, and it often looks back to the French Revolution. The latter, by contrast,

---

[1] Pierre Nora, *Les Lieux de mémoire, Tome 1, La République* (Paris: Gallimard, 1984), p. viii.

focuses on the Republic as an institution and as the incarnation of consensual stability in French politics since the late nineteenth century. Its model is the Third Republic, and the various symbols to which it gave birth, including the republican school, *laïcité* (secularism) and a unified state. This institutional republicanism has been invoked widely on the left and the right, sometimes in conjunction with its transformative counterpart. Nevertheless, they both imply different meanings of republicanism and rest on different readings of modern French history.[2]

As should be clear by now, to make a distinction between different republican narratives is not an exercise in political labelling: the two teleologies overlap and are often invoked simultaneously. However, it is important to separate them as a way of moving beyond fixed models of 'left' and 'right', or 'reactionary' and 'progressive'. Republicanism has always been a unifying political language, which has consistently sought to underplay difference in its efforts to promote national unity, but it has also been ecumenical in its choice of narratives. In recent years, neo-republicanism has had to absorb the divergent languages of Gaullism and socialism – and it has done so by allowing the coexistence of these transformative and institutional narratives.

These two narratives are not a recent invention; the tension between them has been an integral part of French republicanism since the late eighteenth century. Later in this chapter, I shall turn my attention to the construction of the transformative and institutional narratives in contemporary historiography. First, though, I should like to examine these narratives in a longer historical context. This serves a dual purpose: on the one hand, it provides an introduction to French republican historiography since the nineteenth century; on the other, it reminds us that contemporary debates have built on historical divisions, disagreements and tensions. My intention is not to write another exhaustive history of the Republic. Nor do I want to suggest that republicanism is the only lens through which modern French history can be read – a simplification that has become commonplace in neo-republican historiography. Rather, my aim here is to provide a rough sketch of republicanism in modern French history so that we can better understand the background and historical reference points of a neo-republicanism that has become the dominant reading of the French national narrative in the late twentieth and early twenty-first centuries.

---

[2] A number of the arguments in this chapter were initially elaborated in Emile Chabal, 'Memories of the *République* in late-twentieth-century France', in Carolina Armenteros et al. (eds.), *Historicising the French Revolution* (Newcastle: Cambridge Scholars, 2008).

Republicanism in modern French history

It should be clear from the start that my interest is in French republicanism.[3] The Athenian Republic – what the French call the *Cité* – and the republicanism of the early-modern Italian city states bore a genealogical resemblance to French republicanism and were frequently discussed during the French Enlightenment.[4] But, from the late eighteenth century onwards, republicanism in France was constructed with relatively little reference to the outside world. Especially noticeable is the lack of interest in the world's most famous republic – the United States – which acquired that status more than a decade before France.[5] Instead, historians largely agree that French republicanism emerged from a variety of eighteenth-century French debates surrounding the nature of politics and governance. These debates found their most powerful political expression in what, for most French republicans of the nineteenth and twentieth centuries, would become the founding moment of the French Republic: the French Revolution. As Keith Michael Baker has argued, it was in the heady days of the Revolution that the language of classical republicanism became fused with Enlightenment ideals and transformed itself from a language of opposition to a language of government.[6] The development of an anti-monarchic Republic was only one of the possible reactions to France's pre-revolutionary crisis, but, for many later republican historians, republicanism seemed the only possible response to the corruption of the *Ancien Régime*. The year 1789 retrospectively marked the beginning of modern French history.[7]

[3] For comparative studies of republicanism as a concept, see for instance Serge Audier, *Théories de la République* (Paris: La Découverte, 1994); and Philip Pettit, *Republicanism: A Theory of Freedom and Government* (Oxford: Clarendon, 1997). See also the substantial body of historical work surrounding Quentin Skinner's analyses of republicanism, for instance Martin van Gelderen and Quentin Skinner (eds.), *Republicanism: A Shared European Heritage*, 2 vols. (Cambridge University Press, 2005).

[4] On this, see H. Van Effenterre, 'La cité grecque, modèle de *République* des Républicains'; and Claude Nicolet, 'Citoyenneté française et citoyenneté romaine, essai de mise en perspective', in Serge Berstein and Odile Rudelle (eds.), *Le modèle républicain* (Paris: Presses Universitaires de France, 1992).

[5] On perceptions of the United States in France in the eighteenth and nineteenth centuries, see Philippe Roger, *L'ennemi américain: généalogie de l'anti-américanisme français* (Paris: Seuil, 2002).

[6] Keith Michael Baker, 'Transformations of Classical Republicanism in Eighteenth-Century France', *Journal of Modern History* (Vol. 73, No. 1, 2001), pp. 32–53.

[7] Serge Berstein, 'Le modèle républicain: une culture politique syncrétique', in Serge Berstein (ed.), *Les Cultures Politiques en France* (Paris: Seuil, 1999), p. 114.

In addition to providing republicanism with a founding myth, the French Revolution was the crucible of republican 'values'. This was the period during which the distinctive civic and normative dimensions of French republicanism began to take shape. At a rhetorical level, the emphasis on civic virtue was a response to the instability and violence of the years following 1789, but, as Andrew Jainchill has suggested, the same process continued in the 1790s as the Thermidor administration tried to make republicanism into language of government and administration that would stabilise a nation still in revolutionary turmoil.[8] The result was that, by the mid-nineteenth century 'unlike the term "republic" in the United States, "republic" in France meant more than simply a juridical and legal system. It referred to a complex set of *values*'.[9] These values would subsequently form an integral part of French republicanism, especially during the long periods of non-republican government in the nineteenth century.

What exactly these values were has, understandably, been a matter of intense debate. Nevertheless, it is possible to make some general points. In his well-known book, *Political Traditions in Modern France* (1994), the political historian Sudhir Hazareesingh identified five ways in which the revolutionary heritage contributed to the construction of French republicanism: it established the principle of popular sovereignty; it affirmed the possibility and the desirability of creating a rational political order; it emphasised the universality of principles; it projected a specific conception of patriotism and nationalism; and it suggested structures that could be used to promote equality.[10] These broad themes crystallised around five key positions that were common to many, if not all, republicans in the nineteenth century: universal (male) suffrage, a commitment to Enlightenment rationality, secularism and anti-clericalism, a (limited) interest in social conditions, and a civic conception of patriotism.[11] In the dark days of the Restoration (1815–30), the July Monarchy (1830–48) and the Second Empire (1852–70), these were the principles that set republicans apart from their political counterparts. These were also the principles at stake during the tempestuous Second Republic (1848–51), which enacted what appeared at the time to be a truly republican agenda: freedom of the press, universal (male) suffrage,

---

[8] Andrew Jainchill, *Reimagining politics after the Terror: The Republican Origins of French Liberalism* (London: Cornell University Press, 2008).

[9] Maurice Agulhon, *République, Tome 1: 1880–1914* (Paris: Hachette, 1990), p. 8 (emphasis added).

[10] Hazareesingh, *Political Traditions*, p. 68.

[11] Philippe Darriulat, *Les Patriotes: la gauche républicaine et la nation, 1830–1870* (Paris: Seuil, 2001), p. 8.

the abolition of slavery, the recognition of certain social rights and the offer of moral support to people abroad.[12] The collapse of the Second Republic left republicans to rue both political defeat and the partial reversal of their programme. It was not until the 1870s and the advent of the Third Republic that republicanism once again became a language of government.

As we shall see below, the last thirty years have seen an extensive rehabilitation of the Third Republic (1870–1940).[13] To many neo-republicans, it has come to represent the apogee of the Republic. There is something to this view. The Third Republic did indeed see the rebirth and implementation of certain republican values – especially in education. This was intertwined with a growing assortment of republican symbolism that contributed to a process of nation-building and continues to exert a powerful hold on French politics.[14] But this myth of the Third Republic has obscured the fact that it also represented the success of a highly contested 'bourgeois' republicanism, which underplayed the Republic's revolutionary heritage. Republicans were never as united as late twentieth-century historiography of the Third Republic has suggested. During the course of the Third Republic, the central values of republicanism moved from a radical fringe to the consensual centre of French politics, but only because they were adopted by a wide variety of groups (such as the Orleanists) who had hitherto been opposed to republicanism and democratisation.

The early years of the Third Republic support this view, with divided republicans forced to make difficult alliances to defend the Republic. It was not until the turn of the century that some kind of wider consensus was achieved. The Dreyfus Affair of the 1890s gave a reason for the left to rally to the defence of the Republic in the name of a 'rational' and 'secular' justice, which was seen to stand in stark contrast to the obscurantist anti-Semitism of the anti-Dreyfusards.[15] And by the first decade of the twentieth century, the rise of the 'Radicals' Republic' seemed to indicate that a republican vision was in the ascendant.[16] Nevertheless,

---

[12] Claudine Goldstein, *République et républicains en France de 1848 à nos jours* (Paris: Ellipses, 2000), pp. 15–19.
[13] Bertrand Taithe, 'Should the Third Republic Divide Us the Least?', *French History* (Vol. 18, No. 2, 2004), pp. 222–33.
[14] Philip Nord, 'La Troisième République', in V. Duclert and Christophe Prochasson (eds.), *Dictionnaire Critique de la République* (Paris: Flammarion, 2002).
[15] On Dreyfus, see Michel Winock, 'Le mythe fondateur: l'affaire Dreyfus', in Berstein and Rudelle, *Le modèle républicain*. For a revisionist perspective see R. Harris, *The Man on Devil's Island: Alfred Dreyfus and the Affair that Divided France* (London: Penguin, 2011).
[16] Philip Nord, *The Republican Moment: Struggles for Democracy in Nineteenth-Century France* (London: Harvard University Press, 1995).

this dominance was fragile and revolved largely around anti-clericalism, a political issue which seemed far less potent after the 1905 legislation that guaranteed the separation of church and state. Long before it collapsed in 1940, the Third Republic had many public enemies. The extreme left continuously denounced it as insufficiently republican and excessively 'bourgeois' or 'opportunist', while those on the far right – whether 'fascist' or not – regularly condemned republicanism as a dangerously divisive, democratic and godless political form.[17]

Yet, despite its divisions, the Third Republic provided a political framework for the implementation of what a number of historians have described as republicanism's 'modernising determinism', albeit purged of much of its revolutionary fervour.[18] In an attempt to reconstruct France along rational lines, the Third Republic and its advocates set about creating institutions that have since become powerfully associated with republicanism.[19] By far the most significant was the state school (*l'école républicaine*). As we shall see later, this has exerted an almost mystical hold on neo-republicanism, but, even a century earlier, the school was already a unique battleground in French politics.[20] It was through education that nineteenth-century republicans' hitherto abstract commitment to progress and the centrality of reason found its practical expression.[21] Jules Ferry is remembered as the architect of the education reforms of 1879–86, which created a system of elementary education and began a complete overhaul of the country's higher education system.[22] In reality, the implementation of rural schooling was subject to an infinite number of accommodations and compromises with local elites, but the symbolic power of the school as a republican symbol has remained overwhelming.[23]

Another key legacy of the Third Republic to capture a symbolic place at the heart of French republicanism was *laïcité* – an idea intimately tied up with *l'école républicaine*. Again, even if the reality of republican

---

[17] On the debate surrounding 'fascism' under the Third Republic, see Zeev Sternhell, *Ni droite ni gauche: l'idéologie fasciste en France* (Paris: Fayard, 2000). For an overview of the historiography, see Sean Kennedy, 'The End of Immunity? Recent Work on the Far Right in Interwar France', *Historical Reflections* (Vol. 34, No. 2, 2008), pp. 25–45.

[18] Claude Nicolet, *L'idée républicaine en France. Essai d'histoire critique (1880–1924)* (Paris: Gallimard, 1982), pp. 245–6; Berstein, 'Le modèle républicain', p. 115; Hazareesingh, *Political Traditions*, p. 72.

[19] Sudhir Hazareesingh, *Intellectual Founders of the Republic: Five Studies in Nineteenth-Century Political Thought* (Oxford University Press, 2001).

[20] Mona Ozouf, *L'école, l'église et la République* (Paris: Editions Cana, 1982).

[21] Hazareesingh, *Political Traditions*, p. 66.

[22] Odile Rudelle, 'De Jules Ferry à Raymond Poincaré ou l'echec du constitutionalisme républicain', in Berstein and Rudelle, *Le modèle républicain*.

[23] Mona Ozouf, *L'école, l'église et la République: 1871–1914* (Paris: Seuil, 2007).

anti-clericalism was of extraordinary complexity – and few nineteenth-century republicans were as thoroughgoing anti-clericals as neo-republican historiography would have us believe – the slow separation of church, state and school played a vital role in late nineteenth-century French politics.[24] Today, it is the official separation of 1905 that is remembered above all. But there were a whole range of other legal measures implemented in the previous decade, primarily related to schooling. These constituted something of a 'secular pact [pacte laïque]' between the church and state, which was characterised as much by mutual compromise as opposition.[25]

Alongside these two highly symbolic areas of legislation, both of which have become part of republican mythology, the Third Republic was associated with a number of other significant changes. For instance, the local *mairie* (town hall) became a powerful monumental symbol of the French republican state. In many smaller villages and towns, the school and *mairie* were located in the same building, symbolically and literally tying together secular pedagogy and secular administration. In some cases, *mairies* were buildings converted from other uses; in other cases, they were built specially for their new purposes; in all cases, they symbolised the growing interaction between the Third Republic and the daily life of the French people.[26] Finally, it should be emphasised that the Third Republic coincided with France's high colonial period. Military service was extended and the army became a powerful integrative tool for the Republic. [27] This was a time when France was to bring 'enlightenment' and 'liberation' to its colonies; republicanism – which had abolished slavery in 1848 – was invoked as an emancipatory ideology of peculiar force. Here, more than anywhere, the gulf between theory and practice was immense, but, as we shall see in later chapters, the legacy of this republican idea of empire profoundly influenced France's relationship with all its colonies and territories well into the twentieth century.[28]

---

[24] An interesting perspective on the accommodation of the Catholic Church to the Republic can be found in Christian Amalvi, 'Marianne dans les manuels scolaires confessionnels: une histoire singulière (1880–1964)', in Maurice Agulhon, A. Becker and E. Cohen (eds.), *La République en Représentations: autour de l'oeuvre de Maurice Agulhon* (Paris: Publications de la Sorbonne, 2006), pp. 147–58.
[25] Jean Baubérot, *Laïcité 1905–2005, entre passion et raison* (Paris: Seuil, 2005).
[26] Maurice Agulhon, 'Mairie', in Nora, *Les Lieux de mémoire, Tome 1*, pp. 168–79.
[27] On this, see Robert Tombs, *France 1814–1914* (London: Longman, 1994), pp. 302–20.
[28] This is an enormous topic that merits a great deal more discussion than space will allow. Later chapters deal with the question of colonial memory, but, for some perspectives on republicanism's relationship to empire in the nineteenth and twentieth centuries, see Alice Conklin, *A Mission to Civilise: The Republican Idea of Empire in France and West Africa, 1895–1930* (Stanford University Press, 1997); Jennifer Pitts, *A Turn to Empire: The Rise of Imperial Liberalism in Britain and France* (Princeton University Press, 2005);

This proliferation of national symbols in a colonial age was in no way peculiar to France. The late nineteenth century saw new attempts to 'invent' traditions across Europe, as governments attempted to direct the rise of mass nationalism.[29] But, alongside Bonapartist, royalist and Catholic narratives, the Third Republic pushed the republican narrative into France's political mainstream.[30] However, this consensus was never entirely secure. The most painful and difficult exception to the primacy of republicanism was the implosion of the Third Republic and the Vichy government (1940–44).[31] By rejecting the heritage of 1789, Vichy was seen to betray core republican principles. It dismantled the *état de droit* (rule of law) on which the Republic was built. But it did so using the institutions, administrative traditions and often the personnel of the Third Republic. Vichy made republicanism and statism appear dangerously similar.[32] This tarnishing of republicanism during the Second World War undoubtedly provides an important explanation for the waning of a republican discourse in the post-war period. The Fourth Republic (1946–58) can be credited with several reforms that seemed to be inscribed in a republican trajectory, most notably the introduction of universal female suffrage and the foundation of the Ecole nationale d'administration (ENA) in 1945 to train France's elite republican cadres. But the post-war period also saw France embroiled in brutal colonial wars in French Indochina and Algeria, which severely damaged France's reputation at home and abroad. At the same time, the strength of the PCF reached its apogee in the post-war period, buoyed by worker unrest, the economic changes of post-war reconstruction and Soviet geopolitical strength.[33] There was little space for republican rhetoric between a language of Marxism that condemned the Republic as 'bourgeois' and

Carole Paligot, *La République Raciale: paradigme racial et idéologie républicaine* (Paris: PUF, 2006); Laurent Dubois, 'La République Métisée: Citizenship, Colonialism, and the Borders of French History', *Cultural Studies* (Vol. 14, No. 1, 2000), pp. 15–34.

[29] On this see Eric Hobsbawm, 'Mass-Producing Traditions: Europe, 1870–1914', in Eric Hobsbawm and Terence Ranger (eds.), *The Invention of Tradition* (Cambridge University Press, 1983). Some examples (festivals, flags) can be found in Raoul Girardet, 'Les trois couleurs', C. Amalvi, 'Le 14 Juillet' and M. Vovelle, 'La Marseillaise', in Nora, *Les Lieux de mémoire, Tome 1*.

[30] Robert Tombs (ed.), *Nationhood and Nationalism in France* (London: HarperCollins, 1991).

[31] Robert Paxton, *Vichy France: Old Guard and New Order, 1940–44* (London: Barrie & Jenkins, 1972); and Julian Jackson, *France: The Dark Years, 1940–44* (Oxford University Press, 2001).

[32] On the relationship between republicanism and the Vichy period, see Gérard Noiriel, *Les origines républicaines de Vichy* (Paris: Hachette, 1999).

[33] Tony Judt, *Marxism and the French Left: Studies on Labour and Politics in France 1830–1981* (Oxford: Clarendon, 1989); and Sunil Khilnani, *Arguing Revolution: The Intellectual Left in Post-war France* (London: Yale University Press, 1993).

the political pragmatism of the Fourth Republic's administrators.[34] By the mid 1950s, it seemed as if republicanism was being confined to a previous era of French history – at least in metropolitan France.[35]

The early years of the Fifth Republic (1958–) did not exactly see a rebirth of republicanism, but Charles de Gaulle's presidency occupies a significant place in contemporary republican mythology.[36] Where the Dreyfus Affair (1898) had been one of the primary mechanisms by which the left found a home in French republican discourse, Gaullism provided the basis for what many historians have called a 'republicanism of the right'.[37] To many on the republican left at the time, de Gaulle's constitution, with its provision for a directly elected president, appeared deeply anti-republican, since the principle of an executive power subservient to a legislative power had long been a central part of the republican tradition. Yet de Gaulle was not anti-republican. In many ways, he embodied certain crucial republican values without necessarily explicitly speaking the language of republicanism. Nowhere was this republican heritage more apparent than in his construction of a strong, interventionist and dirigiste state. Great public works were given a tremendous boost in this period – for example, the high-speed rail network (developed in the late 1960s and inaugurated in 1981) and nuclear power (developed in the 1950s–60s and implemented in the Messmer Plan of 1974) – while France grandly played its role as arbiter in Europe and go-between in the Cold War.[38] Even the direct election of a president, and de Gaulle's insistent use of referendums throughout his presidency, could be interpreted as a form of republican popular sovereignty, although it could equally be associated with the Bonapartist tradition of plebiscites.[39] Crucially, it was under de Gaulle that the right could finally complete its conversion to republicanism, and regain some of the legitimacy it had

---

[34] Richard Vinen, *Bourgeois Politics in France, 1945–1951* (Cambridge University Press, 2002).

[35] There is a good deal of evidence that the language of republicanism remained important with respect to the colonies under the Fourth Republic, and was also significant in anti-colonial struggles. For perspectives on republicanism and the colonies, see Todd Shepard, *Invention of Decolonization: The Algerian War and the Remaking of France* (London: Cornell University Press, 2008); and Tony Chafer, *The End of Empire in French West Africa* (Oxford: Berg, 2002).

[36] On the mythology of de Gaulle and Gaullism, see Sudhir Hazareesingh, *Le mythe gaullien* (Paris: Gallimard, 2010).

[37] Maurice Agulhon, *République, Tome 2: 1914 à nos jours* (Paris: Hachette, 1990), p. 298.

[38] Philip Cerny, *The Politics of Grandeur: Ideological Aspects of de Gaulle's foreign policy* (Cambridge University Press, 2008 [1980]); Stanley Hoffmann, *Decline or Renewal? France since the 1930s* (New York: Viking, 1974).

[39] Neil Rogachevsky, 'Are plebiscites constitutional? A disputed question in the plebiscite campaign of 1870', *French History* (Vol. 27, No. 2, 2013), pp. 249–70.

lost after the discrediting of the Vichy regime. This was an important
change: in earlier periods, republicanism had been used as a philosophy
of revolution, but the Gaullist-inspired republicanism of the right had a
different emphasis. It included elements of post-war Christian democracy and thereby offered those on the right a way of speaking the language
of nationalism and national pride at a time when older forms of nationalism were still taboo because of their associations with Vichy.[40]

By the time of de Gaulle's death, however, France was changing. The
economy looked dangerously fragile in the face of the oil shocks of the 1970s
and unemployment began to rise, alongside growing – and now unwanted –
immigration. These socio-economic changes were mirrored by political
transformations. The protests of 1968 saw the shattering of a left-wing
consensus, and a decade and a half later the PCF was in terminal decline.[41]
Gaullism after de Gaulle struggled to maintain its ideological unity and
was eventually defeated by François Mitterrand's Union de la Gauche
(Union of the Left) in 1981. The grand ideologies which had governed
post-war French politics – Gaullism, socialism and communism – began
to fade as France entered its self-proclaimed 'crisis'. It was at this point
that some public figures began to talk about republicanism again – not as a
historical passion confined to the pages of history books, but as a living
political ideal that could offer real solutions to intractable socio-economic
and political problems. By the 1990s, republicanism and the Republic
had become unavoidable reference points in French political discourse.
Never before in France had a particular conception of the Republic been
so vigorously and widely discussed, and not since the early years of the
twentieth century had republicans been so ready to define themselves as
such.[42] Republicanism, it seemed, was born again.

The institutional narrative: the Republic
as *lieu de mémoire*

It is appropriate that the first signs of a republican revival were to be
found among historians. This is because the genesis of neo-republicanism

[40] Agulhon, *République, Tome 2*, pp. 295–352.
[41] On the eclipse of the PCF, see Sudhir Hazareesingh, *Intellectuals and the French
    Communist Party: Disillusion and Decline* (Oxford: Clarendon, 1991).
[42] For a perspectives on this revival, see Chapters 1–4 in this book, as well as Hugues Jallon
    and Pierre Mounier, *Les enragés de la République* (Paris: La Découverte, 1999); Justine
    Lacroix, 'Le national-souverainisme en France et en Grande Bretagne', *Revue
    Internationale de Politique Comparée* (Vol. 9, No. 3, 2002), pp. 391–408; and Alastair
    Cole and Gino Raymond (eds.), *Redefining the French Republic* (Manchester University
    Press, 2006).

lies first and foremost in a rehabilitation of republicanism and the Republic by historians in the late 1970s. In subsequent chapters, we shall examine the roots of neo-republicanism in party politics and French intellectual life, but here I should like to focus on the writing of history. Like nine-teenth- and early twentieth-century republicanism, neo-republicanism has relied very heavily on a specific reading of French history in order to secure its political legitimacy. We have already seen how republicanism's rise to prominence in the nineteenth century was highly contested: repub-licans' struggle to gain political power was simultaneously a struggle over the French national narrative. This was no less true at the end of the twentieth century. If the Republic was not fundamentally at risk in the same way as it was in 1851 or 1914, the fight for control over France's national narrative remained fierce.

It was historians of France who first began the task of revitalising and celebrating the Republic, and especially the Third Republic. This was all the more striking because, as we saw above, the Third Republic had previously been seen in a much more negative light as a regime of chronic instability. By the late 1980s, however, there had been a wide-spread reassessment of the Third Republic's achievements: it appeared now as the institutional model and inspiration for contemporary France, and as the crucible of republican stability. This gave renewed strength to what I earlier described as the institutional narrative of republicanism. By rewriting the history of modern France to celebrate the role of the Third Republic, a number of highly influential French historians were simultaneously reinforcing an institutional narrative that once again made republicanism a legitimate language of government, rather than simply a language of opposition.

By far the most spectacular historiographical example of neo-republicanism's institutional narrative was the highly influential and widely read *Les lieux de mémoire* (1984–92), edited by Pierre Nora. An influential figure in French intellectual life, Nora had been a senior editor of the publishing house Gallimard since the mid 1960s and had helped to found the journal *Le Débat* in 1980. Born out of a seminar Nora convened between 1979 and 1981 at the Ecole des hautes études en sciences sociales (EHESS), the aim of the *Lieux de mémoire* project was to examine and classify key sites of French memory in order to counteract what Nora saw as the 'rapid disappearance of national memory'.[43] In this, it succeeded handsomely: what began as a relatively small seminar eventually became a monumental, seven-volume work of academic

---

[43] Nora, *Les Lieux de mémoire, Tome I*, p. vii.

history that brought together essays by a bewildering number of highly respected French historians.[44] Moreover, the work had a significant impact outside the academy: by the mid 1990s, the term *lieu de mémoire* had passed into common usage, and it was soon clear that Nora's vast historiographical project had itself become a *lieu de mémoire*.

Despite a good deal of praise, there were inevitably voices of dissent – particularly outside France.[45] Perry Anderson called the *Lieux de mémoire* 'one of the most patently ideological programmes in post-war historiography, anywhere in the world'.[46] Others pointed out – with good reason – that France's colonial memory was all but absent from the seven volumes, a problem I discuss in greater detail below.[47] Still others were astonished that there was next to nothing on Bonapartism and the Bonapartist legacy.[48] If nothing else, the fact that not a single foreign historian had contributed to a work chronicling the vast inventory of French national symbols was an indication of its fundamentally parochial orientation.[49] But it is precisely this parochialism which makes Nora's project a useful starting point for an examination of the changing conceptions of the nation in late-twentieth-century France.[50]

The *Lieux de mémoires* project was built around three conceptual frameworks for the nation, which Nora used to structure the volumes: *la République, la Nation* and *les France*. It is of more than passing relevance that Nora chose to begin with the most recent of these: the Republic, he argued, is the 'most complete form of the nation'.[51] The Republic's success has been to absorb the entire national tradition into the service of republican goals; it has become, in Nora's rather controversial words,

---

[44] The English edition compressed the work into three volumes, and included forty-six of the original 132 entries. Pierre Nora (ed.), *Realms of Memory: Rethinking the French Past*, trans. Arthur Goldhammer (London: Columbia University Press, 1996). In English, the three volumes are entitled 'I. Conflicts and divisions', 'II. Traditions' and 'III. Symbols'.

[45] It should be said that some foreign historians were much more positive than others. See for instance Stefan Collini, 'Un antidote à la manie de la célébration', *Le Monde*, 5 February, 1993.

[46] Perry Anderson, 'Union Sucrée', *London Review of Books* , 23 September 2004.

[47] An example of this criticism is Hue Tam Ho Tai, 'Remembered Realms: Pierre Nora and French National Memory', *American Historical Review* (No. 106, 2001), pp. 906–22.

[48] Steven Englund, 'The Ghost of Nation Past', *Journal of Modern History* (Vol. 64, No. 2, 1992), p. 305.

[49] By volume 3, Nora had become aware of this criticism, although he does not address it satisfactorily. Pierre Nora (ed.), *Les Lieux de Mémoire, Tome 3, Les France: I. Conflits et partages* (Paris: Gallimard, 1992), p. 19.

[50] On this, see also Judt's excellent essay, '*À la recherche du temps perdu*: France and its pasts', in Tony Judt, *Reappraisals* (London: Penguin, 2008), pp. 196–218.

[51] Pierre Nora (ed.), *Les Lieux de Mémoire, Tome 2, La Nation: I* (Paris: Gallimard, 1986), p. ix.

'the only conceivable image of the nation'.[52] Although he went on in the next six volumes to explore older, more 'primordial', *lieux de mémoire*, he began with its most obviously contemporary and political form. Significantly, Nora's image of the Republic in the first volume was disproportionately biased in favour of the Third Republic. As he put it,

[I]t seemed legitimate to present [republicanism's] central and indivisible tradition, without burdening ourselves with the multiple republics of which it is formed. It also seemed legitimate to emphasise the Third Republic, *the real if not the only one for all French people*, and especially its founding years, during which a veritable memory strategy was constructed that marginalised two other moments: the revolutionary period, and the period from the Popular Front to the Resistance.[53]

As a declaration of historiographical intent, this is unusually strong. The Republic is endowed with a genesis myth and placed within strict chronological boundaries. For Nora, there is a clear vision of a 'true' Republic – imperfect, perhaps, but of paramount symbolic importance. As Englund points out, this meant that Nora's project resembled those of earlier republican historians such as Ernest Lavisse and Jules Michelet.[54] But Nora's innovation was to make the Third Republic the 'real' manifestation of republicanism. In so doing, his project made a substantial contribution to a reassessment and rehabilitation of the memory of the Third Republic in late-twentieth-century French historiography.

The importance of the Third Republic was further reinforced by the entries in the first volume of *Les lieux de mémoire*. Each one was devoted to the 'forest of symbols' that were said to make up republican memory. In keeping with the historiographical project, the majority of these symbols were drawn from the Third Republic.[55] From Lavisse and Buisson to Victor Hugo's funeral and the centenary of the French Revolution, the importance of the Third Republic was repeatedly highlighted. While most of the individual entries demonstrated a critical awareness of their subject matter, the editorial vision was of a Third Republic that was the true embodiment of the Republic, complete with its own political form

---

[52] Nora, *Lieux de Mémoire: Tome 1*, p. 652.   [53] Ibid., p. xiii (emphasis added).
[54] Englund, 'Ghost of Nation Past', p. 306.
[55] The table of contents of Volume 1 is divided into five sections as follows: 1. *Symboles*: – Les trois Couleurs – Le calendrier républicain – 'La Marseillaise'; 2. *Monuments*: – Le Panthéon – La mairie – Les monuments aux morts; 3. *Pédagogie*: – Le 'Grand Dictionnaire' de Pierre Larousse – Lavisse, instituteur national – 'Le Tour de la France par deux enfants' – La bibliothèque des Amis de l'instruction du IIIe arrondissement – Le 'Dictionnaire de pédagogie' de Ferdinand Buisson; 4. *Commémorations*: – Les centenaires de Voltaire et de Rousseau – Le 14 Juillet – Les funérailles de Victor Hugo – Le Centenaire de la Révolution française – L'Exposition coloniale de 1931; 5. *Contre-mémoire*: – La Vendée, région-mémoire – Le Mur des Fédérés.

and symbolic 'canon' of institutions and personalities. The picture that
emerged from the first volume of the *Lieux de mémoire* was one of a
project that actively sought to make a positive ideological contribution
to a new (republican) conception of the nation.[56] For Anderson to
criticise it on the grounds of its 'patently ideological' character was, in
some senses, to miss the point: Nora explicitly saw himself as a republican 'half-priest' and 'half-soldier' with the clear ideological goal of
giving republicanism a new-found legitimacy.[57] Thus, despite its chronic
instability and damaged reputation, the Third Republic appeared in the
Lieux de mémoire as the regime which gave birth to the memorialisation
of memory in the service of national unity. And it is the Third Republic
that Nora chooses to retain as 'true' – a 'true' model of unity, and the
'truest' of all Republics.

The implication was clear: France can and should seek the kind of
unified national narrative to which the Third Republic aspired. Indeed,
Nora goes on to say in the third volume that his use of the plural *les
France* does not imply an acceptance of 'diversity' or multiple 'identities';
rather, he wants all of the 132 entries in the *Lieux de mémoire* to contribute to an understanding of the 'whole of France'.[58] Nora's project
became one designed to unify France's national narrative or, as one
American reviewer put it, to bring 'significant cohesion and order in
the national project'.[59] Ultimately, the *Lieux de mémoire* sought not only
to deconstruct the 'age of commemoration' and the 'memorialisation' of
historical symbols, but also provide a new (and superior) republican
memory in its place, one that took inspiration from the Third Republic.[60]

In the following chapters, we shall see how this celebration of the
Republic's origins spread into the wider political space. But it is important to note that the *Lieux de mémoire* was a powerful statement about the
politics of historiography in France. By emphasising the overwhelming
symbolic importance of a political system, Nora was launching an attack

[56] F. Hartog, 'Pierre Nora', in L. Kritzmann (ed.), *The Columbia History of Twentieth-
Century French Thought*, (New York: Columbia University Press, 2006), pp. 629–31.
[57] Nora, *Les Lieux de Mémoire: Tome 1*, p. xxxi.
[58] Nora, *Les Lieux de Mémoire, Tome 3, Les France: I. Conflits et partages*, pp. 22–3.
[59] John Bodnar, 'Pierre Nora, National Memory and Democracy: A Review', *Journal of
American History* (Vol. 87, No. 3, 2000), pp. 951–63. Other reviewers – especially in
France – highlighted the importance of Nora's project as an attempt to 'revisiter le
monument national qu'a toujours été l'histoire de France'. J.-P. Rioux, 'La déesse
mémoire', *Le Monde*, 18 March 1993.
[60] Nora examines the 'age of commemoration' in his conclusion to the seven volumes.
Pierre Nora, 'L'ère de la commemoration', in Pierre Nora (ed.), *Les Lieux de Mémoire,
Tome 3, Les France: III. De l'archive l'emblème* (Paris: Gallimard, 1992), pp. 977–1012.

on the Annales school of historiography from which he had emerged.[61] Where the Annales school had highlighted the *longue durée* – and especially the deep, physical continuities in landscape and geography – Nora's project began with the ephemeral symbols of a political regime (calendars, festivals, anthems ...), and only in the final volumes dealt sporadically with the geography of the nation (forests, coastlines ...) Even here, the political organisation of the land (*départements, régions* ...) remained more important than its mere physical existence; the focus was above all on human intervention or, as he put it, the 'division of space and time [*le partage de l'espace-temps*]'.[62] This resurrection of political history from the embers of the Annales goes some way towards explaining the renewed appeal of histories of the Third Republic in the 1980s and 90s. Neither a traditional Marxist historiography, nor an Annales-influenced approach, had given much attention to politics and its symbols. A new interest in these questions allowed French historians to turn their attention to the hitherto neglected study of the Third Republic and its obsession with national symbols.

This was evident in the work of another highly influential historian, Maurice Agulhon. Agulhon, who died in 2014, had a long and distinguished career as one of France's most important political historians, with publications ranging from local studies of politics in the Var to broad histories of modern France. He taught at the Sorbonne in the 1970s, before being elected to a professorship at the Collège de France from 1986 to 1997.[63] Of particular interest here are his rich studies of Marianne as a symbol of the Republic, which were published in the late 1970s and 80s.[64] These were altogether less political texts than the *Lieux de mémoire*, even if Agulhon was involved with Nora's project from its inception, and openly expressed his admiration for it. Nevertheless, Agulhon's attempts to rehabilitate the history of political symbols, and his general history of the Republic (in his two-volume contribution to

---

[61] On Nora's role in the 'new history' see Jean-Pierre Le Goff and Pierre Nora (eds.), *Constructing the Past: Essays in Historical Method* (Cambridge University Press, 1985 [1974]).

[62] Nora (ed.), *Les Lieux de Mémoire, Tome 3, Les France: I. Conflits et partages*, section 3 ('Partages de l'espace-temps').

[63] For a concise summary of Agulhon's career, see Peter McPhee, 'Maurice Agulhon (1926–)', in Philip Daileader and Philip Whalen (eds.), *French Historians 1900–2000: New Historical Writing in Twentieth-Century France* (London: Blackwell, 2010).

[64] See his trilogy Maurice Agulhon, *Marianne au combat: l'imagerie et la symbolique républicaine de 1789 à 1880* (Paris: Flammarion, 1979); Maurice Agulhon, *Marianne au pouvoir: l'imagerie et la symbolique républicaines de 1880–1914* (Paris: Flammarion, 1989); and Maurice Agulhon, *Les métamorphoses de Marianne: l'imagerie et la symbolique républicaines de 1914 à nos jours* (Paris: Flammarion, 2001).

Hachette's *Histoire de France* series), has echoed the kind of shifts visible in Nora's work.[65] This is in addition to a number of other essays and lectures – including Agulhon's inaugural lecture at the Collège de France in 1986 – that have openly defended the memory of the French Revolution against accusations of totalitarianism, encouraged a return to 'civic' republican responsibility and criticised the 'relativism' of multicultural philosophies.[66] Indeed, in a memorable moment of (neo-)republican rhetoric during his 1986 lecture, he described 1789, 'the decisive year of the French Revolution, which was itself a French form of universal liberalism [*l'exigence libérale universelle*]', as France's foundational 'melting pot'.[67] Clearly, then, for Agulhon (as for Nora) the rediscovery of politics after the Annales school was central; so, too, was what Agulhon described as a certain *conscience républicaine*.[68] For both historians, the historical project of rehabilitating the Republic and its institutions developed alongside a desire to rebuild France's contemporary national narrative.

A renewed interest in the history of the Republic was visible in the work of a number of other prominent historians as well. An excellent example of this is Claude Nicolet, a historian of Ancient Rome and political adviser to Pierre Mendès-France in 1956 and Jean-Pierre Chevènement between 1984 and 2002. He began to publish works on the Republic from the early 1980s, starting in 1982 with his influential *L'idée républicaine en France: essai d'histoire critique (1880–1924)*. Predictably, the book's focus was the Third Republic. Before embarking on an extensive analysis of 'the republican ideal', he warned against the French historical establishment's condescension towards the Third Republic and the dangers of contemporary amnesia.[69] His book was designed as a response to both. Conceived at roughly the same time as Agulhon's trilogy on Marianne and Nora's *Lieux de mémoire*, Nicolet's work on republicanism lends further credence to the view that historians played an important role in the re-emergence of republicanism in the 1980s.

---

[65] Agulhon, *La République, Tome I*; and Agulhon, *La République, Tome 2*.

[66] See his essays 'Conscience nationale et conscience régionale en France de 1815 à nos jours' (1981), 'Faut-il avoir peur de 1989?' (1984), 'La Révolution française au banc des accusés (1984)' and his inaugural lecture 'Conflits et contradictions dans la France contemporaine' (1986), in Maurice Agulhon, *Histoire vagabonde II: Idéologies et politique dans la France du XIXème siècle* (Paris: Gallimard, 1988).

[67] Agulhon, 'Conflits et contradictions', p. 294.

[68] On Agulhon's reaction to Nora, and his relationship to the Annales, see the interview 'L'histoire et les pouvoirs; a l'occasion de la parution de plusieurs ouvrages, l'historien Maurice Agulhon livre sa réflexion sur le renouveau du rapport de l'historien au politique', *Le Monde*, 7 February 2003.

[69] Nicolet, *L'idée républicaine en France.*

Moreover, unlike Nora, whose commitment to neo-republicanism was implied in his work rather than stated outright, Nicolet has been particularly outspoken in his support of neo-republicanism. More recent essays have presented a republican case for *laïcité*, while a government report Nicolet wrote in 1984 for the then Education Minister Jean-Pierre Chevènement warned against the disappearance of 'republican' and 'civic' values in schools.[70] Nicolet also helped to found in 1996 the pressure group Comité Laïcité République, which fights for the defence of secularism in all areas of French public life.[71] For Nicolet – as for many earlier generations of republican historians – an academic commitment to his subject matter has gone hand in hand with the politics of engagement.

This elision between history and contemporary politics brings us back to the question of multiple republican teleologies. In different ways, Nora, Agulhon and Nicolet all contributed to a rehabilitation of republican symbols and values in the 1980s; Nora himself was speaking of a 'forceful return of national historiography' by the early 1990s.[72] They also restored to prominence the Third Republic as the institutional realisation of these republican principles. For Nicolet, the Third Republic was the 'foundation' of republican values; for Nora, it was the 'truest' of republics. But, whatever the words used, these historians emphasised not simply republicanism's abstract principles, but its institutional incarnation. This is what I have called the institutional narrative of the Republic – one that sees the Republic as a political regime, historically rooted in the Third Republic. As I shall show in later chapters, this narrative has become an important part of neo-republicanism. Paradoxically, especially given the left-wing politics of historians like Agulhon and Nora, this is because it has allowed the contemporary right to deploy a language of republicanism that traditionally emphasised a more progressive, revolutionary and transformative narrative.

The transformative narrative: the Republic as *laïcité*

Most historians of modern France would agree that, for much of its early life, republicanism was a language of protest. To reduce it simply to its institutional manifestations would be to leave aside its powerful

---

[70] Claude Nicolet, *La République en France: état des lieux* (Paris: Seuil, 1992), pp. 73–99.
[71] All relevant documents can be found on their website, www.laicite-republique.org (last accessed 15 April 2014).
[72] Pierre Nora, 'Comment écrire l'histoire de France', in Nora, *Les Lieux de Mémoire, Tome 3*, p. 13.

normative rhetoric. The Republic has always been invested with 'values', which are said to extend to every aspect of political life. The continuous battle to restart, reassert or re-energise the Republic has, more often than not, been built around a restatement of its core normative principles, and it is these principles which are the foundation of republicanism's transformative narrative. Where the institutional narrative relies on an idealised image of republicanism as a force for stability and national unity, the transformative narrative underlines republicanism's normative ambition and rests on a specific reading of French history that stresses its revolutionary origins and its trans-historical potential. For much of modern French history, this narrative has been the preserve of the left: it has been a language of protest that demands change, or exhorts the state to be more faithful to republican values.[73] But the rise of neo-republicanism in the last three decades has seen it spread to all corners of French politics. In the twenty-first century, even the far-right Front National (FN) has selectively deployed the transformative narrative of republicanism as a way of exhorting the French people to protect their distinctive national 'qualities'.[74]

Again, the writing of history has been instrumental in refashioning a transformative narrative of republicanism. In particular, the last thirty years have seen an extensive reinterpretation of one of republicanism's core values: *la laïcité*. The background to the *laïcité* debate, and especially its relationship to immigration and the rise of the FN, will be discussed in more detail in later chapters. Here, I simply want to explore some of the historical narratives of the Republic that have emerged in constructions of *laïcité*. For this, we need to look beyond the world of academic history to more public debates. One of the most sustained – and certainly the most public – attempt to theorise *laïcité* and place it within the broader sweep of French history was the report of the Commission Stasi in 2003 on 'religious signs' in schools. The Commission was composed of twenty public intellectuals, including a number of historians (such as René Rémond and Patrick Weil). The report they produced would form the basis for subsequent legislation, and it became, in its own way, a text of equal historical significance to Nora's *Lieux de mémoires*. Quite apart from its political consequences – of which more later – the collaborative nature of the text offered a

---

[73] Jacques Julliard, *Les gauches françaises. 1762–2012: Histoire, politique et imaginaire* (Paris: Flammarion, 2012), especially pp. 307–403.
[74] Marine Le Pen, 'Pour une République VRAIMENT française' (video, 4 November 2009), available at www.frontnational.com/videos/republique-vraiment-francaise/ (last accessed 12 January 2014).

unique insight into the teleologies and assumptions that have under-pinned a transformative narrative of neo-republicanism.[75]

The opening sentence of the report was a strong statement of intent: 'The French Republic was built around *laïcité*.'[76] Historically, such a statement is debatable. If the battle with the Catholic Church was an important part of modern French history, particularly in the period 1880–1914, relations between the state and the church were not always viewed through the prism of *laïcité*.[77] By simplifying discussions surround-ing religion in this way, the report situated itself firmly within a neo-republican vision of the Third Republic of the kind outlined earlier in this chapter.[78] Moreover, despite the need to affirm the principles of *laïcité* and inscribe them in the constitutions of 1946 and 1958, the second half of the twentieth century was a period when *laïcité* was not given a great deal of attention, either in politics or among academics. This was no doubt in part related to the lack of interest in the Third Republic.[79] But a rehabili-tation of the Third Republic also meant a rehabilitation of *laïcité*. By the first decade of the twenty-first century, it appeared an incontrovertible and timeless republican value, even if, as Jean Baubérot has pointed out, the 2004 legislation banning 'ostentatious religious signs' in schools was the first in French history to contain the word 'laïcité'.[80]

Not that these historical complexities stopped the authors of the report from restating their central claim a few pages later. *Laïcité*, we are told, is the 'cornerstone of the republican pact [*pacte républicain*]', a 'universal principle', and a 'republican value' that is 'constitutive of [French] collective history'.[81] Significantly for our purposes, this is the point at

---

[75] See chapter 4 for the context of the headscarf controversy. The Commission Stasi was unusual in the surprisingly large number of public consultations that took place over a very short space of time (9 September 2003–5 December 2003). The report was published on 12 December 2003.

[76] Commission de réflexion sur l'application du principe de la laïcité dans la République, *Rapport au Président de la République* (Paris: La Documentation Française, 2003), p. 9.

[77] The question of Catholicism and its relationship to the French state is an enormous field of study. For some pointers see Maurice Larkin, *Church and State after the Dreyfus Affair* (London: Macmillan, 1974); James McMillan, 'Priest hits girl: on the front line in the 'war of the two Frances', in Christopher Clark and Wolfram Kaiser (eds.), *Culture Wars: Secular–Catholic Conflict in Nineteenth-Century Europe* (Cambridge University Press, 2003); Ruth Harris, *Lourdes: Body and Spirit in a Secular Age* (London: Penguin, 1999); and Emile Perreau-Saussine, *Catholicism and Democracy: An Essay in the History of Political Thought* (London: Princeton University Press, 2012).

[78] For instance, after 1918, the legislation of 1905 was not applied to Alsace-Lorraine, an anomaly that still exists.

[79] Jean Baubérot, *L'intégrisme républicain contre la laïcité* (Paris: Editions de l'Aube 2006), pp. 197–210.

[80] Baubérot, *Laïcité 1905–2005*, p. 178.

[81] Commission de réflexion sur l'application du principe de la laïcité, *Rapport*, pp. 9–10.

which *laïcité* is given a strong historical narrative that is initially associated with a Western Enlightenment tradition:

> *Laïcité* refers to ancient Greece, the Renaissance and the Reformation, the Edict of Nantes, the Enlightenment: each of these stages developed in their own ways the autonomy of the individual and freedom of expression.[82]

Such an all-encompassing statement means that *laïcité* belongs not simply to the French, but to Western civilisation as a whole. This is a frequent trope in the transformative narrative of neo-republicanism, which systematically attempts to elevate republicanism into a trans-historical language of politics. Much later in the report, the authors again universalise the question of *laïcité* by drawing parallels with the contemporary political situation in other European countries. Their conclusion is that, whereas 'most European countries opted for a communitarian logic [*logique communautaire*]' in the post-war period, today 'there is the opposite tendency ... [as] they return to a more voluntaristic politics of integration'.[83] In other words, a neo-republican model of integrative *laïcité* remains applicable beyond the borders of France.

Nevertheless, for all its universal qualities, the report clearly identifies the French Revolution as *laïcité*'s 'moment of birth', the Ferry educational laws of 1882 and 1886 as its proving ground, and the 1905 separation law as its culmination. Over this period, *laïcité* went from an impassioned 'battle cry' to a 'widely shared republican value'. The authors accept that today's *laïcité* is more 'liberal' and more 'open', but they are adamant that the 1905 law should not be modified.[84] Instead, they recommend that the French state put together a 'charter' to clarify the practical limits of *laïcité*, above all in the public sector (schools, hospitals, municipal government). Such a charter would obviate the need for a case-by-case approach and would express clearly the secular principles that underpin French society. It would also strengthen France's case for speaking on behalf of the Western world: a transparent statement of intent would be a model for other countries looking for a solution to the problem of religious extremism.

The most visible manifestation of this desire to legislate *laïcité* was, of course, the 2004 ban on the wearing of 'ostentatious religious symbols' in state schools, and we shall look more closely at this in subsequent chapters. But the lengthier task of putting together a written charter along the lines suggested by the Commission Stasi was entrusted to the Haut Conseil à l'intégration, a permanent state commission founded in 1989 and responsible for elaborating state policy towards integration.

---

[82] Ibid., p. 10.   [83] Ibid., p. 33.   [84] Ibid., p. 50.

Not surprisingly, their influential 2007 report, entitled *Projet de charte de la laïcite dans les services publics*, offered further evidence of the historical narratives that have underpinned official conceptions of *laïcité* in France. Once again, the report's point of departure was an idealised image of the French Revolution as the beginning of modern history:

> From the French Revolution onwards, a series of laws guaranteed, for all citizens, the progress of a secular spirit and secular institutions: the Declaration of the Rights of Man and the Citizen in 1789, with its famous article X on the liberty of opinion and faith; the Civil Constitution of the Clergy in 1790; the secularisation of civil administration and marriage in 1792; a first separation of Church and State in 1795.[85]

This was followed by the inevitable passage through the Third Republic and the 1905 law, which was, according to the report's authors, an 'object of astonishment for the world ... [that] aroused interest and spawned multiple imitations'.[86] This was an almost exact replica of the narrative elaborated in the Stasi report and it included all the key aspects of a transformative narrative of the Republic: on the one hand, a reference to the universal applicability and normative aspirations of republican values; on the other, a teleology that begins with the most progressive legacies of the French Revolution. There are elements of the institutional narrative, too; the repeated references to the Third Republic and the school in the Stasi and Haut Conseil à l'intégration (HCI) reports give *laïcité* a temporal and physical *lieu de mémoire*. But the emphasis in both texts is always first and foremost on *laïcité* as a trans-historical phenomenon with universal aspirations.

Of course, the neo-republican conception of *laïcité* found in government reports in the 2000s simply reflected and amplified the renewed interest in republicanism in academic history more generally. We have already seen how professional historians like Nora, Agulhon and Nicolet contributed to the rehabilitation of an institutional narrative inspired by the Third Republic, but they were also quite willing to invoke a transformative narrative when discussing the present. For instance, in Agulhon's 1986 Collège de France inaugural lecture, he claimed that 'the pluralist and secular form [of the nation] ... is the only form of [national community] that is conceivable in the contemporary age'.[87] Nicolet went further still in his homage to the transformative potential of republicanism in an essay from the mid 1980s. Without the slightest hint of irony,

---

[85] Haut Conseil à l'integration, *Projet de charte de la laïcite dans les services publics* (Paris: La Documentation Française, 2007), pp. 16–17.
[86] Ibid., p. 14.
[87] 'Conflits et contradictions', in Agulhon, *Histoire vagabonde II*, p. 294.

he argued that 'the balance sought by the Republic for the happiness of the human race can only truly be achieved and satisfactory if it is global [*planétaire*]'.[88] To his audience at the time such a statement probably appeared outlandish and passé. But, by the time of the Commission Stasi two decades later, it was taken for granted that *laïcité* was a perennial republican value imbued with special trans-historical qualities.

This mixing of narratives should be a reminder that my separation of institutional and transformative narratives is not an exercise in rigid political classification: there is no such thing as, say, a transformative neo-republican. My purpose in this chapter was to uncover different narratives and historiographies in an effort to paint a more complex picture of neo-republicanism. In this, I have followed the lead of a number of French historians, many of whom have tried to show the divisions and tensions inside France's 'republican tradition'. Some have chosen to stress the difference between 'the Republic as ideal' and 'the Republic as a form of government'.[89] Others have identified a conflict between republicanism as 'the common and consensual heritage of the nation' and republicanism as a philosophy expressed with the 'activist vehemence of resuscitated Jacobinism'.[90] Even Agulhon has made a distinction between 'the Republic as a code and the Republic as a value'.[91] But, despite this abundance of frameworks, none of these historians has been able (or willing) to analyse critically the consequences of this historical division for contemporary French politics. By looking at multiple narratives rather than values or ideas, I have tried to bring the historical complexity of republicanism into the more recent past, without becoming trapped in an argument over its 'true' nature.

This is important because recently there has been a good deal of scholarship that has cast French neo-republicanism – and especially *laïcité* – as an intolerable attack on liberal pluralism, or simply as a thinly veiled form of neo-colonial domination targeted at Muslims.[92] I do not

---

[88] Nicolet, *La République en France*, p. 129.
[89] For example Christophe Prochasson, 'Introuvable modèle républicain', *Cahiers Français: Les valeurs de la République* (No. 336, 2007), pp. 3–7.
[90] Mona Ozouf, 'L'idée républicaine et l'interprétation du passé national', *Annales* (Vol. 53, No. 6, 1998), pp. 1075–87.
[91] 'Républicain à la française' (1992), in Maurice Agulhon, *Histoire vagabonde III: La politique en France d'hier et d'aujourd'hui* (Paris: Gallimard, 1996), p. 98.
[92] The claim that *la laïcité* is a way of exercising domination over minorities and has concealed racism has been made for instance in Joan Scott's recent work. See Joan Wallach Scott, *The Politics of the Veil* (London: Princeton University Press, 2007); and Joan Wallach Scott, 'Symptomatic Politics: The Banning of Islamic Head Scarves in French Public Schools', *French Politics, Culture and Society* (Vol. 23, No. 3, 2005), pp. 106–27.

want to dismiss these criticisms entirely; we shall see later how the resurgence of colonial memory has shaped neo-republicanism. Nevertheless, I believe that we should see *laïcité* first and foremost as a strong, teleological reading of French history. That there is significant historical distortion in the Stasi and HCI reports is beyond doubt. But the construction of *laïcité* as a republican value in contemporary France cannot simply be seen as an exercise in 'domination' or as a thin justification for 'racism' or 'exclusion'. Rather, it is a story of republican triumph that rests on partial readings of the Revolution, the Third Republic and the impact of the 1905 law. This has now become a core narrative of neo-republicanism, widely accepted among the political elite, the press and the wider public.

The following chapters will deal in greater detail with the multifarious contexts in which France's national narrative has been rewritten since the 1980s. But the writing of history has played a part in every one of these contexts: as in the past, the interplay between institutional and transformative narratives of republicanism has paved the way for novel and unusual political configurations. For example, figures from the right and the left have joined together to defend *l'école républicaine* as an essential legacy of the Third Republic, or warned of the dangers of multiculturalism on the ground that it compromises national unity. There have been frequent elisions between transformative and institutional narratives depending on the history that is being invoked. It might be tempting to see these differences as just another incarnation of a right–left divide inside neo-republicanism. But a simple right–left equation cannot do justice to this kind of debate; as we shall see, much more sophisticated conceptual tools are required if we are to explain the contemporary writing of the French national narrative.

2 From *nouveaux philosophes* to *nouveaux réactionnaires*: Marxism and the Republic

It is difficult to understand the rise of neo-republicanism without reference to France's Marxist intellectual tradition. This is not because it has been the sole preserve of current or former Marxists. On the contrary, one of its defining characteristics has been its political ecumenism. Nevertheless, the key concerns of neo-republicanism have been profoundly shaped by France's Marxist heritage and, more specifically, by the fragmentation of the French left since the 1970s. By and large, the republican revival of the 1980s was led by people who had been associated with the left at some point in their careers – whether this was historians such as Maurice Agulhon, political figures such as Jean-Pierre Chevènement or the two intellectuals whose trajectories will be the subject of this chapter: Alain Finkielkraut and Régis Debray.

This umbilical connection between neo-republicanism and the left has often been phrased in relatively stark terms: as Marxism became increasingly discredited at the ballot box and in universities, republicanism took its place. In this interpretation, it was a simple case of substitution; class and the proletariat were discarded in favour of the Republic and the citizen. The narrative that emerges from such a reading stresses the decline of the left, and its gradual rightward shift. The story begins in 1968, with the violent attack on the communist left during the protests of May 1968. The result is a near total collapse of the Communist Party by the end of the 1980s, squeezed out at the ballot box by Mitterrand's Socialists and a rejuvenated Gaullist movement.[1] At the same time, a wholesale attack on various forms of intellectual Marxism had begun in the academy. Aronian 'liberalism', cultural history, 'new philosophy' – all these trends flourished in the 1980s and appeared to announce the victory of anti-Marxism. With the collapse of the Soviet Union and the fall of the Berlin Wall in 1989–91, Marxism was finally terminated as a

---

[1] Hazareesingh, *Intellectuals and the French Communist Party*.

political and intellectual force. As if to mark the end of an era, this was precisely when neo-republicanism made its public entry with the *affaire du foulard*, in 1989. It seemed self-evident that the Republic had emerged from the ashes of French Marxism.[2]

This narrative has much to commend it. It is one shared by many (left-wing) commentators on France's intellectual scene, most of whom look back with rose-tinted glasses to a time of Sartrean intellectual engagement, and bemoan today's 'pensée unique' or 'pensée tiède'.[3] Likewise, more scholarly analyses have stressed the importance of neo-republicanism's roots in the reaction to 1968 or as a means to combat the fading legitimacy of Marxism.[4] Unfortunately, the narrative which presents neo-republicanism as simply a weak substitute for Marxism is only one reading of a more complex story. For a start, there were many gradations within French Marxism – most notably between the communist and non-communist (socialist) left – not all of which have been equally involved in, or receptive to, the neo-republican turn. In addition, there is no simple correlation between the delegitimisation of Marxism in the final quarter of the twentieth century, and the return of a language of republicanism. Rather, we should see neo-republicanism – and particularly its 'transformative' narrative – as an attempt to build on and realise some of the key rhetorical elements of French Marxism such as 'revolution' and 'solidarity'. Those who appeared to abandon their Marxist past for a neo-republican future were looking for a way to combine the political engagement of their Marxism with ideas about the nation and the national narrative that had not played a prominent part in their intellectual upbringing. It is certainly the case that the disintegration of a Marxist consensus among France's intellectual class made it possible for republicanism once again to enter the mainstream. But the turn to the Republic was also a sign of the democratisation of French intellectual life. For, unlike the finer doctrinal differences between, say, different kinds of communist groups, the Republic was a

---

[2] In essence, this was the narrative sketched out in Pierre Rosanvallon, 'Malaise dans la représentation', in Furet, Julliard and Rosanvallon, *La République du Centre*, p. 140 ; and Serge Berstein, 'La gauche française entre marxisme et République', paper presented at the conference 'Origine et modernité des valeurs républicaines', Belfort, France, 12–13 November 2010.

[3] Ignacio Ramonet, 'La pensée unique', *Le Nouvel Observateur* (January 1995), and Perry Anderson, *La pensée tiède: un regard critique sur la culture française* (Paris: Seuil 2005). For an overview of these debates see Emile Chabal, 'Writing the French National Narrative in the Twenty-First Century', *Historical Journal* (Vol. 53, No. 2, June 2010), pp. 495–516.

[4] On the legacy of 1968, see the comprehensive Serge Audier, *La pensée anti-68: essai sur une restauration intellectuelle* (Paris: La Découverte, 2008).

concept readily understood, invoked and accepted by many French people.[5] Engaging with neo-republicanism meant descending from the ivory tower into the grubby world of TV chat shows and newspaper columns. It therefore provided an ideal means for French intellectuals to reinvent themselves as public commentators.

One of the best ways of mapping these transformations is by studying individual trajectories. In the previous chapter, I focused on the role of historians and the writing of history more generally, but here I want to turn my attention to political thought and philosophy. I focus on two intellectuals who have played a central role in discussions surrounding the Republic in the past three decades. They are both graduates of France's most elite higher education institution, the Ecole normale supérieure (ENS), and their contrasting intellectual journeys shed light on the relationship between French Marxism and neo-republicanism. As before, this is not an exercise in labelling, although both figures openly identified themselves with neo-republicanism. My purpose is to explore the intellectual climate that surrounded them and some of the debates with which they have been preoccupied. Both Debray and Finkielkraut have had varied interests, only one of which has been the redefinition of the nation. But the reasons that have led them to reassess the nation state are central to an understanding of the wider resurgence of neo-republicanism. Even if the conversion of these two members of France's high intellectual class from Marxism to the Republic might appear to be one that has little relevance to the country as a whole, I shall suggest that the reverse is true.

Before analysing each figure independently, however, I want to high-light some characteristics of post-war French Marxism that laid the foundations for the neo-republican revival. The first point is the extent to which the essential Marxist concepts of theory and practice have been peculiarly separated in the French context. If the practice (and success) of the French left in the twentieth century was largely a product of electoral compromise and organisational strength on the ground, its theory was discussed at extraordinary length in the rarefied atmosphere of the Parisian intellectual scene. The difference could not have been more pronounced, and has been repeatedly commented on by observers outside France, especially those who have worked on the period after 1945.[6] In particular,

---

[5] Tony Judt was one of the strongest critics of the 'irresponsibility' and 'detachment' of post-war French intellectual life, especially in Tony Judt, *Past Imperfect: French Intellectuals, 1944–1956* (Oxford: Clarendon, 1992).

[6] Judt, *Marxism and the French Left*, pp. 230–40; and Khilnani, *Arguing Revolution*, esp. chs. 1–4.

the sharp disjunction between Communist Party activists and the restricted intellectual world of the Party's 'fellow travellers' had important consequences for the development of French Marxism from the 1930s onwards. Two of these are particularly relevant to our discussion: first, the long-standing obsession with a specific reading of Hegel; and, second, the almost complete domination of political Marxism, at the expense of more economic readings of Marx's theories. Both of these peculiarities are central to an understanding of how neo-republicanism could so easily absorb refugees from French Marxism.

The importance of Hegel to French Marxism is now well known. Already in the late 1970s, Vincent Descombes's survey of twentieth-century French philosophy emphasised the extent to which much of it was an extended dialogue with Hegel.[7] This was a legacy of a neo-Hegelian turn that can be traced with remarkable precision to classes given by Alexandre Kojève at the Ecole Normale Supérieure. Kojève was particularly influential in reincorporating Hegel's phenomenology into Marxist thought, an approach given added weight by György Lukács's contemporaneous work and, even more importantly, the discovery and circulation of the 1844 Manuscripts in the 1940s, which demonstrated Marx's engagement with Hegelian thought.[8] The rehabilitation of Hegel and his concept of the *Geist* during this period led later Marxists into an almost obsessive concern with the 'totality', often viewed in the political terms imagined by Hegel.[9] From a generational point of view, the importance of this move is illustrated by the sheer number of French intellectuals who attended Kojève's classes.[10] Jean Hyppolite was later to prolong the life of the neo-Hegelian turn by producing the first French translations of Hegel's *Phenomenology of the Spirit* in 1939 and teaching a second generation of intellectuals at the Sorbonne and the Ecole Normale Supérieure after the Second World War.[11]

The weight of this neo-Hegelianism had a significant impact on French Marxist thought. Not only did it set the linguistic parameters of French Marxism, it also meant that the problem of 'totality' or 'total' theory remained at the heart of French philosophy. The need to

---

[7] Vincent Descombes, *Le même et l'autre: Quarante-cinq ans de philosophie française (1933–1978)* (Paris: Editions de Minuit, 1979).

[8] See Alexandre Kojève, *Introduction to the Reading of Hegel*, ed. Allan Bloom (New York: Basic Books, 1969).

[9] On this see Martin Jay, *Marxism and Totality: the adventures of a concept from Lukács to Habermas* (Berkeley, CA: University of California Press, 1984).

[10] Among whom were Jean Hyppolite, Jean-Paul Sartre, Maurice Merleau-Ponty, Raymond Aron, Georges Bataille, Jacques Lacan, Eric Weil and André Breton.

[11] This second generation included figures such as Michel Foucault, Gérard Granel and Gilles Deleuze.

subordinate history, politics and human existence to a phenomenological totality exacerbated the already acute tendency towards abstraction encouraged by an inward-looking intellectual environment and the highly theoretical philosophical training of the Ecole Normale Supérieure.[12] It also explains why French Marxist thought found itself in such disarray in the late 1970s: it was faced on one side by a post-structuralist reaction that was set on 'deconstructing' the totality and on the other by the possible political reality of socialist rule under Mitterrand. Ironically, just as the first left-wing government of the Fifth Republic was about to come to power, the ideological foundations of the intellectual left appeared comprehensively bankrupt. The generation of *nouveaux philosophes* that came of age in the late 1970s – of whom Alain Finkielkraut, André Glucksmann and Bernard-Henri Lévy were perhaps the best known – embodied the most public voice of this critique of the left.[13] Their subsequent turn to alternative totalities in the 1990s (Finkielkraut found solace in the Republic, while Glucksmann and Henri-Lévy looked to the United States and George W. Bush's Republicans) only confirmed the profound delegitimisation of Marxist thought in France by the turn of the century.[14]

But French Marxism's abstract neo-Hegelian tendencies had another important consequence: a startling absence of reflection on economic questions – and this despite the vital importance of labour and economics to Marxist thought. The more economic later Marx of *Das Kapital* was, for obvious reasons, less appealing to generations of young French philosophers brought up on Kojève and Hyppolite. As a result, almost none of the leading lights of post-war French Marxism had anything more than a perfunctory interest in economic theory. Those on the left who took an interest in economic issues – for instance, André Gorz with his work on the 'end of labour' – produced relatively abstract analyses of economic phenomena, far removed from the empirical obsessions of, say, American modernisation theorists such as Walt Rostow or neo-liberal economists of the Chicago School such as Milton Friedman or Gary Becker.[15]

---

[12] For a sense of the peculiar character of intellectual life at the ENS, see the illuminating discussion in Edward Baring, *The Young Derrida and French Philosophy, 1945–1968* (Cambridge University Press, 2010).

[13] Michael Scott Christofferson, *French Intellectuals against the Left* (Oxford: Berghahn Books, 2004).

[14] André Glucksmann, 'L'étrange renversement d'alliance', *Le Monde* (5 April 2003) ; Bernard Henri-Lévy, *American Vertigo: Travelling America in the Footsteps of Tocqueville* (London: Random House, 2006).

[15] André Gorz, *Métamorphoses du travail* (Paris: Galilée, 1988). On modernisation theorists, see David Engerman (ed.), *Staging Growth: Modernization, Development and the Global Cold War* (Boston, MA: University of Massachusetts Press, 2003).

Beyond the confines of the academy, too, there was a general apathy on the French left towards economics. Thus, in 1954–5, left-wing intellectuals had little to say about Mendès-France's abortive efforts to create a practical left-wing economic agenda.[16] The same was true when Mitterrand attempted to implement a form of French Keynesianism in 1981–3: the painful consequences of these early years, which culminated in a radical shift to austerity policies in 1983, can to some extent be blamed on an intense desire on the part of many socialists at the time to make the minutiae of microeconomics subservient to more general political goals. Even a scholar like Gorz had a tendency to minimise the purely economic dimensions of economic problems. In keeping with his background as an erstwhile disciple of Sartrean phenomenology he repeatedly argued in the 1980s and 1990s that problems related to the 'end of labour' and the disappearance of the 'proletariat' were 'essentially political'.[17] This attitude has begun to change in recent years with the global success of left-wing economists like Thomas Piketty and Emmanuel Saez, but their writings still retain a strong belief in the power of politics (and the state) as the solution to growing inequality.[18] This is a reminder that French Marxism has always remained more interested in politics than economics, if for no other reason than because its most prominent twentieth-century intellectual exponents have been literary critics, philosophers and, more recently, sociologists. By contrast, economists – and economics generally – have been marginalised.

Seen in this light, the rehabilitation of the Republic among France's intellectual elite is easier to understand. Indeed, it is worth remembering that classical French republicanism, dating back to the Revolution, was also largely silent on economic matters.[19] None of the central tenets of republicanism had much to do with economics. Liberty, equality, fraternity: these were political values above all. In the same way that the vital place of economics in Marx's thought was largely ignored by French Marxists, the vital place of economics in Enlightenment thought was never prominent in French republican thinking as it developed in the nineteenth century. Such is the parallel that one is tempted to argue that the French left's lack of interest in economics has more to do with its republican than its neo-Hegelian heritage. Either way, when combined

---

[16] Judt, *Marxism and the French Left*, p. 183.

[17] Gorz, *Métamorphoses du travail*, p. 107. See also André Gorz, *Adieux aux prolétariat: au-delà du socialisme* (Paris: Galilée, 1980).

[18] See for instance Thomas Piketty, *Capital in the Twenty-First Century* (London: Harvard University Press, 2014), esp. Part 4. I discuss some of these issues in more detail in chapter 8.

[19] Baker, 'Transformations of Classical Republicanism in Eighteenth-Century France'.

with a persistent concern with a 'totality', the need to reaffirm the political over the economic made it relatively straightforward for intellectuals such as Debray and Finkielkraut to combine Marxism and the Republic in a new, and sometimes imaginative, synthesis.

Régis Debray's revolutionary Republic

Debray made his name, not as a philosopher, but as a guerrilla *manqué*.[20] After graduating from the Ecole Normale Supérieure, Debray decided to participate actively in the revolutionary struggles in Latin America. In a rare attempt on the part of a French intellectual to live the notional unity between Marxist theory and practice, he travelled to Havana in 1965 and subsequently attempted to join Ernesto 'Che' Guevara in Bolivia. But in 1967 Debray was captured by the Bolivian authorities, put on trial for dissident activities, and subsequently jailed in Bolivia after a highly publicised trial. He was released in 1971 after a long campaign that had been instigated by Jean-Paul Sartre. Although he had become something of an icon during his time in jail – when he was released, he was taken to meet Salvador Allende and Pablo Neruda – one of the main consequences of his period of incarceration was that he was absent from France during the protests of 1968. This gave him an unusual perspective on the ideological changes of the late 1960s. Unmoved by the 'spirit of 68' – and more than a little unhappy that so much activity had taken place in his absence – he became increasingly sceptical of the value of the 1968 protests.

This scepticism culminated in 1978 with the publication of *Modeste contribution aux discours et cérémonies officielles du dixème anniversaire*, which was a blistering attack on the generation that came of age in 1968. Far from being the vanguard of counterculture, Debray argued, this group had enabled the rise of the neo-liberal economy. Their hedonistic and unstructured 'creativity' in 1968 had actually been remarkably conducive to the growth of a consumerist society, not least because ten years later few of them were still willing to countenance truly revolutionary change. As he put it bluntly, 'the strategy of development of Capital demanded a cultural revolution ... [even if] it did not know it', with the result that 'neo-capitalism' was able to 'move forward concealed beneath the virtues of counterculture'.[21] But, alongside his pungent critique of

---

[20] A good biographical overview can be found in Keith Reader, *Régis Debray: A Critical Introduction* (London: Pluto Press, 1995).

[21] Debray's *Modeste contribution* was republished in Régis Debray, *Mai 68, une contrerévolution réussie* (Paris: Mille et une nuits, 2008). The citations here are from pp. 29 and 89 of this version.

the *soixante-huitard* generation, Debray was also in the late 1970s beginning to develop a theory of media power. This owed much to Guy Debord's famous work *La Société du Spectacle* published in 1967 (in *Modeste contribution*, Debray had described Debord as one of the only 'true geniuses' of 1968).[22] In common with other post-Marxist thinkers such as Pierre Bourdieu or Jean Baudrillard, Debray was critical of mass culture and the media. In his *Le Pouvoir Intellectuel en France* (1979), he identified the post-1968 period as the beginning of a pernicious 'media cycle' in French intellectual life.[23] He attacked the alleged stranglehold of Bernard Pivot's popular and highly influential television programme *Apostrophes* and the media presence of the *nouveaux philosophes*.[24]

Yet, for all his radical pretensions, Debray could not conceal his proximity to the Parisian political elite when he was invited to become a presidential advisor on international relations after Mitterrand's election victory in 1981. In a substantial interview for *Le Nouvel Observateur* shortly after his appointment, he struggled to convince his interviewer that his journey from the Bolivian jungle to the Elysée Palace was part of a consistent career trajectory.[25] Instead, it was apparent from his answers that it was not simply his political orientation that had shifted; his intellectual compass had also been reoriented, first by his disenchantment with Marxism in the 1970s and then by his integration into a now governing Parti socialiste (PS).[26] In short, Debray was an intellectual searching for an individual and collective cause. As he put it in 1981, 'a society without a strong belief [*croyance forte*] is a society that is dying'.[27] The question, then, was what kind of belief would be required to re-energise French politics? By the late 1980s, the answer was clear: Debray would henceforth be a vocal advocate of the Republic.

This was consistent with Debray's changing intellectual interests, but it helped that neo-republicanism was also one of the most sustained

---

[22] Guy Debord, *La Société du Spectacle* (Paris: Folio, 2000 [1969]). Debray praised Debord in Debray, *Modeste contribution*, p. 91.

[23] Régis Debray, *Le Pouvoir Intellectuel en France* (Paris: Editions Ramsey, 1979), p. 94.

[24] *Apostrophes* was a television programme presented by Bernard Pivot. Broadcast every Friday evening from 1975 to 1990, it brought authors, journalists, historians, sociologists and other intellectuals together to discuss a book or theme. It was enormously successful and it undoubtedly contributed to bringing 'high' intellectual debate to a wider audience in France (and abroad).

[25] Jean Paul Enthoven, 'La longue marche de Régis Debray', *Nouvel Observateur* (10 October 1981).

[26] A good example of Debray's changing political orientation can be found in a radio debate between Debray and Jean Ziegler from 1985. *Répliques: La raison d'état*, France Culture (16 November 1985).

[27] Enthoven, 'La longue marche de Régis Debray'.

attempts to build a 'croyance forte' in late-twentieth-century France. Still, it took a particular context for Debray to commit his neo-republicanism to paper. This was the so-called *affaire du foulard* (headscarf affair) in September 1989. The wider debate surrounding the *affaire* will be discussed in the next chapter, but here we need only note that, amidst the cacophonous controversy, Debray's texts stood out for their uncompromising nature. The most famous of his interventions was his lengthy article 'République ou démocratie', which was first published in *Le Nouvel Observateur* in November 1989.[28] The core of Debray's argument was that there is a profound normative distinction to be made between a Republic and a Democracy (he capitalises both terms). A Republic corresponds to the public incarnation of enlightened rationalism, while a Democracy is simply the expression of society's collective opinion. In his words,

The Republic is Democracy *plus*. The Republic is Liberty *plus* Reason; the Rule of Law *plus* Justice; tolerance *plus* will [*volonté*]. Let us say that Democracy is what is left of a Republic when the Enlightenment has been taken out.[29]

But Debray did much more than merely construct a normative comparison between a Republic and a Democracy; he also laid out a long list of associations that give us a much sharper view of his own preconceptions. Of particular interest are his discussions of Democracy's supposed relationship with business, advertising and the media. Some examples will suffice to give an idea of his argument. In a Democracy, 'opinion is the law', 'money is sacrosanct' and 'the client is king'.[30] This corresponds to the key personalities of a Democracy: 'lawyers … journalists, publicity moguls, singers, actors, businessmen'.[31] Above all, a Democracy has different priorities. While a Republic focuses obsessively on its 'institutions', a Democracy is ultimately only ever concerned with 'marketing [*communication*]'.[32] Debray recognises that not all democracies are as obviously liberal or consumerist as his ideal type, but he maintains that, in the current period, 'a liberal and consumerist society [is] … so dominant and omnipresent that we believe it to be obligatory'.[33] In this analysis, then, democracy, liberalism and consumer capitalism are all coterminous.

Debray reaffirmed this argument in a number of later texts, including *Que vive la République!* (1989) and *La République expliquée à ma fille* (1998). In *Que vive la République!*, for example, he announced that 'the

---

[28] References here are to the version of Debray's essay republished in Régis Debray, *Contretemps: éloges des idéaux perdus* (Paris: Folio, 1992), pp. 15–54.

[29] Régis Debray, 'République ou démocratie', p. 18 (emphasis in original).

[30] Ibid., pp. 32, 35.   [31] Ibid., pp. 26, 34.   [32] Ibid., p. 33.   [33] Ibid., p. 17.

Republic [is] threatened today by the Image [*l'Image*] and Money [*l'Argent*]'.[34] In this one sentence, he succeeded in highlighting the dangers of the media (*l'Image*) and the potential threat to the political (the Republic) from the economic (*l'Argent*). In a global world that is flooded with televised images, the Republic becomes both an offensive weapon to be used against *l'Argent* and *l'Image* and a protection against their never-ending encroachment. The fact that *l'Argent* and *l'Image* are associated with the United States is a point to which we shall return later; what is important is that Debray's republican model of the nation state carries persistent anti-American overtones.[35] American values – which are the values of *l'Image* – are given powerful negative connotations and placed in direct competition with (French) republican values. His construction of a facile binary opposition between the two countries provides a ready-made conceptual framework and a strong normative foundation for his brand of neo-republicanism.[36]

Most importantly, Debray is unambiguous about the need for a strong, rational central authority in the form of a republican state. As a repository of national memory, cultural heritage and enlightenment values, the Republic is the only possible bulwark against the decadence of Democracy and the warped ethics of financial capitalism. In previous decades, it was 'the State and its censorship that threatened the autonomy of the individual', but 'today it is civil society ... and the rise of more and more intolerant powers – the media, the clerics, the sciences, the administration'. The only way out of this impasse is through a defence of the Republic and its values.[37] For Debray, the Republic and its secular institutions are the preconditions of emancipation. The Republic stands for unity, community and positive values, while Democracy is synonymous with fragmentation and a valueless society. In this sense, the rise of Democracy, the 'media cycle' and the 'reign of the Image' are very much of a piece, as Debray makes abundantly clear in a more recent essay, *L'obscénité démocratique* (2008). Here, the contrast is not so much between Democracy and Republic, but on the ways in which Democracy utilises and manipulates 'theatrical' techniques in order to convey its messages. Debray's central claim is that the ubiquity of *l'Image* has created a narcissistic and individualist society.[38]

---

[34] Régis Debray, *Que vive la République!* (Paris: Editions Odile Jacob, 1989), p. 13.

[35] See chapter 5 on perceptions of the Anglo-American world.

[36] He uses the United States as his straw man in Régis Debray, *La République expliquée à ma fille* (Paris: Seuil, 1998), pp. 1–4. There is a searing critique of Debray's anti-Americanism in Audier, *La pensée anti-68*, pp. 290–300.

[37] Debray, 'République ou démocratie', p. 52.

[38] Régis Debray, *L'obscénité démocratique* (Paris: Flammarion, 2008).

By the time Debray was invited to participate in the Commission Stasi in 2003, his views on the Republic were well known and no one was taken aback to find him wholeheartedly in support of legislation to ban the wearing of 'ostentatious religious symbols' in state schools. As we shall see, some of the arguments he developed in his letter to the Commission about the sanctity of the school had been elaborated in the 1990s in dialogue with Finkielkraut, but his main point about the need for a strong *laïcité* as a bulwark against the fragmentation of collective beliefs was familiar. However, the subtitle to the published version of Debray's letter – *Ce que nous voile le voile: la République et le sacré* (2004) – suggested that a new theme was becoming increasingly prominent in his thought: the role and function of religion.[39] Debray was a tireless defender of *laïcité* from the late 1980s onwards, but over time he became more and more sensitive – in some cases, sympathetic – to religion's role as a form of collective belief. He published widely on religion's role in history and politics, to the point of arguing in a recent text that the basis of fraternity lies in the affective power and longevity of the 'sacred'.[40] Moreover, Debray has not shied away from expressing these opinions in public: in his influential report *L'enseignement du fait religieux dans l'École laïque* (2002), commissioned by the then Socialist Minister of Education, Jack Lang, he defended the teaching of religion in schools and universities, as well as suggesting that it be incorporated more explicitly in the curriculum.[41] To his fellow neo-republicans, such proposals were alarming: surely this eulogy of religion was in contradiction to both his left-wing past and his neo-republican principles?

In fact, the contradiction was not as great as it first appeared. Debray had been interested in religion for some time – at least since the 1970s – and his admiration for its transcendental quality fitted well with the transformative narrative of republicanism that was at the forefront of his writing.[42] Nor had he entirely abandoned his youthful Marxism; it was merely given a new twist. His trenchant denunciation of an individualistic media- and money-based modernity, and his regular reiteration of the collective power of the Republic, owed a great deal to France's Marxist heritage. In Debray's neo-republican turn, Hegelian totality was

[39] Régis Debray, *Ce que nous voile le voile: la République et le sacré* (Paris: Gallimard, 2004).
[40] Régis Debray, *Le moment fraternité* (Paris: Gallimard, 2009).
[41] Régis Debray, *L'enseignement du fait religieux dans l'École laïque* (Paris: La Documentation Française, 2002).
[42] Michael Behrent, 'Religion, Republicanism, and Depoliticization: Two Intellectual Itineraries – Régis Debray and Marcel Gauchet', in Julian Bourg (ed.), *After the Deluge: New Perspectives on the Intellectual and Cultural History of Postwar France* (Lanham, MD: Lexington Books, 2004).

retrieved and repackaged as the 'indivisible unity' of the Republic; the primacy of the political over the economic was reaffirmed; and the post-*soixante huitard* criticism of the media was brought to the fore, alongside a modified form of French intellectual anti-Americanism. Debray even found a way of legitimising revolutionary violence: in the final chapter of *Que vive la République!*, he argued that if 'the redemption of peoples by revolutionary violence was an illusion, the obliteration of this violence is a mere dupery, of which the 'Rights of Man' are often the instrument'[43] – in short, that revolutionary violence (in the name of republican principles) is both acceptable and desirable. This classic Marxist statement of the value of violence was a potent demonstration of the way in which a declining Marxist language of politics was absorbed into an emerging neo-republican idea. It also helps to explain how a Republic which, to many early-twentieth-century French Marxists represented a suspiciously bourgeois form of government, could be so easily rehabilitated at the end of the century by a former Marxist like Debray.

Alain Finkielkraut's Republic of Letters

Finkielkraut's divorce from Marxism was as polemical as Debray's but rather less adventurous. Unlike the hopeful guerrilla fighter, Finkielkraut nursed his revolutionary fantasies on Paris's Left Bank among the Maoist Union des jeunesses communistes marxistes-léninistes (UJC-ML) and its splinter group, the Gauche prolétarienne (GP).[44] In common with many intelligent and impressionable left-wing *normaliens* of his generation, Finkielkraut was drawn to Maoism around 1968. This stimulating, if sectarian, environment of *gauchiste* student politics did not have a lasting effect on the substance of Finkielkraut's thought, but it did play a role in shaping the style of his subsequent intellectual interventions, which were invariably strongly worded, polemical and, at times, uncompromising. In the words of his critics, his Maoism left him with a 'symptomatic' view of the world, in which 'everything is political' and therefore liable to provoke a strong reaction.[45] Nevertheless, within a

[43] Debray, *Que vive la République!*, p. 204. See also 'Résister' in Régis Debray, *Contretemps: éloges des idéaux perdues* (Paris: Folio, 1992).

[44] On French Maoism, see Julian Bourg, *From Revolution to Ethics: May 1968 and Contemporary French Thought* (London: McGill-Queen's University Press, 2007), pp. 45–104; Camille Robcis, '"China in Our Heads": Althusser, Maoism, and Structuralism', *Social Text* (Vol. 30, No. 1, 2012), pp. 51–69; Christophe Bourseiller, *Les maoïstes: La folle histoire des gardes rouges français* (Paris: Points, 2008); and Richard Wolin, *The Wind from the East: French Intellectuals, the Cultural Revolution and the Legacy of the 1960s* (Princeton University Press, 2010).

[45] Christophe Ayad, 'Alain Finkielkraut, bile en tête', *Libération* (29 December 2005).

decade Finkielkraut had firmly renounced the cause of *gauchisme* and launched himself into trenchant and bitter denunciation of totalitarianism, which earned him a place among the media-savvy *nouveaux philosophes* and put him at the forefront of the attack on Marxism that swept across French intellectual life in the late 1970s and early 1980s.

Finkielkraut's main contribution to this movement was a book he co-wrote with Pascal Bruckner entitled *Le nouveau désordre amoureux* (1977), in which they criticised the libertarian ideology behind the 'sexual revolution' of the 1960s and endorsed a greater diversity of sexual experience.[46] This argument was in keeping with the broad critique of totalitarianism on which the *nouveaux philosophes* built their philosophical and political credentials. We shall explore in greater depth in subsequent chapters how they read and misread certain French liberal thinkers in their attempt to construct a powerful critique of Marxism, but it is enough to say here that their anti-totalitarianism was based on a tendentious and partial rereading of the work of, among others, Hannah Arendt, Raymond Aron and Claude Lefort. Their explicit aim was to denounce the totalitarian potential of ideology in general, although the primary target was communism in all of its forms.[47] This reflected a growing scepticism of Marxism amongst France's intellectual elite, but also domestic political concerns – namely, the possibility of a left-wing victory in the legislative elections of 1978 and the fear of communist involvement in a government of the 'Union of the Left'. This political configuration gave added urgency to the message: as the American historian Michael Scott Christofferson has clearly demonstrated, the *nouveaux philosophes* saw themselves locked in a battle to prevent communism from creeping into French politics.[48]

Paradoxically, the victory of the left in 1981 was the beginning of the end of the *nouveaux philosophes*. This group of erstwhile *gauchistes* had focused so much of their attention on the threat of communism that, with the collapse of the PCF in the early 1980s and Mitterrand's ideological about-turn in 1982–3, they were deprived of their arch-enemy. Not to mention the fact that their methodology, approach and conclusions had been severely criticised by other philosophers as simplistic, reductive and facile. In any case, by the mid 1980s, France seemed to be facing much more pressing problems than the remote possibility of a communist

---

[46] Alain Finkielkraut and Pascal Bruckner, *Le nouveau désordre amoureux* (Paris: Seuil, 1977).
[47] A useful analysis of this moment in French thought can be found in K. Reader, *Intellectuals and the Left in France since 1968* (London: Macmillan, 1987).
[48] Christofferson, *French Intellectuals against the Left*.

takeover. Economic contraction had brought an end to post-war economic growth. The parallel rise of minority identity politics, immigration as an electoral issue and the Front National in the 1980s had pushed the idea of the nation centre stage. And historians were eagerly rehabilitating the great symbols of the French republican canon. It makes sense, therefore, that a former *nouveau philosophe* like Finkielkraut should have begun to turn his attention to some of these themes as a way of revitalising the political aspects of his thought and as a means of remaining in the public eye.

Finkielkraut's pre-eminent intervention in the emerging debate surrounding the identity of the French nation – and the essay which made him famous in his own right – was *La défaite de la pensée* (1987).[49] The central argument of the book was that, since 1945, Western thought had abandoned its core principles of rationality and universalism in favour of a diverse and presentist conception of 'culture'. Rather than the elevated notion of culture that had prevailed for much of the nineteenth century, Finkielkraut argued that the horrors of the Second World War, anti-imperialism, and the inexorable rise of the mass media had distorted and debased Western notions of culture and 'civilisation'. The root cause of this 'betrayal' of Western values lay in a loss of nerve: Western societies had revealed themselves to be powerless against the onslaught of relativising consumerist values and the insidious penetration of post-colonial guilt.[50] Finkielkraut believed that this undoing of Western values was most clearly visible in the French school system. Imagined as a space of rational discussion and enlightenment by the administrators of the Third Republic, the present-day school was in danger of becoming nothing more than a mirror of a juvenile and hedonistic society, in which some education specialists were encouraging students to learn 'grammar, history, mathematics and all the fundamental subjects ... [as] rock music', which they would listen to through their Walkmans.[51]

There are obvious parallels between Finkielkraut's paean to Enlightenment Western culture in *La défaite de la pensée* and Debray's defence of the Republic in 'République ou démocratie'. In the first instance, they both adopt a highly critical perspective towards the legacy of 1968. Finkielkraut may have been involved in the protests, but his subsequent

---

[49] Alain Finkielkraut, *La défaite de la pensée* (Paris: Gallimard, 1987).

[50] This idea of 'betrayal' is an explicit reference to Julien Benda's famous attack on the irresponsibility of inter-war intellectuals in *La trahison des clercs* (1927) – Finkielkraut believes that his pamphlet is also a call to arms.

[51] Finkielkraut, *La défaite de la pensée*, p. 170.

anti-totalitarianism changed his perspective. By the late 1980s, his frequent attacks on 'hedonism' and the 'youth' in post-68 France were a sign that he was quite comfortable with his identity as an anti *soixante-huitard*: 'it has taken two decades for dissidence to become the norm, for autonomy to transform itself into hegemony, and for the adolescent lifestyle to become the template for the whole of society'.[52] This attack on 'youth' was tied to a critique of consumerism. But, where for Debray it is *l'Image* that has 'seduced' contemporary society, for Finkielkraut the 'cultural malaise' goes deeper than this. *L'Argent* and *l'Image* are replaced in Finkielkraut's thought by the combined threats of the atomisation of society, the triumph of individualism and the debasement of culture. In *La défaite de la pensée*, there is no specific reference to the Republic, but it was only a small step from an abstract defence of Western culture and rationality to a concrete defence of the French Republic.

Finkielkraut's neo-republicanism took shape in the 1990s, in the wake of the headscarf affair. Through numerous essays and comment pieces, and every week on his radio programme *Répliques* (broadcast on France Culture), he repeated and reinforced his attachment to republicanism. But, in contrast to Debray, his was an overwhelmingly institutional narrative of the Republic, which focused on a criticism of multicultural-ism, and a defence of *laïcité* and the school. Given Finkielkraut's emphasis on culture, it was natural that he should see *l'école républicaine* as a vital (and threatened) institution in contemporary France. The school is 'a place where one learns to think for oneself', but it has been fatally compromised by an all-powerful politics of diversity and individ-ual identity.[53] It represents, through its historical associations, a battle for secularism, positivism and progress – all of which can protect against the perils of post-68 modernity. In the same way that Debray imagined an abstract and idealised image of the school as a bastion of Condorcet-like rationalism, Finkielkraut defended its integrative power.[54] In both cases, a defence of the Republic became the necessary ideological mechanism with which to build this defensive consensus around 'the school as sanctuary [*l'école sanctuaire*]'.[55] For Finkielkraut, it is the school that

---

[52] Ibid., p. 174.

[53] Among others, Finkielkraut discusses the school in *Répliques: Qu'est-ce que la laïcité?* France Culture (23 January 1993), *Répliques: L'école face aux revendications identitaires*, France Culture (27 May 2000), and Alain Finkielkraut (ed.), *Où va la France?* (Paris: Stock, 2007).

[54] Debray suggests that *l'école républicaine* should be modelled on the manuals of Condorcet: Debray, *La République expliquée à ma fille*, p. 42.

[55] The idea of *l'école sanctuaire* found an echo in the political world under the tenures as education minister of François Bayrou and Luc Ferry. See L. Bronner, 'L'illusoire tentation de l'école sanctuaire', *Le Monde* (15 February 2004).

creates the 'secular space' necessary for the construction of a rational, progressive society.[56] Insofar as the *école laïque* is an integral part of the Republic, it needs to be defended against the threat of multiculturalism. The Republic elevates the role of reason. Multiculturalism, and its ideological alibis (post-modernism, relativism ...), do not. Thus while the Republic is required for the enlightenment of the individual and the stability of society, multiculturalism is to be condemned as a dangerous celebration of difference.[57]

This defence of the school was amplified by Finkielkraut's cultural elitism. So, while Debray openly bemoaned in 2004 the 'disappearance in our advanced classes of Chateaubriand, Victor Hugo and Aragon', Finkielkraut reminded us in 2006 that he is 'French through Racine and Diderot'.[58] This emphasis on the transmission of culture through text was a logical extension of their argument that culture – in its written form – can protect against the banality of society and that the only appropriate place for cultural enlightenment is the secular sanctuary of the school. Already in 1990, both thinkers had made their position clear when they signed a collective petition in defence of *l'école républicaine*. It is worth quoting at length.

[Must we] transform teachers into socio-cultural group leaders and schools into everyday life [*lieux de vie*]? ... High schools in good shape are those that are sites of study and training, which does not mean that they are places to rehearse everyday life, but places from which one can escape the clutches of communitarianism, the consumerist obsession, the pressures of the immediate and the hubbub of the audiovisual that fills today's civil society.[59]

Here, in a short extract, are the key elements of a neo-republican theory of the school. For the signatories to the petition, *l'école républicaine* had been buffeted by identity politics and consumerism, which meant that its status as a haven away from the debasement of cultural life and society urgently needed to be protected.

Although Finkielkraut and Debray have openly acknowledged their similar position with respect to the future of the school, this is not their

---

[56] In Finkielkraut's words, 'l'école est essentielle à la laïcité ... parce qu'elle est le lieu par excellence de la médiation, du détour, de l'hétéronomie bienfaisante'. Alain Finkielkraut and Benny Lévy, *Le Livre et les livres: entretiens sur la laïcité* (Paris: Editions Verdier, 2006), p. 90.

[57] Nicole Rachlin, 'Alain Finkielkraut and the Politics of Cultural Identity', *Substance* (No. 76–77,1995), pp. 73–92.

[58] Debray, *Ce que nous voile le voile*, p. 43; Finkielkraut and Lévy, *Le Livre et les livres*, p. 65.

[59] The petition was signed by Elisabeth Badinter, Catherine de Fontenay and Catherine Kintzler (who also signed the petition that brought the *affaire* to national prominence). 'Point de vue: Souvenez-vous des professeurs', *Le Monde* (25 November 1990).

only common ground.[60] They have also both taken a growing interest in the role, function and potential of religion in public life. In Finkielkraut's case, it is the 'Jewish question' that has returned again and again in his work. As the child of a secular, east European Jewish family and a *normalien* steeped in the radically atheist world of 1960s Maoism, a turn to religion was not immediately obvious. But the preponderance of young intellectuals of Jewish origin in the *gauchiste* politics of the time (including Bernard-Henri Lévy, Benny Lévy and André Glucksmann) meant that one of the most significant ways of negotiating and coming to terms with the legacy of the 1960s was through religion. A central part of this process was an engagement with the writings of the Jewish philosopher Emmanuel Lévinas, born in 1906, who emigrated from present-day Lithuania to France in 1930.[61] Lévinas's complex work on being and ontology provided a means by which a whole generation of politically aware French philosophy students in the late 1960s and early 70s could engage simultaneously with the philosophical debates of the time and their Jewish heritage.[62] Along with a rejection of the New Left's anti-Zionism after the Six Day War in 1967, this gave rise to a reimagined Jewish identity that was crucial to the political interventions of Finkielkraut, Lévy and others in the 1980s.[63]

Finkielkraut's best-known theoretical discussion of his Jewish identity is *Le Juif imaginaire* (1980), in which he analysed the difficulty of European Jews in forging an identity after the Holocaust and, especially, the problem of 'authentic' Judaism in a secular world.[64] It was intended as a reflection on contemporary Jewish life, which seemed to be defined by an 'absence' created by past experiences of discrimination and genocide that today's generation could not share. He summarised the main aim of the book clearly in an interview in 2000:

Le Juif imaginaire started from the paradox of a Jewishness [*judéité*] defined by a tragedy [the Holocaust], a tragedy whose memory and trauma protected us from

---

[60] In conversation with Finkielkraut in 2006, Debray accepted that 'sur l'école nous avons des positions assez voisines'. *Répliques: Régis Debray est-il réactionnaire?* France Culture (1 April 2006).

[61] Samuel Moyn, *Origins of the Other: Emmanuel Levinas between Revelation and Ethics* (London: Cornell University Press, 2005).

[62] On the 'Levinassian turn' see Judith Friedlander, *Vilna on the Seine: Jewish Intellectuals in France since 1968* (London: Yale University Press, 1990), and Sarah Hammerschlag, 'Reading May '68 through a Levinasian Lens: Alain Finkielkraut, Maurice Blanchot, and the Politics of Identity', *Jewish Quarterly Review* (Vol. 98, No. 4, 2008), pp. 522–51.

[63] Jonathan Judaken, 'Alain Finkielkraut and the Nouveaux Philosophes: French-Jewish Intellectuals, the Afterlives of May '68 and the Re-birth of the National Icon', *Historical Reflections/Réflexions historiques* (Vol. 32, No. 1, 2006), pp. 1–31.

[64] Alain Finkielkraut, *Le Juif imaginaire* (Paris: Seuil, 1980).

anti-Semitism. I was asking myself, already at that point, how to honour the dead without appropriating their destiny.[65]

Over the course of the 1980s, Finkielkraut was drawn into a number of debates surrounding Holocaust denial and Jewish identity but, by the 1990s, it was clear that his interpretation of the Jewish experience had begun to permeate his neo-republicanism. The Arab–Israeli conflict, the rise of Islamic fundamentalism, the growing number of anti-Semitic attacks in France in the 1990s: all seemed to present a mounting threat to Jews in France. As he put it in his essay *Au nom de l'autre* (2003), 'it takes courage to wear a *kippa* in these ferocious places we call difficult estates [*cités sensibles*] and in the Paris metro: Zionism is being criminalised by an ever greater number of intellectuals'.[66] Yet despite this pressure on Jews, Finkielkraut was adamant that the Republic was the best form of protection. It would shield France from Islamic fundamentalism and multiculturalism, thereby ensuring that anti-Semitism, too, was kept at bay. On more than one occasion Finkielkraut stated unambiguously that 'the multicultural environment' was one of the primary causes of anti-Semitism, and he firmly believed that only neo-republicanism could act as a bulwark against dangerous identity politics and the atomisation of modern society.[67]

This staunch defence of the Republic marked Finkielkraut out from some of his Jewish contemporaries, most obviously someone like Benny Lévy, who was a good friend, and also a former *normalien* and leader of Gauche prolétarienne. In fact, a comparison between the two men is instructive. Both figures engaged more and more with their Jewish heritage after 1968 and both were influenced by Lévinas to the extent that in 2000 they founded an Institut d'Etudes Lévinassien in Jerusalem. But, while Finkielkraut defended *laïcité* and the Republic, Lévy chose the path of orthodox Judaism, eventually moving to Jerusalem in 1997 until his death in 2003. The result of this schism was that Lévy could easily reject the principle of *laïcité*, while Finkielkraut was, time and again, forced to reconcile his Judaism with a strong version of *laïcité* that severely limits religious expression in the public sphere. In their conversations in the 1990s and 2000s, many of which were published as a volume entitled *Le Livre et les livres: entretiens sur la laïcité* (2006), Finkielkraut consistently rejected Lévy's assertion that, without religion, the 'social bond' would

[65] Stéphane Floccari, 'Alain Finkielkraut: la mémoire et son double', *L'Humanité* (18 May 2000).
[66] Alain Finkielkraut, *Au nom de l'autre: réflexions sur l'antisémitisme qui vient* (Paris: Gallimard, 2003), p. 10.
[67] *Répliques: Le destin de la République*, France Culture (14 October 2000).

disintegrate.[68] Yet he was becoming increasingly sympathetic to Lévy's position with each successive encounter. By the 2000s, Finkielkraut appeared to be as attached to the validity of a 'Jewish identity' as he was to a neo-republican conception of *laïcité*. Of course, this tension was hardly unusual; historically, many Jews were instrumental in the construction of the republican state in France, and Finkielkraut has, in this respect at least, conformed to the classic trajectory of the educated French 'secular Jew'.[69] This is no doubt why his defensive position on Zionism – which has been influenced by the transnational pro-Israeli Judaism of the late twentieth century – has remained compatible with a deep commitment to the Republic.

More generally, the rediscovery of religion by Finkielkraut (and Debray) suggests an alternative interpretation for the intellectual origins of neo-republicanism. Obviously, both thinkers developed a post-Marxist critique of modernity and the Enlightenment that led to a strong defence of *laïcité* and the Republic. And it is evident that the disintegration of a Marxist worldview was instrumental in clearing the way for neo-republicanism. But, equally, there was a desire on the part of some neo-republicans to resurrect spiritual and religious belief as a form of social bond. The actual content of this belief – Jewish, Catholic, 'Christian' – was less important than its function. In a France that seemed to be opening on to a period of economic and social crisis in the 1980s and 1990s, religion offered alternative forms of certainty and universalism. It is telling that even thinkers like Marcel Gauchet, who have been less consistently associated with the republican revival, showed a renewed interest in religion in this period; for example, Gauchet's well-known and widely cited *Le désenchantement du monde: une histoire politique de la religion* was published in 1985. This is a reminder that, although neo-republicanism has repeatedly stressed the importance of *laïcité*, this does not mean that its advocates were necessarily anti-religious. Just as historians have shown the extent to which the militant republican secularism of the Dreyfusards at the end of the nineteenth century was compatible with 'spiritual' and 'religious' beliefs, so the same was true of the neo-republicanism of the late twentieth century.[70] One might even

---

[68] Finkielkraut and Lévy, *Le Livre et les livres*, p. 135

[69] Pierre Birnbaum, *Les fous de la République: histoire politique des juifs d'État de Gambetta à Vichy* (Paris: Fayard, 1992); Pierre Birnbaum, *Jewish Destinies: Citizenship, State and Community in Modern France* (New York: Hill & Wang, 2000); Tony Judt, *The Burden of Responsibility: Blum, Camus, Aron and the French Twentieth Century* (London: University of Chicago Press, 1998); and Friedlander, *Vilna on the Seine*.

[70] Ruth Harris, 'Letters to Lucie: Spirituality, Friendship, and Politics During the Dreyfus Affair', *Past and Present* (Vol. 1, 2006), pp. 118–38.

say that neo-republicanism was an attempt on the part of some intellectuals to 're-enchant' the world of politics and give it a renewed ethical foundation: this would certainly be consistent with the transcendental quality of the transformative narrative of republicanism.[71]

For critics of neo-republicanism, however, the turn to religion was a sign of political conservatism rather than intellectual ecumenism. Perhaps the most famous attack on the assumptions that underpinned neo-republicanism came from a polemical pamphlet published in 2002 by the historian Daniel Lindenberg entitled *Rappel à l'ordre: enquête sur les nouveaux réactionnaires*.[72] Seemingly oblivious to the potential for controversy, Lindenberg went fearlessly into battle and indicted a whole raft of thinkers – including Finkielkraut, Debray and Gauchet – as *nouveaux réactionnaires* (new reactionaries). What united them was not their ideas, he argued, but their trajectories: all of them had formerly belonged to the left in some form or another, and were now languishing dangerously close to what he described as the 'reactionary' right. It was not simply that their revolutionary fervour had expired, but that they were now keenly endorsing openly conservative positions. Not surprisingly, with its open nostalgia for the Third Republic and its potent critique of consumerist modernity, Lindenberg lambasted neo-republicanism as one of the finest examples of right-wing reconversion. As he memorably put it,

Behind a certain number of popular targets (moral decadence, the 'new barbarism', Rights-of-Man-ism [*droit-de-l'hommisme*] etc.), there is a new militant [reactionary] synthesis that denounces all those ... who have contributed to the dissolution of the sovereign state in the morass of individual rights, the Nation in a Euro-globalised melting-pot, the 'people' in civil society, and high culture in youthful multi-ethnicism.[73]

Inevitably, Lindenberg's pamphlet provoked a violent response.[74] It is certainly true that his category of 'nouveaux réactionnaires' was of questionable analytical use. It often misrepresented its targets, and flattened out the nuances between different thinkers, disciplines and intellectual

---

[71] In his *From Revolution to Ethics*, Julian Bourg stresses the importance of a fundamental change in French thought from the idea of 'revolution' to a concern with 'rights' and 'ethics' in the decades after 1968. This suggestive analysis could be supplemented by a clearer focus on religion.

[72] Daniel Lindenberg, *Le rappel à l'ordre, Enquête sur les nouveaux réactionnaires* (Paris: Seuil, 2002).

[73] Ibid., p. 32.

[74] Alain Finkielkraut, Marcel Gauchet, Pierre Manent, Philippe Muray, Pierre-André Taguieff, Shmuel Trigano and Paul Yonnet, 'Manifeste pour une pensée libre', *L'Express* (29 November 2002); 'Nouveaux réactionnaires – un manifesto en réplique', *Le Monde* (29 November 2002); and Pierre Birnbaum and Nicolas Weill, 'Ce livre qui brouille les familles intellectuelles', *Le Monde* (22 November 2002).

orientations. Nevertheless, the essay had the merit of pointing out – albeit without realising it – the changing configuration of French politics. The word 'reactionary' itself is notoriously slippery, but is often taken as a category beyond simple definitions of right and left.[75] Even if Lindenberg's polemic rested too strongly on a retelling of the 'rightward drift' interpretation of French politics I presented at the beginning of the chapter, his attempt to understand intellectual politics through a new lens captured an essential feature of contemporary French intellectual life.

In the case of Debray and Finkielkraut, there were certainly a number of openly 'reactionary' elements to their neo-republicanism, and they were quite willing to acknowledge these. In 2006, Finkielkraut invited Debray to participate in a special broadcast of his *Répliques* radio show entitled 'Is Régis Debray reactionary?'[76] The rather self-referential theme notwithstanding, both thinkers found themselves in agreement on issues as varied as the state of the school and the relation between modernity and religion. They also happily agreed that they were 'reactionaries', taking the term as a badge of honour rather than an insult. Nevertheless, we would be wrong to take these self-admissions at purely face value. The multiple influences on both Debray and Finkielkraut's political thought prove that theirs was not a straightforward story of a 'rightward drift', but instead a complex synthesis of political and religious commitments. Marxism was not simply replaced; it was absorbed into a wider narrative of neo-republicanism.

The perennial return of the French intellectual?

Whatever one's opinion of Debray and Finkielkraut, a discussion of their ideas raises an important question: have their cogitations had any effect outside the restricted world of the French intellectual elite? This question takes on particular importance in the context of the role of intellectuals in France since the late nineteenth century. Ever since the Dreyfus Affair, French intellectuals have played a vital role in French society as critics and sounding-boards for significant societal issues such

---

[75] Antoine Compagnon, *Les antimodernes: de Joseph de Maistre à Roland Barthes* (Paris: Gallimard, 2005).

[76] *Répliques: Régis Debray est-il réactionnaire?* France Culture (1 April 2006). It is worth noting, however, that this was not the first time Debray and Finkielkraut had met in discussion, nor was it the first time that Debray had been the sole guest on Finkielkraut's radio programme (which normally has two guests). For instance, Debray was invited by Finkielkraut to talk about his book *Que vive la République!* in 1989. *Répliques: La République est-elle en train de mourir?* France Culture (7 January 1989).

as anti-Semitism, pacifism, communism, and the condition of the working class.[77] In the post-war period, however, the French intellectual elite turned increasingly inward, consumed by its own sectarian tendencies. There were outstanding exceptions such as Raymond Aron, whose legacy is dealt with in chapter 6, but many of the ideological quarrels of the 1950s and 1960s revolved around doctrinal differences that would have seemed opaque, if not entirely irrelevant, to the majority of the French population. Althusserian communism and situationism were significant intellectual movements, but were often entirely detached from the dominant issues of their day. Even when *gauchisme* achieved its greatest public exposure during the protests of May–June 1968, it was still an extremely marginal phenomenon.[78]

Seen in this way, neo-republicanism was actually something of a return to the mainstream for France's intellectual elite. After the rarefied doctrinal disputes in the halls of the Ecole Normale Supérieure in the late 1960s, the rediscovery of the nation and of secularism put French intellectuals back in touch with some of the most pressing public concerns of the 1980s and 1990s. For the first time since an earlier generation had decided to become 'fellow travellers' of the PCF in the 1940s and 50s, the questions that intellectuals like Finkielkraut and Debray were discussing were major electoral issues, and the influence of their pronouncements was felt well beyond higher education. The following chapter will show the extent to which Finkielkraut and Debray's arguments have been reflected, magnified and politicised since the 1980s. But we need not look to the wider political space to see their influence, since both figures have had significant roles to play in policy formation.

Finkielkraut, for example, was interviewed for the Commission de la Nationalité, formed in 1987 to recommend changes to French nationality law. Of all the interviewees, it was his intervention that the Commission used to lay the ideological foundations of their reforms. The authors of the report claimed that they did not want to take a position on the 'philosophical debate on the essence of the nation', but they took up Finkielkraut's wording verbatim when they claimed that

---

[77] David Caute, *Communism and the French Intellectuals, 1914–1960* (London: Macmillan, 1964); Stefan Collini, *Absent Minds: Intellectuals in Britain* (Oxford University Press, 2006); Jean-François Sirinelli, *Les intellectuels en France, de l'affaire Dreyfus à nos jours* (Paris: Armand Colin, 1986); and David Drake, *Intellectuals and Politics in Post-war France* (London: Palgrave, 2002).

[78] For a strongly revisionist account that explores the hegemony of *gauchiste* accounts of 1968, see Chris Reynolds, *Memories of May '68: France's Convenient Consensus* (Cardiff: University of Wales Press, 2011).

France is 'a country in which the highest ethical and spiritual values are proposed to the conscious agreement of all its members'.[79] Obviously, Finkielkraut cannot be held solely responsible for this strong interpretation of citizenship, but his participation in the Commission helped to cement a growing consensus which was eventually formalised in more restrictive nationality legislation passed in 1993.[80] Meanwhile, Debray, already an advisor to Mitterrand in the 1980s, a *maître de requêtes* on the Conseil d'Etat from 1988 to 1992, and the author of his report on the teaching of religion in schools in 2002, found himself at the heart of debates surrounding the Republic in 2003 when he was invited to sit on the Commission Stasi. As we have already seen, the commission's report strongly supported a ban on the headscarf and reproduced all the assumptions of neo-republicanism, including a staunch defence of *l'école républicaine*, deep concerns about the fragmentation of the nation state and an indictment of a debased mass culture. Debray's voice was clearly audible amidst the polemic: it was his vision of secularism and the Republic that had triumphed and would become the foundation of subsequent legislation

Ultimately, then, we are dealing with more than simply the idle chatter of Paris's Left Bank, exchanging one distant Third World cause for another. Finkielkraut and Debray directly contributed to legislative processes and helped to forge a consensus around a strong notion of the Republic. The violent disagreements over Finkielkraut's nomination to the Académie française in 2014 were a reminder that they have not been without their critics – even in the most elevated circles.[81] But, while French intellectuals face ever greater challenges to their legitimacy from the widening French intellectual sphere, they can also boast of a much more intimate relationship with the state than in previous decades.[82] Where once French intellectuals had little or no impact on French government policy, more recently they have found themselves called on in an advisory role. For Debray and Finkielkraut, the journey from Marxism to the Republic has not always been straightforward, but it has brought important political rewards.

[79] Commission de la Nationalité, *Rapport: Etre français aujourd'hui et demain* (Paris: La Documentation Française, 1987), p. 73.

[80] On this see Adrian Favell, *Philosophies of Integration* (London: Routledge, 1998).

[81] Frédéric Joignot, 'Alain Finkielkraut, un Immortel contesté', *Le Monde* (11 April 2014).

[82] On the changing roles of the intellectual see Jeremy Jennings, 'Mandarins and Samurais: The Intellectual in Modern France', in Jeremy Jennings (ed.), *Intellectuals in Twentieth-Century France: Mandarins and Samurais* (London: St Martin's Press, 1993).

3 *La République en danger!* The search for consensus and the rise of neo-republican politics

In the previous two chapters, the emphasis was on the intellectual roots of neo-republicanism, its relationship to the historiography of modern France and the transformation of French Marxism since 1968. Here I want to focus more closely on the daily life of French politics in the past three decades. Once again, my purpose is not to provide an exhaustive account of contemporary French politics; it is, rather, to examine the emergence of the language of neo-republicanism at key political moments since the 1980s. How did neo-republicanism move from the pages of history books and philosophical essays into the political space more broadly? Around which issues did a neo-republican consensus crystallise? By the end of the 1990s, both the French electorate and the country's political elite had developed an instinctive feel for issues that would have seemed anachronistic or alien to a previous generation. But this transition could not have taken place without a penetration of neo-republican discourse into political circles well beyond those of Nora or Finkielkraut. One of the main aims of this chapter, then, is to widen the cast of characters from intellectuals and academics to politicians, commentators and journalists, all of whom played a crucial role in manipulating, repackaging and disseminating the themes that lay at the heart of neo-republicanism.

There are many good reasons for anchoring neo-republicanism within a more general interpretation of French political change since 1980. First, as I suggest below, the search for consensus in the 1980s goes a long way towards explaining why the Republic became an attractive ideal for a wide range of political actors. Over the course of the 1980s, the progressive decline of a number of key reference points in French politics led to a search for new unifying languages and ideas. In particular, 1989 was an obvious turning point. This was the year during which France celebrated the controversial bicentennial of the Revolution and experienced a profound ideological and geopolitical reorientation in the wake of the fall of the Berlin Wall. It was also the year of the *affaire du foulard*, which brought immigration and secularism directly into the public eye, alongside a rejuvenated republicanism. Inevitably, then, much of the discussion of politics in this chapter will focus on the period after 1989 when neo-republicanism became a ubiquitous part of the political landscape and the most prominent interpretation of the national narrative.

The second reason for anchoring our story in French politics is to counteract a strong tendency towards abstraction in many of the debates that have involved neo-republicans. This has been especially true of, say, the headscarf debates, or France's attitude towards multiculturalism, both of which have provoked a wide range of responses from French and foreign commentators. For historical reasons, these debates have often relied on the use of abstract and decontextualised models. We shall see in subsequent chapters that these models are well worth analysing in their own right, but this chapter will focus on the exigencies of party-political engagement and specific policy issues such as the French state's attitude to female representation in politics and regional languages. I shall demonstrate how neo-republicanism has become intertwined in even apparently unrelated policy questions. In this way, it is possible to avoid one of the most common pitfalls in the literature on contemporary French politics, which often takes at face value abstract theories of the kind that have been championed by the likes of Finkielkraut and Debray without putting them in their political context. Neo-republicanism emerged as an idea with a complex intellectual genealogy, but it has simultaneously been a political strategy. This means that apparently abstract debates between defenders and critics of the Republic reveal as much about the reformulation of contemporary French politics as they do about the threshold of 'liberal tolerance', the potential for 'critical republicanism' or the dangers of 'Western secularism'.

Adieu 89? The search for political consensus in the 1980s

It is now widely accepted that the Fifth Republic has been marked by a search for consensus. Whether in the form of de Gaulle's battle to put to rest the ghosts of the Algerian War in the 1960s or Mitterrand's efforts to marginalise the Parti communiste français (PCF) in the 1980s, there has been a consistent cross-party project to build a stable and consensual polity. This has not been entirely successful: since the early 1980s, the persistence of a radical anti-globalisation rhetoric on the far left and the presence of the Front National on the far right have repeatedly disrupted attempts to foster political consensus.[1] Nevertheless, the Fifth Republic

---

[1] Pascal Perrineau, 'The great upheaval: left and right in contemporary French politics', and Jim Shields, 'The Front National since the 1970s: electoral impact and party system change', in Emile Chabal (ed.), *France Since the 1970s: History, Politics and Memory in an Age of Uncertainty* (London: Bloomsbury Academic, 2014).

already counts as the most stable and long-lasting of France's political regimes. Initially, much of this was the result of economic prosperity and the stabilisation of European politics in the three decades following the end of the Second World War. But, as the foundations of the Fifth Republic came under attack from global economic contraction and political apathy in the 1970s and 1980s, there was an ever greater need to look for an ideology that might unite an increasingly disparate France. It was in this context that neo-republicanism emerged as one of the pre-eminent languages of consensus in French politics, both in reaction to political and social fragmentation, and as a means of bringing together a diverse electorate.

Specifically, the revival of interest in republicanism coincided with the longest period of left-wing rule in French history. This was no coincidence. In the same way that French Marxism provided a vital intellectual framework for neo-republicanism, so the reformulation of Socialist politics in the 1980s largely determined its political expression. As we saw in the opening chapter, the nineteenth century cemented a complex and fractured relationship between revolution, republicanism and radicalism. Some left-wing groups challenged the legitimacy of the republican state – such as anarchists in the early nineteenth century and communists during the Third Republic – but, by and large, anti-state socialism was consistently marginalised in France.[2] This created an unusual ideological framework for the French left in the twentieth century. On the one hand, there were repeated references to the French left's revolutionary and Marxist heritage. In times of relative stability, this produced a yearning for revolutionary change and a consistent critique of the 'bourgeois Republic'. On the other hand, many on the left acknowledged the strength and legitimacy of the Republic as a defender of rational, progressive values. This tendency was noticeable especially in times of crisis such as the Dreyfus Affair and the Vichy regime, when the left rallied to the powerful idea of the *pacte républicain* (republican pact) against the threat of the far right.

This unresolved tension was brought into sharp relief by Mitterrand's electoral victory in 1981 and the Socialist landslide in the legislative elections of the same year. For the first time since the Popular Front, the left was the Republic. There was now an urgent need to move away from a Marxist language of opposition to a more natural language of governance – and neo-republicanism was essential in this transition. Nowhere was this more apparent than in the career of François Mitterrand, the post-war French left's most emblematic figure until his death in

---

[2] See Judt, *Marxism and the French Left*, p. 6, and Julliard, *Les gauches françaises*, pp. 565–700.

1996. A complete discussion of Mitterrand's complex political personality is not possible here.[3] I merely wish to highlight ways in which Mitterrand's presidency created a framework favourable to a reaffirmation of republican values. It is a point that has been made by a number of other commentators, both French and foreign. In the words of the historian and journalist Jacques Julliard, 'the invocation of republican values facilitated in the case of François Mitterrand ... the shift from an ideology of class struggle and revolutionary rupture to one of national union and consensus'.[4] Likewise, the political scientist Alastair Cole has talked of 'a restored reference to republicanism as the *raison d'être* of Mitterrand's presidency', while the historian Serge Berstein has argued that 'the renewed support for the republican model' was the consequence of the left's inability to 'throw up any new political ideas'.[5]

Leaving aside the normative dimension of Berstein's rather severe judgement, there can be little doubt that Mitterrand turned more and more to symbols of national unity over the course of his presidency. Even his 1981 election campaign posters – which showed him above the caption 'la force tranquille', with a village and church spire in the background – made clear the extent to which he relied on symbols that were not those traditionally associated with the left.[6] His 1988 - campaign slogan – 'la France unie' – drew even more directly on a call for unity. This is perhaps not surprising, given that, in 1986, the Socialists had been defeated in the legislative election by the centre-right Rassemblement pour la République–Union pour la Démocratie Française (RPR–UDF) coalition under Jacques Chirac, thereby inaugurating the first period of 'cohabitation' under the Fifth Republic, with a president and prime minister from different parties. Openness was a prerequisite for Mitterrand at a time when he ruled alongside a government of the right, and his invocation of republican unity was a

---

[3] There are already many such studies. See for instance Wayne Northcutt, *Mitterrand* (London: Holmes & Meier, 1992); Máiri Maclean (ed.), *The Mitterrand Years: Legacy and Evaluation* (London: Macmillan, 1998); Alastair Cole, *François Mitterrand: A Study in Political Leadership* (London: Macmillan, 1997); Eric Duhamel, *François Mitterrand: l'unité d'un homme* (Paris: Flammarion, 1998).

[4] Jacques Julliard, 'La course au centre', in Furet, Julliard and Rosanvallon, *La République du Centre*, p. 105.

[5] Cole, *François Mitterrand*, p. 66. Serge Berstein, 'The Crisis of the Left and the Renaissance of the Republican Model, 1981–1995', in Maclean, *The Mitterrand Years*, p. 46.

[6] Contrast this with his 1965 election campaign poster, which showed a young Mitterrand against a backdrop of electricity pylons and distant industrial smokestacks – images much more reminiscent of a left-wing constituency.

way of underplaying political difference. Take, for instance, this speech he gave on Bastille Day in 1987:

> We must avoid permanent political confusion [*trouble*] and self doubt, which seems to be a common affliction of the French ... a great country can only be great if it knows how to unify itself around important goals. In the run-up to the presidential election, the smear campaigns [*campagnes à ras de terre*] and the encouraging of the basest passions, all of which are instinctive reflexes, must give way to a higher conception of the public interest, which begins with the Republic.[7]

Gone was the Marxist language of class and confrontation that Mitterrand had adopted in the 1970s. By 1987, this had been replaced by an appeal to a republican unity that celebrated the *grandeur* of France and owed as much to de Gaulle as it did to the French left.[8]

But Mitterrand's invocation of republican symbols and language transcended mere contingency; it was part of his wider political outlook. This can partly be explained by his unusual political trajectory. He was not a traditional man of the left: he was born and brought up in a Catholic family in rural Charente in western France. His early political career saw him flirt with right-wing groups later associated with Vichy and, for much of the Fourth and early Fifth Republics, he was a politician of the centre, unwilling to join any political party.[9] He came to prominence with his famous pamphlet *Le coup d'état permanent* (1964), which was highly critical of de Gaulle's return to politics in 1958.[10] His opposition was based on eminently republican principles, namely that de Gaulle's seizure of power had been illegal according to a republican constitution. This cemented Mitterrand's reputation as a politician committed to republicanism – but it also made him acceptable to a left that had always seen de Gaulle's rise to power as illegitimate. Using this to boost his credentials, Mitterrand gravitated towards the non-communist left and gradually rose to the top of a divided socialist bloc in the 70s. His detractors saw his belated 'conversion' to socialism as rampant opportunism but, by the late 1970s, he had become the obvious choice to lead a newly reunited PS.

---

[7] 'Un certain nombre de pensées politiques sont menaçantes pour la République', *Le Monde* (16 July 1987).

[8] Stanley Hoffmann, 'Gaullism by Any Other Name', *Foreign Policy* (No. 57, 1984), pp. 38–57.

[9] Mitterrand's involvement with the pre-Second World War right was discussed most clearly (and publicly) in Pierre Péan, *Une jeunesse française. François Mitterrand, 1934–1947* (Paris: Fayard, 1994).

[10] François Mitterrand, *Coup d'état permanent* (Paris: Plon, 1964).

Historians are still unclear as to the extent of Mitterrand's opportunism, and much depends on one's political perspective. However, what is beyond doubt is that, even throughout his 'socialist period' from the early 1970s to the 1990s, Mitterrand remained firmly attached to his republican credentials. In a 1991 article, the historian Wayne Northcutt identified a number of key republican symbols which Mitterrand had mobilised thus far in his presidency, including his use of the Panthéon during his inauguration and his starring role in the 1989 bicentennial of the French Revolution.[11] When called on to defend Culture Minister Jack Lang's grand plan for the bicentennial, Mitterrand enthusiastically endorsed the proposals, adding that it should be a 'a magnificent celebration of the Republic'.[12] Similarly, in a speech in 1992, Mitterrand claimed that a commitment to socialism was secondary to a commitment to the Republic: in his words, 'one must first serve the Republic'.[13] Of course, it would be hard to describe Mitterrand as a neo-republican in the sense in which I have used the term thus far. Mitterrand belonged to a different generation – one that lived through and remembered the Third Republic, and his republicanism was more of an ambiguous and historically accessible call for unity. Nevertheless, his fourteen-year presidency provided a political framework for the resurgence of a neo-republican language, and laid the groundwork for the rehabilitation of a whole range of republican values in contemporary French politics.

His presidency also coincided with the upheavals of 1989. For the French left, in particular, 1989 was a year of intense soul-searching as the Berlin Wall fell, and the Soviet Union began to unravel. With the legitimacy of communism rapidly fading, it became clear even to its most ardent supporters that Marxism was in terminal decline.[14] If Marxism had long been under threat in French intellectual life, it was only in the late 1980s that it became firmly marginalised in French politics as a

---

[11] Wayne Northcutt, 'François Mitterrand and the Political Use of Symbols: The Construction of a Centrist Republic', *French Historical Studies* (Vol. 17, No. 1, 1991), pp. 141–58.

[12] 'M. Mitterrand au conseil des ministres: le Bicentenaire doit être "une célébration grandiose de la République"', *Le Monde* (15 July 1989).

[13] The text runs as follows: 'c'est Jaurès qui a dit à peu près que sans la République il n'y a pas de socialisme ... et c'est vrai: il faut d'abord servir la République, c'est-à-dire protéger les conquêtes d'un système qui s'est imposé à la France dans une grande tourmente révolutionnaire mais qui a eu, dès le premier moment, une déclaration des droits de l'homme si péniblement rédigée et adoptée [*sic*]'. François Mitterrand, '19 Novembre 92: Allocution Lors De L'Inauguration Du Centre Culturel de Carmaux', *Anthologie Sonore des discours de François Mitterrand (1981–95)* (France Inter/Editions Frémeaux).

[14] A pithy contemporary summary of this feeling can be found in an editorial in the journal *Esprit* in 1989. 'Sortir du communisme', *Esprit* (June–July 1989), pp. 3–4.

whole. With the obliteration of the PCF as a national political force, Mitterrand's ideological volte-face in 1982–3 and the success of liberal politics on the right (under Chirac in 1986–8) and the left (under Rocard in 1988–91), the signs of decline were already clearly visible. But it was 1989 that precipitously confined Marxist politics in Europe to the past rather than the present. With the historical framework of the left falling away, it was inevitable that newer issues would fill the ideological vacuum. Two of these proved to be especially significant: the bicentennial of the French Revolution and the *affaire du foulard*.

As we have already seen, Mitterrand enthusiastically supported the idea of the bicentennial as a gigantic public relations exercise. It was to be a moment of celebration and self-congratulation. The fact that the 1989 G7 summit was to be held in Paris around the time of the two-hundredth anniversary of the storming of the Bastille only heightened the expectations surrounding the event. Sure enough, the bicentennial saw public pageantry and festivities on a national scale, while leaders from around the world were invited to share in a celebration of France's historical greatness with a photograph and festivities on the Place du Trocadéro in Paris on 13 July 1989.[15] All but the most cynical observers could see that this was an attempt by Mitterrand to reaffirm France's world-historical stature at a time of growing uncertainty. The recent opening of archives has revealed the extent to which Mitterrand was privately unsettled by the fall of the Berlin Wall and the prospect of German unification but, at the time of the bicentennial, the intention was to show how the roots of 'human rights' and emancipation from authoritarian rule lay in the French Revolution.[16] As Mitterrand put it in his end of year address in December 1989,

[W]e were proud to celebrate this year the bicentenary of our revolution and to commemorate the role played by France in the fight for liberty, equality, and the defence of the rights of man; we find now that, two hundred years later, *the same words carry the same hope and have helped to topple other Bastilles*.[17]

Just as the Commission Stasi would later claim that the French conception of *laïcité* was an 'inspiration' to others, so Mitterrand tied together the bicentennial of the French Revolution with current events happening

---

[15] 'Cérémonie officielle de la commémoration du Bicentenaire de la Révolution Française et de la Déclaration des Droits de l'Homme et du Citoyen', *Antenne 2* (13 July 1989).

[16] Frédéric Bozo, *Mitterrand, la fin de la guerre froide et l'unification allemande: de Yalta à Maastricht* (Paris: Odile Jacob, 2005), and Samy Cohen (ed.), *Mitterrand et la sortie de la guerre froide* (Paris: Presses universitaires de France, 1998).

[17] François Mitterrand, 'Voeux au Français', *Antenne 2* (31 December 1989) (emphasis added).

beyond France's borders. The bicentennial provided grand symbolic confirmation of the continuous relevance of France's revolutionary ideals and their universal validity. It also placed centre stage the Revolution's greatest legacy – the Republic – and provided an excellent opportunity to re-emphasise the transformative narrative of the Republic, especially the relationship between revolution, republicanism and human rights.[18]

It was not simply the context that guaranteed the bicentennial's neo-republican overtones; there were also a number of prominent neo-republican figures on the organising committee, including Régis Debray and the historian Max Gallo. Nevertheless, for Claude Nicolet, this wasn't enough. In his view, the conception of the Republic that emerged from the bicentennial was 'desperately bland'.[19] This sentiment was echoed in a number of different circles, especially on the left, where the apparent triumph of François Furet's reinterpretation of the French Revolution at the expense of a Marxist model was indicative of an equally pernicious historiographical blandness.[20] Others – including Alain Finkielkraut – criticised the celebrations as being little more than a picturesque publicity stunt, in thrall to a misguided commercial 'modernity'.[21] Yet, despite the significant criticisms from France's intellectual and academic elites, the festive atmosphere of the celebrations drew millions of tourists to Paris to celebrate a Revolution whose legacy no longer provoked violently partisan reactions. Indeed, as a number of outside commentators noted, it seemed as if the bicentennial had fused the most potent elements of Gaullist *grandeur* with the venerable tradition of revolutionary festivals.[22]

But popular celebrations could not hide a deeper political unease. Even more than the bicentennial, it was the *affaire du foulard* that placed France's present in direct relation to its past and provided perhaps the most explicit articulation of a neo-republican agenda. The actual narrative of the affair is, by now, well known. In October 1989, three girls at the Lycée Gabriel Havez in Creil – Samira Saidani, Leila Achaboun and her sister Fatima Achaboun – were suspended by the school headmaster Ernest Chenière for refusing to remove their headscarves in class. The issue, quickly reported in the national press, took on a life of its own with

---

[18] For an analysis of Mitterrand's role in the celebrations, see Northcutt, 'François Mitterrand and the Political Use of Symbols'.

[19] Claude Nicolet, 'Faut-il larguer la République?', *Le Monde Diplomatique* (June 1989).

[20] By far the most sustained description of the disagreements surrounding the bicentenary is Steven Kaplan, *Adieu 89* (Paris: Fayard, 1993).

[21] 'La nation disparait au profit des tribus: Un entretien avec Alain Finkielkraut', *Le Monde* (13 July 1989).

[22] On this see *Le Monde*, 12–15 July 1989.

the publication in November 1989 of the famous manifesto 'Profs, ne capitulons pas!' in the left-leaning magazine *Le Nouvel Observateur*.[23] It was signed by Debray, Finkielkraut and three prominent female intellectuals – Catherine Kintzler, Elisabeth Badinter and Elisabeth de Fontenay. Seemingly a return to the grand French intellectual tradition of the petition, this call to arms made a vigorous and sustained case in support of Chenière's decision, on the grounds that the headscarf was an instrument of female oppression and inimical to a French tradition of *laïcité*. In an oft-quoted moment of rhetoric, the authors warned of the 'Munich of the republican school', thereby conflating Islam, feminism, Nazism and the language of humiliated capitulation in one sentence.

For the next three months the *affaire du foulard* occupied an unprecedented amount of media space. From a political perspective, what was especially noteworthy was the realignment of political affiliations. Although the petition of the five intellectuals did little to further a pragmatic debate around the issue – a point made by many at the time – it did expose France's changing political landscape: for the first time, neo-republicanism carried political weight.[24] This shift was reflected in the career of politicians like the dissident socialist Jean-Pierre Chevènement. A founder of the orthodox Marxist Centre d'études, de recherche et d'éducation socialiste (CERES) in 1966, Chevènement was subsequently Education Minister (1984–6), Defence Minister (1988–91) and Interior Minister (1997–2000). By the 1990s, his neo-republican credentials were well known.[25] Defence Minister at the time of the *affaire*, he did not hesitate to add his voice to that of the original petition in a piece entitled 'Le débat sur la laicité' published in November 1989, while the political youth group close to him – Socialisme et République – demonstrated in favour of Chenière's position.[26] In later years, he consummated his separation from the mainstream PS by forming his own political party. He even

---

[23] Elisabeth Badinter, Régis Debray, Alain Finkielkraut, Elizabeth de Fontenay and Catherine Kintzler, 'Profs. ne capitulons pas!', *Le Nouvel Observateur* (2 November 1989).

[24] See in particular the 'counter-petition' signed by Joëlle Brunerie-Kauffmann, Harlem Désir, René Dumont, Gilles Perrault and Alain Touraine, 'Pour une laïcité ouverte', *Politis* (9 November 1989). Among other dissenting voices we can also include those of Cheikh Haddam (the rector of the Mosquée de Paris) and the sociologist Farhad Khosrokhavar. For reactions at the time see e.g. 'La polémique sur le port du foulard islamique à l'école', *Le Monde* (24 October 1989); Harlem Désir, 'Une loi-cadre pour l'intégration', *Le Monde* (10 November 1989); and Alain Touraine, 'France: société forteresse', *Le Monde* (23 November 1989).

[25] Jean-Pierre Chevènement, *Une certaine idée de la République m'amène à...* (Paris: Albin Michel, 1992).

[26] Jean-Pierre Chevènement, 'Le débat sur la laicité', *Le Monde* (9 November 1989). 'L'affaire du foulard islamique divise la gauche', *Le Monde* (2 November 1989).

presented himself as an independent presidential candidate in 2002 under the political banner of the Pôle Républicain, thereby contributing to the failure of Lionel Jospin to reach the second round of the 2002 presidential election.[27] Nevertheless, Chevènement's journey indicated that, by 1989, neo-republicanism could become a party-political position (albeit a relatively unsuccessful one).

Chevènement undoubtedly represented the most radical neo-republican strand in the PS at the time and his move from the orthodox Marxism of the CERES in the 1970s to neo-republicanism in 1990s mirrored the transition of an intellectual like Debray. But, even among those who were associated with moderate socialist reformism, reactions were mixed. Michel Rocard and Pierre Mauroy agreed with the spirit of the petition that 'a multi-confessional school is not a secular school [école laïque]'.[28] Others, such as the Socialist Education Minister at the time – Lionel Jospin – adopted a more cautious position. In his public statement on the matter, he asked that decisions be made at a local level and that 'the public school ... prioritise its tradition of welcoming and respecting [individual] conscience over any systematic and premature exclusionary measures'.[29] Jospin's position was later upheld by the Conseil d'Etat, which refused to support Chenière's decision to exclude the three girls.[30] The debate was equally polarised among prominent left-wing female voices: Kintzler, Badinter and Fontenay had already declared their position in the petition – and reinforced it in later interviews – but others, such as Danielle Mitterrand (the wife of the former president), called for 'toleration', while the Algerian writer Leïla Sebbar denounced the generalised 'panic' surrounding discussions of the headscarf and Islam in France.[31]

Many of the disagreements took place within the intellectual and political left, but all political allegiances were blurred by the *affaire*.

---

[27] He received 5.33 per cent of votes in the first round. The fact that he fell in line behind Ségolène Royal's candidacy in 2007 is evidence that the Socialists have yet to forgive him for his role in Jospin's downfall.

[28] 'Polémique sur le voile: "Une école multiconfessionelle n'est pas une école laïque" déclare Michel Rocard', Le Monde (21 November 1989).

[29] 'Le communiqué du ministre', Le Monde (5 November 1989).

[30] Le Conseil d'Etat, No. 346.893: Port de signe d'appartenance à une communauté religieuse (foulard islamique) (27 November 1989) (www.conseil-etat.fr/cde/media/document/avis/346893.pdf; last accessed 1 August 2011).

[31] On the feminist/gender debate, see the analyses in Florence Rochefort, 'Foulard, genre et laïcité en 1989', Vingtième siècle (No. 75, 2002–3), and Norma Claire Moruzzi, 'A Problem with Headscarves: Contemporary Complexities of Political and Social Identity', Political Theory (Vol. 22, No. 4, 1994). See also Frédéric Gaussen, 'Les deux écoles de la gauche', Le Monde (7 November 1989), and Leïla Sabbar, 'Pourquoi cette peur?', Le Monde (24 October 1989).

Politicians from the centre-right RPR and UDF such as Raymond Barre, Jacques Chaban-Delmas and Bernard Pons supported Chenière's position on republican grounds, although the right-wing invocation of the Republic often went hand in hand with an alarmist discourse about the threat of Islamic 'fundamentalism'.[32] Yet even this was not always sufficient to distinguish right and left: the original petition – signed by openly left-leaning intellectuals – also emphasised the rising oppression of women by Islamic 'fundamentalists'. The troubling post-colonial implications of such a position will be discussed in the following chapter, but what is noteworthy is that the language used on both sides called on a transformative republican narrative of 'liberation' from religious oppression. That this narrative was now common to personalities as different as Alain Juppé and Elisabeth Badinter demonstrated that the *affaire du foulard* had, by 1989, brought neo-republicanism to the attention of a much wider range of political actors.

La République à l'attaque! Headscarves, *parité* and regional languages

After 1989, the language of neo-republicanism began to appear in a whole range of public debates. One of the most significant was the (ongoing) discussion surrounding the integration of migrants – a subject that forms the basis of the next chapter. However, neo-republicanism was clearly evident in a number of other key debates, three of which I should like to examine briefly here: the headscarf and the *burqa*; the law on the equal representation of women in politics (*loi sur la parité*); and the question of regional languages.

Predictably, the issue of the headscarf did not go away after 1989. Throughout the 1990s, sociologists of Islam and women, historians of religion and anthropologists were all invited to join a wide-ranging debate that explored empirical evidence largely ignored by the five signatories to the original petition.[33] Numerous analyses pointed out that the question of the headscarf involved only a few hundred students at most,

---

[32] 'La polémique sur l'affaire des "foulards" islamiques: La classe politique divisée sur l'interprétation de la laïcité', *Le Monde* (31 October 1989).

[33] The debate has been varied and stimulating. See, for instance, Fatima Lalem-Hachilif and Chahla Chafiq-Beski, 'Voile, la crise des valeurs', *Libération* (16 December 2003); Alain Renaut and Alain Touraine, *Un débat sur la laïcité* (Paris: Stock, 2005); Jean Baubérot, Alain Houziaux, Dounia Bouzar and Jacqueline Costa-Lascoux, *Le voile, que cache-t-il?* (Paris: Les Editions Ouvrières, 2004); and Farhad Khosrokhavar, 'L'universel abstrait, le politique et la construction de l'islamisme comme forme d'altérité', in Michel Wieviorka (ed.), *Une société fragmentée: le multiculturalisme en débat* (Paris: La Découverte, 1996).

and that reasons for wearing the headscarf varied depending on the background of the wearer. But these dissenting voices were not enough to stop the question returning to the heart of French politics. Fourteen years after the original *affaire du foulard*, it was a centre-right president who finally succumbed to public pressure to set up a commission to investigate the wearing of religious symbols in schools. It was placed under the direction of erstwhile UDF deputy Bernard Stasi and, as we know, brought together an all-star cast of France's intellectual class.[34] The composition of the commission gave it a strong neo-republican flavour: in addition to Debray, it included the philosopher Henri Peña-Ruíz (a specialist on *laïcité*) and Marceau Long, who had been head of the commission in charge of reforming nationality law in 1987. All three figures had made clear their commitment to the emerging language of neo-republicanism in previous years, while other members, such as specialist on nationality law Patrick Weil, would later vigorously defend the commission's recommendation to ban religious symbols in schools.[35] Ultimately, there was only one abstention in the final vote on the commission's report: that of *laïcité* expert Jean Baubérot. He subsequently denounced what he described as the 'republican fundamentalism' of the commission. He noted, for instance, how sociologist Alain Touraine, who had hitherto defended forms of French multiculturalism and opposed any legislation, was brought 'rapidly into line' with the commission's conclusions.[36] For Baubérot, the implication was clear: the Commission Stasi was a triumph of neo-republican logic over empirical reasoning.

Baubérot's opinion would have remained largely academic were it not for the fact that the commission's report was quickly made into law. Less than a year after the report was published, the French parliament approved a bill banning 'ostentatious religious signs' in public schools. With one piece of legislation, France became the first country in western Europe to take a strong legislative stance towards the Islamic headscarf. True to the transformative language of neo-republicanism, France was once again a beacon of rationality against religious obscurantism.

---

[34] The twenty members of the commission were Mohammed Arkoun, Jean Baubérot, Hanifa Cherifi, Jacqueline Costa-Lascoux, Régis Debray, Michel Delebarre, Nicole Guedj, Ghislaine Hudson, Gilles Kepel, Marceau Long, Nelly Olin, Henri Peña-Ruíz, Gaye Petek, Maurice Quénet, René Rémond, Rémy Schwartz (*rapporteur*), Raymond Soubie, Bernard Stasi (chair), Alain Touraine and Patrick Weil.

[35] Patrick Weil, 'A nation in diversity: France, Muslims and the headscarf', opendemocracy.org (25 March 2004). On Weil's (strongly neo-republican) attitude towards the question of republican integration in general, see for instance, P. Weil, *La République et sa diversité* (Paris: Seuil, 2005).

[36] Personal interview with the author (13 February 2007).

Unfortunately, the legislation brought with it a deluge of unfavourable publicity. Foreign commentators lined up to explain why the legislation was a bad idea and show how it was little more than a thinly veiled form of neo-colonial racism that threatened to endanger the foundations of liberal pluralism.[37] Even those who had endorsed a rehabilitated form of republicanism opposed the passing of legislation.[38] In contrast, the predicted Muslim backlash to the legislation in France never took place, almost certainly because the vast majority of France's sizeable Muslim population had no interest in drawing attention to themselves while attempting their difficult integration into French society.[39]

This silence on the part of Muslims could not prevent a third incarnation of the *affaire du foulard* from exploding in 2009. On this occasion, it was not the Islamic headscarf (*hijab*) but the 'full veil' (*niqab* and *burqa*) that was the object of attention, but this had little effect on the debate itself, which followed entirely predictable lines and continued to confuse political allegiances.[40] Unusually, it was a Communist deputy – André Gerin – who proposed in June 2009 that a commission be set up to investigate a ban on the wearing of the *burqa* in public.[41] His proposition – signed by fifty-eight deputies from all parts of the political spectrum – reproduced exactly the kind of mix between a transformative and institutional narrative that we saw in previous discussions of *laïcité*. Thus the proposition began with an appeal to *laïcité*'s roots in the Declaration of the Rights of Man of 1789, and went on to affirm that 'when *laïcité* is threatened, so is French society in its entirety and in its capacity to offer a

---

[37] On the 'repressive' aspects of the headscarf legislation and French *laïcité* in general, see the strongly argued Scott, *The Politics of the Veil*, and Talal Asad, 'Trying to understand French secularism', in Hent de Vries (ed.), *Political Theologies* (New York: Fordham University Press, 2006). For a more considered view see John Bowen, *Why the French don't like headscarves: Islam, the State and the Public Space* (Princeton University Press, 2007); or, for a feminist perspective, Bronwyn Winter, *Hijab and the Republic: Uncovering the French Headscarf Debate* (Syracuse University Press, 2008).

[38] For instance, Cécile Laborde, *Critical Republicanism: The Hijab Controversy and Political Philosophy* (Oxford University Press, 2008), p. 254. Despite her opposition to the ban, Laborde makes a strong case *for* republicanism in her essay Cécile Laborde, *Français, encore un effort pour être républicains!* (Paris: Seuil, 2010).

[39] John Laurence and Justin Vaïsse, *Integrating Islam: Political and Religious Challenges in Contemporary France* (Washington, DC: Brookings Institution, 2006).

[40] There was some disagreement over the exact term used to describe the form of dress in question: in popular discourse, the problem was the 'burqa', whereas for specialists the form of dress was closer to the 'niqab'. The term ultimately chosen by the commission was *voile intégral*.

[41] Proposition No. 1725 was entitled 'Proposition de Résolution tendant à la création d'une commission d'enquête sur la pratique du port de la burqa ou le niqab sur le territoire national' (9 June 2009) (www.assemblee-nationale.fr/13/propositions/pion 1725.asp; last accessed 15 April 2014).

common destiny [to its citizens]'. The proposition provoked an immediate and vigorous reaction, coming as it did in the middle of a 'big debate on national identity' led by the then president of the republic, Nicolas Sarkozy. But, while Sarkozy's 'big debate' was a project quite clearly led by him and his party – the Union pour un mouvement populaire (UMP) – the debate over the 'full veil' crossed party lines. On the left, it took until late January 2010 for the PS finally to come out 'against' a full ban, while still openly condemning the 'full veil'. On the right, the general secretary of the UMP, Xavier Bertrand, came out in support of a 'soft' line, while Fadela Amara, Jean-François Copé and the convenor of the Gerin commission, Eric Raoult, were in favour of legislation.[42]

Beyond the world of partisan politics, the French press was once again filled with battles between proponents of a rigid reaffirmation of neo-republican values, and those worried about the 'Islamophobic' nature of any legislation, or simply the danger of legislative 'stigma'.[43] The reaction in the foreign press was particularly vitriolic, with a *New York Times* editorial claiming that the 'Taliban would applaud' legislation banning the 'full veil', while British journalists pleaded 'France, don't ban the niqab'.[44] It is likely that at least some of this negative publicity had an impact on the commission itself: its report, published on 26 January 2010, did not recommend a ban, but only proposed that the government should seek 'the advice of the Conseil d'Etat in advance of a potential examination of a legislative project which would prohibit the covering of the face in a public space'.[45] Nevertheless, the vast 644-page report, which included the full text of all the interviews and round tables conducted by the commission, was a remarkable document. It demonstrated not only an exceptional desire on the part of the commission to open up a public discussion, but also the extent to which the principles of neo-republicanism which emerged in the 1980s had become a consensual part of the language of French politics. Even though a number of political groupings opposed an outright ban (especially the PS and PCF,

---

[42] A summary of these positions can be found in Ségolène Gros de Larquier, 'Le "combat républicain" d'André Gerin', *Le Point* (19 June 2009), and Stephanie Le Pors, 'Les dégâts collatéraux du débat sur le port du voile intégral', *Le Monde* (4 February 2010).

[43] Raphaël Liogier, 'La chasse à la burqa est-elle ouverte? Un arsenal juridique existe déjà inutile de faire de la surenchère', and André Bercoff, 'Les républicains devrait s'unir contre l'aberration du voile intégral. Resistons à la politique de l'autruche', *Le Monde* (13 January 2010).

[44] 'The Taliban Would Applaud', *New York Times* (26 January 2010). M. White, 'France, don't ban the niqab', guardian.co.uk (1 February 2010).

[45] Eric Raoult, *Rapport d'information fait en application de l'article 145 du Règlement: Au nom de la mission d'information sur la pratique du port du voile intégral sur le territoire national* (Paris: La Documentation Française, 2010), p. 188.

which accused the right of using the issue to distract attention from government policies), there were few who disputed the commission's logic: that the 'full veil' posed a fundamental threat to the Republic, its institutions and its values.[46]

While the commission made efforts to include dissenting voices – such as Jean Baubérot or Farhad Khosrokhavar – there was also the usual strong neo-republican representation, from Elisabeth Badinter and Henri Peña-Ruíz to a round table entirely composed of presidents of France's many 'secular organisations [*associations laïques*]'.[47] Thus, in spite of its commendable diversity, the report on the 'full veil' demonstrated how neo-republicanism had become the dominant discourse in all discussions of *laïcité* – and one which led inexorably to further legislation. And so it was that, in October 2010, the Assemblée Nationale and the Sénat approved a new law that 'prohibited the concealment of the face in a public space'.[48] The law was widely condemned as a transparent form of Islamophobia, but it achieved a broad cross-party consensus. After all, by this time, *laïcité* was no longer an issue of right and left: the original *affaire du foulard* first came to prominence in 1989 under Rocard and Mitterrand's centre-left administration, but returned in 2004 and 2009 during the centre-right administrations of Sarkozy and Chirac. Twenty years of public engagement with the language of neo-republicanism had ensured that its interpretation of *laïcité* would transcend traditional political fault lines.

Yet it has not only been through *laïcité* and the *foulard* that neo-republicanism has found its way into contemporary French political life. Many of the figures who had sharpened their swords in the debate surrounding the *foulard* found themselves once again in the spotlight in the mid 1990s – this time, opposing the law on *parité*, a provision to ensure the equal representation of women in national elections. The difference in this instance was that republicanism was used both to defend and to attack the proposed law, which added an additional layer of complexity to the subsequent debates. As with the *affaire du foulard*, the disagreements over the *loi sur la parité* ignored right–left divisions, although the fiercest debates were within the left. The majority of the proposal's critics, as well as the two principal organisers of the

---

[46] For the party-political position 'letters' solicited by the commission see Raoult, *Rapport d'information*, pp. 195–233.

[47] This included, for example, the Comité Laïcité République, founded by Claude Nicolet.

[48] 'Loi n° 2010–1192 du 11 octobre 2010 interdisant la dissimulation du visage dans l'espace public', available at www.legifrance.gouv.fr/affichTexte.do;jsessionid= EB787F209B3911905B192A25782398E3.tpdjo03v_1anddateTexte=?cidTexte= JORFTEXT000022911670 (last accessed 8 March 2014).

Mouvement pour la Parité – Françoise Gaspard and Claude Servan-Schreiber – had either been actively involved in the PS or had long-standing commitments to the left. Significantly, however, both Gaspard and Servan-Schreiber had represented the *droit à la différence* wing of the Socialists in the early 1980s.[49] As we shall see in the chapter on the politics of post-colonialism in France, this post-1968 tendency within the so-called *deuxième gauche* (second left) was associated with the promotion of difference during the early years of Socialist rule after 1981. It was dealt a severe blow by the rise of neo-republicanism in the 1980s, but its openness to cultural, ethnic and gender pluralism laid the groundwork for the *parité* movement. For supporters of the law on the left, it was a continuation of a long-standing project to make French politics more representative and diverse.

As for those opposing the law on neo-republican grounds, the cast was relatively familiar. Aside from Fontenay, Kintzler and Badinter, it included Peña-Ruíz; author and journalist Danièle Sallenave; political scientist and author Evelyne Pisier; highly respected historian of the French Revolution, Mona Ozouf; and Bernard-Henri Lévy. These critics of the law invoked a wide range of arguments. Central to almost all of them was the fear of a disintegration of the Republic into separate communities, an echo of the vigorous debate surrounding the validity of 'multiculturalism' in France, which will receive close attention in the following chapter. In Badinter's words,

[The argument for *parité*] carries within it the seeds of a dangerous tendency [*dérive*] for our secular and universalist Republic . . . [it] will inevitably give rise to new equality claims [*revendications paritaires*] from other racial, religious, cultural and sexual communities.[50]

Badinter was the most strident in denouncing the proposed law as inimical to the Republic, but her argument was amplified in Kintzler and Ozouf's interventions. Meanwhile, Lévy joined his fellow ex-*nouveau philosophe* Finkielkraut in warning of the risks of having 'this or that community' demand separate representation from the state.[51] Just as there had been fears of a 'communitarian drift' in discussions surrounding *laïcité*, so these same concerns were at the heart of a neo-republican critique of the *parité* law.

---

[49] On this, see Joan Wallach Scott, *Parité! L'universel et la différence des sexes* (Paris: Albin Michel, 2005).

[50] Elisabeth Badinter, 'Non au quotas des femmes', *Le Monde* (12 June 1996).

[51] Catherine Kintzler, 'La parité, ou le retour de la "nature"', and Mona Ozouf, 'Une bienheureuse abstraction', in Micheline Amar (ed.), *Le piège de la parité: textes pour un débat* (Paris: Hachette Littératures, 1999); Bernard Henri-Lévy, 'Oui à l'égalité, non à la parité', *Le Point* (13 February 1999).

Moreover, it was argued that, since legal equality was necessary to guarantee the fair treatment of women, the *parité* law, by undermining the principle of equality, would disadvantage women. As Pisier put it,

Equality before the law is the only idea that allows us to fight against the prejudices that still ... justify the inferiority of women.[52]

The consequences were clear:

[Although] it has come from women, *parité* will turn against them. For segregation, whether on the grounds of sex, gender or race, always gives rise to discrimination.[53]

There was, of course, something of a paradox here: on the one hand, a law guaranteeing equal participation of women was seen to compromise the legal equality of women; on the other, neo-republicans were clamouring for clear legislation on the headscarf. Why was legislation necessary in order to clarify the limits of religious expression but unnecessary – even dangerous – for women? In the event, such questions remained purely theoretical since, to general surprise, *parité* became enshrined in French law.[54] In June 2000, the Assemblée Nationale approved a modification to the French constitution that forced political parties to ensure that women made up 50 per cent of their candidates for legislative elections conducted by proportional representation or face financial sanctions.[55] The effect on the political representation of women has been painfully slow and most political parties have preferred to pay fines rather than move towards any kind of *parité*.[56] Still, the law seemed, at first sight, to go against the growing post-1989 neo-republican consensus.

In hindsight, things are not so clear. Even in defeat, neo-republicans succeeded in imposing their language on the debate. As Joan Scott has persuasively argued, the only way that the Mouvement pour la Parité was able to survive the neo-republican onslaught was by skilfully avoiding the pitfalls of an 'affirmative action' position and framing their arguments along republican lines. Supporters of the law argued that the masculine

---

[52] Evelyne Pisier, 'Universalité contre parité', *Le Monde* (8 February 1995).
[53] Elisabeth Badinter, Evelyne Pisier and Danièle Sallenave, 'Trois arguments contre la parité', *L'Express* (11 February 1999).
[54] The PS itself 'resisted' the republican line and the bill passed through the Sénat with an almost unanimous vote. See 'La parité: la direction du Parti Socialiste reste imperméable au "badinterisme"', *Le Monde* (18 February 1999).
[55] The text of the legislation is available at www.legifrance.gouv.fr/WAspad/UnTexteDe Jorf?numjo=INTX9900134L (last accessed 4 January 2010).
[56] Observatoire de la Parité, *Effets directs et indirects de la loi du 6 juin 2000* (Paris: La Documentation Française, 2005).

character of the state was itself a distortion, thereby turning the neo-republican position on its head. Rather than argue that *parité* was designed to redress a 'historic' imbalance between the sexes, supporters of the law maintained that it would recognise the 'universality of sexual differences'. The *parité* law would therefore help to redefine the woman as an individual (rather than as a community) and, ultimately, contribute to the more complete realisation of republican democracy. In addition, a law guaranteeing *parité* would more closely represent the reality of the Republic and would, therefore, unite rather than divide the state.[57] That such a creative reinterpretation of the French republican tradition was required to defend *parité* merely reaffirmed the dominance of neo-republicanism in the mid 1990s: it was only through this kind of argument that supporters of *parité* could package a piece of legislation that looked suspiciously like an anti-republican form of 'affirmative action'.

We can put this achievement in perspective if we compare the success of the *parité* law with the almost complete failure of any kind of 'affirmative action' policies, even broadly conceived, in France's higher educational institutions. The only example of such policies so far have been the attempts by the Institut d'études politiques, Paris (otherwise known as Sciences Po), to facilitate entry for those students applying from under-privileged urban areas since 2001. Needless to say, Sciences Po's approach was extremely controversial and only possible because of the institution's relative autonomy.[58] Attempts to implement forms of 'affirmative action' in other French universities and *grandes écoles* have met with stiff resistance on the grounds that they pose a fundamental threat to a republican principle of equality.[59] In the realm of education reform, a neo-republican language strongly opposed to any undermining of the (theoretical) meritocracy of the French education system has remained powerful, but in debates surrounding *parité*, campaigners were able to sidestep the neo-republican critique and push through legislation.

[57] Scott, *Parité!*, pp. 7–12, 90–6.
[58] For an overview and contextualisation of the reforms at Sciences Po, see Bernard Toulemonde, 'La discrimination positive dans l'éducation: des ZEP à Sciences-Po', *Pouvoirs* (No. 111, 2004), pp. 87–99. For opinions from the initial debate in 2001, see for instance Nathalie Guibert, 'Les conventions ZEP en débat à Sciences-Po', *Le Monde* (10 March 01); Hervé Baro, 'Démocratisation de Sciences Po: attention aux fausses solutions', *Le Monde* (4 April 2010); and Pascal Combemale and Olivier Coquard, 'La gifle de Sciences Po', *Le Monde* (15 March 2001).
[59] For an overview of Sciences Po's historical trajectory – and what has made it an unusual higher educational institution in France – see for instance Philip Nord, 'Reform, Conservation, Adaptation: Sciences Po from the Popular Front to the Liberation', in Sudhir Hazareesingh (ed.), *The Jacobin Legacy in Modern France* (Oxford University Press, 2002).

In so doing, they demonstrated, not the weakness of neo-republicanism, but the imagination required to transcend its powerful normative and historical narratives.[60]

The *parité* law was something of an exception. There have been other areas where a language of neo-republicanism has more successfully stalled reform. One of the best examples of this is the debate over France's regional languages. As before, the debate began in the 1980s, when it seemed that a growing acceptance of regional languages would become the norm. The Socialist victory in 1981 promised what some foreign commentators described as 'an evolution away from the traditional Jacobinism of most of the French ... elite'.[61] The decentralisation policies enshrined in the Loi Defferre of 1982 suggested that regional autonomy – both political and cultural – might become a reality for France's peripheral areas (such as Alsace, Corsica, Brittany or the *départements d'outre-mer*). Jack Lang – Socialist Culture Minister from 1981 to 1986 – further raised the hopes of advocates of decentralisation by commissioning the Rapport Giordan and Rapport Queyranne in 1982.[62] Both argued for further regional autonomy and stressed the importance of supporting regional languages. To some extent, these claims were heard: there was increased funding for classes in regional languages throughout the 1980s, and the first official teaching qualification for a regional language (the CAPES for Breton) was inaugurated in 1985.[63]

But the backlash was not long in coming. It was one thing to support the teaching of regional languages; it was quite another to accept legislative or constitutional amendments that would recognise their legitimacy. Just as member states of the European Community were preparing to

---

[60] There are interesting comparisons to be made with the debates surrounding gay rights, the Contrat d'union sociale (CUS) and the Pacte civil de solidarité (PACS). Here, too, neo-republicans argued that alternatives to marriage would encourage communitarianism and undermine the 'republican' family. See Camille Robcis, 'Republicanism and the critique of human rights', in Chabal, *France since the 1970s*.

[61] William Safran, 'The Mitterrand Regime and its Policies of Ethnocultural Accommodation', *Comparative Politics* (Vol. 18, No. 1, 1985), p. 41.

[62] Henri Giordan, *Démocratie culturelle et droit à la différence: Rapport au ministère de la culture* (Paris: Documentation Française, 1982). J.-J. Queyranne, *Les régions et la décentralisation: Rapport au ministère de la culture* (Paris: Documentation Française, 1982).

[63] From 2011, the CAPES was offered for the teaching of Corsican, Basque, Breton, Catalan, Créole, Occitan-langue d'oc and Tahitien. *Arrêté du 30 avril 1991 fixant les sections et les modalités d'organisation des concours du certificat d'aptitude au professorat de l'enseignement du second degré* (28 June 2009) available at www.legifrance.gouv.fr/affichTexte.do?cidTexte=JORFTEXT000000709273anddateTexte= (last accessed 8 March 2014).

acknowledge the role of regional languages in the 1992 Charter for Regional and Minority Languages, the French were moving in the opposite direction. On 23 June 1992, the Assemblée Nationale adopted a constitutional amendment to make French the official language – the first time any such clause had been added to a French constitution. Article 2 was amended to include the words: 'The language of the Republic is French.' Alongside this highly symbolic gesture, in November the same year the French chose not to sign the 1992 European Charter for Regional or Minority Languages.[64] France did ultimately sign the Charter in May 1999, but, the following month, the Conseil Consitutionnel ruled that it would run counter to the revised Article 2 of the Constitution.[65] In their conclusions, they reproduced the familiar neo-republican argument that the recognition of regional languages would 'confer specific rights to "groups" of regional language speakers inside "territories" in which these languages are spoken'. This would, by extension, 'violate the constitutional principles of the indivisibility of the Republic, of equality before the law, and the unity [unicité] of the French people'.[66] Still today, France has not ratified the Charter.

There was further evidence of the penetration of neo-republicanism in language policy in the groups and personalities that influenced the legislative process. The 1992 amendment to the constitution was a direct consequence of the work of the pressure group Avenir de la Langue Française (ALF), one of whose founding members was Debray. In a matter of months, the ALF elevated the question of the constitutional status of French from a non-issue to a proposed legislative measure. The first mention of a 'proposal' submitted to ministers – including Jean-Pierre Chevènement – was in early May 1992.[67] A little over two months later, the original proposal had been reduced to its final version and had passed through the Assemblée Nationale and the Sénat with relatively little opposition. This did not stop the ALF from issuing two further petitions in Le Monde shortly after the constitutional amendment was passed and, in 1994, playing a key role in the elaboration of

---

[64] Lynne Wilcox, 'Coup de langue: The amendment to Article 2 of the Constitution: An equivocal interpretation of linguistic pluralism?', Modern and Contemporary France (Vol. 2, No. 3, 1994), pp. 269–78.

[65] Béatrice Jerome, 'La France signe la Charte européenne des langues régionales', Le Monde (8 May 1999).

[66] Décision n° 99–412 DC du 15 juin 1999 of the Conseil constitutionnel, www.conseil-constitutionnel.fr/conseil-constitutionnel/francais/les-decisions/depuis-1958/decisions-par-date/1999/99–412-dc/decision-n-99–412-dc-du-15-juin-1999.11825.html (last accessed March 2010].

[67] Jean-Pierre Péroncel-Hugoz, 'La Francophonie dans la constitution?', Le Monde (8 May 1992).

the so-called Loi Toubon, which was designed to ensure the use of French in the workplace.[68]

The ALF itself never made any special claim to embody neo-republican values; its purpose was limited to the protection of the French language. It is nonetheless hard to ignore the relationship between a growing neo-republican discourse in the 1990s, and the protection of the French language. Indeed, the link was made quite explicit in an editorial in *Le Monde* in August 1994 by the centre-right deputy and minister Jacques Toubon that sought to justify the legislation named after him:

> To govern ... is to prefer ... the superiority of culture over the imperatives of the market [and] the will of the people to live together over individualism and communitarianism ... This is the republican tradition ... This is why the overwhelming majority of French people ...approved the law which I put forward, and which was adopted, without any opposition, in parliament.[69]

The subsequent debates in 1999 over the signing of the Charter for Minority or Regional Languages provoked an even stronger wave of neo-republican protest. On the left, Chevènement and Georges Sarre – who were founder members of the Mouvement des Citoyens – registered their disapproval of Jospin's decision to sign the Charter, alongside other less thoroughgoing neo-republican figures such as the Socialist politician Michel Charasse.[70] The latter declared:

> [B]y meddling with our justice system, our language, the principle of equality, the unity of the French and the indivisibility of France, it is the Republic [itself] that we are unravelling, one thread at a time.[71]

Similar complaints were heard elsewhere on the political spectrum. The centre-right deputy Xavier Deniau, who had been instrumental in the passing of the constitutional amendment in 1992 – attacked the Charter as a threat to the 'unity of the Republic', a position he shared with the secretary of the ALF, Thierry Priestley, for whom the signing of the Charter was the clearest indication yet of the 'hammer of

---

[68] 'L'Avenir de la langue française', *Le Monde* (8 July 1992), and 'Avenir de la langue française', *Le Monde* (1 December 1992). On the changes since 1992 more generally, see William Safran, 'Politics and Language in Contemporary France: Facing Supranational and Infranational Challenges', *International Journal of the Sociology of Language* (Vol. 137, 1999), pp. 39–66.

[69] Jacques Toubon, 'La langue de tous', *Le Monde* (4 August 1994).

[70] Georges Sarre, 'Langues régionales: ouvrir les yeux', *Le Figaro* (1 September 1999), and 'Un entretien au 'Figaro': les quatre vérités de Chevènement', *Le Figaro* (6 July 1999).

[71] 'Charasse: 'On ne revise pas la République', *Le Figaro* (24 June 1999). Michel Charasse, a politician very active in his native Puy-de-Dôme region, became a member of the Conseil constitutionnel in 2010.

communitarianism'.[72] Even intellectuals such as Sallenave, who had already attacked the *parité* law, and the eminent sociologist of the nation Dominique Schnapper denounced the potentially deleterious consequences of the Charter for national unity.[73]

It was left to an odd and equally ecumenical range of personalities to defend the Charter, among whom were the current Prime Minister Jospin, Henri Giordan, a long-time supporter of regional autonomy and language reform, and conservative philosopher Alain de Benoist. They all argued in different ways that it was time to reform France's 'Jacobin' tendencies and to accept linguistic diversity within the Republic.[74] Predictably, this reform has been slow in coming. A major step towards recognition took place in July 2008, when the following clause was added to the Constitution: 'Regional languages belong to the heritage [*patrimoine*] of France.' But this still fell short of a legal recognition of the validity of regional languages, and France has yet to ratify any part of the Charter on the grounds that it would enforce just such a legal recognition.[75]

What was true for regional languages was also true for proposals to develop regional autonomy. Here the picture was more complex, in large part because of the range of different territories that fall under French jurisdiction. In the final chapter, I shall explore how a more liberal approach to decentralisation resulted in the successful implementation of various projects for local autonomy in places like Nouvelle-Calédonie in the 1990s and 2000s. But, in the same period, there was also sustained opposition to greater decentralisation from political and intellectual figures who used the language of neo-republicanism for their own political purposes. One example of this was the aborted project for Corsican devolution proposed by Pierre Joxe, Socialist Minister of the Interior, in 1990–1. His first mistake was to make mention of the rights of a 'Corsican people' in the proposed legislation. This earned him an immediate sanction from France's highest judicial body, the Conseil constitutionnel:

---

[72] Xavier Deniau, 'Langues régionales: non à la Charte', *Le Figaro* (19 October 1999), and T. Priestley, 'Contre la Charte européenne: le marteau du communautarisme', *Nouvel Observateur* (1 July 1999).

[73] Dominique Schnapper on *A Voix Nue* (Radio France/France Culture, 8 April 2009), and Danièle Sallenave, 'Partez, briseurs d'unité!', *Le Monde* (3 July 1999).

[74] Henri Giordan, 'Langues régionales: un peril communautariste?', *Le Monde* (7 July 1999). Alain de Benoist, 'Jacobinisme ou fédéralisme?', translated and published in a Dutch right-wing publication as Alain de Benoist, 'Jacobinisme of federalisme. Beschouwingen over Frankrijk, Europa en de regio's', *TeKos* (No. 108, 2002), pp. 3–17.

[75] Xavier Ternisian, 'L'entrée des langues régionales dans la Constitution suscite des espoirs', *Le Monde* (1 August 2009).

Given that France is ... an indivisible, secular, democratic and social Republic that guarantees equality before the law to all citizens, regardless of their origin ...[any] mention by legislators of a 'Corsican people, a component part of the French people' is contrary to the Constitution, which only recognises the French people, made up of all French citizens without any distinction of origin, race or religion.[76]

This eminently neo-republican line of reasoning – a striking precursor to the Conseil's attitude towards the Charter for Regional or Minority Languages – found a wide echo among France's political elite, on both the left and the right.[77] Within a few months, Joxe's proposals were dead in the water.

Even in Corsica itself, a neo-republican language of unity had powerful political backing in the form of Emile Zuccarelli – Socialist deputy for Haute-Corse in 1986–2007 and mayor of Bastia since 1989. Zuccarelli was instrumental in mobilising the campaign against Joxe's proposed changes to the status of Corsica in 1990–1. He subsequently opposed the Matignon reforms proposed by Jospin in 2000, and led the opposition to Interior Minister Sarkozy's unsuccessful referendum in Corsica on administrative reform in 2003.[78] Given his long-standing republican credentials, it was no surprise to find that Zuccarelli supported Chevènement in the 2002 presidential elections (after the latter's resignation from the Jospin government precisely over the question of Corsican devolution).[79] While critics have argued that Zuccarelli's attachment to France has been motivated mainly by his desire to retain personal control over his Corsican fiefdom, his vocal opposition to projects for Corsican devolution demonstrated how neo-republicanism could be reshaped in order to give meaning to 'peripheral' regional narratives and their relationship to central authority.[80] At the same time, the various ways

---

[76] Décision n° 91–290 DC du 09 mai 1991 of the Conseil constitutionnel, available at www.conseil-constitutionnel.fr/conseil-constitutionnel/francais/les-decisions/acces-par-date/decisions-depuis-1959/1991/91–290-dc/decision-n-91–290-dc-du-09-mai-1991.8758.html (last accessed, 1 February 2010).

[77] See Thierry Brehier, 'Dans le project Joxe, la notion de "peuple corse" deplaît à nombreux socialistes', *Le Monde* (16 November 1990), and Jean-Louis Andréani, 'Malgré l'hostilité accrue de l'opposition, l'Assemblée nationale rétablit la notion de "peuple corse"', *Le Monde* (15 April 1991).

[78] For a brief profile of Zuccarelli, see Raphaëlle Bacque, 'Emile Zuccarelli, dit Milou, s'est revélé en tombeur de Sarkozy', *Le Monde* (9 July 2003).

[79] On the 'Corsican question' in 2000, and its relation to neo-republican politics, see Olivier Mongin, 'L'été corse: Matignon et la réforme', *Esprit* (October 2000), pp. 186–92.

[80] I have explored some of these issues in relation to local politics in Montpellier under the Fifth Republic in Emile Chabal, 'Managing the Postcolony: Minority Politics in Montpellier, c. 1960–c.2010', *Contemporary European History* (Vol. 23, No. 2, 2014), pp. 237–58.

in which a powerful neo-republican language of unity has prevented the expression of regional difference is yet another example of how neo-republicanism had begun to reshape the French political landscape by the turn of the twentieth century.

The all-conquering Republic?

This chapter did not set out to be a political history of France since 1980, nor was it designed as an exhaustive account of every major political debate of recent years. The aim was to explore three areas where the language of neo-republicanism has been particularly influential, as well as place this new language in its wider political context. It is clear that neo-republicanism has become an increasingly important political reference point. Even those who attempted to overturn powerful neo-republican narratives – such as supporters of the *parité* law – found themselves either thwarted altogether or forced to repackage their proposals. Indeed, the strength of neo-republicanism has been amply demonstrated by the fact that it is one of the few languages to have survived in the unstable ideological climate of the 1980s and 1990s.[81] Yet, for all its strength, neo-republicanism has flourished without an obvious institutional or party-political base. Chevènement's attempts to make neo-republicanism an explicit political platform were a failure, and few political figures would make 'republicanism' their primary political identity (for the simple reason that no one today, even on the far right, would claim the mantle of 'anti-republicanism'). Instead, the language of neo-republicanism has become a conglomerate of words, phrases, ideas and symbols freely available to France's political class.

Does this mean that neo-republicanism has become a new language of consensus? Certainly, the political scientist Pierre Rosanvallon's prophecy in 1989 seems more apposite now than ever before:

In order to give meaning to its slow descent into pragmatism, [France's] political class has almost unanimously draped itself in a double reference to Gaullism and the Third Republic. The left in particular has restructured its [collective] memory around this improbable base and political life seems to have been driven by a desire for a consensual return to its 'origins'.[82]

---

[81] Pascal Perrineau, *Le choix de Marianne: pourquoi, pour qui votons-nous?* (Paris: Fayard, 2012).

[82] Rosanvallon, 'Malaise dans la représentation', in Furet, Julliard and Rosanvallon, *La République du Centre*, p. 140.

But, while this explanation captures the deeply consensual aspirations of neo-republicanism, it fails to recognise that neo-republicanism has also provided the French political class with an important new ideological dividing line. In an age when the right/left cleavage appears of limited relevance, neo-republicanism has created a new political space in which to discuss such pressing concerns as the role of religion in public life, the fate of the nation state, the modalities of political representation and the challenges of democratic pluralism. Rather than see it simply as a weak example of consensus and apolitical pragmatism, we should see neo-republicanism as a sustained attempt to re-energise French politics in the face of new challenges. In recent years, few challenges have been more pressing than France's post-colonial predicament – and it is to this that we must now turn.

4   Post-colonies I: integration, disintegration and citizenship

Regardez les portugais, ils ne font pas tant d'histoires!
A humorous definition of *intégration* from a 1989 study of second-generation immigrants in France[1]

From a purely academic point of view, post-colonialism came late to France. French historians, political scientists and sociologists resisted attempts to understand modern French history through a post-colonial lens until the early 2000s. Imperialism and its consequences were put to one side as France 'silenced' memories of its colonial encounters in North and West Africa, Indochina and beyond.[2] Yet, if post-colonialism seemed invisible inside the academy, outside it was omnipresent. France received an enormous influx of migrants from its former colonies and elsewhere from the 1960s onwards. Soon, second- and third-generation immigrant children were reclaiming what they perceived as 'their' colonial memories. Whether in the form of 'reparations' for slavery, or a recognition of police violence against Algerians in Paris in 1961, there was a growing number of demands from a wide variety of pressure groups, organisations, individuals and political movements.[3] Alongside the resurgence of colonial memory, other major problems began to surface. Institutionalised racism blocked access to housing and the labour market, while spatial segregation turned many French *banlieues* (suburbs) into areas where unemployment, violence and social exclusion were the norm. It seemed that the problem was not simply one of silenced memories; the post-colonial predicament had become an integral part of French society.

---

[1] Jean-Marie Térrasse and Virginie Linhart, *Génération Beur* (Paris: Plon, 1989), p. 10.
[2] On this, see for instance, Pascal Blanchard, Nicolas Bancel and Sandrine Lemaire, *La fracture coloniale: La société française au prisme des heritages coloniaux* (Paris: La Découverte, 2005). I discuss this in more detail in chapter 8.
[3] On the memory of slavery in France, see Françoise Vergès, *La mémoire enchaînée* (Paris: Albin Michel, 2006). On Paris 1961, see Jim House and Neil Macmaster, *Paris 1961: Algerians, State Terror and Memory* (Oxford University Press, 2006). On France's memory wars more generally, see Pascal Blanchard and Isabelle Veyrat-Masson (eds.), *Les Guerres de Mémoires: La France et son histoire* (Paris: La Découverte 2008).

One of the main consequences of this change was that France's post-colonial immigrant communities became increasingly visible. This, in turn, has led to impassioned debates over immigration and colonial memory – two of the most pressing political issues in contemporary France. Not a week goes by without, for example, a public debate over the right of non-EU citizens to vote (a long-standing Socialist electoral pledge that has still not been fulfilled), a disagreement over whether there should be public funding for mosques (an area of considerable legal ambiguity), or a polemical exchange over the Algerian War. It is only natural, therefore, that neo-republicanism – which developed in the 1980s at the same time as many of these questions and focused heavily on definitions of citizenship and the nation – should have become intimately tied up with this emerging post-colonial challenge to French national identity. As neo-republicanism has become a vital part of the symbolic vocabulary of French politics, it has been repeatedly deployed in the face of the bleeding of the colonial past into the present.

This has been most clearly visible in a variety of words and ideas that have gained wide currency in France. The most potent of these is *intégration* (integration) – a word whose myriad meanings will form the basis of this chapter. The struggle to define *intégration* and its opposites (*désintégration, fracture sociale, communautarisme* . . .) has structured debates surrounding post-colonial minorities. It has provided a means through which political actors of every persuasion have been able to understand social problems and the rise of identity politics in France. Not all of this has been related to immigration, ethnicity or the legacy of colonialism. But, for various reasons, *intégration* has become indelibly associated with a cluster of debates that focus on these issues, such as racism, nationality law and Islamic fundamentalism. Significantly for our purposes, the idea of *intégration* also provides an excellent case study of how neo-republicanism has penetrated political discourse and policy practice in France. In this chapter, we shall see how discussions about the meaning of *intégration* reveal the umbilical relationship between neo-republicanism and France's post-colonial predicament – a relationship that was already implicit in previous chapters. And we shall see how the most common definition of *intégration* has come to rely on a specifically neo-republican historical narrative, sociological theory and conception of citizenship.

Dividing the nation: immigration, the Front National and *la fracture sociale*

No threat has traditionally been perceived as more dangerous to a republican vision of national unity than that of 'désintégration', which in French carries the double meaning of the 'disintegration' of the state and the failure of citizens to 'integrate'. Since the 1980s, one of the most prominent perceived causes of disintegration in France has been immigration.[4] Of course, France is not unique in this. The emergence of immigration as an issue has been well documented across Europe. It has been intensified by the rise of anti-immigrant populist politics in the past three decades. The Europe-wide collapse of the far left has led disgruntled voters to vote in large numbers for the extreme right in a geopolitical climate that has created a new, more confrontational attitude towards Europe's Islamic minorities. For all its similarities, however, the French experience is distinct in two important respects. First, despite its long history as a country of immigration, the issue of immigration has – until recently – played little or no part in the writing of a national narrative in which the question of 'origin' has always been subservient to a project of 'social' and 'national' integration. Second, France has been unusual in the strength and persistence there of an organised extreme right-wing party since the 1980s.[5] As we shall see, these are the two crucial contexts that have underpinned the French political class's feeling of 'disintegration'.

France has long been a country of immigration. Yet, surprisingly, scholarly interest in the subject is a relatively new phenomenon. Part of the explanation for this silence was a singular lack of academic work on the subject until the late 1970s. As the historian Gérard Noiriel pointed out in his seminal volume *Le creuset français* (1988), academic studies presented immigration as 'external' to France – a transitory or fleeting economic phenomenon. It was absent from textbooks, and academic historians left the subject largely to students of law. For Noiriel, the explanation for this lies in the fact that the modern idea of the nation in France came into being during the French Revolution, before the widespread use of the term 'immigration'. This meant that foreigners were not considered an integral part of the nation.[6] By the time immigration became a significant phenomenon in France in the later part of the nineteenth century, the nation had been ideologically 'fixed'. There was no space for the experience of immigrants or foreigners within the French national narrative, despite the fact that France had a higher rate

---

[4] Alec Hargreaves, *Immigration, 'Race' and Ethnicity in Contemporary France* (London: Routledge, 1995), p. 151.

[5] Emmanuel Godin, 'Does it make sense to treat the Front National as a French exception?', in Emmanuel Godin and Tony Chafer (eds.), *The French Exception* (Oxford: Berghahn, 2004).

[6] Michael Rapport, *Nationality and Citizenship in Revolutionary France: The Treatment of Foreigners 1789–99* (Oxford: Clarendon, 2000), pp. 327–43.

of immigration in relation to the overall population than the United States for long periods in the nineteenth and twentieth centuries.[7] It was only in the 1970s that French historians began to look at this major social phenomenon, in response to the obvious contemporary import-ance of immigration as a political and social issue. But even then there was nothing like the public memorialisation of sites of immigration like Ellis Island in the United States or the complex empirical research on immigrant communities of the kind that has long existed in Britain or the United States.

Today, there is relatively little disagreement about Noiriel's arguments as they relate to his analysis of immigration studies in France. Nor can there be much doubt that *Le creuset français* marked a watershed in French studies of immigration, after which an entire school of students inside and outside France began to look at the question in much greater detail.[8] Nevertheless, Noiriel's book simultaneously (and inadvertently) revealed some important assumptions about French attitudes towards immigration and the integration of migrant communities. Even though this was the first detailed and empirical investigation into a phenomenon long pushed aside in a French republican narrative of national unity, it still held to two important tenets of this narrative: first, it underplayed the importance of France's colonial encounter and, second, it maintained that the challenges of 'ethnic' integration are little different from those of social integration. The following passage highlights the first of these two assumptions:

The fact that the [latest wave] of mass immigration ... is from the colonial world ... is indeed unprecedented. For the first time, individuals whose family life has been marked by wars that were started by French people ... are confronted with the question of naturalisation and this can provoke particularly acute problems of conscience.[9]

Such a statement would have appeared profoundly uncontroversial to most British academics writing about this subject in the late 1980s, especially given that well-known scholars such as Paul Gilroy and Stuart Hall were writing about the interrelationship of race, post-colonialism and immigration at the same time.[10] In France, by contrast, the same intellectual traditions were almost entirely absent and Noiriel could

---

[7] Gérard Noiriel, *Le Creuset Français* (Paris: Edition du Seuil, 1988), pp. 16–30.
[8] For outside perspectives on the question of immigration and integration in twentieth-century French history, see e.g. Mary Dewhurst Lewis, *Boundaries of the Republic: Migrant Rights and the Limits of Universalism, 1918–1940* (Stanford University Press, 2007).
[9] Noiriel, *Creuset Français*, p. 211.
[10] Most famously, perhaps, Paul Gilroy, *There Ain't No Black in the Union Jack: the Cultural Politics of Race and Nation* (London: Hutchinson, 1987).

quickly pass over the issue of France's colonial past without arousing suspicion. Indeed, it is astonishing that this brief mention of the colonial encounter was the only time in his 500-page book that he acknowledged the role of France's colonial heritage and its relation to immigration. The implication was clear: that colonialism and the discourse of superiority that accompanied it were relatively insignificant to an understanding of French immigration – be it in the 1920s or the 1990s.[11] In this sense, *Le creuset français* clearly rehearsed a traditional republican narrative of 'colour-blind' integration. By downplaying the relevance of the colonial encounter to contemporary immigration, Noiriel was suggesting that migrant identity and memory were of negligible importance, even though there was ample evidence at the time that racism and colonialism were vital factors in understanding immigrant responses to French society.

This brings us directly to Noiriel's second claim in *Le creuset français*, that immigration should be viewed as a 'social' rather than an 'ethnic' problem. As he put it,

Is not the clearest proof of the effectiveness of the French melting pot illustrated precisely by the fact that the diversity of its origins today passes unnoticed by specialists of immigration themselves ...?[12]

With this statement, Noiriel was evidently trying to counter political rhetoric from the extreme right about the 'explosion' of migrants in France. He wanted to stress that immigration is an old problem that need not provoke hysterical panic. In so doing, however, he summarily dismissed current problems of integration as simply another manifestation of France's social problems, and reduced feelings of alienation among young ethnic minorities to a generalised 'crisis of hope' affecting the current generation.[13] Paradoxically, in trying to defuse the apocalyptic talk of a 'crisis of integration' and a 'flood' of migrants, he pushed the question of 'ethnic' integration into the same category as 'social' integration – a strategy that would subsequently be enthusiastically taken up by neo-republicans seeking to counteract the corrosive effect of identity politics in France.

Some of Noiriel's blind spots can be explained with reference to his political allegiances and intellectual trajectory. Noiriel's training was as a Marxist historian who worked on the northern French working class, and, even though he has drawn on a very wide range of influences since then, his work on immigration has always been driven by what he calls

---

[11] For a more critical perspective see Neil Macmaster, *Colonial Migrants and Racism* (London: Macmillan, 1997).
[12] Noiriel, *Creuset Français*, p. 341.   [13] Ibid., p. 356.

'socio-history'.[14] This has resulted in an overwhelming interest in the empirical facts of immigration and relations of power inside French society. He has left to one side questions of 'identity', 'discourse' and 'belonging'. Inevitably, this strict social approach, and some of his later essays denying, for instance, the double identity of second-generation immigrants, made his work popular with neo-republicans.[15] He recently acknowledged this and, in an effort to correct his image, wrote a book specifically on racial discourse in nineteenth- and twentieth-century France.[16] But he still remains resolutely hostile to analyses of contemporary France that emphasise its 'post-colonial' character, writing in 2009:

[T]he ritual invocation of the 'colonial imaginary' as a way of analysing the social problems that affect today's young people from deprived backgrounds [*jeunes des quartiers*] has the effect of inhibiting our understanding of *existing* power relations, and the role that professional opinion-formers play in the construction of stereotypes.[17]

Thus, while Noiriel can hardly be considered an unreconstructed neo-republican, the argumentative thrust of much of his work on immigration has helped to rehabilitate one of the central assumptions of neo-republicanism, namely that problems of ethnic integration are the same as those of social integration. Moreover, by dismissing France's 'post-colonial turn', Noiriel has reinforced the sense that the legacy of colonialism is largely irrelevant, and possibly even dangerous, to an understanding of contemporary French politics. In the context of a renewed political interest in the integration of migrant and ethnic minority communities, it is telling that the scholar who did most to rehabilitate immigration as an object of serious study in 1980s France simultaneously found himself reproducing a number of neo-republican assumptions.

Alongside the rediscovery of immigration in the academy, and the (often well-meaning) tendency to conflate 'ethnic' and 'social' integration, there was also a very real political concern, which forced immigration and integration to the top of the political agenda: the rise of the FN. This was vital

---

[14] His early work was published as Gérard Noiriel, *Longwy: immigrés et prolétaires* (Paris: Presses Universitaires de France, 1984). On Noiriel's influences see Gérard Noiriel, *Penser avec, penser contre: itinéraire d'un historien* (Paris: Belin, 2003). On socio-history, see Noiriel, *Etat, nation, immigration*, and Gérard Noiriel, *Sur la crise de l'histoire* (Paris: Belin, 1996).

[15] 'Les jeunes 'd'origine immigrée' n'existent pas', in Gérard Noiriel, *Etat, nation, immigration: vers une histoire du pouvoir* (Paris: Bélin/Folio 2001).

[16] Gérard Noiriel, *Immigration, antisémitisme et racisme en France: discours publics, humiliations privées* (Paris: Seuil, 2007).

[17] Ibid., p. 681 (emphasis in original).

both in placing immigration at the heart of political discussion but also in helping to create a renewed consensus around republican values.[18] Since the FN's first publicised success – in the municipal elections in Dreux in 1983 – the party has posed a constant threat to the consensual character of France's post-Gaullist political landscape. Gathering strength in legislative and presidential elections, the FN's most spectacular success was on 21 April 2002, when its presidential candidate, Jean-Marie Le Pen, squeezed past the Socialist Lionel Jospin in the first round of the presidential elections. But Le Pen's success was only the most striking manifestation of the FN as a political protest movement. With the collapse of the PCF, the FN became at once an inheritor of the erstwhile *poujadisme* of provincial France's lower middle class and of a wide-ranging critique of the supposedly complacent consensus of the Parisian elites.[19] The party's most popular slogan – 'la France au Français' – not only ran counter to the abstract, non-ethnic conception of the French Republic but was also an attack on the country's elites. The FN posed, therefore, a double threat: first, to the ideal of the Republic and, second, to the institutions and personalities who make up the Republic. Hence, perhaps, the vehemence with which political figures associated with the revival of a republican discourse denounced the FN.

At the same time, Le Pen's sometimes frenzied attacks on Muslims, Arabs, *sans-papiers* and *clandestins* (illegal immigrants) took the logic of French immigration policy to its most extreme conclusion.[20] In common with other European countries, the official discourse in France surrounding immigration throughout the 1980s increasingly emphasised immigration as 'transgression' by using a discourse of illegality to marginalise both economic migrants and asylum seekers.[21] The unfortunate expression 'the threshold of tolerance [*seuil de tolerance*]' – picked up by Mitterrand in December 1989 to describe the limits of France's immigration policy – indicated the degree to which this view had become widespread, even on the left, where the idea would previously have been condemned as racist.[22] Of course, it is debatable whether France's

[18] On this see especially Favell, *Philosophies of Integration*.

[19] For an analysis of the Front National's role in the context of the French right, see Jim Shields, *The Extreme Right in France, from Pétain to Le Pen* (London: Routledge, 2007).

[20] A famous example of this hysteria is Le Pen's statement that 'Demain, les immigrés s'installeront chez vous, mangeront votre soupe et coucheront avec votre femme, votre fille ou votre fils.' From a speech by Jean-Marie Le Pen on 14 February 1984 in 'Dossier Société – Le Front National: c'est ça', *Le Monde* (21 March 1998).

[21] On this, see the analysis in Max Silverman, *Deconstructing the Nation: Immigration, Racism and Citizenship in Modern France* (London: Routledge, 1992).

[22] Excerpts of Mitterrand's original speech on illegal immigration can be found in 'L'immigration clandestine ne doit pas être tolérée', *Le Monde* (12 December 1989).

increasingly repressive immigration policy can be attributed to the influence of the FN alone; European, geopolitical and economic imperatives have also played a crucial part in the worsening climate for migrants. Still, the FN concentrated the fears of France's political elites and gave neo-republicans a clear enemy. From a purely philosophical perspective, to stress the integrative power of the Republic against the FN's 'ethnic' conception of the nation was to suggest that immigrants can and should have a place in French society. More pragmatically, the electoral successes of the FN created the conditions for a new defensive *pacte républicain* in the 1990s that was designed to protect French politics from the influence of the extreme right.

By the mid 1990s, the political and social problems surrounding immigration, identity politics and the extreme right seemed to have come to a head. It was at this point that the term *fracture sociale* came to prominence, both as a way of understanding the fragmentation of French society and as a basis on which to build policy. There is no satisfactory translation for *fracture sociale* in English. The English terms 'social fracture' and 'social cohesion' are vague, while 'inequality' suggests a primarily economic phenomenon.[23] In French, however, *fracture sociale* implies a breakdown, dissolution or disintegration of the body politic. Such a notion provided the ideal counterpoint to a neo-republican project of nation-building. As we shall see, for neo-republicans of all stripes, *intégration* was the logical solution to *la fracture sociale*. But the enthusiasm with which French political figures in the 1990s adopted the word 'fracture' to describe the ills of the nation was in itself an indication of the penetration of a neo-republican language of national unity into the French political space.

The first use of the term *fracture sociale* was attributed (incorrectly) to the geographer, Emmanuel Todd, in the early 1990s, but it came to prominence in the 1995 presidential election campaign, when Jacques Chirac called on 'republican discipline' to counter the threat of the Front National.[24] This gave Chirac the political legitimacy to invoke the traditional rallying cry of the Republic: that the Republic was in danger. Alongside the threat from Le Pen, there was a growing sense of

On the penetration of far-right discourse into French politics, see Pierre Tévanian and Sylvie Tissot, *Mots à Maux: le dictionnaire du lepénisation de l'esprit* (Paris: Dagorno, 1998).

[23] There are echoes of the French idea of 'social fracture' in the writings of Anglo-American conservatives such as Charles Murray and Theodore Dalrymple, but they focus much more on a negative view of 'culture' than politics and citizenship.

[24] Emmanuel Todd, 'Rien ne sépare les enfants d'immigrés du reste de la société', *Le Monde* (12 November 2005).

insecurity. In particular, rising unemployment and unrest in France's *banlieues* had once again brought to the fore issues of social exclusion, racism and spatial segregation. Employing an analytical term that was in vogue at the time, Chirac grouped these numerous problems under the term *fracture sociale*. The success of the phrase was immediate. After Chirac won the election, variants of the term began to appear regularly across a variety of media.[25] For example, the sociologist Michel Wieviorka, in his work on the strikes of 1995, used it to describe the kind of social divisions that had led to the confrontational politics of the strikers.[26] The writer Azouz Bégag, whose fictional writing had played a major role in bringing the problems of second-generation immigrant children to public attention in the 1980s, talked of a *fracture éthnique*.[27] Others, particularly those on the losing left, denounced the growing *fracture politique*, the most important aspect of which was the right's neglect of 'popular sovereignty'.[28]

As the millennium approached, the term appeared to have lost none of its urgency. When asked in a 1997 opinion poll, the overwhelming majority of respondents claimed that the *fracture sociale* had either remained as bad as it ever was or had worsened.[29] By 1999, the French had, according to another opinion poll, become the 'most morose' of west European nations, which the then head of the French polling organisation IPSOS, Pierre Giacometti, attributed to the continuing fracture.[30] On the right, figures such as Henri Guiano used the concept to suggest that France was going through a 'moral and intellectual crisis'.[31] On the left, the term was employed both to undermine Chirac's policies and to understand Jospin's failure in the 2002 presidential elections. The riots of 2005 in the *banlieues* and the rejection of the European Constitution in the same year saw the idea return to prominence: an

[25] For a multifarious interpretation of the 'fracture sociale', see Claude Julien, 'Brève radiographie d'une fracture sociale', *Le Monde Diplomatique* (6 June 1995).

[26] Michel Wieviorka, 'Le sens d'une lutte', in Alain Touraine (ed.), *Le Grand Refus* (Paris: Fayard, 1996), pp. 250–5.

[27] Bruno Causse, 'Intégration: M. Chirac face aux fractures sociale et éthnique des banlieues', *Le Monde* (14 October 1995).

[28] Jerôme Lèbre, 'Vers une fracture politique', *Le Monde* (20 September 1995).

[29] The poll revealed that 48 per cent of respondents thought that the *fracture sociale* had not improved, while 42 per cent thought that it had worsened. Only 5 per cent felt that there had been any improvement. 'Scepticisme des français sur la "fracture sociale"', *Le Monde* (17 April 1997).

[30] 'La France: Pays de la fracture sociale', *Le Figaro* (23 June 1999).

[31] Henri Guiano, 'L'opinion et les responsables politiques: Comment en est-on arrivé à cette crise générale de la confiance? La fracture morale', *Le Figaro* (4 November 2000); Henri Guiano, 'La crise actuelle n'est ni technique, ni économique, ni sociale. Elle est intellectuelle et morale. Plaidoyer pour le principe d'autorité', *Le Figaro* (18 June 2001).

editorial in *Le Monde* in late 2005 suggested that the *fracture sociale* had not been addressed and that both the right and the left were responsible for the 'destruction [*déchirure*] of the republican pact' in the *banlieues*.[32] In the meantime, scholars of French colonial history coined the term *fracture coloniale* to describe the initial suppression and subsequent resurgence of France's colonial memories at the turn of the twentieth century, while the political scientist Pierre Rosanvallon used *fracture sociale* to describe France's social problems.[33] Claims in 2001 that the term *fracture sociale* had been replaced by 'insécurité' (insecurity) in the electoral vocabulary were premature, and there have been few signs that the earlier concept has passed its political sell-by date. For example, editorials in *Le Monde* in 2007 and 2008 again invoked various fractures – 'social, educational, ethnic, urban' – to explain the worsening state of the Parisian *banlieues*.[34] Within a decade, the idea of fracture had become deeply ingrained in academic and political debates.

The continuing relevance and use of the term *fracture sociale*, and the zeal with which it was adopted by France's political and intellectual elite in the mid 1990s, was a testimony to both the fear of fragmentation and the continuing pre-eminence of a neo-republican language of national unity. In some cases, the link was made explicit – as was the case when philosopher Blandine Kriegel came up with the term 'fracture républicaine' in 2002 – but, in the majority of cases, it was simply assumed that any 'fracture' would, by definition, compromise national unity.[35] Above all, the notion of a *fracture sociale* was a means by which new and disruptive post-colonial narratives of second-generation identity politics or post-colonial racism, could be understood and fitted into an existing neo-republican framework. Just as Noiriel's arguments had minimised the role of colonialism by underplaying the importance of 'ethnic' identities, so the idea of the *fracture sociale* reduced disruptive post-colonial narratives to one part of a much wider narrative of generalised socio-economic crisis. Even if there was widespread popular recognition that a number of France's social ills were in some way related to the country's colonial legacy, the idea of *fracture sociale* made it possible

---

[32] 'Fracture urbaine', *Le Monde* (8 November 2005).
[33] Blanchard, Bancel and Lemaire, *La fracture coloniale*; Pierre Rosanvallon and Thierry Pech, 'Introduction', in Pierre Rosanvallon and Thierry Pech (eds.), *La nouvelle critique sociale* (Paris: Seuil, 2006), p. 16.
[34] 'Banlieues, la fracture', *Le Monde* (26 October 2007); 'Banlieues, la rage', *Le Monde* (17 June 08). In an interview in March 2002, the sociologist Robert Rochefort claimed that the term 'insécurité' had replaced that of a *fracture sociale*; Robert Rochefort and Emmanuel Todd, 'Interview avec Robert Rochefort, Emmanuel Todd: Le thème d'insécurité a pris le relais de la fracture sociale', *Le Monde* (10 March 02).
[35] Blandine Kriegel, 'Non à la fracture républicaine!', *Le Figaro* (23 April 2002).

to understand this within a familiar narrative of the breakdown of the Republic and the threat of disintegration. What, then, was the solution? How could the French state repair a broken society? It was in response to France's multiple fractures that neo-republicans in the 1990s began to elaborate a new, more strident project of national integration.

Repairing the nation: the Haut Conseil à l'intégration

It has become commonplace to speak of a 'French model of integration'. Under the banner of a unifying Republic, and stressing the need to integrate immigrant communities, this French model has generally been placed in contrast to an Anglo-American 'multicultural' model that celebrates community identities and ethnic difference. The debate – often revolving around the emotive issue of Islam – usually takes on a partisan tone. To its critics, 'multiculturalism' is a dangerous celebration of fragmented multi-ethnic communities, while the 'French model' is little more than an updated version of an old assimiliationist colonial ideology. Unfortunately, this easy dichotomy has too often been accepted by the French and non-French alike. The result has been to confuse a debate surrounding citizenship that has been marked by an inadequate understanding of the way concepts such as 'multiculturalism' and 'integration' have been deployed in different political contexts. Moreover, the tendency of French intellectuals to raise discussions of specific issues (such as the headscarf) to a high level of abstraction has often been misread beyond the confines of France as an invitation to further abstraction rather than as part of a political debate within the French elites. The problem with a decontextualised treatment of France's model of integration is that it ignores the importance of successive nation-building projects in modern French history. Seen in a short-term perspective, it was the complex relationship between the rise of the FN, the growing 'problem' of immigration and the legacy of France's colonial encounters that made the elaboration of a new model of integration particularly urgent. But, in a long view, current debates over national integration are simply part of an ongoing political debate which has drawn on previous attempts to unify France across religious and class lines. When the French elite talk about 'intégration', therefore, they are not merely referring to the absorption of disparate 'ethnic' communities into France; they are endorsing a nation-building project that, on paper at least, involves all French citizens.

In order to gain a clearer view of what 'intégration' means, the obvious starting point is the work of the Haut Conseil à l'intégration, some of whose reports we examined in the opening chapter. In order to gain a clearer view of what *intégration* means, the obvious starting point is the work of the Haut Conseil à l'intégration, some of whose reports we examined in the opening chapter. The HCI provided an institutional framework for the implementation of state integration policies from 1989 until its effective dissolution in 2013 (to be replaced by the Observatoire de la Laïcité). At the time of its creation by the Socialist Prime Minister Michel Rocard in December 1989, it was seen to be a positive, state-driven response to the perceived crisis of integration. Its stated aim was to

give advice and make any useful proposition at the request of the Prime Minister or the inter-ministerial committee on integration on any question related to the integration of foreign residents or French residents of foreign origin.[36]

To this end, it gathered together a number of important public personalities, of whom many have been associated with neo-republicanism, including the commission's presidents Marceau Long (1990–7) and Blandine Kriegel (2002–8). Nevertheless, unlike the Commission Stasi, where the presence of neo-republicans was overwhelming, the HCI is interesting precisely because its eclectic (and changing) composition gives us an insight into a more consensual, official definition of 'intégration'. Fortunately, it is not necessary to infer the HCI's interpretation of the term, since it gave a quite explicit definition:

The term 'intégration' (generally used to describe the situation of immigrants who have settled permanently in their host country) refers both to a [social] process and policies that are put in place in order to facilitate it ... The process requires the effective participation of all those called to live in France in the construction of a society that brings [its citizens] together around shared principles (liberty of thought and conscience, equality between men and women for example) as they are expressed in equal rights and common responsibilities ... To lead a policy of integration is to define and develop actions that tend towards the maintenance of social cohesion.[37]

This excerpt has the benefit of capturing succinctly some of the very important aspects of the term 'intégration' and is entirely consistent with the definition found in the HCI's reports. What emerges strongly is its explicitly political dimension; there is a contractual element to the idea of 'shared principles'. If *intégration* is something which depends on a certain 'social cohesion', this is primarily political in nature. The unity of the body

---

[36] Article 1 du Décret no 89–912 du 19 décembre 1989 portant création d'un Haut Conseil à l'intégration, *Journal Officiel* (23 December 1989).

[37] This definition is taken from the glossary of terms on the HCI website, www.hci.gouv.fr/-Mots-de-l-integration-.html#I (last accessed 10 March 2014). Significantly, this definition has found its way into a wide variety of other documents, including those produced by the erstwhile Ministère de l'Emploi, de la Cohésion Sociale et du Logement, the INSEE statistics agency, and a slew of local government documents

politic is the implicit assumption behind any 'policy of integration', for no integration can take place where there is no unity in which to integrate.

The consequence of such a conceptual framework is, to quote an HCI report from 2003, that

> *intégration* is not only destined for French citizens of immigrant origin, but concerns any individual who participates in the public space [*espace civique*] ... National identity is experienced through shared values: it is not enough to be born on French soil to feel French. In order to come together, we must forget our particularities and discover what we have in common with others.[38]

This is a strong form of citizenship, which passes through the state – hence the HCI's continuous emphasis on the role of a 'public debate' instigated by the state.[39] It is also what one might describe as a 'total' form of citizenship, insofar as it brings together the social (*insertion sociale*), the economic (*exclusion*) and the 'ethnic' (*origine*) under the specifically political notion of *intégration*, which takes as its basis a 'republican pact'. Unlike the English 'inequality', which carries economic connotations, *intégration* suggests a wider civic project.

Any policy that promotes *intégration* also necessitates the reconstruction of what has become known as the *lien social* (social bond), a subject to which the HCI devoted an entire report in 1997. It becomes obvious from the report's introduction that the weakening of the *lien social* is one of the most significant components of the *fracture sociale*, and that it is intimately tied to the fate of the nation:

> The weakening of the *lien social* ... is a consequence of the search, by those belonging to the most fragmented social classes, for a collective identity that they no longer find in the nation.[40]

In this analysis, the *lien social* depends on the nation. It is through the nation that the 'fragmented social classes' find their collective identity. The weakening of the *lien social* poses a fundamental threat to the body politic, since it leads to identities that 'affirm themselves against others, either through the development of a group identity and verbal aggression, or through discrimination'.[41] Any weakening must therefore simultaneously entail a fragmentation of the nation itself. Of course, this logic

---

[38] Haut Conseil à l'intégration, *Le contrat et l'intégration* (Paris: La Documentation Française, 2003), p. 104.

[39] For example, the HCI chose not to recommend the collection of statistical data along ethnic grounds, instead arguing for a greater civic debate around the issue of discrimination. See Haut Conseil à l'intégration, *Les parcours de l'intégration* (Paris: La Documentation Française, 2001).

[40] Haut Conseil à l'intégration, *L'affaiblissement du lien social* (Paris: La Documentation Française, 1997), p. 26.

[41] Ibid., p. 26.

rests on an eminently neo-republican elision between nation, state and identity – and it is the same logic that we find in the notion of *intégration*. The 'total' citizenship required by the HCI's definition of *intégration* thus becomes the obvious response to the 'total' disintegration of the *lien social* and the resulting *fracture sociale*.

It was noticeable that the HCI's reports articulated an increasingly sophisticated conceptual framework from 1995 onwards, in an attempt both to respond to the critics of a monolithic republican universalism and to present a coherent ideological justification of the notion of *intégration*.[42] The result of this increasing conceptual clarity did not, however, give rise to a questioning of the fundamental assumptions behind *intégration*. If anything, the HCI's conclusions became more militant in tone. In 2002, the commission argued that

We must maintain the French republican tradition in its secular and contractualist version, but we must reject assimiliationism, which represented its hidden organicist dimension ... Disintegration [*désintégration*] remains a threat to the Republic. [The battle for integration] is a constant struggle and public authorities must be vigilant.[43]

Quite apart from the difficulty of distinguishing between *assimilation* and *intégration* – a problem the HCI tries to deal with in the report – this particular passage lays out quite explicitly the relationship between disintegration and republicanism. It claims that the Republic is under threat, a rallying cry that has long been part of republican language. At the same time, the HCI's calls for vigilance on the part of 'public authorities' places a heavy burden on the state, whose responsibility it is to tackle the threat of disintegration.

This question of responsibility was made more explicit still in an HCI report in 2009 entitled *Études et intégration – faire connaître les valeurs de la République*. The report's aim was to offer guidelines on measures designed to stimulate 'the understanding of republican values and symbols among immigrants'.[44] The report's recommendations included the mass distribution of small French flags at sporting events, and the more 'systematic' display of Marianne in public buildings.[45] Aside from these symbolic proposals – strikingly reminiscent of late-nineteenth-century republican attempts to bring the Republic to the provinces – the report also provided a reassertion of the necessity of 'total' citizenship. While

---

[42] See in particular the philosophical discussion in ch. 3 of Haut Conseil à l'intégration, *Le contrat et l'intégration*, pp. 104–22.

[43] Ibid., pp. 111–12.

[44] Haut Conseil à l'intégration, *Études et intégration: faire connaître les valeurs de la République* (Paris: La Documentation Française, 2009), p. 19.

[45] Ibid., pp. 24, 27.

recognising that 'the return of . . . the republican model in the 1980s was marked by a form of nostalgia for a supposedly unified doctrine of republicanism', the report nevertheless set about rehearsing its own neo-republican vision. In keeping with a transformative narrative of the Republic, it insisted that republicanism is built on its 'emancipatory force', but reminds us that

Through his engagement with the collectivity and his fellow citizens, . . . the citizen embodies a type of universality which everyone can recognise. The participation of citizens in the *res publica* leads to the formation of a republican identity that brings together and unites [*solidarise*] citizens in a common political project.[46]

The implication is clear: integration and disintegration are political processes, which require a political response.[47]

The reason for emphasising this strongly political dimension to the concept of integration in the HCI's reports is that it is often underplayed by foreign commentators who focus on France's 'model of integration' in relation to ethnic minorities. While there can be little doubt that a fear of disintegration and a renewed interest in national integration are direct consequences of France's post-colonial challenges, *intégration* cannot be compared unproblematically to the Anglo-American world's response to the same problems. So-called 'multiculturalism', even in its most clearly articulated form, separates the process of individual and community identity formation from the nation state. A neo-republican concept of *intégration* does precisely the opposite: it makes 'ethnic' (and other) group claims subservient to a narrative of social integration, and makes the state responsible for carrying out such integration. In so doing, the state also restores the *lien social*, which ultimately serves to re-energise the nation. This being the case, any discussion of the French 'model of integration' cannot limit itself, as it might in the Anglo-American world, solely to 'ethnic minorities' – a concept that anyway is taboo in France. As the work of the HCI makes abundantly clear, *intégration* is seen as a much wider process, involving a form of 'total' citizenship in which all French citizens are summoned to participate.

To recognise this is not to ignore the crucial importance of the post-colonial or the 'ethnic'; it is simply to recognise that 'ethnic' exclusion is seen to be only one part of a crisis of integration that has much wider implications for French society. Moreover, discussions surrounding

---

[46] Ibid., p. 21.
[47] Despite this general hardening of attitudes on the subject of *l'intégration*, it is notable that in 2000 the HCI was unwilling to recommend a ban on the headscarf in schools, despite heated debate. Haut Conseil à l'intégration, *L'islam et la République* (Paris: La Documentation Française, 2000), pp. 6–8.

intégration in France remind us that, despite numerous emerging post-colonial narratives, the nation has remained the over-arching reference point in contemporary French politics. Through such terms as *la fracture sociale* and *intégration*, French politics has continued to absorb – some might say, deflect – post-colonial questions with remarkable success. In the same way as Noiriel in *Le creuset français*, the HCI's reports tried to absorb the 'problem' of immigration into a wider narrative of social integration. This made it possible to underplay its specifically post-colonial dimensions and emphasise the renewed importance of the nation in the process of integration.

From *intégration* to *communautarisme*: the language of integration and the French elite

While there are good reasons for focusing on the HCI's reports as the most thoroughgoing attempts to define *intégration* there is ample evidence to suggest that the HCI was not so much imposing its vision from above as piecing together fragments of existing languages circulating in the political space. Indeed, in another of its reports, the HCI itself uncovered the powerful hold of a 'republican rhetoric' in the public and private sectors, which made managers and civil servants extremely reluctant to talk about the problems of racial or ethnic discrimination. They almost all used a republican discourse of colour-blind integration to minimise the role of job discrimination and explain away the need for various forms of positive discrimination.[48] This same 'colour-blind' logic has been used to justify the refusal to collect statistics on ethnic grounds, an issue which has regularly provoked sustained confrontation between those who see ethnic statistics as necessary, and those who see them as a potentially dangerous acknowledgement of community identities.[49] Not surprisingly, opponents of ethnic statistics have usually been those associated with other aspects of the neo-republican turn. So, for instance, demographer Hervé Le Bras – whose book *Le démon des origines* (1998) pushed the issue into the limelight in the late 1990s – recently published another book with Elisabeth Badinter denouncing the 'return of race' in statistical collection.[50] The HCI, too, was extremely reluctant to

---

[48] On this, see Haut Conseil à l'intégration, *Les parcours de l'intégration*.

[49] See for instance Centre d'analyse stratégique, *Colloque sur les statistiques éthniques* (Paris: Centre d'analyse stratégique, 2006), and Henri Héduin, 'Faut-il inventer des categories "ethniques"?', in *Différences* (June/July 2002), pp. 36–7.

[50] Hervé Le Bras, *Le démon des origines: la démographie et l'extrême droite* (Paris: Editions de l'Aube, 1998). On the initial controversy in 1998, see 'Une virulente polémique sur les données éthniques divise les démographes', *Le Monde* (6 November 1998). For more

endorse the use of ethnic statistics, in 2007 describing such a task as 'anachronistic and of little use in learning about integration'.[51] Even the Conseil constitutionnel cast serious doubt on their use when, in the same year, it ruled that any data collection based on ethnic or racial criteria would run counter to Article 1 of the Constitution.[52] This opposition has hampered attempts on the part of French researchers to construct a picture of French ethnic diversity.[53] On this issue, as with others, the language of neo-republicanism has proved too great a barrier to overcome.

Even among France's (rather limited) 'ethnic' elite, the language of republican integration has often taken pride of place. Two good examples are Jacky Dahomay, a Guadeloupean philosophy teacher and member of the HCI in 2006–8, and Malika Sorel, a writer of Algerian descent who was nominated to the HCI in 2009. Although Dahomay resigned from the HCI in protest at the creation of a Ministry of National Identity, both have vigorously defended *intégration* and 'republican identity' in the press, on the internet and in the media in recent years.[54] They are not alone: other prominent non-white public figures have stressed republican integration as the primary means for immigrants to surmount their social and political disenfranchisement. For instance, Socialist politician Bariza Khairi, since 2004 a member of the Sénat, one of only two Muslim members, has attacked the idea of ethnic statistics on neo-republican grounds.[55] In the same vein, Kofi Yamgnane, who was elected in 1989 as the first black mayor of a predominantly white French

recent interventions see Hervé Le Bras, 'Inutiles statistiques éthniques', *Le Monde* (14 July 2009), and Hervé Le Bras and Elisabeth Badinter, *Retour de la race* (Paris: La Découverte, 2008).

[51] Haut Conseil à l'intégration, *Les Indicateurs de l'intégration: statistiques ethniques, enquêtes sur les patronymes, mesure de la diversité, baromètre de l'intégration* (Paris: La Documentation Française, 2007), p. 18.

[52] Décision n° 2007–557 DC du 15 novembre 2007, available at www.conseil-constitutionnel.fr/conseil-constitutionnel/francais/les-decisions/acces-par-date/decisions-depuis-1959/2007/2007–557-dc/decision-n-2007–557-dc-du-15-novembre-2007.1183. html (last accessed March 2010].

[53] For critical voices, see for instance Michèle Tribalat, 'La connaissance des faits: est-elle dangereuse?', *Le Monde* (5 November 1998).

[54] For Dahomay, see Jacky Dahomay, 'Pour une nouvelle identité républicaine: point de vue', *Le Monde* (15 April 2005), and J. Dahomay, 'Le cynisme des chiens', *Libération* (17 December 2008). For Sorel – whose tone is altogether more shrill, see her blog www. malikasorel.fr and her presentation before the Veil Commission on the subject of diversity and integration. Comité de reflexion sur le préambule de la Constitution, *Redécouvrir le préambule à la Constitution: rapport de la commission présidé par Simone Veil* (Paris: La Documentation Française, 2008), pp. 164–73.

[55] See, for instance, her position in Bariza Khiary and Patrick Lozès, 'Pour ou contre les statistiques éthniques', *Nouvel Observateur* (19 October 2006).

town (Saint Coulitz) and a Socialist secretary of state in 1991–3, founded
a Fondation pour l'intégration républicaine in 1993. He used the Foundation to promote his strongly neo-republican reading of *intégration*.[56]
As he put it in 1995, 'integration can only take place through the values
of the Republic … The integration that we are proposing is positive
and mobilising since it is the binding element of social cohesion'.[57] At
the other end of the political spectrum, too, there has been a strong neo-
republican current among non-white political figures such as the deputy
Rachid Kaci, who is of Kabyle origin. In 2002, he founded La Droite
Libre, which described itself as 'liberal and republican' and developed
a strong discourse of republican integration mixed with Gaullist nationalism and a hostility to economic interventionism.[58]

Another excellent example of a trajectory strongly marked by the neo-
republican turn is that of Malek Boutih. His career in the anti-racism
organisation SOS Racisme – as vice-president (1985–92) and then president (2001–3) will be examined in more detail later. What is relevant
here is that, after his involvement with SOS Racisme, he has been
a prominent member of the PS and has been instrumental in the formulation of the party's immigration policy.[59] Rather like the party with
which he has been so closely involved, his attitude to the question of
immigration and integration has taken on increasingly neo-republican
overtones, to the point that in his essay *La France aux français? Chiche!*
(2001), he denounced the inexorable logic of *communautarisme* and
defended a strong version of republican *intégration*.[60] This is all the more
striking given that SOS Racisme, as we shall see, emerged at a time in the
early 1980s when the centralising Jacobinism so dear to neo-republicans
was under attack from the emerging anti-racism and *beur* movements.

---

[56] The Fondation was set up, in his words, to 'soutenir les projets de jeunes issus de
l'immigration … Les premiers projets de la fondation consistent à parrainer des jeunes
dans des entreprises, à ouvrir des appartements partagés et des 'cafés-rencontre' … à
organiser plusieurs manifestations artistiques … destinées à valoriser l'apport culturel
des jeunes issus de l'immigration'. 'Kofi Yamgnane crée une Fondation pour
l'intégration républicaine', *Le Monde* (28 May 1993).

[57] Kofi Yamgnane, 'Intégration. Adapter le modèle républicain', *Le Monde* (23 September
1992), and Kofi Yamgnane, 'Exclure l'exclusion', *Le Monde* (14 August 1995).

[58] Kaci was a member of a minority rights NGO, France-Plus, and a fervent defender of the
anti-*foulard* position during the *affaire*. He has been involved in the Gaullist right since
the early 1990s. See, in particular, his blog (http://rachidkaci.over-blog.com/) and R.
Kaci, *La République des lâches* (Paris: Editions des Syrtes, 2003).

[59] For a useful profile of Malek Boutih, see Claude Patrice, 'Malek Boutih, Le
Désillusioniste', *Le Monde* (13 June 2002).

[60] Malek Boutih and Elisabeth Lévy, *La France au français? Chiche!* (Paris: Fondation 2
Mars/Mille et une nuits, 2001). Nicolas Weill, 'Entre Malek Boutih et la philosophe
Chantal Delsol, un accord presque parfait sur l'intégration', *Le Monde* (15 November
2002).

Boutih's subsequent conversion demonstrates the irresistible attraction of neo-republicanism, even to its erstwhile detractors.

Of course, we should not be especially surprised to find that political figures who have emerged from France's immigrant communities have been attached to a notion of republican *intégration*, since it is this very model that, in their view, made it possible for them to participate in French political life. Moreover, evidence suggests that France's minority communities have traditionally been extremely favourable to the political contract implied by *intégration*. In a recent survey, the Pew Global Research Centre found that French Muslims were much more likely than their counterparts in other European countries to value their 'French' identity and demonstrate a willingness to 'adopt French customs'.[61] The merits of such a broad longitudinal study notwithstanding, it served to emphasise the fact that both France's ethnic minorities, and its 'ethnic' elite, have often taken their own *intégration* seriously. The historians Jim House and Neil Macmaster are surely right when they argue that 'some racialised colonial and post-colonial groups within the French polity [have] questioned elements of Republicanism … based upon their lived experiences of [a] political model, which has treated them with profound ambivalence'.[62] By the same token, successful members of these same groups have regularly aspired to precisely the model of integration that historically treated them with indifference and even hostility.

But the spread of a neo-republican conception of *intégration* in the past three decades has not been confined to France's ethnic elite alone. Nor has it been the sole preserve of those involved in party politics in some way. The resurgence of interest in *intégration* also had intellectual roots. This has been most clearly visible in the work of Dominique Schnapper. The daughter of the most important non-Marxist intellectual in post-war France, Raymond Aron, Schnapper made her name through a series of books on citizenship, the Other and the sociology of the nation.[63] Having pursued a highly successful academic career, with a doctorate in sociology and a position at the EHESS since 1980, she embodies the intellectual involved at the highest levels of decision-making. She has sat on a number of government commissions (including the 1987 Commission de la Nationalité), and was a member of the Conseil constitutionnel

---

[61] Pew Global Attitudes Project, *Muslims in Europe* (7 June 2006), available at http://pewglobal.org/reports/display.php?ReportID=254 (last accessed March 2010].

[62] House and Macmaster, *Paris 1961*, p. 332.

[63] On this, see especially Dominique Schnapper, *La communauté des citoyens: sur l'idée moderne de nation* (Paris: Seuil, 1994), and Dominique Schnapper, *La relation à l'autre: au cœur de la pensée sociologique* (Paris: Seuil, 1998).

in 2001–10. This commitment to public service extends to her work. A number of her books have essentially been textbooks designed for a wide market and, in much of her more recent work, there has been a consistent interest in political (or, what we might call in English, 'civic') integration.[64]

From the 1980s onwards – and especially after 1987 – she became increasingly outspoken in her defence of a neo-republican conception of citizenship (which she calls a 'tolerant republicanism') as the best response to the crisis of integration.[65] As Schnapper put it herself in 2005,

[C]itizenship is the foundation of political legitimacy; it is also the source of the *lien social*. To live together is not to participate in the same church or to be subjects of the same monarch, it is to be citizens together.[66]

In this definition, republican citizenship forms the basis of the political community – a community in danger of fragmenting under pressure from the unravelling of social bonds. Citizenship is the theoretical foundation of a (French) model of *intégration*, which in turn means that the political process of nation-building is the most effective response to the (dis)integration of the national community. As she puts it, the integration *of* a society is as important as integration *to* that society – in other words, the integration into society of any external element (such as foreigners) can only take place when each constituent part of that society is integrated into a whole. In short, the integration of different classes, sexes, ages or regions is as significant as the integration of 'ethnic' and 'foreign' communities. Like others, Schnapper believes that the integration of society relies on political foundations: citizenship rests on a political consciousness of the citizen, and the understanding of political rights and responsibilities.

It is true that Schnapper has remained more sensitive than many other defenders of *intégration* to the changing meaning of concepts. Her empirical approach has offered a critical view of the development of neo-republicanism and she has even softened her position on the

---

[64] This is true of her most recent summary of the sociology of the nation. Dominique Schnapper, *Qu'est-ce que l'intégration?* (Paris: Folio, 2005).

[65] Schnapper herself claims that her participation in the Commission de la Nationalité was a turning point (personal interview with the author, June 2011). This is confirmed by her earliest statements on this subject that date from this period, such as Dominique Schnapper, 'Unité nationale et particularismes culturels', *Commentaire* (Vol. 10, No. 38, 1987), pp. 361–7. See also Schnapper, *La communauté des citoyens*, and Dominique Schnapper, 'La République face aux communautarismes', *Études* (Vol. 2, 2004), pp. 177–88.

[66] Schnapper, *Qu'est-ce que l'intégration?*, p. 132.

question of ethnic statistics.[67] Nevertheless, these critical reflections have not significantly modified her view, which has conformed to some of the central assumptions of neo-republicanism and found a wide audience among other intellectuals. For instance, although radically different in approach and focus, the philosopher and sociologist Pierre-André Taguieff has looked to Schnapper to support his staunch defences of the Republic. A product of the 'new' university in Nanterre, and a child of the *gauchiste* atmosphere of 1968, Taguieff has also followed the path of a career academic.[68] He now teaches at Sciences Po Paris, and is a member of the influential Centre de recherches politiques de Sciences Po (CEVIPOF). He has also, since 2002, been a member of the Cercle de l'Oratoire – a think tank created to support the war in Iraq and combat French anti-Americanism.[69] Taguieff's earlier works dealt with French anti-Semitism, and the development of the anti-racism movement, but it was in the mid 1990s that he began to write on the future of the Republic.[70] His work has become increasingly outspoken and polemical, not least in his recent 600-page attack on Lindenberg's essay on the *nouveaux réactionnaires* entitled *Les contre-réactionnaires* (2008), but he has remained a staunch neo-republican.[71]

However, where Schnapper has focused on the necessity of civic integration, Taguieff has brought to the fore the fear of fragmentation. For Taguieff, the most important reason to defend France's unitary and unified concept of the Republic is that it is increasingly under threat from the atomising tendency of multiculturalism.[72] This, as well as the ideologies of cultural relativism and cosmopolitanism, has led to a dangerous disintegration of the nation. He claims that France must protect a republican conception of the nation in order to restore the 'civic bond'

---

[67] While still remaining very resistant to their use, she now reluctantly accepts their value as an expression of a certain 'democratic aspiration'. See Dominique Schnapper, 'Les enjeux démocratiques de la statistique ethnique', *Revue française de sociologie* (Vol. 49, No. 1, 2008), pp. 133–9.

[68] Christopher Flood, 'National Republican Politics, Intellectuals and the Case of Pierre-André Taguieff', *Modern and Contemporary France* (Vol. 12, No. 2, 2004), pp. 353–70.

[69] A list of members of the Cercle de l'Oratoire can be found at www.lemeilleurdesmondes. org. The Cercle also produces a journal, *Le meilleur des mondes*.

[70] See especially Pierre-André Taguieff, *La force du préjugé: essai sur le racisme et ses doubles* (Paris: Gallimard, 1987); Pierre-André Taguieff, *Les fins de l'antiracisme* (Paris: Editions Michalon, 1995); and Pierre-André Taguieff, *Sur la Nouvelle Droite: jalons d'une analyse critique* (Paris: Descartes, 1994).

[71] Pierre-André Taguieff, *Les contre-réactionnaires: le progressisme entre illusion et imposture* (Paris: Denoel, 2007). And see, for instance, Pierre-André Taguieff, *La République enlisée: pluralisme, communautarisme et citoyenneté* (Paris: Syrtes 2005), and Pierre-André Taguieff, *La République menacée: entretien avec Philippe Petit* (Paris: Textuel, 1996).

[72] Taguieff, *La République enlisée*, pp. 23–4.

and defend against 'tribalisation'.[73] One example of this 'tribalisation' is the threat of Islam: the issue of 'the Islamo-terrorist threat' looms in the background, and there is a clear sense that a breakdown in social relations will make space for militant Islam.[74] Hence the Republic is invoked as both a protection against outside threats and a way of combating internal fragmentation.

Alongside Taguieff's rather apocalyptic vision of fragmentation, his work on the Republic also highlights neo-republicanism's eclectic intellectual roots. We saw earlier how Debray and Finkielkraut travelled from the 'radical' left to neo-republicanism. In a similar way, Taguieff's work shows a strong – if not always clearly argued – link between consumer society, the atomisation of social relations under capitalism, and the unravelling of the nation. Here, Taguieff betrays his intellectual roots in a post-1968 situationist critique of consumerism.[75] This critique pushes him to defend the centrality of the nation as a counterweight to consumer society.[76] It is logical, therefore, that Taguieff's work has been placed among those of other *nouveaux réactionnaires*, whose journey from left to right has been well documented. But this is to simplify the issue. Not only does Taguieff deny that he has taken a partisan political position – he has been described, rather confusingly, as a 'libéral social conservateur' – but he also represents something more complex.[77] He is an intellectual who has used a defence of the Republic to bring together a traditional anti-capitalist language of the left with many of the traditional concerns of the right (a critique of 'progressivism', the fear of immigration, the 'Islamic threat', etc.)

Taguieff's work also draws attention to another argument that has further strengthened the neo-republican consensus around the notion of integration: the threat of *communautarisme*. We shall see in the following chapter the extent to which this unusually loaded term has involved a repackaging of long-standing stereotypes of the Anglo-American world, but it is worth clarifying here that the French *communautarisme* carries much stronger connotations than its English translation 'communitarianism'. It is seen to be the culmination of the logic of multiculturalism: a fearful descent into isolated and discrete communities that would run

---

[73] 'La première des ces conditions est le sentiment de coappartenance à une communauté métacommunautaire, dotée d'une identité méta-identitaire: la nation, où s'inscrit et s'épanouit, dans la modernité, ce qu'il est convenu d'appeler le principe civique'. Taguieff, *La République enlisée*, p. 115. References to 'tribalisation' can be found on pp. 64 and 169.
[74] Ibid., p. 342.   [75] See especially ibid., p. 282.
[76] On this, see the excellent analysis in Audier, *La pensée anti-68*, pp. 331–49.
[77] George Weyer, 'Taguieff', *Le Figaro* (11 December 2004)

counter to even the most flexible definition of *intégration*. This is the definition of *communautarisme* we find in the work of Taguieff, and it is one that has been widely popularised in the political space more generally. So, for example, in 1989, Finkielkraut deplored the fact that 'the nation is disappearing in favour of tribes ... [and] the cultural unity will make way for a juxtaposition of ghettos'.[78] In a similar vein, in 1999 Danièle Sallenave borrowed the expression 'community of citizens' from Schnapper's work to argue that it was important to oppose the Charter for Regional Languages because this also meant

[o]pposing the division of the national community, which is a 'community of citizens' and not a conglomeration of ethnic, linguistic and religious groups ... [the Charter] would bring French law in line with *communautarisme* and differentialism [*différentialisme*].[79]

This kind of critique also found an echo in the media. Journalists and commentators such as Christian Jelen (who died in 1998) and Joseph Macé-Scaron – the former an editor at *Le Point*, the latter a regular contributor to *Le Figaro* – denounced what they describe as *la tentation communautaire*.[80] Jelen, in particular, took up Finkielkraut's reasoning by indiscriminately indicting polygamy, homosexuality, 'the Islamic chador' and the danger of multiculturalism at the hands of 'dangerous' academics such as Farhad Khosrokhavar or Michel Wieviorka.[81] They were all, according to him, responsible for a growing communitarian logic in contemporary France.[82]

In politics, too, a fear of *communautarisme* has become a common rhetorical tool, from Jean-Pierre Chevènement's left-wing republicanism to Philippe de Villiers's defence of a rural France against the inexorable onward march of Islamic fundamentalism. From 2003 until 2011, there was even a semi-political pressure group entitled Observatoire du communautarisme, dedicated to protecting France from its pernicious effects. Its founder, Julien Landfried, has published a number of articles on the subject, including an essay entitled *Contre le communautarisme*

---

[78] Alain Finkielkraut, 'La nation disparait au profits des tribus', *Le Monde* (13 July 1989).

[79] The expression 'communauté de citoyens' is borrowed from the title of Schnapper's early work on the sociology of the nation. Danièle Sallenave, 'Partez, briseurs d'unité', *Le Monde* (3 July 1999).

[80] Joseph Macé-Scaron, *La tentation communautaire* (Paris: Plon, 2001). See also a 2003 television debate on the subject involving Macé-Scaron, alongside Yves Calvi, Manuel Valls, Michel Wieviorka and Catherine Wihtol de Wenden. *C dans l'air*, France 5/La Cinquième, (28 March 2003).

[81] France Culture, *Répliques: La République est-elle une idée de neuve?* (2 November 1996).

[82] Christian Jelen, *Les casseurs de la Republic* (Paris: Plon, 1997), one of several books on this topic.

(2007), and the Observatoire's website brought together articles by almost every neo-republican public figure.[83] At its height, the website claimed to receive up to 40,000 visitors each month, which, even allowing for exaggeration, suggests that there was a sustained interest in the topic for at least a decade.[84] The proliferation of essays, articles, pamphlets and editorials dealing with the subject suggests that, like *fracture sociale* and *intégration*, the term has been a powerful response to a number of existing concerns. Today, the fear of communitarian fragmentation has become a widely recognised political argument throughout the French political space and, while it might be easy to dismiss its more radical manifestations as hyperbole, it has proven a powerful means by which the key tenets of neo-republicanism have been vulgarised.

Intégration à la française: a political paradigm

It might seem strange that an entire chapter devoted to France's post-colonial predicament has dealt relatively little with the lives of France's migrant and minority communities. It is customary, at the very least, to highlight migrant or minority counter-narratives, and show how these have undermined or delegitimised existing narratives such as neo-republicanism. Very often, it is expected that a post-colonial approach will cast a strongly critical eye on precisely the kind of 'hegemonic' ideology embodied in the neo-republican notion of *intégration*. But a critical approach – however valuable it may be – only tells part of the story. We also need a much finer appreciation of the ways in which national narratives have absorbed and adapted to the reality of a post-colonial nation. In later chapters, I shall try and show how various counter-narratives have in fact been written in contemporary France, but here I have chosen to emphasise the longevity, and indeed resurgence, of *intégration* as a rehabilitation of the French national narrative. Against the backdrop of growing numbers of settled immigrants and the significant presence of an extreme-right party, the late twentieth century saw a reinterpretation of *intégration* as a neo-republican nation-building project. The importance of political participation was re-emphasised, accompanied by a renewed notion of 'strong' citizenship based on the values of the Republic. From a neo-republican perspective, there was no need to modify France's model of integration: the processes of

---

[83] Julien Landfried, *Contre le communautarisme* (Paris: Armand Colin, 2007).

[84] The Observatoire du communautarisme's website – www.communautarisme.net – has since been taken down. It is not clear whether this is because the organisation has folded or because it is going to be redesigned.

integration that had united rural populations, the working classes and early immigrants in the nineteenth century could once again be used to absorb incoming immigrants at the end of the twentieth.

Contemporary definitions of *intégration* have thus provided both an account of France's past and a blueprint for its future. The problem is that the reality of identity politics, socio-economic exclusion and the battle over the memory of the French empire have all posed a formidable challenge to neo-republican definitions of *intégration*. Despite Noiriel's assurances that first-, second- and third-generation immigrants are underprivileged groups like any other, the economic integration of agrarian populations within the nation state in nineteenth- and twentieth-century Europe is not the same as the social integration of ethnic minorities today. Some of the processes may be similar but there are important differences, notably in perception on the part of the receiving nation. In seeking to minimise the challenges of 'ethnic' integration in favour of a language of 'social' and 'civic' integration – by refusing even to give ethnic minorities a name – those who have defended a strongly neo-republican model of *intégration* have caught themselves in the discourse they are trying to take apart. A relative silence about the colonial encounter until the late 1990s, the systematic and historical marginalisation of foreigners, the fear of Islam and a repressive Europe-wide migration policy have hampered France's ability to find a solution to its own ideological impasse. For the foreseeable future, foreigners will continue to arrive in France. The majority will continue to integrate with some success. Most will continue to carry around with them their multiple identities.[85] The question, then, is the extent to which these identities will be recognised by the Republic and exactly how they will be incorporated into a neo-republican national narrative that continues to emphasise unity over difference.[86]

[85] Riva Kastoryano, *Negotiating Identities: States and Immigrants in France and Germany* (Oxford: Princeton University Press, 2002).
[86] Sophie Guérard de Latour, 'Cultural Insecurity and Political Solidarity: French Republicanism Reconsidered', in Chabal, *France since the 1970s*.

5 The Republic, the Anglo-Saxon and the European project

La supériorité des Anglo-Saxons! Si on ne la proclame pas, on la subit et on la redoute ...   Edmond Demolins, *À quoi tient la supériorité des Anglo-Saxons* (1898)[1]

[Le] 'modèle' anglo-saxon, porté aux nues par les institutions économiques et financières internationales et par leurs innombrables relais médiatiques, est partout à l'offensive.   Richard Farnetti, in *Le Monde Diplomatique* (1997)[2]

It has become commonplace to argue that nationalisms require an 'other' against which to build their identity. Nations and 'imagined communities' forge their collective identities in opposition to or at war with another community. 'We' get invested with particular – and usually superior – characteristics; 'they' become demonised or distorted in an effort to magnify 'our' superiority. In the majority of cases, this form of negative nationalism – 'we' are what 'they' are not – is the keystone around which national identity is constructed.[3] In modern times, France has often been seen as one of the oldest and most consistent examples of a nation. Since the eighteenth century, its relatively stable territorial boundaries, its apparently increasingly homogenous culture and its strongly centralised political authority have given it an imagined unity of which (sometimes fledgling) neighbouring European nations could only dream. That this discourse of unity should have obscured some of the very real challenges of uniting France is of secondary significance

---

[1] Edmond Demolins, *À quoi tient la superiorité des Anglo-Saxons* (Paris: Firmin-Didot, 1898), p. i.

[2] Richard Farnetti, 'Dossier: Grande Bretagne. Excellents indices économiques pour un pays en voie de dislocation', *Le Monde Diplomatique* (February 1997).

[3] For four varied discussions of nationalism, its origins and its dynamics, see Ernest Gellner, *Nations and Nationalism* (Oxford: Blackwell, 1996), Eric Hobsbawm, *Nations and Nationalism since 1780* (Cambridge University Press, 1990), Benedict Anderson, *Imagined Communities* (London: Verso, 1991), and Keith Minogue, *Nationalism* (London: Batsford, 1967).

here.[4] Instead, what is striking is that almost every form of modern French nationalism – whether of the Catholic right, the communist left or the republican centre – has viewed the anglophone world as one of its most potent and consistent enemies.

It is for this reason that any discussion of the writing of France's national narrative in the past three decades must take into account the role and function of the Anglo-American world in French political discourse. Behind almost all of the debates analysed in previous chapters has lurked an Anglo-American 'counter-model' and, as has often been the case in the past, it has acted as both a foil and a mirror for French perceptions of themselves. In crucial disagreements that have defined contemporary discussions of the national narrative – such as those surrounding integration, multiculturalism, the future of Europe, and the global role of French culture and language – the Anglo-American world has been consistently invoked on all sides. This does not mean that perceptions of Britain and the United States have always been one and the same thing, but the resurgence of the term 'Anglo-Saxon' has ensured that the two countries have been frequently and easily conflated. In the same way that the steady return of colonial memory has acted as a powerful counter-narrative, the Anglo-Saxon has offered another alternative narrative that has come to trouble the unifying discourse of neo-republicanism. The ways in which it has been absorbed, manipulated and rejected help us to understand the tensions at the heart of France's contemporary national narrative.

The anti-France? Economics and the *modèle anglo-saxon*

Today, the term 'Anglo-Saxon' has passed into common usage in France.[5] There are Anglo-Saxon economic models, Anglo-Saxon educational philosophies, and a widely recognised Anglo-Saxon 'mentality'. Despite the fact that few Britons or Americans would be inclined to celebrate their Anglo-Saxon identity, the French use the term to cover a wide range of stereotypes, preconceptions and judgements about the Anglo-American world. It is used by politicians, serious academics and political commentators, and in everyday conversation on the street. The fact that its meaning has remained relatively stable since the 1870s

---

[4] The classic text on this is Eugen Weber, *Peasants into Frenchmen: the modernization of rural France, 1870–1914* (Stanford Unviersity Press, 1977).
[5] For a more extensive discussion of the historical roots of the term 'Anglo-Saxon', see Emile Chabal, 'The Rise of the Anglo-Saxon: French Perceptions of the Anglo-American World in the Long Twentieth Century', *French, Politics, Culture and Society* (Vol. 30, No. 3, 2012), pp. 24–46.

has no doubt helped it to become one of the most widely used terms to describe both Anglo-American society and the ideal type of the Anglo-American individual.

Almost as surprising as the widespread use of the term is the paucity of work on the subject. There have been significant attempts to document the long history of Franco-British and Franco-American relations, but there have not been more than a few published and unpublished articles specifically on the notion of the Anglo-Saxon.[6] This relative absence of scholarly interest has made the task of interpretation that much more urgent.[7] That the French continue to use the term uncritically is an indication that the Anglo-Saxon represents more than a passing fad. On the contrary, the term contains a renewable repertoire of symbols and ideas, all of which can be mobilised for specific political causes. So, in the late nineteenth century, when a fear of 'Anglo-Saxon superiority' became an important popular trope, the Anglo-Saxon offered a counterpoint to French nation-building under the Third Republic. Today, *le modèle anglo-saxon* is not simply a socio-economic vision loosely inspired by market liberalism and multiculturalism; it is also (and sometimes primarily) an image of individualism, enterprise and atomisation.

We cannot say exactly when the term 'Anglo-Saxon' began in France to describe something more than an early medieval language and people. Our best guess is that it gained a new meaning in the 1850s and 60s.[8] Its inclusion in the revised 1877 edition of Emile Littré's *Dictionnaire de*

---

[6] The most significant attempt to document Franco-British relations is Robert Tombs and Isabelle Tombs, *That Sweet Enemy: the French and the British from the Sun King to the present* (London: Heinemann, 2006). On perceptions of America and anti-Americanism more specifically, see Roger, *L'ennemi américain*; Denis Lacorne (ed.), *The rise and fall of anti-Americanism: a century of French perception* (Basingstoke: Macmillan, 1990); Jean-Philippe Mathy, *Extrême Occident: French Intellectuals and America* (London: University of Chicago Press, 1993); David Strauss, *Menace in the West: the rise of French anti-Americanism in modern times* (London: Greenwood Press, 1978); Richard Kuisel, *Seducing the French: The Dilemma of Americanization* (Berkeley: University of California Press, 1993); and Jean-François Revel, *L'obsession anti-américaine: son fonctionnement, ses causes, ses inconséquences* (Paris: Plon, 2002).

[7] On the notion of the Anglo-Saxon more specifically, Alan Pitt's article is very informative but only covers the period up to 1914: A. Pitt, 'A Changing Anglo-Saxon Myth: Its Development and Function in French Political Thought, 1860–1914', *French History* (Vol. 14, No. 2, 2000), pp. 150–73. Jeremy Jennings's article focuses primarily on the economic aspects of the Anglo-Saxon model: Jeremy Jennings, 'France and the Anglo-Saxon Model: Contemporary and Historical Perspectives', *European Review* (Vol. 14, No. 4, 2006), pp. 537–54. Colin Jones has also done research on the term Anglo-Saxons – I thank him for sending me an unpublished paper of his entitled 'Les Anglo-Saxons in French Culture', first presented at Cambridge University in 2005.

[8] Maike Thier, 'The View from Paris: "Latinity", "Anglo-Saxonism", and the Americas, as Discussed in the *Revue des Races Latines*, 1857–1864', *International History Review* (Vol. 3, No. 2, 2011), pp. 1–31.

la langue française was a good indication that the term had achieved some kind of public respectability. In addition to its historical definitions as they related to medieval Anglo-Saxon history and language, Littré's *Dictionnaire* indicated that 'when speaking of the race to which the English and the Americans of the United States belong, it is often said that they are Anglo-Saxons'.[9] This definition crystallised over the next few decades, above all in the late 1890s with a vigorous public debate surrounding the relative merits of Anglo-Saxons and Latins. It was at this point that older conceptions of the Anglo-American world were mixed with a new racialised language of politics and brought together under the term 'Anglo-Saxon'. The most emblematic text in the 'Anglo-Saxon' debate was undoubtedly the polemical pamphlet *À quoi tient la supériorité des Anglo-Saxons?* (1898). It was written by Edmond Demolins – a noted commentator on French history and politics, and a disciple of sociologist Frédéric Le Play. Using a mix of rather alarming statistics, perfunctory observation and ethno-racial typologies, Demolins argued that the Anglo-Saxon race was particularly well suited to world dominance – a point made abundantly clear by the fact that most editions carried a map on the first page designed to show the Anglo-Saxon's sphere of influence. Even though the ethno-racial premise on which Demolins's argument was based – namely that the Anglo-Saxon 'race' was dominant both in the British Isles and the United States – was questionable at best, the elision between the two countries was highly significant, for it cemented a relationship in the French mind that has been largely impervious to the very obvious differences between the two countries over the course of the twentieth century.[10]

This sense of a combined Anglo-American threat remained at the heart of the notion of the Anglo-Saxon through the first half of the twentieth century. It was a term that appeared frequently in the press, and in works by authors as different as Charles Maurras, Paul Vidal de la Blache and André Siegfried. Because of the close relationship between the British and the Americans during the Second World War and the Cold War, it continued to be used regularly in the 1950s and 60s, especially in the writings and speeches of de Gaulle, who used the term when he was both in and out of power. Indeed, the historian Colin Jones

---

[9] Emile Littré, *Dictionnaire de la langue française, Tome I* (Paris: Hachette, 1877).

[10] On this, and nineteenth century French liberalism's perceptions of Britain, see e.g. Larry Siedentop, 'Two Liberal Traditions', in Alan Ryan (ed.), *The Idea of Freedom: Essays in Honour of Isaiah Berlin* (Oxford University Press, 1979); Lucien Jaume, *L'individu effacé, ou le paradoxe du libéralisme français* (Paris: Fayard, 1997); and Jeremy Jennings, 'Conceptions of England and its Constitution in Nineteenth Century Political Thought', *Historical Journal* (Vol. 29, No. 1, 1986), pp. 65–85.

has argued that it was de Gaulle who 'more than any other single individual . . . Anglo-Saxonised Britain in French eyes'.[11] Even if Britain and the United States retained distinct identities, the second half of the twentieth century confirmed their umbilical relationship in French eyes. Perceptions of Britain slid into and came to reinforce those of the United States. The differences in perception of the two countries remained more a matter of scale than substance. Britain was often portrayed as the United States' 'Trojan Horse' in Europe, while the United States appeared simply to be a more extreme version of Britain.[12] After 1970, the term 'Anglo-Saxon' found its way into a bewildering range of contexts. As its ethno-racial connotations were buried, it became increasingly used as an adjective that could be attached to fields as varied as cultural policy and economic theory. Over time, its usage began to revolve around a phrase that has now become extremely common: *le modèle anglo-saxon*. Its simplistic and reductive implications notwithstanding, the prevalence of the expression *le modèle anglo-saxon* has made it impossible to ignore. It has provided a counterweight to an (equally mythical) *modèle français*, and has offered an almost endless repertoire of tropes, metaphors, images and words that have simultaneously reinforced and undermined French perceptions of themselves. Inevitably, because of its very broad scope, *le modèle anglo-saxon* is not an easy phrase to define. But my intention here is to give a sense of both its economic connotations and its social connotations.

That the adjective 'Anglo-Saxon' has become more widely used in France in the past three decades is beyond doubt. A careful examination of text-searchable online databases for a diverse range of daily and monthly publications – including *Esprit, Le Figaro, Libération, Le Monde, Le Monde Diplomatique* and *Nouvel Observateur* – all show a steep rise in the use of the term 'Anglo-Saxon' from the early 1980s onwards.[13] On the basis of these figures, it is fair to conclude that the term is used several times a day in the French press – in articles, editorials, interviews and comment pieces. However, looking more closely at the deluge of results reveals that the term 'Anglo-Saxon', and especially the phrase *modèle anglo-saxon*, has carried with it strong economic connotations. These have usually revolved

---

[11] Jones, 'Les Anglo-Saxons in French Culture'.
[12] On this, see for instance, George Wilkes (ed.), *Britain's Failure To enter the European community, 1961–63* (London: Frank Cass, 1997).
[13] I examined a variety of databases, including the complete digitised archives of *Le Monde Diplomatique, Esprit* and *Commentaire*; the online archives of *Le Monde* and *Nouvel Observateur*; and the LexisNexis Academic database, which has a complete archive of *Le Monde* since 1990, and a number of other French publications from the mid-1990s onwards.

around an implicit or explicit association between Anglo-Saxon and '(neo-)liberalism', 'free market', 'monetarism', or 'free trade'.

This has been particularly true on the left of the political spectrum. A search in the archives of the left-leaning *Le Monde Diplomatique* from 1978 turns up references to the 'monetarist myopia that reigns in the Anglo-Saxon world' (in 1981), the 'global hegemony of Anglo-Saxon capitalism' (in 1982) and the 'Anglo-Saxon capitalist model – the privileged choice of multinationals' (in 1992).[14] These are complemented by frequent references to 'Anglo-Saxon liberalism', which was usually seen to be a dangerous affront to a French 'social model': as a journalist put it in a flattering review of a book on the subject in 1993, 'France is in danger of sliding towards a social model inspired by Anglo-Saxon ultra-liberalism'.[15] As the 1990s wore on, this language became increasingly shrill: contributors warned of the hegemony of an 'Anglo-Saxon neo-liberalism' or a predatory 'Anglo-Saxon capitalism', particularly in the wake of the public-sector strikes of 1995. It is at this point that we began to hear more and more about a *modèle anglo-saxon*. Articles warned of the 'generalised flexibilisation of the labour market according to the Anglo-Saxon model' (in 1996) and the decision of the French government to fall in line with 'the Anglo-Saxon model ... the deleterious consequences of which are by now plain to see' (in 1997).[16] In a neat summary, the well-known journalist (and current editor of *Le Monde Diplomatique*) Serge Halimi argued in 1998 that

Armed with a feeble intellectual programme and a toolbox that contained only four blunt instruments (deregulation, privatisation, tax reductions, free trade), international economic organisations launched themselves [into the task] of transforming the world in the image of the 'Anglo-Saxon model'.[17]

Here, in a nutshell, are the economic aspects of the *modèle anglo-saxon* – driven by four blunt instruments, but nonetheless threatening and all-powerful.

There are many references to a *modèle anglo-saxon* outside the pages of a left-wing publication like *Le Monde Diplomatique* as well. Since the 1990s, there have been scholarly books and articles with titles such as

---

[14] Georges Corm, 'La prépondérance absolue du dollar', *Le Monde Diplomatique* (August 1981); Guy Martinière, 'La "latinité" de l'Amérique', *Le Monde Diplomatique* (July 1982); Raymond Van Ermen, 'Intérêts capitalistes et responsabilité planétaire', *Le Monde Diplomatique* (May 1992).

[15] 'Social, par ici la sortie', *Le Monde Diplomatique* (April 1993).

[16] Hubert Bouchet, 'L'Arlésienne du social', *Le Monde Diplomatique* (July 1996); Jacques Robin, 'Repenser les activités humaines à l'echelle de la vie', *Le Monde Diplomatique* (July 1997).

[17] Serge Halimi, 'Le naufrage des dogmes libéraux', *Le Monde Diplomatique* (October 1998).

Le modèle anglo-saxon en question and *Forces et faiblesses du capitalisme anglo-saxon*, and a steady stream of academic conferences and papers that have examined the *modèle anglo-saxon*, especially in contrast to a *modèle nordique*, *modèle rhénan*, *modèle scandinave* and, of course, a *modèle français*.[18] Inevitably, this tendency to essentialise an Anglo-Saxon economic model has been further exacerbated by political contingency: as we have seen, the left has frequently invoked the spectre of an 'Anglo-Saxon ultra-liberalism' in discussions on reform of the welfare state and public-sector institutions, and the spectre of Anglo-Saxon capitalism in all its forms has provided a powerful mobilising symbol. Nowhere was this more evident than in the discussions surrounding the European Constitution in 2005, when the fear of an 'Anglo-Saxonisation' of Europe was an important factor in securing a 'no' vote. Already before the referendum President Jacques Chirac had sought to reassure voters that

[T]he solution of laissez-faire, in other words a solution that would lead to a Europe led by an ultra-liberal, Anglo-Saxon and Atlanticist current ... is not the Europe we want. The alternative way is a humanist Europe.[19]

Shortly after the referendum, the first line of a front-page editorial in *Le Monde* reinforced the sense that the fear of the Anglo-Saxon had been at the heart of the campaign:

The strength of the 'no' vote in the referendum of 29 May can be explained, in large part, by a rejection of the 'Anglo-Saxon model', seen by French workers as a world of pitiless competition, where the reward for employment is very poor salaries, precarious jobs and the hyper-flexibility of the labour market. All this underpinned by levels of social inequality that are acceptable to the British but would be unbearable here.[20]

By this time, the *modèle anglo-saxon* had become a significant political battleground. To take a stand for or against the Anglo-Saxon 'way' was to take sides in a pressing debate about the ethics of economic development.

---

[18] Richard Farnetti and Ibrahim Warde, *Le modèle anglo-saxon en question* (Paris: Economica, 1997); 'Forces et faiblesses du capitalisme anglo-saxon', *Cahiers Français* (No. 349, 2009). Some comparative articles include Patrick Artus, 'Capitalisme anglo-saxon et capitalisme européen continental: une question d'aversion au risque', *Revue d'économie politique* (Vol. 112, No. 4, 2002), pp. 545–56, and Jean Gadrey, 'Modèle nordique vs. Modèle anglo-saxon', *L'Economie politique* (No. 19, 2003), pp. 72–89. An example of a gathering to discuss the relative merits of the *modèle français* and its Anglo-Saxon counterpart is a panel discussion organised by *Le Monde* in 2004. 'Où va le capitalisme français?', *Le Monde* (25 March 2004).

[19] The full text of the president's speech is reproduced in 'N'ayez pas peur, vous n'avez aucune raison d'avoir peur!', *Le Monde* (16 April 2005).

[20] Jean-Louis Andréani, 'Les raisons d'un rejet', *Le Monde* (5 June 2005).

This interest in the economic aspects of the *modèle anglo-saxon* was renewed in the economic crisis of 2008–9. Already in 2005, Eric Besson – Socialist secretary in charge of economic affairs – had argued that it was up to the French to show that 'there exists another economic model than the Anglo-Saxon model'.[21] Likewise, the Socialist Pierre Moscovici had warned in the same year that, if Sarkozy were to be elected president in 2007, he would take as his reference 'the Anglo-Saxon model ... and advocate a market society without rules, which will inaugurate a brave new world of the free market'.[22] And, on this issue at least, they were right: Sarkozy's election victory in 2007 relied on an astute combination of anti-immigration populism, an open endorsement of American culture and an enthusiasm for neo-liberal economics.[23] At the level of rhetoric, however, the economic crisis turned this calculation on its head: all of a sudden, Sarkozy himself was singing the praises of the 'modèle français' in 2009.[24] Even the traditionally free-market British weekly *The Economist*, in a rare use of the term 'Anglo-Saxon' outside France, had to admit in a 2009 editorial that the financial crisis had been a highly effective way of 'laying low *les Anglo-Saxons*'.[25] It appeared that the *modèle anglo-saxon* was finally on the back foot; in the words of one journalist, the financial crisis seemed to mark the 'defeat of Anglo-Saxon capitalism'.[26]

How long this will last is, of course, open to question. In all likelihood, the pendulum will soon swing back the other way, and the *modèle anglo-saxon* will once again be an object of fear and envy. Either way, it is quite clear that the construction of an imagined Anglo-Saxon economic model has been one of the most powerful counter-narratives to Gaullist and post-Gaullist economic nationalism. Critics of French economic policy, whose interventions will be analysed in more depth in chapter 9, have frequently invoked the Anglo-Saxon world in their attempts to undermine some of the 'sacred cows' of the French economy (state planning, high taxation ...). By contrast, defenders of the economic status quo (in particular public-sector workers) have painted an image of an

---

[21] Sylvia Zappi, 'Il existe un autre modèle économique que le modèle anglo-saxon – Eric Besson', *Le Monde* (9 September 2005).

[22] Pierre Moscovici, 'Pour un nouveau compromis économique et social français', *Les Echos* (31 August 2005). At the time, Moscovici was a member of the European Parliament, and he has since been re-elected as a deputy in the Doubs.

[23] On the roots of Sarkozy's liberalism, see chapter 10. See also Nicholas Hewlett, *The Sarkozy Phenomenon* (London: Imprint Academic, 2011).

[24] Claire Guélaud, 'Dans la crise, le modèle français, naguère décrié, retrouve des couleurs', *Le Monde* (31 January 2009).

[25] 'Europe's new pecking order', *The Economist* (7 May 2009).

[26] Thierry Philippon, 'La défaite du capitalisme anglo-saxon', *Le Nouvel Observateur* (3 April 2009).

Anglo-Saxon economic dystopia of rampant inequality, unbridled entre-preneurialism and atrophying public services. Perhaps inevitably, it is also the latter who have been the strongest supporters of a neo-republican *modèle français*, a claim confirmed by the 2005 referendum, when growing opposition to the European Constitution among lower-level public-sector workers helped to carry the 'no' vote.[27]

Dystopias: Anglo-Saxon society

For all its economic connotations, it would be reductive to limit the contemporary definition of the Anglo-Saxon to economics alone. The apparent superiority of the Anglo-Saxon has been expressed as much in social organisation as in economic ideology. More often than not, the *modèle anglo-saxon* has been seen as a potent mix of an economic ideal (free market capitalism) and a social model (multiculturalism). Just as Anglo-Saxon economic successes have been heightened by France's supposed decline, so, too, the benefits of Anglo-Saxon multiculturalism have been thrown into sharp relief by France's crisis of integration. While the majority of the references to the Anglo-Saxon in the past three decades focused on economics, a significant proportion involved social policy – and, in particular, the integration of migrants. It is here that the connection between perceptions of the Anglo-Saxon world and neo-republicanism are clearest. Despite lengthy protestations by sociologists who have bemoaned the unsophisticated and unempirical juxtaposition of French and Anglo-Saxon models, the debate surrounding integration has seen almost as complete a rehabilitation of the adjective 'Anglo-Saxon' as in the realm of economic policy.[28]

Even in the world of more scholarly articles in publications such as *Esprit*, there are frequent and relatively unproblematic uses of the term 'Anglo-Saxon' with reference to the question of integration. In a startling moment of comparative reductionism, the journal's readers were informed in 1993 that 'the Anglo-Saxon, Dutch and German models [of integration] are all communitarian [*communautariste*] to different degrees'.[29] Five years later, another article argued that

[27] Dominique Goux and Eric Maurin, '1992–2005: la décomposition du oui', *CEPREMAP Working Papers* (2005) (www.cepremap.fr/depot/docweb/docweb0507. pdf, last accessed 24 March 2014).

[28] Philippe D'Iribarne, 'L'intégration des immigrés: modèle français et modèle anglo-saxon', *Cahiers Français* (No. 352, 2009).

[29] All the more surprising because the author, Olivier Roy, is a sophisticated and subtle scholar of transnational Islam and the problem of 'ethnic minorities' in Europe. O. Roy, 'Les immigrés dans la ville: peut-on parler de tension "ethniques"?', *Esprit* (May 1993).

[D]ebates on the future of society ... are more and more often a confrontation between an Anglo-Saxon model that privileges one's relationship to economics, the integration of individuals through market forces, and the acceptance of growing inequality, and a purely political European reading [of integration] that stresses solidarity ... the Anglo-Saxon model pushes to the limits the benefits of a close relationship between the social and the economic.[30]

In addition to highlighting the supposed assumptions behind an Anglo-Saxon philosophy of integration, this quotation has the benefit of making clear the intimate relationship between the social and the economic, which lie at the heart of the *modèle anglo-saxon*.

It is only one of many examples. The well-known geographer Emmanuel Todd in his *L'illusion économique* (1998) constructed a complete anthropological and economic theory on the basis that German and Japanese family structures differ fundamentally from 'the absolute, liberal and non-egalitarian nuclear family [that] is characteristic of the Anglo-Saxon world'. He assures readers that the Anglo-Saxon family combines 'a precocious autonomy among children with the absence of strict rules of inheritance', which results in a peculiar propensity for 'individualistic capitalism of the Anglo-Saxon type'.[31] In his book, Todd strongly suggests that the secret of the success of Anglo-Saxon capitalism lies in the family and that Anglo-Saxon-style integration depends on Anglo-Saxon capitalism (and vice versa). The parallels with Demolins's late-nineteenth-century essay are striking. After all, it was the latter who had argued in 1898 that Anglo-Saxon home and family life encouraged 'the sense of dignity ... independence ... and effort'.[32] The reproduction of this argument almost a century later demonstrated the extent to which Anglo-Saxon society and economics could still represent an essentialised counter-model.

But, where Todd's theory implied that an Anglo-Saxon society was incompatible with France, many others believed that it had already penetrated French society. In Taguieff's *La République enlisée*, several pages are devoted to the supposed 'Anglo-Saxonisation of social relations' within French society. The author takes this process to mean a growing sense of atomisation and the celebration of discrete community identities. Perhaps inevitably, these are both seen to be caused by the inexorable rise of an Anglo-Saxon market and consumer capitalism.[33]

---

[30] Jacques Roman and Joël Donzelot, '1972–1998: les nouvelles donnes du social', *Esprit* (March–April 1998).
[31] Emmanuel Todd, *Illusion économique. Essai sur la stagnation des societés développées* (Paris: Folio, 1999), especially pp. 69–96 ('Les deux capitalismes').
[32] Demolins, *À quoi tient la superiorité des Anglo-Saxons*, pp. 196–7.
[33] Taguieff, *La République enlisée*, pp. 117–9.

Likewise, Jelen, whose fierce attacks on *communautarisme* were analysed in the previous chapter, warned the French in 1997 that 'the communitarianisation of society ... is like hell, paved with good intentions' and that inveterate 'multiculturalists' risked undoing 'the national bond [*lien national*] and dissolving what they refuse to call French culture'.[34] In this analysis, nation and Republic appear to be natural partners, while the threat of American-style *communautarisme* is used to bind the two together. It is significant, too, that Jelen invokes American historian Arthur Schlesinger's critique of multiculturalism, *The Disuniting of America* (1992), a book referred to by other neo-republican intellectuals. Schlesinger's thesis has found a natural home among those who denounce the fragmentation of France into communities, in the same way that a highly-selective use of Alexis de Tocqueville's *Democracy in America* has long been invoked by those passing judgement on the United States.[35]

Thus, while the previous chapter demonstrated the extent to which discussions of multiculturalism and *communautarisme* have responded to the growth of immigrant and colonial counter-narratives, a second perspective emerges here, namely that one of the reasons for the virulent reactions to the imagined rise of multiculturalism in France has been a long-standing French distrust of a *modèle anglo-saxon*. As we have seen, *communautarisme* has usually referred to an unusually dystopic reading of Anglo-American multiculturalism that emphasises its tendency towards fragmentation along community lines, and its encouragement of radical ethnic and religious identities. But such a dystopian vision has always rested on a juxtaposition of a neo-republican model of integration with an Anglo-Saxon model that threatens to bring *communautarisme* to France. This mixing of cultural sterotypes and an essentialised clash of models has made for powerful political rhetoric. As Prime Minister Dominique de Villepin put it in 2005, 'we do not aspire to becoming an Anglo-Saxon country ... we have a republican model without equivalent anywhere in the world'.[36]

The spectre of *communautarisme* never seemed as ominous as it did in the months following the urban unrest of 2005. But, where the debate surrounding the referendum on the European Constitution a few months before had led to intense criticism of an Anglo-Saxon economic model, the riots and violence in many French cities seemed to cast Anglo-Saxon multiculturalism in a better light. To some, the conclusion was clear: 'the

---

[34] Jelen, *Les casseurs de la République*, p. 13.   [35] Roger, *L'ennemi américain*, pp. 90–3.
[36] Eric Zemmour, 'Tradition républicaine contre schema américain: communautarisme et intégration', *Le Figaro* (2 June 2005).

French model of integration is finished' announced an opinion piece by the demographer Michèle Tribalat, in which she argued that it was no longer possible for France to pretend that it could avoid riots *à l'anglo-saxonne*.[37] For others, such as Blandine Kriegel, this was the occasion to defend a French republican model against a version of 'the modern "fashionable" democratic republic [*cité*] ... that is practised by our Anglo-Saxon neighbours'. In a memorable passage, she launched a three-pronged attack on the *modèle anglo-saxon*:

The more we are enthusiastically told about the Anglo-Saxon model [of integration], the more we forget certain things. (1) The United States, and not the French Republic, wrote segregation ... into the laws of their southern states. (2) The United States began the battle against segregation forty years ago. Only a year ago, the Cour des comptes [in France] argued that French society had not yet really thought about immigration. (3) Those responsible for the communitarian model [*modèle communautariste*] in Holland and England are asking themselves questions about the murder of Theo van Gogh and ethnic violence.[38]

Hyperbole notwithstanding, this sentiment was echoed elsewhere: the lawyer Robert Badinter complained that journalists were taking great pleasure in generalising from the experiences of individuals who had failed to integrate into an argument for the 'supposed superiority of the Anglo-Saxon model', while Malek Boutih deplored the 'administrative machinery that creates Anglo-Saxon communitarianism'.[39] On both sides of the debate, the term 'Anglo-Saxon' was being mobilised and manipulated to fit a specific political context. Without losing many of its fundamental associations, the term was being attached to a wide range of processes, ideas, theories and problems related to French society on issues as varied as the question whether to allow the collection of statistical data on 'ethnic' grounds and affirmative action policies in French higher education. In each case, one's attitude towards the *modèle anglo-saxon* became a marker of political affiliation, with neo-republican sympathisers lining up to attack it and critics of neo-republicanism using it to undermine an ossified *modèle français*.

In the realm of culture, too, the Anglo-Saxon has played a crucial role in defining recent approaches towards French 'civilisation', language and

---

[37] Michèle Tribalat, 'Le modèle d'intégration à la française, c'est fini', *Le Figaro* (19 November 2005).
[38] Blandine Kriegel, 'La crise des banlieues: faillite du modèle républicain?', *Le Figaro* (23 November 2005).
[39] Ariane Lacroix, 'Badinter – Rémond: le "modèle français", un universalisme singulier', *Le Figaro* (20 November 2005). Weill, 'Entre Malek Boutih et la philosophe Chantal Delsol un accord presque parfait'.

modernity. None of this is especially new; as a number of scholars have argued, The function of the United States as a fascinating but disturbing example of capitalist modernity has been prevalent since at least the 1930s.[40] Predictably, with a growing concern over what constitutes the French national narrative in the twenty-first century, these stereotypes and images have re-emerged at the hands of neo-republicans like Finkielkraut and Debray.[41] For instance, Finkielkraut's attacks on anti-racism groups or the gay 'lobby' in the 1980s carried with them strong anti-American overtones. Likewise, the marginalisation of the nation and the Republic in the bicentennial celebration in 1989 suggested to Finkielkraut an imminent descent into an Americanised nightmare:

With a sumptuous 'multi-tribal' Bastille celebration, today's France is celebrating the 'real revolution', ... the birth of a global soundscape, what the Anglo-Saxons call 'world music'. There is nothing left of the literary nation of France: the nation is disappearing in favour of tribes, and literature is giving way to global 'music'.[42]

In this analysis, 'world music' becomes the debased expression of a globalised Anglo-Saxon hegemony – and a debasement of culture itself. It was a sentiment echoed by Debray, whose work has repeatedly manu-factured a dichotomy between a money-driven, selfish and superficial Anglo-Saxon culture and a rational (French) Republic. Such a view became something of a parody when, in 2004, Debray claimed that the inclusion in *Le Monde* of a condensed version of the *New York Times* once a week meant that people 'have turned their back on civic life [*la chose publique*]'.[43] The penetration of an organ of the American media into the heart of the French established press evidently seemed to Debray to be an impossible affront to the nation.[44]

Such feelings have not solely been the preserve of France's rarefied intellectual elite, however: various French political positions on the international stage have reinforced the sense that French approaches to culture differ fundamentally from those of their Anglo-Saxon counter-parts. A good example was the defence of the 'cultural exception' at the Uruguay Round of GATT talks in 1993. It brought head to head the mercantile belligerence of American negotiator Jack Valenti and the defence of what the then Culture Minister Jacques Toubon described as

---

[40] On this, see especially Mathy, *Extrême Occident*.
[41] Jean-Philippe Mathy, *French Resistance: The French-American Culture Wars* (Minneapolis: University of Minnesota Press, 2000).
[42] 'La nation disparait au profit des tribus: Un entretien avec Alain Finkielkraut', *Le Monde* (13 July 1989).
[43] Debray, *Ce que nous voile le voile*, p. 71.
[44] Debray directly tackles the issue of anti-Americanism (and his form of 'intelligent' anti-Americanism) in 'Un "antiaméricain" à New York', in Debray, *Contretemps*.

the 'elementary liberty' needed to protect the French culture industry against the unfair competition of American cultural imports.[45] The French delegation that articulated the specific demand for a cultural exemption from the GATT free trade accord did so on the basis that European cultural products could not compete with large American corporations such as the major Hollywood studios. This position was criticised by Hervé Bourges, the then director of France Télévisions, in the pages of *Le Monde*. He maintained that the French reaction to changes in the audiovisual market was 'astonishingly conservative'.[46] The response he got from songwriter Pierre Delanoë, film-maker Guy Seligmann and screenwriter Claude Brule captured perfectly the supposed dichotomy between the cultural life of France and the Anglo-Saxon world:

The Americans know that the 'cultural exception' is a brake on their conquest of the world market because, behind the French objection [to free trade], it is Europe's entire audiovisual [sector] that is beginning to take root and develop.[47]

In this case, it is 'the Americans', whose imperialist tendencies ('conquest') are being held in check by a 'French objection', which also speaks for the rest of Europe. Already in 1981, the Socialist Culture Minister Jack Lang had denounced American 'cultural imperialism'. That his charge should have found echoes on the right (Jacques Toubon) and among members of France's artistic elite in 1993 was a testimony to the central importance of opposition to the United States in defining what the Republic represented.[48] France was not only protecting itself but was adopting a moral high ground against the American economic machine.

This debate found its way back into television, radio and newspaper debates in the mid 2000s with Google's project to digitise books. Once again, it was French critics who led the attack on the digital behemoth. In a stinging comment piece in 2005, historian and former head of the Bibliothèque Nationale de France Jean-Noël Jeanneney saw clearly the link between Google's project and the mythical Anglo-Saxon:

[Google's] criteria for inclusion will be powerfully influenced ... by an Anglo-Saxon perspective on the diversity of civilisation ... Anglo-Saxon publications,

---

[45] 'M. Toubon prêt à se battre pour l'exception culturelle', *Le Monde* (11 May 1993).
[46] Hervé Bourges, 'La vraie réponse: produire et franchir les frontières', *Le Monde* (17 November 1993).
[47] Guy Seligmann, Pierre Delanoë and Claude Brule, 'Réponse à Hervé Bourges', *Le Monde* (2 December 1993).
[48] For Lang's position, see Nicolas Vulser, 'Depuis les années 1920, l'Europe tente de résister à l'emprise américaine', *Le Monde* (29 December 2001), and J. Rigaud, *L'exception culturelle: culture et pouvoirs sous la Ve République* (Paris: Editions Grasset, 2001).

which are already dominant in a large number of fields, will automatically be over-represented, with a crushing advantage of Anglophone [texts] compared with other, especially European, languages.[49]

This wide-ranging quotation brings together many of the key meanings and associations behind the term 'Anglo-Saxon'. There is the fear of superiority, expressed both in the 'over-representation' of Anglo-Saxon scientific production, and in the 'crushing' hegemony of the English language. There is an implicit criticism of 'diversity' (both social and cultural), which is placed in contrast to a more thoroughgoing French notion of 'civilisation'. There is even the implication that the Anglo-Saxon is watching over the world's cultural production. We are left with the impression that Google has become a predatory and omniscient virtual Anglo-Saxon.

This kind of alarmist language might appear better suited to the opinion pages of daily newspapers than reasoned political discussions, but it is not so easy to draw these straightforward distinctions. The plasticity of the Anglo-Saxon in French political language should not conceal the fact that it has played a crucial role in defining political allegiances – and has done so for some time. From the nineteenth century onwards, the logical counterpart to a view of the Anglo-Saxon world as mercantile, commercial and anti-humanist was that it lacked culture and spiritual value. The United States was seen as a land of standardised mass-consumer goods.[50] The same was true of Britain: critics drew an implicit distinction between the 'civilisation' of the French and the pragmatic British command of 'nature'.[51] The barren cultural wasteland of the United States and the pragmatic world of British mercantilism were supposed to be a stark contrast to the humanity – and moral superiority – of France. This assumption permeated post-war French Marxism and Gaullism – and has continued in today's anti-globalisation and post-Gaullist movements. More than ever, it has also become inextricably tied up with French national identity. The cynical might be inclined to argue that, given France's geopolitical impotence, it can only resort to occupying a 'moral high ground' of the type taken by Villepin and Chirac over the 2003 Iraq War or of the type expressed in Chirac's plea to 'humanise globalisation' after the G8 summit in Genoa

---

[49] Jean-Noël Jeanneney, 'Quand Google défie l'Europe', *Le Monde* (24 January 2005). With thanks to Colin Jones for pointing out this article (and Jeanneney's subsequent book on the same subject).

[50] Denis Lacorne and Jacques Rupnik, 'La France saisie par l'Amérique', in Denis Lacorne, Jacques Rupnik and M-F. Toinet, *L'Amérique dans les têtes: un siècle de fascinations et d'aversions* (Paris: Hachette, 1986), pp. 31–2.

[51] Tombs and Tombs, *That Sweet Enemy*, p. 449.

in 2001.[52] But I think it would be more accurate to see this as an expression of a deeply held belief in the moral superiority of French (neo-) republicanism over an 'inhuman' Anglo-American capitalism.

The Anglo-Saxon in Europe

The construction of Europe has added a new dimension to the battle between Anglo-Saxon and French models of economy, society and culture.[53] While the United States has often been perceived as a distant counter-model, the same cannot be said of Britain – a state that is not only part of Europe but also increasingly popular as a destination for thousands of highly skilled French migrants of all ages. The opening of the Channel Tunnel in 1994 encouraged a new wave of French migration to the United Kingdom, and recent estimates suggest that around 250–300,000 French citizens were living in the Greater London area in the late 2010s – the size of a large city in metropolitan France.[54] For the first time, it seemed that Britain had become a counter-model sufficiently attractive that it could lure the French away from a stagnant and unchanging *modèle français*.[55] The perceived dynamism of the United Kingdom under Margaret Thatcher in the 1980s and Tony Blair in the early 2000s lent additional credence to the fears of a 'brain drain'. Not to mention that, since joining the European Economic Community in 1973, the British have been the most obstinate opponents of French-inspired projects to reform and extend European integration. In return, the French have cast the British as Europe's advocates for Anglo-Saxon capitalism. The 'no' to the 2005 referendum marked the culmination of these fears, but it concealed a longer history of confrontation which has formed another crucial element in the writing of the neo-republican national narrative.

---

[52] 'M. Chirac pour une "conscience citoyenne"', *Le Monde* (20 July 2001). A scathing analysis can be found in Revel, *L'obsession anti-américaine*, pp. 70–2.
[53] Some of the themes in this final section are developed in more detail in Emile Chabal, 'Just Say "Non"? France, Britain and Europe Since the 1980s', in B. J. Sudlow (ed.), *National Identities in France* (London: Transaction Press, 2011).
[54] For a comprehensive discussion of these estimates see Wesley Stephenson, 'Is London Really France's Sixth Biggest City?', 1 April 2014, available at www.bbc.co.uk/news/magazine-26823489 (last accessed 5 November 2014).
[55] Some scholars have begun working on the French community in London. See e.g. Adrian Favell, *Eurostars and Eurocities* (Oxford: Wiley, 2008), and Jon Mulholland and Louise Ryan, 'Trading Places: French Highly Skilled Migrants Negotiating Mobility and Emplacement in London', *Journal of Ethnic and Migration Studies* (Vol. 40, No. 4, 2014), pp. 584–600.

Since its inception, Britain has been a reluctant partner in Europe. From the 1950s onwards, there were suspicions in France that Britain was intent on undermining attempts at European integration. Famously, it was de Gaulle who most explicitly articulated the challenge Britain posed to the European project by twice, in 1963 and 67, rejecting the British application to join the Common Market. It was abundantly clear that, in additional to a residual Anglophobia, de Gaulle feared both the dilution of his (French-led) vision of Europe and Britain's very different attitude towards the United States, the free market and political integration.[56] Nevertheless, with de Gaulle's death in 1970, the way was open for Britain to join the Common Market in 1973. This did not, however, mean that the French and British shared a common approach to Europe; on the contrary, they were on rapidly diverging paths. As Tombs and Tombs put it, 'rarely since the first Napoleon had they embodied such clear differences, or tried to remake Europe in their own contrasting images', and this despite the fact that France and Britain were becoming more and more similar economically and demographically.[57] This clash between British and French 'models' in Europe has been integral to the writing of the contemporary French national narrative. We have already seen how a *modèle anglo-saxon* has acted as a vital foil in discussions surrounding integration and economic reform. But battles inside Europe have made the threat of the *modèle anglo-saxon* very real.

The contrast between France and Britain became most pronounced in the 1980s, as Thatcher followed an aggressive policy of 'liberalisation' and privatisation, accompanied by the militant language of neo-liberalism, while Mitterrand pushed for a form of 'socialism in one country' after his election in 1981. If these appeared to be merely political differences between right and left, once transposed into the European arena they reflected national 'characters' as much as partisan politics. Indeed, many have argued that the failure of Mitterrand's economic policy led directly to a renewed interest in Europe; it was hoped that France's standing could be reinvigorated by a strengthened Europe.[58] Mitterrand delegated the task of 'renewing' Europe to Jacques Delors – a former Confédération française démocratique du travail (CFDT) trade unionist, democratic socialist and Finance Minister in 1981–4. Delors's presidency of the European Commission (1985–95) resulted in some of the most

---

[56] On this see Cerny, *The politics of grandeur*; Hoffmann, *Decline or Renewal?*
[57] Tombs and Tombs, *That Sweet Enemy*, p. 637.
[58] In Delors's words, 'C'est donc à partir de son choix decisive de mars 1983 qu'il [Mitterrand] a vraiment chaussé les bottes du grand Européen qu'il était'. Jacques Delors, *Mémoires* (Paris: Plon, 2004), p. 179.

far-reaching European legislation (the Single European Act and the Maastricht Treaty, among others) but also some of the most public battles between British and French models of Europe, vividly captured in the frequent exchanges between Delors and Thatcher throughout the 1980s.[59]

This clash is most clearly embodied in speeches by Thatcher and Delors given at the Collège d'Europe in Bruges in the late 1980s. In 1988, the British Prime Minister laid out her vision for Europe in one of her most famous speeches. She reaffirmed her hostility to the Common Agricultural Policy (CAP) – perhaps the longest-standing policy disagreement between France and Britain – emphasised Europe's connections to the North Atlantic Treaty Organization, and made plain her vision of a 'liberalised' 'union of nations'. In one of the most frequently quoted passages, she told her audience:

> We have not successfully rolled back the frontiers of the state in Britain, only to see them reimposed at a European level, with a European super state exercising a new dominance from Brussels. Certainly we want to see Europe more united and with a greater sense of common purpose. But it must be in a way which preserves the different traditions, parliamentary powers and sense of national pride in one's own country.[60]

There would be no clearer statement of an Anglo-Saxon Europe than this – as Delors perceptively observed in his memoirs, 'her speech was specifically Thatcherite [*thatchérien*] but against a backdrop of familiar English ideas that have been articulated before and have continued to be articulated until the present day'.[61] Still, at the time Delors took Thatcher's Eurosceptic call to arms seriously, and delivered his own reply at the Collège d'Europe a year later, in which he stressed the European 'ideal', and the need for European sovereignty and pluralism in equal measure. The contrast with Thatcher was stark. Where she had urged Europe not to be 'distracted by Utopian goals', Delors proclaimed that 'it is time for an ideal Europe to be reborn!'[62] This was not simply a war of words between rival political orientations; this was a battle over whose national narrative could most successfully be extended to a growing Europe.

When it came to policy, the rhetoric was just as confrontational. Thatcher's opposition to the CAP and continuous requests for budget

---

[59] On the Delors presidency see George Ross, *Jacques Delors and European Integration* (London: Polity, 1995).

[60] Margaret Thatcher, *The Collected Speeches of Margaret Thatcher* (London: HarperCollins, 1997), pp. 315–57.

[61] Delors, *Mémoires*, p. 350.

[62] 'Reconcilier l'idéal et la nécessité (devant le Collège d'Europe à Bruges, le 17 octobre 1989)', in Jacques Delors, *Le nouveau concert européen* (Paris: Odile Jacob, 1992), p. 319.

rebates from the European Community provided ample opportunity for disagreement. But, above all, it was Delors's desire to build a 'social Europe' that met sustained resistance. From the moment he became head of the Commission, Delors set about building a 'European model of society', which included workers legislation and a European Bill of Rights.[63] The Conservative governments of Thatcher and John Major opposed these developments, and opted out of the Social Chapter of the 1992 Maastricht Treaty, which was part of these changes. Tony Blair eventually ratified the Social Chapter in 1997, but Britain's decision to stay out of the eurozone and not to sign the Schengen agreements on free movement of European citizens were further blows to Delors's vision of an increasingly united and interdependent Europe. As the pro-Europeanism of the early Blair years faded, it became apparent that a British conception of Europe remained very different from that of the French.[64] Although the Anglo-Saxon was now in Europe, this did not mean that Britain no longer posed a threat; on the contrary, the desire to rewrite the French national narrative through the European project made a response to the *modèle anglo-saxon* that much more urgent.

The response to this perceived Anglo-Saxon threat in Europe has been varied. In many cases, it has led to increasingly defensive positions on issues that have been seen to compromise French national identity, such as agricultural policy and language. We saw earlier, for instance, how the campaign to protect the French language took off in the 1980s, and resulted in various laws designed to ensure the use of French in the public space. From its inception, the campaign used the spectre of an Anglo-Saxon Europe to strengthen its case. The founding document of Avenir de la Langue Française in 1992 made quite clear the connection between the rise of English and the changing nature of Europe:

In short, there is a more and more enterprising group of fanatics of 'all-English' in France ... When these Anglophiles [*angloglottes*] deign to explain themselves, they generally invoke efficiency and economic explanations; but, recently, they have begun to talk about Europe ... As for Europe itself, it has fewer anglophones than francophones and, in any case, if Europe needs one language, it is hard to see why this should be the language of the United States.[65]

---

[63] See especially 'Nourrir le dialogue sociale (au Congrès de la Confédération européene des syndicats à Stockholm, le 12 mai 1988)' and 'Construire l'Europe sociale (au Congrès des Syndicats britanniques à Bournemouth, le 8 septembre 1988)', in Delors, *Le nouveau concert européen.*

[64] On differing attitudes inside the European bureaucratic elite, see for instance Olivier Costa and Jean-Pascal Daloz, 'How French Policy-Makers See Themselves', in Helen Drake (ed.), *French Relations with the European Union* (London: Routledge, 2005).

[65] 'Appel: Avenir de la Langue Française', *Le Monde* (30 July 1992).

In addition to highlighting the threat to the French language from an increasingly 'anglophone' Europe, this passage also demonstrates the conceptual relationship between the spread of English and 'Americanisation' more generally – an association entirely consistent with the assumptions behind the notion of the Anglo-Saxon. For those defenders of the French language who founded ALF, theirs was a battle to preserve the French national narrative from regional fragmentation and from an Anglo-Saxon threat for which Europe was the vehicle.

The fear of an Anglo-Saxon Europe was not limited simply to the world of French-language politics. By the late 1990s, a number of groups and publications were articulating a novel form of French Euroscepticism that questioned what many in France felt was the increasing penetration of an Anglo-Saxon model into European politics. While British Euroscepticism, which has been embodied by elite think tanks such as the Bruges Group (founded in 1989) and popular political parties such as the UK Independence Party (founded in 1993), has frequently attacked the European project as a whole, much of French Euroscepticism has questioned more specifically the direction Europe is taking.[66] This tendency was given a voice with the launching of the weekly magazine *Marianne* in 1997 and the setting up of the Fondation Marc Bloch think tank in 1998, both of which articulated a critical – though not necessarily anti-European – position towards the expansion and development of the European project.

Marianne was set up by the long-time publicist and journalist Jean-François Kahn. Kahn, who worked for France 2, Europe 1 and *Le Monde* in the 1980s and 90s, had already in 1984 founded a weekly magazine entitled *L'Évènement du jeudi*, famous for its tabloid-style presentation, dramatic 'scoops' and anti-elitism. *L'Évènement du jeudi* collapsed in 1999, but, by this time, Kahn had set up *Marianne*.[67] Its aim was to act as a critical voice in opposition to the conformism of the 'pensée unique', and its position was described from the outset as 'republican' and 'anti-capitalist'.[68] Over the next few years, *Marianne* would become a platform for a wide variety of intellectuals and commentators to engage in discussions about the future of Europe and the French nation.[69]

---

[66] On the Bruges Group, see their website www.brugesgroup.com (last accessed 19 June 2010).

[67] Philippe Bonnet, 'L'Evènement du Jeudi veut retrouver ses anciens lecteurs', *Libération* (8 June 1995).

[68] Alain Salles, 'Jean-François Kahn prépare un nouvel hebdomadaire pour le printemps 1997', *Le Monde* (2 October 1996).

[69] *Marianne* does not publish exact circulation figures. It claimed an average of 280,000 copies sold for each of the first nine issues. More recently, this figure appears to have

The editorial line was unambiguous: in the face of the unravelling of the nation state, the time had come to defend and promote republican values and aspire once again to a heroic national unity. As Kahn put it in 1997, 'it is time to rehabilitate patriotism'.[70] Unsurprisingly, the magazine supported Chevènement's presidential campaign in 2002, but despite his electoral failure, *Marianne* has nevertheless continued to be at the forefront of contemporary neo-republicanism, issuing regular calls for greater 'republican' responsibility in French politics.[71]

At the same time, the magazine has adopted a critical stance towards Europe. In an article in 2001, Kahn claimed that he spoke on behalf of the magazine's editorial team as a whole when he argued for a 'United States of Europe' and against 'a purely mercantile Europe', a reminder that in this context federalism and Euroscepticism were perfectly compatible.[72] Significantly for our purposes, however, Kahn laid the blame for a 'mercantile' Europe squarely at Britain's door: '[when] sovereign nations develop relations between them that are governed by economic and commercial priorities – for instance, in a free-trade zone ... this is a British-style Europe'. A year later, Kahn was more explicit still. In an editorial on the potential dangers of European enlargement without greater political integration, he stated that 'the first mistake was no doubt to have tied ourselves to England, always hostile to the emergence of a true European power'.[73] By the time of the 2005 referendum, *Marianne* claimed to be the only magazine or newspaper offering a 'real' debate on the European Constitution, which in this case meant giving a platform to those campaigning for a 'no' vote, despite disagreements among staff.[74] Yet again, this was an opportunity for regular contributors to the publication to find fault with a 'British approach' to Europe. As one commentator put it,

dropped to around 150,000, reflecting an overall decline in the news weekly market in France. However, since its inception, the vast majority of copies of *Marianne* are sold at newsstands and newsagents, unlike other weeklies, which rely on subscriptions. For early circulation figures, see Alain Salles, 'Marianne a trouvé ses lecteurs et cherche des annonceurs', *Le Monde* (25 July 1997); for a more recent analysis see Xavier Ternisien, 'Le modèle éditorial de 'Marianne' s'essouffle', *Le Monde* (5 March 2010).

[70] Jean-François Kahn, 'Ces Français qui haïssent la France', *Marianne* (3 November 1997).

[71] See, for instance, an 'appel républicain' signed in 2008 by prominent politicians including François Bayrou, Dominique de Villepin, Bertrand Delanoë and Corinne Lepage. 'L'Appel républicain de Marianne', *Marianne* (15 February 2008).

[72] Jean-François Kahn, 'Quelle France dans quelle Europe?', *Marianne* (6 August 2001).

[73] Jean-François Kahn, 'Notre Europe', *Marianne* (16 December 2002).

[74] 'Marianne et la constitution européene', *Marianne* (9 April 2005).

[S]ince the entrance of Great Britain, Europe has been trapped. Great Britain is the 'Trojan Horse' of the United States, only participating here and there when it has seemed in its interest to do so. I knew, in my youth, that crazy European dream and, as long as we were only six countries, everything was possible.[75]

The message was clear: yes to Europe, but no to an Anglo-Saxon Europe.

Despite slowing sales, *Marianne* has held true to its editorial policies. In addition to its frequent 'republican calls', it has continued to argue for referendums on Europe, most notably on the Lisbon Treaty of 2007. But it has not only been in the pages of weekly magazines that this anti-Anglo-Saxon French Euroscepticism has found a voice: within a year of the foundation of *Marianne*, a public think tank was created with similar aims and even greater intellectual legitimacy. The Fondation du 2 mars – initially entitled the Fondation Marc Bloch, until it was forced to change its name because of a legal attack from Bloch's family – was set up in 1998.[76] The foundation – with a strong anti-European core – had the express aim of

bringing together all those who, in the intellectual world and the world of action (party politics, trade unions, civil society) are determined to elaborate new political, economic, social, diplomatic and cultural perspectives within the framework of the Republic and humanism.[77]

Like *Marianne*, it was politically ecumenical, but its ranks were swelled by many figures associated with the neo-republican revival. Three of its presidents (Pierre-André Taguieff, Philippe Raynaud and Elisabeth Lévy) were quite open neo-republicans, while other prominent members – such as politician, political advisor and civil servant Henri Guiano, the geographer and intellectual Emmanuel Todd, the historian Max Gallo and the journalist Joseph Macé Scaron – had all made their neo-republican credentials well known to a wider public.[78]

As a think tank, the Foundation's aim was to act as a forum for the development of a 'pensée critique' and oppose the hegemony of the Fondation Saint-Simon, an earlier think tank set up in 1982 under the auspices of François Furet.[79] The Fondation Marc Bloch's first annual

[75] Denis Peneaud, 'Referendum: et si le non était le vrai vote européen', *Marianne* (26 February 2005).

[76] On this see 'L'étrange défaite de Marc Bloch', *Le Monde* (10 October 1998).

[77] See http://notre.republique.free.fr/amisafmb.htm (last accessed 2 February 2008. Note that access to certain parts of the site is sporadic).

[78] However, its founding members also included figures who have criticised various aspects of the neo-republican turn (such as Michèle Tribalat, who has been an advocate of 'ethnic' statistics in the census).

[79] On the Fondation Saint-Simon, see chapter 9. Ariane Chemin, 'Une fondation Marc-Bloch pour mettre fin au monopole des saint-simoniens', *Le Monde* (18 February 1998).

conference in September 1998 indicated the degree to which it had succeeded in mobilising France's intellectual elite: it was, in the words of one journalist, by far the most 'intellectual' think tank annual conference that year, bringing together the likes of Régis Debray and Max Gallo under the common banner of republican values and an opposition to the single currency and greater European integration.[80] In the years following its inauguration, the foundation acted as a vital vehicle for the diffusion of neo-republican ideals with a strongly Eurosceptic bent. It sponsored a wide range of publications, including works by Taguieff, Peña-Ruíz, Chevènement and Boutih.[81] Some titles dealt directly with the European 'problem', such as Daniel Cohn-Bendit and Henri Guiano's pamphlet *La France est-elle soluble dans l'Europe?* (1999).[82]

As in the case of *Marianne*, the foundation was to be a voice for a specifically neo-republican form of Euroscepticism. Or, to put it in the words of Philippe Cohen, its first secretary-general, in 1998, 'our beliefs are not, for that matter, necessarily anti-European, but rather anti-Europeist [*antieuropéistes*], in the sense of an opposition to Europe as it is being constructed today'.[83] This quotation captured in a nutshell the conceptual relationship between neo-republicanism, Euroscepticism and the notion of the Anglo-Saxon, which has often been at the heart of contemporary French criticisms of the European Union. It makes it clear that it is the European component of France's national narrative that has been threatened by a mythical *modèle anglo-saxon*. The only adequate response to this threat is a return to the nation and the Republic.

The foundation suffered a setback in 2002 with the failure of Chevènement's presidential candidacy. But it has nevertheless tried to reinvent itself, by its own admission moving away from the strictly republican position it held, to a broader critique of the *pensée unique*.[84] A colloquium organised in 2003, which brought together the Socialist politician Hubert Védrine, psychologist Michel Schneider and Finkielkraut, was a reminder of its intellectual orientation, but a number of positions have also changed since 1998. So, for instance, Philippe

[80] Ariane Chemin, 'Des intellectuels de droite et de gauche entrent en résistance contre la pensée unique', *Le Monde* (29 September 2010).

[81] Pierre-André Taguieff, *Résister au bougisme* (Paris: Fondation du 2 Mars, 2001); H. Peña-Ruíz, *La laïcité pour l'égalité* (Paris: Fondation du 2 Mars, 2001); Jean-Pierre Chevènement, *La République prend le maquis* (Paris: Fondation du 2 Mars, 2001); Boutih, *La France aux Français? Chiche!*

[82] Daniel Cohn-Bendit and Henri Guiano, *La France est-elle soluble dans l'Europe?* (Paris: Albin Michel/Fondation Marc Bloch, 1999).

[83] Philippe Cohen, 'Les idées républicaines de la Fondation Marc-Bloch', *Le Monde* (29 May 1998)

[84] Pierre Philippe, 'La Fondation du 2 mars fait sa mue', *Marianne* (24 November 2003).

Raynaud, president of the foundation in 2003–5, preferred the epithet 'Euro-agnostic' to that of 'Eurosceptic', while Emmanuel Todd argued in a 2001 interview that 'Europeists [*européistes*]' and 'nation-ists [*nation-ists*]' now have a common enemy, namely the absence of a 'collective belief' in French society.[85] This fragmentation in the early 2000s reflected a broader trend in French intellectual politics, as debates surrounding the national narrative became more diffuse, and a larger number of actors got involved in political and civic discussions. But the 'no' vote in the referendum on the European Constitution in 2005 indicated that the unease expressed by intellectuals in the late 1990s was more than simply a minority concern. The hostile response to the Constitution proved that the concerns of the intellectual elite and those of the French electorate could converge. The fear of an Anglo-Saxon Europe could be a powerful tool of political mobilisation at the ballot box and it could have a profound effect on French politics.

The global Republic?

The Fondation du 2 mars has not fared well in recent years. Its media presence has declined and the flight of some its members into the orbit of Sarkozy's UMP encouraged influential members like Emmanuel Todd to distance themselves from the organisation.[86] But French Euroscepticism has now found a permanent home in the FN, which since 2011 has ramped up its protectionist and anti-European discourse under its new leader Marine Le Pen.[87] Moreover, the broad themes discussed in this chapter have remained largely intact: large numbers of French people continue to emigrate to Britain to work and study; the fear of an Anglo-Saxon economic model remains deep among a French electorate which remains, according to recent polls, the most hostile to capitalism of any major industrialised nation; British policies towards Europe are often still diametrically opposed to those of France; and the French continue to use the term 'Anglo-Saxon' to describe their Anglo-American counterparts. The persistence of these themes is an indication that the manipulation

[85] Nicolas Weill, 'L'opposition des souverainistes s'est assagie', *Le Monde* (29 April 2004); 'Retour sur la fracture sociale: Emmanuel Todd', *Le Monde* (17 September 2001).
[86] Todd discusses his changing attitude towards in an interview with Gérard Desportes and Sylvain Bourmeau of Médiapart. 'Todd: sarkozysme et les nationaux-républicains', *Médiapart* (www.dailymotion.com/video/xc95ii_todd-sarkozysme-et-les-nationaux-re_news, last accessed 24 March 2014).
[87] Jim Shields, 'Marine Le Pen and the "New" FN: A Change of Style or of Substance', *Parliamentary Affairs* (Vol. 66, No. 1, 2013), pp. 179–96.

of foreign models is a vital part of the construction of the national narrative in contemporary France.

In the previous chapter I dealt with the legacies of colonialism; this chapter offers another perspective on France's post-colonial predicament. For, while we tend to assume that studies of post-colonialism should deal with relations between a (former) coloniser and a (post-) colony, an examination of the Franco-British relationship suggests that we ought also to pay significant attention to the interaction between former colonial powers. Of course, I did not set out to present an exhaustive picture of Franco-British relations. I have focused squarely on French debates and the various ways in which they have distorted and adapted supposed Anglo-Saxon norms, values and models. But even a focus on France alone reveals a complex interplay between transnational and national priorities. We saw, for example, how the battle between an Anglo-Saxon and French social model in Europe was simultaneously a battle over the integration of (largely post-colonial) migrants and a fierce debate over the nature of citizenship. By the same token, discussions over the enlargement of the European Union to Turkey – something which the majority of French electors oppose – have raised questions both about an apparently Anglo-Saxon desire to dilute the Union by expanding it, and whether a Muslim country can be considered truly 'European'. In each case, classic post-colonial issues such as migration and the role of Islam combined with existing Franco-British squabbles over Europe to form a complex picture of two countries searching for their roles after the disappearance of their empires and forced to reckon with a powerful Germany.

The emergence of neo-republicanism, then, was not simply a response to changing intellectual and political currents within France; it was also an attempt on the part of some French elites to give France a truly post-colonial identity. Yes, this was often framed in terms of a defensive reaction against a hostile and predatory Anglo-Saxon or Muslim threat, but neo-republicanism's attempts to reinvigorate the nation raises issues common to many European countries. How to protect local traditions in a globalising world? How to rebuild a grand ideology and 'collective belief' after the collapse of communism? What responsibility should the state have in policing the public space? We need not subscribe to the occasionally starry-eyed universalism of neo-republican rhetoric to see that these questions remain unanswered – a fact which undoubtedly explains why many of the issues raised by neo-republicans still dominate electoral campaigns in France and elsewhere.

Nevertheless, it would be wrong to think that neo-republicanism has gone unchallenged. Numerous groups within the French elite have worked hard to separate themselves from the dominant discourse of neo-republicanism. The questions they ask about the state of the nation and the integration of society are similar, but the answers they give are different. As we shall see, for this group, the Anglo-Saxon world is not a threat but an opportunity, and if France is to survive, it needs to learn from foreign models rather than ward them off. Yet they are grappling with the same issues that we have explored in these first five chapters, and they, too, must reckon with France's post-colonial identities and an overwhelming sense of national decline. For both advocates and sceptics of a strong nation, contemporary France has been thoroughly globalised, and its fate rests as much on its relationship with others as it does on its relationship with itself.

Part II

Liberal critics of contemporary France

Le libéralisme introuvable?

Any use of the term 'liberalism' or 'liberal' in contemporary French politics is extremely controversial. This is largely because French liberalism has long suffered from an image problem. As a political tradition, it has appeared irremediably lost in a French political landscape already over-populated with grand ideologies. In the twentieth century, liberalism never had the powerful and flexible appeal of statist, Jacobin republicanism, nor did it have the potent impact of socialism or communism. The same is true as we move to the right of the political spectrum. The counter-revolutionary tradition, which finally imploded in the Vichy period, had very little to do with what we would recognise as liberalism. And even if France's perennial Bonapartist tradition – best embodied in the twentieth century by Charles de Gaulle – was occasionally supported by liberals such as Raymond Aron, it had few liberal pretensions. The increasingly strong associations between liberal and Anglo-Saxon in the post-war period only made matters worse: the term was – and is still – largely a term of abuse used by those on the left to describe the policies of those to their right.

Why, then, have I chosen to use 'liberal' to describe the ideas, concepts and languages that form the basis of this second part of the book? The answer is simple: because it is the most effective way to bring together what are otherwise disparate and varied counter-narratives in contemporary French politics. In the previous part, it was possible to look at the question of the national narrative through the lens of neo-republicanism – a clearly articulated French political language, with which many politicians, intellectuals, journalists and public figures have identified in the past three decades. This is not the case with French liberalism. Although I shall argue, in common with a number of other outside observers, that there has been a 'liberal revival' since the late 1970s, I recognise immediately that locating French liberalism is a difficult and delicate process and that many of the figures whose ideas I discuss would reject the term if it was applied to them.

It is for this reason that I have chosen here to adhere to a contextual definition of liberalism. I do not use the term in its doctrinal or ideological sense. Instead, I use it to describe a set of counter-narratives that have sought to nuance, rewrite and undermine the neo-republican narrative I presented in Part I. As we have seen, this narrative has attempted to restore the legitimacy of the nation as a historical, political and philosophical construction. It has emphasised the primacy of the political – for instance, in discussions surrounding integration – and it has built a powerful defence of the 'French model' against its Anglo-Saxon counterpart. By contrast, I shall argue that the political language of liberalism during the same period has acted as an increasingly articulate counter-narrative. In some cases, the clash has been very public: this has been true, for example, in the battle between supporters of *intégration*, and advocates of 'diversity' and 'multiculturalism'. In other cases, it has been more subtle, such as Pierre Rosanvallon's attempts to move modern French history away from its Jacobin and republican master narratives and restore to prominence the role of 'civil society' and intermediary bodies between state and society. Of course, this does not mean that all the figures discussed below share the same political opinions, or even the same approach to particular questions. As with liberals in the past, there is a great diversity of opinions.[1] But this should not prevent us from identifying an important – and too often hidden – liberal counter-narrative.

There are a number of unifying threads that help us to identify the contemporary variant of this liberal counter-narrative. It has usually sought either to minimise the importance of the nation – say, through a multicultural or post-colonial critique – or to undermine a neo-republican reading of French history. At the same time, it has frequently emphasised economics as a significant explanatory factor in politics. This is in contrast to a neo-republican narrative, which, as we have seen, has downplayed the role of economics in understanding political phenomena. Finally, it has consistently shown itself to be more open towards outside ideas – in particular, those associated with the Anglo-American world. This is perhaps inevitable given that liberalism (and so-called 'neo-liberalism') has since the 1980s found greatest legitimacy in the United States and the United Kingdom. But it has also been part of an internal critique of the French state: many of those whose ideas I discuss below have been highly critical of what they see as a 'blocked', 'stagnant' or simply 'out-of-date' French model. Where neo-republicanism has stressed its benefits – in the form of a strong nation state, a strong

---

[1] The variety of liberalisms in the context of nineteenth-century France is expertly summarised in Jaume, *L'individu effacé*, pp. 7–21.

language and a strong form of political citizenship – liberal critics have called, at the very least, for a reassessment of this model.

These unifying threads run throughout this second part, which, in many ways, mirrors the first. Once again, I open with chapters on the philosophical and institutional roots of the liberal revival in the late 1970s and 1980s, and on recent attempts to rewrite French history to include actors neglected in the neo-republican teleologies discussed in chapter 1. This is followed by a survey of the potent 'post-colonial' critiques of (neo-)republicanism, the nation and citizenship that began with the *droit à la différence* movement in the early 1980s and have led in the battles of the early twenty-first century over colonial memory. The penultimate chapter looks at the language of 'crisis', which I argue has since the 1980s laid the groundwork for a reform of the state. Finally, I assess the very slow progress of this liberal counter-narrative in the world of French party-politics, from Mitterrand's 'about-turn' in 1983–4 to Sarkozy's self-styled liberal 'rupture' in 2007. As before, I move between political ideas, personalities, events and philosophy in order to bring out the extent to which the liberal counter-narrative has influenced French politics. I believe that it is only by attempting to reconstruct these disparate and fragmented critical voices that we can avoid reducing contemporary French politics to a neo-republican national narrative alone. Even if it is clear that the liberalism I describe below has been built in opposition to some of the key tenets of neo-republicanism, it is not simply derivative. On the contrary, capturing its contours is, to my mind, the necessary counterpart to an analysis of neo-republicanism, for they both provide contrasting ways of conceptualising the relationship between nation, state and citizen in contemporary France. While I do not believe that these are the only two possible starting points for an exploration of the French political space, the tension between liberalism and neo-republicanism does much to illuminate some of the central debates in contemporary French politics.

6   In the shadow of Raymond Aron: the 'liberal revival' of the 1980s

- *Vous êtes le dernier libéral?*

- *Non. Aujourd'hui il y en a beaucoup qui me rejoignent. À la limite, je pourrais être à la mode.*   Raymond Aron in an interview in 1981[1]

In the history of twentieth-century French liberalism, few figures feature as prominently as the philosopher and sociologist Raymond Aron.[2] And yet, despite being recognised as one of post-war France's most prominent intellectuals, he felt himself to be a lonely voice in his home country.[3] A fiercely independent figure, he had both the intelligence and analytical courage to abide by his deepest convictions. But these convictions could only lead him to uncertainty: his interpretation of history and contemporary society were defined by a scepticism and realism that marked him out sharply from his contemporaries.[4] He could never endorse the messianism that he saw as the defining characteristic of French Marxism in

---

[1] Raymond Aron, *Le spectateur engagé: entretiens avec Jean-Louis Missika et Dominique Wolton* (Paris: Livre de Poche, 2005 [1981]), p. 447.

[2] On Aron's liberalism see especially Raymond Aron, *Essai sur les libertés* (Paris: Calmann-Lévy, 1973). These lectures were given in 1963. His misgivings over Hayekian liberalism are laid out most effectively on pp. 117–25. For later analyses, see Daniel J. Mahoney, 'The Politic Liberal Rationalism of Raymond Aron', *Polity* (Vol. 24, No. 4, 1992); Jeremy Jennings, 'Raymond Aron and the Fate of European Liberalism', *European Journal of Political Theory* (Vol. 2, 2003); Cécile Hatier, 'The Liberal Message of Raymond Aron: A Substantial Legacy', *European Journal of Political Theory* (Vol. 2, 2003); Pierre Manent, 'Raymond Aron', in Pierre Manent et al., *European Liberty: Four Essays on the Occasion of the 25th Anniversary of the Erasmus Prize Foundation* (Berlin: Springer, 1983); Nicolas Baverez, *Raymond Aron: un moraliste au temps des idéologues* (Paris: Flammarion, 1993); and the extensive analysis in Iain Stewart, 'Raymond Aron and the Roots of the French Liberal Renaissance', unpublished PhD thesis, University of Manchester, Department of History (2011).

[3] See, for instance, Dominique Wolton's description of him as a 'balancement ... entre tristesse et joie de vivre'. Dominique Wolton, '"Je ne suis pas la conscience universelle ..."', *Commentaire* (Vol. 8, No. 28–9, 1984), pp. 109–11. For a more scholarly perspective, see Judt, *The Burden of Responsibility*.

[4] On this see Raymond Aron, *Introduction à la philosophie politique: démocratie et révolution* (Paris: Editions de Fallois, 1997 [1952]).

both its Leninist and neo-Hegelian incarnations; nor could he condemn the democratic, bourgeois society he saw around him. Until the end of his life, he remained acutely aware of the fragility of the various historical contingencies which had created western Europe. The botched and messy compromise of liberal democracy was one for which he was always willing to fight and this meant endorsing many of the political and ethical tenets of European liberalism.[5]

He did this in the face of formidable opposition, most famously from his erstwhile *petit camarade* at the Ecole Normale Supérieure, Jean-Paul Sartre. His non-Marxist interpretation of history, politics and contemporary society immediately marginalised him. Vilified by the communist and *gauchiste* left, he was not always comfortable on the right of the political spectrum either. He lent his support to de Gaulle in the immediate post-war period, but by the 1960s he had become a consistent critic of the style (if not always the substance) of Gaullist politics.[6] Most often branded as a 'conservative' in France's left-leaning intellectual world, he nevertheless sits awkwardly with any of the traditional right-wing traditions identified by historians.[7] The complexities of his life and work consistently defied attempts to classify him, even if his opponents repeatedly tried to squeeze him into an ideological straitjacket of their choosing. While few at the time denied Aron's immense contribution to French intellectual and political life, the memoirs he wrote shortly before his death in 1983 betrayed a sense of failure and melancholy that belied his achievements.[8]

But Aron's time was to come. He may have died six years before the Berlin Wall came down but his posthumous legacy has been immense. One might go so far as to say that he has defined what it has meant to be liberal in France in the last thirty years. This has been reflected in the arguments and political positions taken by contemporary scholars and in the academic institutions, research groups and prizes that have all, in some way, tried to honour his memory. Moreover, by founding the influential journal *Commentaire* in the late 1970s, Aron left an important inheritance for those of future generations who have tried to remain true

---

[5] On this see for instance Raymond Aron, *Démocratie et totalitarisme* (Paris: Folio, 1965). These lectures were given in 1957–8.

[6] On Aron's complex relationship to Gaullism, see especially his journalistic writing. Raymond Aron, *Les articles de politique internationale dans Le Figaro de 1947 à 1977*, 2 vols. (Paris: Editions du Fallois, 1997).

[7] I refer here to René Rémond's typology of the French right in René Rémond, *Les droites aujourd'hui* (Paris: L'Audibert, 2005).

[8] On this see especially Raymond Aron, *Mémoires* (Paris: Julliard, 1983), pp. 731–50 (Epilogue).

to what they consider his legacy. Even if his direct influence on his disciples has often been overstated, it is evident that the constellation of figures that emerged around Aron was central to the rehabilitation of liberalism in French intellectual life. Many of those who either had close academic relationships with or were taught by Aron became prominent exponents of various facets of the liberal counter-narrative.

This, then, is not a chapter about Aron as such, but an examination of the ways in which he has been read, misread, interpreted, celebrated, memorialised and remembered. At the same time, this chapter is an introduction to many of the key protagonists in the so-called 'liberal revival'. This revival has generated a small, but stimulating secondary literature, the central argument of which is that, after many years in the wilderness, liberalism began to reappear as an intellectual reference point for a new generation of young intellectuals in the late 1970s.[9] This notion of revival rests on a negative reading of liberalism as an absent tradition within modern French political culture. Most historians now agree that liberalism in France all but disappeared under the Third Republic, as liberals and liberal 'values' were absorbed into an all-encompassing republican narrative. Until the 1940s, the strength of the French state's nation-building project, the paucity of an individual rights-based discourse, and the battle between the Republic and its 'illiberal' opponents on the extreme right and extreme left meant that there was scarcely any space for liberalism.[10] Things were little better after the end of the Second World War. The left – ideologically opposed to liberal capitalism, hostile to the Anglo-American economic axis and sceptical of the foundations of liberalism – provided little support for a liberal resurgence.[11] Nor was Gaullism a suitable home: presidential centralisation of power and an emphasis on French *grandeur* were anathema to a classic liberal sensibility.

By the late 1970s, however, the intellectual landscape was changing – and these changes were more obviously favourable to a resurgence of interest in liberalism. The partial conversion of the centre right to a more

---

[9] The idea of 'new liberal thought' in France has been most clearly articulated by Mark Lilla. See Mark Lilla, 'New Liberal Thought', in Kritzmann, *Columbia History of Twentieth-Century French Thought*, pp. 67–9, and Mark Lilla (ed.), *New French Thought: Political Philosophy* (London: Princeton University Press, 1994). For other perspectives, see Iain Stewart, 'France's Anti-68 Liberal Revival', in Chabal, *France since the 1970s*, and Audier, *La pensée anti-68*.

[10] For different perspectives on the failure of French liberalism, see Judt, *Past Imperfect*; Hayward, *Fragmented France*; Jaume, *L'individu effacé*; and Hazareesingh, *Political Traditions in Modern France*.

[11] On the peculiarities of France's liberal tradition, see Siedentop, 'Two Liberal Traditions'.

138 The liberal revival of the 1980s

liberal policy agenda and the precipitous collapse of Marxism opened new spaces for debate and discussion. One way in which French intellectuals filled the void was by turning to the Republic and the nation, but liberalism, too, experienced a revival. Whether in the form of the *nouveaux philosophes* – who toyed with a radical anti-totalitarian liberalism – or through a renewed interest in the work of Alexis de Tocqueville or François Guizot, the 1980s saw the rehabilitation of a number of liberal texts, ideas, concepts and figures. The fact that this occurred at the same time as the neo-republican turn is no coincidence: it was at this time that French intellectuals and academics were searching for new ways to understand contemporary history and politics. And, although the liberal revival had begun well before the collapse of communism in the late 1980s, the geopolitical transformations of the late 1980s gave liberalism an enormous boost. After more than a century in the wilderness, could it be that liberalism had finally made a durable impression on French politics?

Celebrating Raymond Aron, 1983–2010

The philosopher Paul Thibaud was no doubt correct when he argued, a few months after Aron's death in 1983, that 'in the context of the current grand return of liberal values [in France], Raymond Aron played much more the role of the spectator, or of a benchmark, than that of an active promoter'.[12] The vast majority of the eulogies to him that were published in 1984–5 stressed that Aron did not seek to influence those who surrounded him: in the words of the historian Alain Besançon, 'we were not disciples'.[13] Indeed, Aron had often been sceptical of projects – such as the journal *Contrepoint* – which were founded with the aim of promoting 'his' values and principles.[14] Nevertheless, Aron's anti-ideological stance should not obscure the fact that he had a profound influence on those who were taught by him at the Ecole Nationale d'Administration (1945–7) and Sciences Po, Paris (1948–54), as well as those who attended his now legendary seminar series at the EHESS in the 1970s.

---

[12] Paul Thibaud, 'L'oeil du cyclone: Raymond Aron', *Esprit* (May 1984), p. 59.
[13] Alain Besançon, 'Raymond Aron à l'oral', *Commentaire* (Vol. 8, No. 28–9, 1985), p. 74.
[14] He is reported to have told the journal's founder, Georges Liébert, 'Vous n'avez aucune chance. Mais essayez toujours!' The journal was founded in 1970 and dismantled in 1978–9. It was 'replaced' by *Commentaire* – a journal founded by Aron himself. On the genesis of *Contrepoint* and *Commentaire*, see Gwendal Châton, 'Désaccord parfait: le *Contrepoint* libéral dans la configuration intellectuelle des années soixante-dix', in Jean Baudouin and François Hourmant (eds.), *Les revues et la dynamique des ruptures*, (Rennes: Presses Universitaires de Rennes, 2007), pp. 131–64.

I shall deal below with two of the most concrete manifestations of the memorialisation of Aron in the form of the journal *Commentaire* (founded by Aron himself in 1978), and the work of the Institut Raymond Aron at the EHESS. I should like to begin, however, by looking more closely at the numerous commemorations and eulogies of Aron since his death. These reveal the extensive and influential networks that were developing between 'Aronians', despite their varied political and intellectual inclinations.

In many ways, the post-war French intellectual elite's attitude towards Aron was a good indicator of the changing political priorities of the age. In the immediate post-war years, he was the one of the most prominent critics of those intellectuals who decided to become 'fellow travellers' of the PCF. Later, he succeeded in antagonising a new generation of students when he published his pungent attack on the protests of 1968 in *La revolution introuvable* (1968), in which he famously cast students' revolutionary fantasies as a 'psychodrama'.[15] The distaste was mutual, with students in the late 1960s arguing that 'it is better to be wrong with Sartre than to be right with Aron' – in short, that it was better to stick with the principle and polemic of an intellectual like Sartre than descend to the level of Aron's pragmatic empiricism.[16] Nevertheless, Aron was already widely recognised within his profession by this time. His articles in *Le Figaro* were widely read by the political elites and, in 1970, he was appointed to the sociology chair at the Collège de France – the pinnacle of France's intellectual establishment. But it was not until the publication of his *Mémoires* in summer 1983, and his death a few months later, that his influence became clear. Suddenly, there was an enormous outpouring of goodwill, with many former enemies lining up alongside his most faithful followers to pay tribute. François Furet's glowing assessment of the *Mémoires* as the testimony to an 'successful life [*existence réussie*]' was emblematic of the acclaim that accompanied the release of Aron's last book.[17] The numerous obituaries that followed over the next few months confirmed Aron's canonisation. Even those publications that had traditionally been hostile to him – such as the Communist daily *L'Humanité* – had kind words for their 'loyal adversary'. Serge July, in left-wing daily *Libération*, bemoaned the loss of 'France's number one professor', while

---

[15] Raymond Aron, *Révolution Introuvable* (Paris: Fayard, 1968).
[16] The origins of this famous phrase are unclear. The founder of *Nouvel Observateur*, journalist Jean Daniel, claimed in 1987 that it originated in a statement he made about Sartre and Aron in the aftermath of May 1968. J. Daniel, 'Camus contre l'air du temps', *Nouvel Observateur* (17 April 1987).
[17] François Furet, 'Quand Aron raconte notre histoire', *Nouvel Observateur* (2 September 1983).

the sociologist's former colleagues at *Le Figaro* and *L'Express* brought together a number of Aron's former friends and students to write about their memories of him.[18]

This commemorative wave reached its apogee with the publication of a special edition of *Commentaire* in winter 1984, which included over 250 pages of testimonies and homages to Aron. We shall look more closely below at the role of *Commentaire* as a vector for French liberal thought in the period after Aron's death, but, even taken in isolation, the issue devoted to Aron provides a revealing picture of 'Aronians' throughout the academy and beyond in the early 1980s. Among the fifty-two homages, different generational strands emerge. The first is made up of those who knew Aron as a young man – the generation born between 1890 and 1920. These usually have a more personal tone, describing Aron before or during his time at the Ecole Normale Supérieure.[19] Yet, even in these earlier texts, there is a sense that he was always *right* – a trope that appears time and again as his followers celebrated his political commitments. Thus the former diplomat, and expert on the Soviet Union, Jean Laloy praises Aron for seeing into the future: 'Aron began a battle [against communism] that has not yet been won out in the field. Intellectually, on the other hand, the battle is won and, in France, this owes much to Aron.'[20]

This vision of Aron as a member of an enlightened intellectual vanguard becomes even more apparent if we look at the second group of testimonies, written by members of the generation who came of age after the war, many of whom were students of Aron in some form or another. The philosopher Julien Freund, whose doctoral thesis was directed by Aron, describes how he turned to him after Jean Hyppolite declined to supervise him. The quotation Freund chooses to highlight Aron's intellectual rectitude is revealing: he is reported to have told Hyppolite that 'you prefer to destroy yourself rather than recognise that politics obeys rules that do not correspond to your ideal norms'.[21] Not only was Aron historically 'correct', he appears here as an intellectual of unimpeachable integrity, a view of him that was to become powerfully embedded by the

[18] 'Premier Prof de France', *Liberation* (18 October 83). For a contemporary critical perspective on the way Aron was being remembered, see Philippe Raynaud, 'La mort de Raymond Aron', *Esprit* (May 1984).
[19] See for instance, Pierre Bertaux, 'Amitiés normaliennes', *Commentaire* (Vol. 8, No. 28–9, 1985), pp. 13–15.
[20] Jean Laloy, 'Un libéral passionné', *Commentaire* (Vol. 8, No. 28–9, 1985), p. 37. Laloy, born in 1912, died in 1994; he was elected to the Académie des sciences morales et politiques in 1975.
[21] Julien Freund, 'Raymond Aron: Directeur de thèse', *Commentaire* (Vol. 8, No. 28–9, 1985), p. 57.

1990s. Perhaps inevitably, the testimonies of this second generation focus heavily on his qualities as a teacher. His seminar series at the EHESS (1968–77) features prominently in the texts of several writers. The historian Alain Besançon – who would become a member of the senior editorial board of *Commentaire* in 1986 – offers a three-page eulogy to the seminars as an example of Aron's remarkable capacities of synthesis and critique, while Jean Baechler – who was on the general editorial board of *Commentaire* from its inception in 1978 – describes the seminars as 'a work of art'.[22] Consistent with many of the other texts, Aron's students stress that he did not seek to create 'disciples'. But there is little doubt that, to quote Besançon, a *bande d'aroniens* had emerged by the early 1980s. According to him, this group was composed of Jean Baechler, Jean-Claude Casanova, Annie Kriegel, Eugène Fleischmann, Ion Elster, Martin Malia, Pierre Manent, Raymonde Moulin, Kostas Papaioannou, François Bourricaud, Raymond Boudon, Georges Liebert and Jerôme Dumoulins.[23] Almost all of these figures have had an important influence on French political thought in the decades since Aron's death.

To take but a few examples of those whose texts appear in the commemorative issue, Baechler and Besançon went on to have successful academic careers, and were both elected to the Académie des sciences morales et politiques in the 1990s. The economist Jean-Claude Casanova, who co-founded *Commentaire* with Aron and wrote for *Le Monde* and *L'Express* in the 1980s and 90s, became involved with a number of think tanks (such as the Fondation Saint-Simon, founded by François Furet) and government commissions (such as the Commission économique et sociale in 1994–2004). The sociologists Raymond Boudon and François Bourricaud – both of whom claimed a liberal and 'Aronian' heritage – collaborated in the 1980s and 90s in their influential elaboration of 'methodological individualism' and a French form of rational choice theory.[24] Finally, there was Pierre Manent, who was Aron's assistant at the Collège de France and, in the commemorative issue, reproduced a piece published a year earlier entitled 'Raymond

---

[22] Besançon, 'Raymond Aron à l'oral', pp. 74–6. Jean Baechler, 'Maître et disciple', *Commentaire* (Vol. 8, No. 28–9, 1985), pp. 62–5.

[23] Besançon, 'Raymond Aron à l'oral', p. 74.

[24] In his eulogy, Bourricaud writes that 'Aron fut celui qui m'aida à ouvrir un peu les fenêtres d'une France qui, dans l'immédiat après-guerre, restait claquemurée'. François Bourricaud, 'Entre 1947 et 1950', *Commentaire* (Vol. 8, No. 28–9, 1985), p. 34. Boudon chooses to write an analysis of Aron's sociological thought rather than a straightforward eulogy. Raymond Boudon, 'Raymond Aron et la pensée sociologique: le non-dit des *Etapes*', *Commentaire* (Vol. 8, No. 28–9, 1985), p. 222–5. On Boudon's relationship to 'liberalism' see Raymond Boudon, 'Pourquoi les intellectuels n'aiment pas le libéralisme', *Commentaire* (Vol. 26, No. 104, Winter 2003), pp. 773–85.

Aron, éducateur' in which he argued for Aron's place alongside other great European liberals of the twentieth century.[25] Over the next two decades, Manent would prove instrumental in rehabilitating liberalism in French academia with books such as *Une histoire intellectuelle du libéralisme* (1987) and his anthology of liberal texts entitled *Les libéraux* (1986).[26] These attempted to bring together, interpret and make accessible the work of liberal thinkers such as Adam Smith, François Guizot and Alexis de Tocqueville. Despite his diverse career – and, notably, his recent growing interest in the nation state as a historical and philosophical concept – Manent is still today seen as one of Aron's most prominent followers.[27]

Beyond this restricted inner circle of 'Aronians' described by Besançon, there were a number of other contributors to *Commentaire*'s commemorative issue who carried forward what the philosopher and writer François George described in his homage as Aron's 'style' and 'method'.[28] One such figure was the political scientist Philippe Raynaud, whose contribution came in the form of an essay comparing Aron and Max Weber.[29] Raynaud became a member of the general editorial board of *Commentaire* in 1986 and since then he has published widely on French and German philosophy and has regularly reiterated his commitment to liberalism in the pages of *Commentaire* and elsewhere.[30] The same is true of Pierre Hassner, the specialist in international relations, whose contribution to the commemorative issue also appeared in the form of an essay rather than a eulogy.[31] Aron supervised Hassner's doctoral thesis and the student became a willing Aronian in the 1990s and 2000s. He has frequently cited his teacher as a major influence on his

[25] Pierre Manent, 'Raymond Aron, éducateur', *Commentaire* (Vol. 8, No. 28–9, 1985), p. 155–68. On his close relationship to Aron, see for instance P. Bouretz, 'Pierre Manent', *Nouvel Observateur* (14 December 1989).
[26] Pierre Manent, *Les libéraux* (Paris: Hachette, 1986); Pierre Manent, *Histoire intellectuelle du libéralisme* (Paris: Calmann-Lévy, 1987).
[27] On Manent as Aron's 'disciple', see for instance Elisabeth Levy, 'Manent: libéral-patriote', *Le Point* (2 March 2006), and J. Saint Victor, 'Pierre Manent: avoir raison avec Aron', *Le Figaro* (11 October 2010). On Manent's growing interest in the nation state, see for instance Pierre Manent, 'La démocratie sans la nation', *Commentaire* (Vol. 19, No. 75, 1996), pp. 569–77.
[28] 'Si je suis devenu aronien, c'est au sens d'un style ou d'une méthode'. François George, 'Un trop bref dialogue', *Commentaire* (Vol. 8, No. 28–9, 1985), p. 111.
[29] Philippe Raynaud, 'Raymond Aron et Max Weber. Epistémologie des sciences sociales et rationalisme critique', *Commentaire* (Vol. 8, No. 28–9, 1985), pp. 213–22.
[30] See for instance Philippe Raynaud, 'Qu-est ce que le libéralisme?', *Commentaire* (Vol. 30, No. 118, 2007), pp. 325–36, and Philippe Raynaud, 'Les dilemmes du libéralisme', *Le Monde* (7 September 2007).
[31] Pierre Hassner, 'Aron et l'histoire du XXème siècle', *Commentaire* (Vol. 8, No. 28–9, 1985), pp. 226–34.

work and as his 'intellectual mentor [*maître d'hygiène intellectuelle*]'.[32] Moreover, he has regularly tried to show the value and pertinence of Aron's theory of international relations in the post-communist world.[33]

Aron's influence has also been felt in the world of economics. In particular, two contributors to the commemorative issue are worth highlighting: Thierry de Montbrial and Nicolas Baverez. In his homage, de Montbrial describes Aron as the intellectual figure of the twentieth century with the greatest 'depth and ... political coherence', and he praises his 'liberal values'.[34] Since the mid 1970s, de Montbrial has had a glittering career at the head of a number of governmental and non-governmental organisations, such as the highly regarded think tank Institut français des relations internationales (IFRI). He founded the economics department at the Ecole polytechnique in 1974, and taught there until 2009.[35] Along with Besançon, Baechler and Boudon, he was also elected to the Académie des sciences morales et politiques in the 1990s, and was the Académie's president in 2001.[36] Nicolas Baverez, who was born in 1961, represents the youngest generation of 'Aronians'. Like Hassner and Manent, he chose to submit a scholarly essay in memory of Aron and, like them, he has had a significant impact on French political life. He has become best known for his powerful criticisms of the 'French economic model' in his widely read essay *La France qui tombe* (2003), but he had already made a name for himself as the author of the first major biography of Aron in French, *Raymond Aron: un moraliste au temps des idéologues* (1993).[37] More generally, Baverez's liberal critique of the French state and his concern about 'decline' reflect some of Aron's concerns in his last works, notably *Plaidoyer pour une Europe décadente* (1977).[38] Given that he has been outspoken in his acknowledgement of Aron's influence, it is perhaps not surprising that

---

[32] For a recent portrait of Hassner, see Anne Muratori-Philip, 'Pierre Hassner, d'une rive à l'autre', *Le Figaro* (7 October 2003).

[33] On this see, for instance, Pierre Hassner, 'Raymond Aron et la philosophie des relations internationales', *Commentaire* (Vol. 31, No. 122, 2008), pp. 638–43.

[34] Thierry de Montbrial, 'Aron et l'action politique', *Commentaire* (Vol. 8, No. 28–9, 1985), p. 106.

[35] His reflections on almost four decades of teaching at Polytechnique were published as T. de Montbrial, 'La géopolitique entre guerre et paix', *Commentaire* (Vol. 33, No. 131, 2010), pp. 619–28.

[36] He was elected to the Académie in 1992. From 1973–8, de Montbrial was the head of the Centre d'analyses et préventions, set up by the French Foreign Ministry in 1973. Since 1979, he has been the head of the Institut français des relations internationales (IFRI), widely regarded as one of the most influential French think tanks in the world.

[37] Nicolas Baverez, *La France qui tombe* (Paris: Perrin, 2003); Baverez, *Raymond Aron*.

[38] Raymond Aron, *Plaidoyer pour l'Europe décadente* (Paris: Editions Robert Laffont, 1977). See also chapter 9 on the language of crisis in France.

some outside commentators have described him as the 'rising star of the new generation of Aronians'.[39]

Lastly, it is worth mentioning Aron's foreign connections, which were well represented in the commemorative volume. Given his thoroughgoing anti-communism, Aron was fêted by a number of dissident anti-communist east European intellectuals such as Branko Lazitch and François Fejtö. There were also glowing homages from the other side of the Atlantic. A number of scholars have noted Aron's close relationship with American neo-conservative ideologues of the post-war period, and it is therefore unsurprising to find a flattering obituary of Aron by Norman Podhoretz.[40] But Aron's friendships spanned the whole political spectrum of intellectuals – from the avowed anti-communist hawk Henry Kissinger, who wrote that 'no one had a greater intellectual influence on me than Raymond Aron', to the long-time expert in international relations at Harvard, Stanley Hoffmann.[41] The latter, in particular, was extremely influenced by Aron – as he admitted in another obituary of his teacher in the *New York Review of Books* in December 1983.[42] He has consistently been one of the United States' most prominent liberal commentators on global conflict and the changing dynamics of international relations, and has argued on numerous occasions for Aron's formative role for the discipline as a whole.[43]

Taken together, the list of contributors to *Commentaire's* commemorative issue on Raymond Aron is both formidable and ecumenical. A number of the French and foreign figures mentioned above have stood at very different points of the political spectrum, as well as in different fields. Yet, if this diversity is a testimony to Aron's exceptional breadth and intellectual open-mindedness, it should also remind us that those who gathered around Aron, especially towards the end of his career, went

---

[39] Gwendal Châton, 'La Libertée Retrouvée: Une histoire du libéralisme politique en France à travers les revues aroniennes 'Contrepoint' et 'Commentaire', unpublished PhD thesis, Université de Rennes-I: Faculté de Droit et de Sciences Politiques (2006), p. 634. I thank Gwendal Châton for sending me his thesis. On Baverez's position vis-à-vis Aron, see e.g. Nicolas Baverez, 'Raymond Aron face a Mai 68: l'effort pour comprendre, la passion d'agir', *Le Figaro* (14 May 1998).

[40] Norman Podhoretz, 'Combattre pour la liberté', *Commentaire* (Vol. 8, No. 28–9, 1985), pp. 130–1. On Aron's relationship to neo-conservative thought in the United States, see Justin Vaïsse, 'République impériale, démocratie impériale: Aron et les néoconservateurs', in Jean-Claude Casanova (ed.), *Raymond Aron et la démocratie au XXIe siècle* (Paris: Editions de Fallois, 2007).

[41] Henry Kissinger, 'My teacher', *Commentaire* (Vol. 8, No. 28–9, 1985), p. 129.

[42] Stanley Hoffmann, 'Raymond Aron, 1905–1983', *New York Review of Books* (8 December 83).

[43] Stanley Hoffmann, 'Raymond Aron and the Theory of International Relations', *International Studies Quarterly* (Vol. 29, No. 1, 1985), pp. 13–27.

on to make influential contributions to French political and intellectual life. This is evident if we look at two other institutions that, since 1984 have stood out in their (ongoing) attempts to 'do justice' to Aron's memory – and which have provided a home for Aron's followers. The first is the Société des amis de Raymond Aron, which was founded in 1985.[44] It was set up to preserve Aron's memory, and encourage the republication and archiving of his works and correspondence. Until his death in 2009, its patron was the renowned anthropologist Claude Lévi-Strauss, who famously declared in an interview the day after Aron's death that 'Aron was a good man [*un esprit droit*], Sartre was a fake [*esprit faux*]'.[45] The president of the society is Jean-Claude Casanova and its executive committee was at the time of writing composed of Pierre Manent, Nicolas Baverez, Pierre Hassner and the sociologist of poverty and social exclusion Serge Paugam. Through its 'Bulletins d'informations', it has offered a regular insight into the state of research into Aron since the early 1980s. Since 1997, it has extended its reach by endowing the Prix Raymond Aron, given to the best doctoral thesis on Aron in France or abroad.[46] Above all, however, it has been involved in organising Aron's archives. First under the direction of the historian Perrine Simon and, from 1986, the historian Elisabeth Dutartre, the Fonds Raymond Aron has become a comprehensive corpus of Aron's works, correspondence and manuscripts now housed at the Bibliothèque Nationale de France.[47]

The second institution, which has been intimately connected to the Société des amis de Raymond Aron, is the Centre d'études sociologiques et politiques Raymond Aron (CESPRA), formerly known as the Institut Raymond Aron. It was founded in November 1984 with the financial assistance of the EHESS and the Fondation Thyssen, and in characteristically Aronian fashion, this important research institution has reflected both the unity and the diversity of Aron's followers.[48] François Furet was

---

[44] 'Société des amis de Raymond Aron', *Commentaire* (Vol. 8, No. 31, 1985), p. 980. Société des amis de Raymond Aron, *Bulletin d'information – juin 1985* (Paris: Société des amis de Raymond Aron, 1985).

[45] Interview in the *Nouvel Observateur* (21 October 84) reproduced in C. Lévi-Strauss, 'Aron était un esprit droit', *Commentaire* (Vol. 8, No. 28–9, 1985), p. 122.

[46] Winners have included Daniel Mahoney (1999), Serge Audier (2001) and Gwendal Châton (2007). On the current state of the Fonds Raymond Aron, see Société des amis de Raymond Aron, *Bulletin d'information – septembre 2009* (Paris: Société des amis de Raymond Aron, 2009).

[47] Société des amis de Raymond Aron, *Bulletin d'information – juin 1987* (Paris: Société des amis de Raymond Aron, 1987). For details of the collection, see E. Dutartre (ed.), *Fonds Raymond Aron: Inventaire* (Paris: Editions BNF, 2007).

[48] For a summary of the Institut's activites in 1984–6, see Perrine Simon, 'Raymond Aron dans l'histoire du siècle', *Vingtième Siècle* (No. 9, 1986), pp. 124–6.

the Institut's first president until 1992, when the research centre merged with the politics section of the Centre d'études transdisciplinaires Sociologie, Anthropologie, Politique (CETSAP) under the direction of the philosopher Claude Lefort. The joint research unit – now under its new name – was reabsorbed into the EHESS, and expanded its activities. Between 1992 and 2005, it was headed by Pierre Rosanvallon, and since then has been directed by Patrice Gueniffey (2005–9), Olivier Remaud (2009–10) and Philippe Urfalino (2010–). In the next chapter we shall look in more detail at how Furet and Rosanvallon's intellectual interests and institutional networks contributed to certain aspects of the liberal revival but, right from its inception, the Institut Raymond Aron combined Furet's research interests and an Aronian approach.

This is evident in Furet's summary of the Institut's research orientations between 1984 and 1988: the three research topics during that period were 'The history of the subject', 'The study of the philosophical and historical foundations of modern democracy' and 'Research on the political history of the French Revolution'.[49] As Furet put it in 1988,

These fields of research are both broad and diverse. Their unity is derived, not so much from the period under consideration, which is European history from the seventeenth to the nineteenth century, but from the re-examination of the classic question of the *origins of modern individualism*.[50]

These research interests have subsequently evolved, but this core interest in the 'political' and the need for a critical appraisal of the relation between individualism and modernity has continued to define the orientation of the Institut and subsequently the CESPRA. Thus the choice of research themes for the period 2008–12 included 'Political history and political philosophy: forms, regimes, institutions', which quite explicitly set out to 'extend the original vocation of the Centre Aron' by looking at 'new perspectives ... that examine in particular the workings of democracy, the political organisation of the world and new strategic rationalities'.[51]

Not surprisingly, this unity of purpose has led to a convergence of research interests among the CESPRA's members. Its most prominent figures today include some of those who were part of the original 'bande d'aroniens' – such as Pierre Manent and Philippe Raynaud – and other well-known scholars such as Monique Canto-Sperber and Marcel

---

[49] François Furet, 'L'institut Raymond Aron', *Les Cahiers du Centre de Recherches Historiques* (No. 2, 1988).

[50] Furet, 'L'institut Raymond Aron' (emphasis added).

[51] 'Axes de recherches, 2008–12', available at ⟨http://cespra.ehess.fr/document.php?identifiant=axes, accessed 2 November 2010⟩.

Gauchet, both of whom have been associated with various attempts to rehabilitate liberalism in the contemporary French academy. In the case of Canto-Sperber – who was president of the Ecole Normale Supérieure (Ulm) from 2005 to 2012 – this has come in the form of work looking at the relationship between liberalism and the left.[52] In the case of Marcel Gauchet, whose vast corpus of work has also touched on many themes of interest to neo-republicans, it has come in the form of a critique of totalitarianism, extended reflections on Tocqueville and democracy, and research focusing on the relationship between religion, modernity and individualism.[53] Moreover, since the CESPRA is a research unit, it also houses doctoral students, many of whom have worked in greater depth on issues close to the Centre's research agenda. A good example of this younger generation is Emile Perreau-Saussine, who in 2000 completed a doctoral thesis on Alisdair Macintyre's critique of liberalism under Manent's supervision at the CESPRA.[54] He subsequently joined the general editorial board of *Commentaire* in 2004 and, despite leaving France to teach in the United Kingdom, had begun work on one of the Centre's major interests – the interaction between religion and modernity – until it was cut short by his untimely death in 2009.

Given the influence of many of the CESPRA's members, it is not surprising that it has been a controversial institution. Perry Anderson, in his survey of France's intellectual landscape published in 2004, claimed that the Institut had been Furet's fiefdom and 'a committed outpost of anti-totalitarian reflection', while Lindenberg branded a number of the CESPRA's most prominent members – especially Gauchet, Rosanvallon and Manent – as *nouveaux réactionnaires*.[55] Neither of these two criticisms fairly reflects the goal of the Centre. As we shall see in the next chapter, Furet's influence was vital in defining the orientations of the liberal revival; and it is certainly true that many of the CESPRA's members distanced themselves from the left in the 1980s. However, it would be more accurate to say that the Centre's aim has always been to provide an intellectual forum for the development of a French form of 'political liberalism'. Broadly speaking, this has involved sustained reflection on

---

[52] Monique Canto-Sperber, *Le libéralisme et la gauche* (Paris: Hachette, 2008).

[53] Gauchet's career is complex. For his work on contemporary society, history and politics, see his collections of articles in Marcel Gauchet, *La condition politique* (Paris: Gallimard, 2005), and Marcel Gauchet, *La démocratie contre elle-même* (Paris: Gallimard, 2002), as well as extended interviews on his life in Marcel Gauchet, *La condition historique* (Paris: Gallimard, 2003).

[54] Emile Perreau-Saussine, *Alasdair Macintyre: une biographie intellectuelle: introduction aux critiques contemporaines du libéralisme* (Paris: Presses Universitaires de France, 2005).

[55] Perry Anderson, 'Dégringolade', *London Review of Books* (Vol. 26, No. 17, 2004), pp. 3–9. Lindenberg, *Le rappel à l'ordre, Enquête sur les nouveaux réactionnaires*.

the value (and limits) of democracy and individualism – often drawing on a 'neo-Tocquevillean' reading of the individual – and a critique of any form of totalitarianism or extremist politics.[56]

This spirit was well captured in an interview with Rosanvallon in 2002. Ironically, it was Rosanvallon who was in charge of the series in which Lindenberg's book was published.[57] When asked about Lindenberg's claims, he not only defended the publication of the book but also provided a concise insight into the contemporary role of the CESPRA:

> We live in an intellectual landscape that has indeed changed a great deal. The proximity of those of who were involved in the founding of the Centre Aron in the 1970s lay in two common interests: the critique of totalitarianism and the sense that traditional [political] ideas were exhausted, which necessitated a reappropriation of a liberal tradition. This explains the republication and reinterpretation of the works of Constant or Tocqueville. Twenty years later, this recovery project is complete and, even if it is never quite certain, the question of totalitarianism is behind us![58]

This was a clear acknowledgement of the Centre's vocation as an anti-totalitarian, liberal melting-pot. Even if Lindenberg's uncritical use of the term *réactionnaire* did not do justice to its diversity, it is clear that the CESPRA (and the Institut Raymond Aron before it) made a significant contribution to the so-called liberal revival. The commemoration of Aron's death acted as an institutional catalyst for this revival. Of course, the orientation of the CESPRA was not defined by Aron's legacy alone – notably, Lefort's work on democracy, the *lieu vide* ('empty space') and totalitarianism has been extremely influential. But Aron's legacy has remained a focal point for his followers. As one of his most vocal standard-bearers, Alain Besançon, put it in 2005,

> Today, all those who claim with pride the patronage [of Raymond Aron] form a sort of implicit club, in which we emphasise the qualities and habits that he exemplified in his life and work ... We do not all follow a single doctrine (Aron himself did not), but rather a discipline and respect for a certain kind of morality ... This was guided by one overriding commandment: to prioritise the truth.[59]

[56] On 'néo-tocquevillisme' and the rehabilitation of Tocqueville, see Serge Audier, *Tocqueville retrouvé: genèse et enjeux du renouveau tocquevillien français* (Paris: Editions EHESS/Vrin, 2004).

[57] The series is entitled 'La République des Idées'. For a further discussion of this series, see chapter 9.

[58] Jean Birnbaum, 'Il faut refaire le bagage d'idees de la democratie française', *Le Monde* (22 November 2002).

[59] Alain Besançon, 'Pourquoi nous aimions tant Raymond Aron', *Commentaire* (Vol. 28, No. 110, 2005), p. 476.

There have been few clearer descriptions of the long – and supposedly 'non-ideological' – shadow Aron has cast over his disciples.

Securing the liberal revival: the journal *Commentaire*

If the Institut Raymond Aron allowed the *bande d'aroniens* to come into contact with and influence numerous other members of France's intellectual world, so, too, did the journal *Commentaire*. Founded in 1978 by Aron himself, and edited by him until his death, it is not surprising that *Commentaire* has been the major publication most consistent in supporting an explicitly liberal political and intellectual agenda since the 1980s. We have already seen how it played an important role in commemorating Aron's life and work, but its liberalism has also been reflected in its political positions and the platform it has provided, in particular for economists and sociologists who have been critical of France's excessive reliance on statist economic policy.

The most comprehensive study of *Commentaire* is without a doubt the work of the political scientist Gwendal Châton. Despite the fact that he does not look in detail at the period after 1992, his reconstruction of the genealogy and trajectory of the journal offers a valuable insight into the 'prehistory' of the liberal revival.[60] He traces the roots of *Commentaire* in the earlier and less successful journal *Contrepoint*, which had been inspired, but not endorsed, by Aron. It was out of the networks of contributors to *Contrepoint* that *Commentaire* was formed, this time with Aron's active participation. As Aron admitted himself in his very first article for the journal, the prospect of a left-wing government coming to power in 1978 in collaboration with the PCF had acted as a powerful incentive for the development of the journal.[61] Over the next few years, *Commentaire* would maintain this centrist, anti-communist line, especially after 1981 when Aron's fear of a Socialist and Communist coalition had come true. Throughout the 1980s, the journal provided a platform for criticisms of post-1968 *gauchisme* and offered a range of 'democratic' and 'liberal' solutions to contemporary France's most pressing problems.[62]

Of course, as Châton points out, Aron's direct influence on the journal was weak.[63] Rather, we should place *Commentaire* alongside the other

---

[60] See Châton, *La Libertée Retrouvée*.

[61] Raymond Aron, 'Incertitudes françaises', *Commentaire* (Vol. 1, No. 1, 1978), pp. 7–16.

[62] Iain Stewart strongly emphasises the anti-68 dimensions of *Commentaire* in Stewart, 'France's anti-68 liberal revival', in Chabal, *France since the 1970s*.

[63] Châton, *La Libertée Retrouvée*, p. 623.

commemorative efforts discussed above. Casanova made this quite clear in 1984 when he laid out the reasons for continuing to publish the journal despite its founder's death:

> We know ... that he would not have wanted this journal to disappear. Not so that a cult of personality could be organised around him. He would have hated such an idea. But rather so that his ideals could continue to be defended ... [above all] the need to understand the world and love liberty for itself.[64]

After Aron's death, the purpose of *Commentaire* was for the *bande d'aroniens* to continue the 'fight' against the forces of illiberalism that Aron had identified and condemned. This is not to hide the great diversity among the journal's contributors. The editor Jean-Claude Casanova – whom Châton describes as 'an English-style liberal, very anti-statist and anti-Jacobin, a centrist liberal and an advocate of a federal Europe' – stands in contrast to those like Schnapper and Manent, who have been sceptical of the European project and keen to see the rehabilitation of the nation state.[65] Nevertheless, their commitment to a diverse liberal project has been consistent to the extent that *Commentaire* has become a mature part of the French political space and an influential voice for an Aronian 'political liberalism'.

This voice has taken many forms. One of the ways in which *Commentaire* has tried to remain true to its mission is by publishing hundreds of articles since the early 1980s that have looked explicitly at liberal thinkers and at the concepts and meanings of liberalism. Many of these have appeared in the series 'Les Classiques de la Liberté', which was inaugurated in the journal's second issue in 1978. By the editors' own admission, the series was to be 'devoted to the great figures of liberalism' such as 'Gibbon, Voltaire, Kant, Condorcet, Taine, Elie Halévy ... '.[66] In 1981 the editors reinforced this claim: 'From the very start, *Commentaire* has been attached to the study of the foundations and ambiguities of liberalism.'[67] In some cases, the 'Classiques' series has featured reproductions of original or unpublished primary texts. More frequently, it has featured analyses of liberal political thought by historians and political scientists. In both cases, the accent has been on the contemporary value

---

[64] Jean-Claude Casanova, 'Pour Raymond Aron', *Commentaire* (Vol. 6, No. 24, Winter 1983), p. 700.

[65] Châton, *La Libertée Retrouvée*, p. 628.

[66] This one-paragraph introduction to the series was included as a header to A. Fabre-Luce, 'Benjamin Constant et ses partenaires', *Commentaire* (Vol. 1, No. 2, 1978), pp. 193–9.

[67] From the editorial introduction to Patrice Rolland, 'Equivoques du libéralisme: à propos de Benjamin Constant', *Commentaire* (Vol. 4, No. 15, 1981), pp. 411–19.

of liberal thought. Since the early 1980s, the range of 'liberal' thinkers covered has included Taine, Constant, Montesquieu, Renan, Friedrich Hayek, Aron himself (after his death) and, of course, Tocqueville. As a leader of the so-called 'Tocqueville revival', it is hardly surprising that *Commentaire* devoted a number of articles to his work, particularly in the early 1980s.[68] Indeed, the emphasis placed on nineteenth-century French liberals mirrored a renewed interest in this topic in French academia as a whole: with its 'Classiques' series, *Commentaire* put itself at the vanguard of this rediscovery of France's liberal heritage.

The 'Classiques' series – and the pages of *Commentaire* in general – also provided a platform for a number of figures whose work is already familiar to us. In addition to his role on the journal's senior editorial board, Manent, for instance, has been a regular contributor to the series. His articles have shown a consistent interest in the fate of liberalism – from a glowing review of Gauchet's edition of Constant's writings in 1980 to his reflections on liberalism and modernity in 2008.[69] Typical of his interventions was an influential article published in 1986, in which Manent reflected positively on the emerging liberal consensus, especially after the right's victory in the recent legislative elections:

The significance of the current liberal revival ... goes beyond the political and economic policies it has inspired. Today, it is liberalism that provides the conceptual tools with which Europeans and Americans formulate the problems of social life: it is liberalism that sets the tone.[70]

He goes on to suggest that, while this liberalism resurgence poses certain challenges, 'liberals are right, even if their reasons are not always good'.[71] As Châton points out, Manent's increasing interest in the nation state has given his liberalism a 'Gaullist' sensibility, but there is no denying that his association with the journal has reinforced his commitment to

---

[68] See in particular the dossier 'Alexis de Tocqueville', featuring articles by Alain Peyrefitte and Raymond Aron, and a text by Tocqueville, in *Commentaire* (Vol. 3, No. 10, 1980), pp. 280–6; François Furet, 'Le système conceptual de la Démocratie en Amérique', *Commentaire* (Vol. 3, No. 12, 1980), pp. 605–14; Jean-Claude Lamberti, 'Tocqueville et les deux démocraties', *Commentaire* (Vol. 5, No. 19, 1982), pp. 476–84; Jean-Claude Lamberti, 'Tocqueville et la constitution de 1848', *Commentaire* (Vol. 7, No. 25, 1984), pp. 141–52; François Furet, 'Quinet et Tocqueville: un dialogue posthume à propos de l'Ancien Régime', *Commentaire* (Vol. 7, No. 26, 1984), pp. 341–51.
[69] Pierre Manent, 'Aux origines du libéralisme: Benjamin Constant', *Commentaire* (Vol. 3, No. 11, 1980), pp. 483–90. Pierre Manent, 'Le philosophe et l'Etat', *Commentaire* (Vol. 31, No. 121, 2008), pp. 155–63.
[70] Pierre Manent, 'Situations du libéralisme', *Commentaire* (Vol. 8, No. 35, Autumn 1986), p. 388.
[71] Manent, 'Situations du libéralisme', p. 396.

liberalism.[72] As well as Manent, a number of other commentators have shown their political and intellectual colours in *Commentaire* since the early 1980s. Boudon, Furet, Besançon, Baechler, Perreau-Saussine: all have contributed to an eclectic discussion about the historical roots and continuing value of liberalism to contemporary French society.

This has been augmented by outside voices: one of *Commentaire*'s biggest coups was to be the first to publish in French Fukuyama's controversial essay on the 'end of history' in late 1989.[73] Predictably, given the strength of the Hegelian tradition in twentieth-century French thought, the fact that Fukuyama's reading of Hegel was heavily influenced by that of Kojève and the omnipresence of history in the form of the bicentennial of the French Revolution, the article provoked strong reactions.[74] The next three issues included more than twenty responses from French and foreign scholars, many of which were favourable to the thrust of Fukuyama's piece but hostile to its methodology, implications or (mis)use of Hegel. Thus despite significant reservations Hassner believed Fukuyama's thesis to be 'more right than wrong', while the journalist and philosopher Jean-François Revel, who was one of post-war France's most significant liberal thinkers, announced that 'I am in complete agreement with Francis Fukuyama's thesis'.[75] Others were more cautious, or even hostile, notably Besançon and the conservative philosopher Alain-Gérard Slama.[76] Either way, by publishing Fukuyama and his critics, *Commentaire* placed itself at the heart of the emerging liberal-democratic debate of the late 1980s.

Not long after the 'end of history' moment in the early 1990s, what optimism had existed in the pages of *Commentaire* began to evaporate. By the twentieth anniversary edition in 1998, the majority of those writing were bemoaning a generalised 'melancholy' (Raynaud), 'decadence' (Baverez), 'French illness' (Jacques Lesourne) or even, to use Slama's words, the 'crisis of French happiness'.[77] We shall see later how this

---

[72] '[Manent] est plus proche d'une sensibilité "gaulliste au sens large".' Châton, *La liberté retrouvée*, p. 532.

[73] Francis Fukuyama, 'La fin de l'histoire', *Commentaire* (Vol. 22, No. 50, 1989), pp. 457–70.

[74] On this, see especially Descombes, *Le même et l'autre*. I am also grateful for the comments of Adam Tooze during a seminar course entitled 'The End of History: from Kojève to Fukuyama', held in Cambridge in 2006–7.

[75] Pierre Hassner, 'Fin de l'histoire ou fin d'un cycle?', *Commentaire* (Vol. 21, No. 47, 1989), pp. 473–6. Jean-François Revel, 'Raison pure et raison pratique', *Commentaire* (Vol. 21, No. 48, 1989), pp. 669–74.

[76] Alain-Gérard Slama, 'Le triomphe de l'idée', *Commentaire* (Vol. 22, No. 49, 1990), pp. 78–81. Alain Besançon, 'Le drame est encore devant nous', *Commentaire* (Vol. 21, No. 47, 1989), pp. 476–8.

[77] These articles were published in *Commentaire* (Vol. 20, No. 81, 1998), pp. 5–137.

discourse of crisis took hold among France's liberal critics in the 1990s, and examine its roots in a liberal pessimist tradition, but here we can simply note how *Commentaire* acted as a vector for this 'declinism'. In the same way that Aron's later work was marked by a deep sense of pessimism about the future of Europe, even as it was ridding itself of totalitarianism, it seemed that the *bande d'aroniens* who led *Commentaire* were unable to bask for long in the triumph of liberal values in 1989–91. Still, pessimism notwithstanding, *Commentaire*'s commitment to liberalism has remained consistent. This was succinctly reaffirmed in a 'Libéralisme' section in the thirtieth anniversary edition in 2008. Alongside Manent's piece on liberalism, modernity and the state mentioned above, there was an article by Gil Delannoi on the present-day meaning of the word 'liberal', and three other articles on Pascal, Châteaubriand and Rémusat.[78] This mix perfectly encapsulated the journal's original vocation, which was to restore to prominence the (predominantly French) founders of liberalism, and extend their relevance into contemporary politics.

But *Commentaire*'s liberalism has not only been expressed in terms of political philosophy and French history. The journal has also provided a platform for economists. Already by 1988, outside observers had noticed the extent to which 'the world of economics has become increasingly prominent in "generalist" journals that hitherto focused on politics or the humanities'.[79] *Commentaire* was no exception to this trend, and several names stand out in the journal's attempts to give a fair hearing to economic problems and policy. So, for instance, the Johns-Hopkins-based Hungarian economist Béla Balassa was commissioned to write careful assessments of the French economy every year from 1978 until his death in 1991. Following a broadly free-market approach, he argued on numerous occasions that France's lack of competitiveness, slow economic growth and high corporate tax burden would be detrimental to the French economy. This led him to criticise severely the first years of the Mitterrand presidency, while looking more favourably on the reforms led by the right in 1986–8 and by the left, under Michel Rocard's tutelage, in 1988–93.[80]

These same criticisms were echoed by French scholars. Two of the most emblematic economists to write in the pages of *Commentaire* have

---

[78] These articles were published in *Commentaire* (Vol. 30, No. 131, 2008), pp. 151–98.

[79] Jean-Luc Pouthier, 'Du Débat à Commentaire: quand les patrons sont de la revue', *Nouvel Observateur* (3 November 1988).

[80] Béla Balassa, 'Après cinq ans. Bilan de la politique économique socialiste', *Commentaire* (Vol. 8, No. 33, 1986), pp. 66–76; Béla Balassa, 'L'économie française à l'aube du nouveau septennat', *Commentaire* (Vol. 10, No. 42, 1988), pp. 420–9; Béla Balassa, 'L'économie politique de Rocard', *Commentaire* (Vol. 13, No. 54, 1991), pp. 307–15.

been Christian Stoffaës and Paul Mentré, both members of the general and senior editorial boards respectively. Stoffaës is a *polytéchnicien* and has been an *haut fonctionnaire* in the Corps des Mines, the Industry Ministry and, more recently, at Electricité de France (EDF). He summed up his attitudes towards liberal economic change in the tenth anniversary edition of *Commentaire* in 1988, when he reflected positively on the end of the 'Keynesian consensus' and the French 'taming of liberal ideology'.[81] Since then, he has continued to show an interest in the fate of liberalism (and anti-liberalism) in various publications, and he is a prominent member of the influential think tank Le Cercle des économistes.[82] Another *polytéchnicien* and *haut fonctionnaire* in the Finance Ministry, Mentré is best known for his book *Gulliver enchaîné, ou Comment déréglementer l'économie* (1982), the first chapter of which was reproduced in *Commentaire* in the year of its publication.[83] In the excerpt he suggested that what the French economy desperately needs is a 'liberation of its productive forces' alongside lower taxes and reduced state intervention. A few years later, in 1987, he wrote admiringly of the 'Thatcherite revolution' in Britain and warned of a 'return of the myths of the old left' if the PS and Mitterrand were to be re-elected in 1988.[84] In 1992, he wrote a glowing assessment of privatisation in Britain and elsewhere, and he reiterated his message of privatisation and competitiveness in a 2002 article addressed to the newly elected right-wing government of Jean-Pierre Raffarin.[85]

Alongside these two noteworthy figures, the benefits of free enterprise, competition and economic growth have been developed by others on the editorial board. Baverez, for instance, lent his support to Sarkozy's presidential campaign in 2007 on the grounds that he was the only leader who could embody the 'reforming' spirit necessary to implement a liberal economic agenda. Once Sarkozy was elected, Baverez explained his victory as a reflection of French voters' enthusiasm for an 'ambitious programme of modernisation that combines the restoration of political

[81] Christian Stoffaës, 'Apprivoiser le libéralisme', *Commentaire* (Vol. 10, No. 41, 1988), p. 46.
[82] See for instance the edited volume Christian Stoffaës et al. (eds.), *Psychanalyse de l'antilibéralisme: les Française ont-ils raison d'avoir peur?* (Paris: Saint-Simon, 2006).
[83] Paul Mentré, *Gulliver enchaîné, ou Comment déréglementer l'économie* (Paris: Table Ronde, 1982). Paul Mentré, 'Les trois corbeaux ou le dilemme de l'économie française', *Commentaire* (Vol. 4, No. 19, 1982), pp. 432–6.
[84] Paul Mentré, 'Les politiques économiques libérales: bilan d'une décennie', *Commentaire* (Vol. 9, No. 41, 1988), pp. 276–83.
[85] Paul Mentré, 'Les privatizations. Bilan et perspectives', *Commentaire* (Vol. 14, No. 60, 1992), pp. 861–70. Paul Mentré, 'La politique économique du gouvernement Raffarin', *Commentaire* (Vol. 24, No. 99, 2002), pp. 619–24.

authority with economic and social liberalisation'.[86] Thus, almost thirty years after *Commentaire* was founded, we find one of its most prominent economic commentators still endorsing an avowedly liberal economic and political agenda – and this despite the widespread critique of 'neoliberalism' that emerged in the 1990s in the United States and Europe. There could be few better examples of *Commentaire*'s sustained and passionate commitment to liberalism. As we saw in the reception of Fukuyama's piece, this liberalism has not been a unified ideology but, in whatever form, it has had a reliable and influential platform in the pages of Jean-Claude Casanova's journal.

A mature French liberalism at last?

One of the clearest signs of the success of the liberal revival among France's intellectual elite was the growing number of liberal 'fellow travellers' in the 1980s. In the world of France's journals alone, two other influential publications helped to bring to prominence many of the themes championed by the *bande d'aroniens*. The first was *Le Débat*. Founded in 1980 by Pierre Nora and Marcel Gauchet, the journal has been at least as influential as *Commentaire*, if not more. Despite Aron's initial hostility to the journal when it was founded – Aron is said to have seen it as a direct competitor – *Le Débat* has contributed some important elements to the liberal revival. Less obviously political than *Commentaire*, and focused more on history and literature than economics, *Le Débat* has nonetheless reflected the increasing liberalisation of intellectual life. It has done so above all by endorsing an explicitly 'new' form of politics that would transcend the divisions between socialist left and Gaullist right.[87] It aimed to offer a 'neutral' forum for the discussion of contemporary issues – such as the future of the welfare state – and, since its inception, it has steered clear of any overt political affiliations. Unsurprisingly, this moderation has often proved the ideal environment for those whose ideas we have examined in this chapter, not least Gauchet himself, but also such figures as François Furet and the economist Alain Minc. Unlike *Commentaire*, however, *Le Débat* has not focused solely on liberals and liberalism, especially given Nora's own interests in the neo-republican turn. It has also given a voice to prominent neo-republicans such as Régis

---

[86] Nicolas Baverez, 'L'année du réveil français', *Commentaire* (Vol. 29, No. 119, Autumn 2007), p. 701.

[87] On Nora's vision for *Le Débat*, see Pierre Nora, 'Le Débat', *Le Débat* (No. 1, 1980), p. 1. Nora discusses Aron's reaction to *Le Débat* in Pierre Nora, 'Continuons "Le Débat"!', *Nouvel Observateur* (28 September 1995). See also Dominique Dhombres, 'Un adolescent en pleine forme', *Le Monde* (3 July 1998).

Debray, Alain Finkielkraut, Christian Jelen and Hervé Le Bras. This is a reminder that the republican and liberal revivals had common intellectual roots in the reconfiguration of the intellectual landscape of the 1970s. It was, as we shall see in subsequent chapters, perfectly possible for individual scholars like Gauchet or Manent to absorb and engage with both of these emerging political languages in their work.

The second journal to participate actively in the liberal revival was *Esprit*. A much older publication, founded by Emmanuel Mounier in 1932 and with roots in the Catholic 'personalism' of the inter-war years, the journal has already been the subject of a number of historical studies.[88] All of these agree that under the stewardship of Jean-Marie Domenach (1956–76), Paul Thibaud (1976–89) and Olivier Mongin (1989–), the journal became an increasingly prominent voice for the anti-totalitarian 'second left'. As the editors themselves put it in a recent history of *Esprit*, '[the journal was] continuously a part of the anti-totalitarian front'.[89] So, while *Esprit* was less explicitly liberal than *Commentaire*, its commitment to the anti-totalitarian movement and its attachment in the 1980s and 90s to what Winock describes as 'the principles of political liberalism and democracy' led to a sustained convergence with *Commentaire*. This has been reflected in a vigorous engagement with some key debates that began in *Commentaire* – notably those surrounding Fukuyama and the 'decline of culture' – as well as the occasional (cautious) homage to *Commentaire* and the work of some members of its editorial board.[90]

If the intellectual convergence between these three journals was clear as early as 1980, their symbolic reunion came in summer 1986, when *Commentaire* was invited to participate in a week of debates and discussions at the prestigious 'Rencontres de Pétrarque' at the Féstival de Radio-France in Montpellier, alongside journalists from *Le Débat, Esprit* and *La liberté de l'esprit*. The topics covered included the fate of democracy, the role of religion in contemporary society and the

---

[88] The most comprehensive histories of *Esprit* are Michel Winock, *Histoire politique de la revue Esprit* (Paris: Seuil, 1975), and Goulven Boudic, *Esprit, 1944–1982: les métamorphoses d'une revue* (Paris: Editions de l'IMHC, 2005). For a summary, see Michel Winock, 'Esprit', in Kritzmann (ed.), *Columbia History of Twentieth-Century French Thought*, pp. 699–702.

[89] D. Lindenberg et al., *Esprit, 1932–2002: une revue dans l'histoire* (Paris: Editions Esprit, 2002), p. 61.

[90] Particularly indicative of this kind of 'cautious homage' is Paul Thibaud's contribution to *Commentaire*'s 10th anniversary volume in 1988. Paul Thibaud, 'Rendre plus sobre', *Commentaire* (Vol. 10, No. 41, 1988), p. 23. See also, for instance, the cautious but broadly positive reviews of works by Pierre Manent and Nicolas Baverez in the pages of *Esprit*: Olivier Mongin, 'Commentaire et le liberal catholicisme', *Esprit* (September, 1988), pp. 120–2, and Olivier Mongin, 'Nicolas Baverez: A consommer avec modération', *Esprit* (November, 2003), pp. 163–5.

transformation of the French intellectual landscape in the 1970s and 80s.[91] The message was clear: *Commentaire* now belonged to the political mainstream. As Raynaud put it in an interview with Châton in 2005,

There was a moment, which corresponds roughly to the Rencontres de Pétrarque in 1986, when it is was possible to feel ... that we were entering a new phase in the liberation of thought and expression, in which one could talk reasonably and agree on many things, while still diverging on political questions.[92]

This sense of a flourishing liberal revival echoed throughout the political space by the late 1980s.[93] Aron would no doubt have been surprised to read the editor of *Esprit*, Olivier Mongin, arguing in 1988 that 'it is something of a paradox that French intellectual life [today] suffers from an excess of agreement and consensus – something that would have been unimaginable only a few years ago'.[94] But he would also have had to recognise that this consensus crystallised around his legacy and that French liberalism of the 1980s was built in his shadow.[95]

[91] See 'Les Rencontres de Pétrarque', *Commentaire* (Vol. 8, No. 34, 1986), p. 382.
[92] Raynaud in an interview in November 2005. Quoted in Châton, *La liberté retrouvée*, p. 519.
[93] Indeed, the virulence with which the liberal revival was attacked in the 1990s, above all in the idea of a *pensée unique* or *pensée tiède*, was indicative of its success. On this see, for instance, L. Bonelli, 'Les revues, metronomes de la vie intellectuelle', *Le Monde Diplomatique* (April–May 2009).
[94] Mongin, 'Commentaire et le libéral catholicisme', p. 120.
[95] For contemporary approaches and attitudes to Aron and his legacy, see for instance a broadcast on France Culture, entitled 'Aron à tort ou à raison', in *Radio Libre* (15 March 2003). The invited guests were Nicolas Baverez, Pierre Hassner, Jean-Claude Casanova, François George, Jacques Julliard, Albert Palle and Yves de Belleville.

7 Rewriting Jacobinism: François Furet, Pierre Rosanvallon and modern French history

Those who have been involved with a journal like *Commentaire* have usually been more than willing to describe themselves as liberals. For them, it is an honour to follow in the footsteps of Aron. However, as I suggested earlier, such a clear statement of intent is unusual. The heavy stigma attached to the term 'liberal' in France has meant that a majority of political and intellectual actors have avoided using the term in relation to their work or policies.[1] Thus, if we are to understand fully the extensive and diverse liberal critique of contemporary France, we must look beyond the limited confines of those who explicitly use the term. One of the most effective ways of doing this is by examining the changing contours of French historiography. This echoes themes from the first part of the book, where I showed some of the ways in which *Les lieux de mémoire* and the return of politics in French historiography led to a renewed interest in the nation state and the Republic. I adopt a similar approach here in relation to two other highly influential historians: François Furet and Pierre Rosanvallon. I argue that their work has, in different ways, attempted to restore to modern French history a liberal sensibility. Often – although not always – this has entailed a subtle critique of neo-republican teleologies and historiographies. But, more than that, both these figures have sought to open new interpretations of French history that make space for France's liberal tradition.

An engagement with the life and work of Furet and Rosanvallon immediately raises another issue, namely the diverse origins of contemporary French liberalism. Whereas Aron – and many of his followers – were typecast as figures of the right, the same cannot be said of either of these two historians, whose left-wing credentials were well established early on in their careers. We cannot, therefore, reduce French liberalism simply to the dominant ideology of the French right. On the contrary, an

---

[1] For instance, Gauchet's awkward reply to the question 'êtes-vous libéral?' in an interview in 2003 reflects the uneasiness associated with the term in France. See Gauchet, *La condition historique*, pp. 340–2.

anti-communist and anti-totalitarian 'liberalism of the left' was critical to
the slow spread of liberal values in France. Even if later chapters will
show that this movement – which has often been called the 'second left' –
has had mixed success at the party-political level, its influence on
French intellectual life is unquestionable. Indeed, its importance represents one of the singularities of the French liberal revival. In both the
United Kingdom and the United States, for instance, the revival of
liberalism in the 1980s took on distinctly right-wing overtones. Ronald
Reagan and Margaret Thatcher and their advisors, who took intellectuals such as Friedrich Hayek and Milton Friedman as their ideological
reference points, brought to the fore a highly market-orientated interpretation of liberalism, emphasising a limited state, individual enterprise and the primacy of economic growth. This is not to say that this
was the only possible reading of a rich and contradictory liberal political
tradition, but it is the interpretation of liberalism that entered common
political parlance in the 1980s, often under the umbrella term of 'neo-
liberalism'.

Given this widespread perception of (neo-)liberalism as an overwhelmingly right-wing phenomenon, my claim that Furet and Rosanvallon are
liberals might appear misplaced. Neither their political affiliations nor
their political thought showed an affinity with market-oriented liberalism. But, within a broader and more contextually sensitive definition of
liberalism, the tension between their left-wing principles and their commitment to liberalism is easier to reconcile. By taking seriously the roots
of the French liberal revival in the post-war Marxist left, we are better
able to appreciate the differences between contemporary French liberalism and its Anglo-American counterpart. These differences lie in both
form and content. Whereas in the United Kingdom and the United
States neo-liberalism emerged from the right as a critique of the traditional conservative right and the statist left, in France we shall see how a
good deal of contemporary liberalism emerged as critique of the left *from*
the left. Thus Furet's journey from communist fellow-traveller to anti-
orthodox 'revisionism' – in his case, a bold new interpretation of the
French Revolution – was shared by many intellectuals of his generation
and became a central narrative of the liberal revival. Likewise, where
American and British neo-liberalism revolved heavily around economics
and economic theory, in France some of the fiercest battles were fought
over the writing of history. It is therefore hardly surprising that Furet and
Rosanvallon developed their liberal critiques through their interpretations of French history, especially given that battles over historiography
have often preceded and formed the basis of political engagement in
modern French history. Seen in this light, Furet's work on the French

Revolution and Rosanvallon's reinterpretation of nineteenth- and twentieth-century French history both offered means of reviving and legitimising French liberalism.

The melancholy liberalism of François Furet

Born in 1927 into a left-leaning republican and bourgeois Parisian family, François Furet was a talented student in school. After a brief period of involvement in the French Resistance at the end of the Second World War, he failed his entrance examination for the Ecole Normale Supérieure in 1946 and decided, after much soul-searching, not to try again. Instead, he enrolled at the Sorbonne and became increasingly interested in the study of history. Like many others of his generation, he contracted tuberculosis in 1950 and spent the following four years being treated for and recovering from the illness. Yet these were still productive years, during which he got involved in communist politics and discussed history with his peers (including Emmanuel Le Roy Ladurie and Maurice Agulhon). He eventually passed his *agrégation* examination in history in 1954 and, after a brief period of secondary school teaching, embarked on a life-long academic career. In retrospect, there were already some signs of dissent: his early setbacks had left a strong imprint on his relations with the academy and it was not until the 1980s and his prominence at the newly founded EHESS that he could consider himself part of the academic elite. This situation was exacerbated by the fact that he abandoned, unfinished, his *doctorat d'État* on the bourgeoisie under the Ancien Régime – something which his enemies would later hold against him. A victim rather than a beneficiary of the French educational system, the stage seemed to be set for him to break away from its orthodoxies.[2]

Not that this was especially apparent at the time. In fact, his trajectory resembled that of almost all of his colleagues. His increasingly dissident reading of the French Revolution notwithstanding, much of his early academic career revolved around the kind of straightforward statistical and empirical social history that had been championed by his mentor, the Marxist historian Ernest Labrousse. With hindsight, it is hard to imagine that the same scholar who transformed the historiography of the Revolution was, for most of the late 1960s and 70s, working on large-scale data studies and 'serial history' at the Sixth Section of the Ecole pratique des

---

[2] For a discussion of Furet's early years see Christophe Prochasson, *François Furet: les chemins de la mélancolie* (Paris: Stock, 2013), pp. 19–78.

hautes études (EPHE, which was to become the EHESS in 1975).[3] In politics, too, Furet's choices appeared conventional and he followed the vast majority of his contemporaries by joining the PCF in 1949. Although it is clear that, by 1958–9, he was no longer a thoroughgoing communist, the speed with which he left the confines of the Party and the extent of his commitment have remained subjects of some debate. Furet's student, the historian Ran Halévi, suggests that he was a relatively uncommitted communist who showed little interest in the party after 1956: it was a political home to which he was attached for affective, rather than political reasons.[4] This is certainly the way in which Furet later presented his involvement: in 1978, he said that he had joined the Party 'like everyone else' because of its association with anti-fascism:

> For my generation it was a classic progression. Add to this the fact that the Communist world, especially in its Stalinist incarnation, is a reassuring world for those of a worried disposition … in the [Communist] Party, [the intellectual] could rediscover the mythical bond with the people and the working class, and received as a bonus an all-encompassing and exhaustive explanation of a society in which he felt himself to be uncomfortable … This was the case for me between 1947 and 1954.[5]

Furet's account, like many of those at the time, emphasised the extent to which his engagement had been a 'mistake' and there is an evident ironic distance in his description of his involvement with communism. There is even the suggestion that it was an aberration of his youth.[6]

Recent work on the anti-totalitarian movement, however, cautions us against accepting this narrative at face value. Unlike Halévi, who follows Furet's own account, the American historian Christofferson suggests not only that Furet remained a Party member until 1958–9 but that he was much more committed than he later recognised.[7] According to this interpretation, Furet's disavowal of his communist past

---

[3] A number of biographical details and interpretative insights in this chapter were drawn from the seminar course 'Autour de François Furet', organised by Vincent Duclert and Chrisophe Prochasson at the EHESS from October 2010 to February 2011. I am grateful for their assistance and critical comments.

[4] Ran Halévi, *L'experience du passé: François Furet dans l'atelier de l'histoire* (Paris: Gallimard, 2007), pp. 22–33.

[5] François Furet, 'La Révolution et ses fantômes', *Nouvel Observateur* (20 November 1978).

[6] On numerous occasions he commented on his involvement with the PCF in these rather dismissive terms – especially after 1989. See for instance an interview with Furet in 'Interview (8 juin 1995)', *Derrière Le Mur. Revue universitaire de sciences sociales* (Spring 1996), p. 10, or François Furet, *Le passé d'une illusion*, reproduced in François Furet, *Penser le XXème siècle* (Paris: Robert Laffont, 2007), p. 513.

[7] Christofferson bases this on a claim made by Emmanuel Le Roy Ladurie. Michael Scott Christofferson, *French Intellectuals against the Left* (Oxford: Berghahn, 2004), p. 233.

was part of the 'hegemonic' narrative of the anti-totalitarian movement as a whole, which sought to discredit communism by indicting it as a form of 'totalitarianism'.[8] In my view, this is to overstate the case. While there was undoubtedly an important element of political contingency – perhaps even opportunism – in Furet's later anti-communism, Christofferson underestimates the extent to which, in his case, the move away from communism was bound up with an increasing affinity with liberal thought. Indeed, in the very same 1978 interview quoted above, Furet went on to say: 'even if I was born and have my roots on the left, I feel quite close to the most enlightened advocates [représentants] of liberal thought'.[9] Again, we might be tempted to see in such statement a tardy appropriation of liberalism to fit with the prevailing ideological climate, but, since the late 1950s, there had been various indications that he was relatively comfortable with certain strands of liberal thought.

This was noticeable, for instance, in his attitude to Aron. Already, in 1959, Furet had written in a review of two of Aron's books that

[T]he history of the first half of the twentieth century obviously seems to confirm Aron's analyses, as does our present fear when confronted with two contrasting types of industrial society . . . After a global panorama of the modern world, Aron brings us back to fundamental philosophical questions.[10]

Even if his review retained a cautious and slightly distant tone, it was a relatively strong endorsement of Aron's theoretical and conceptual approach, particularly given that Aron was seen, in this period, as the anti-communist intellectual par excellence. As time passed, Furet made clearer still his admiration for Aron. In a 1967 essay on French intellectuals' and structuralism, Furet deplored that the end of the 'ideological age' announced by Aron still seemed far off: it is with some disappointment that he wrote: '[I]t is not Raymond Aron who reigns but Lévi-Strauss; it is not a liberal and empirical reading of Marxism [that dominates], but a hyper-intellectual and systematic reading of Marxism.'[11] Almost a decade before the anti-totalitarian wave engulfed the French intellectual class, Furet was invoking Aron and calling for a

---

[8] Christofferson, *French Intellectuals against the Left* and his article on the same theme, Michael Scott Christofferson, 'An Antitotalitarian History of the French Revolution: Francois Furet's "Penser la Revolution Française" in the Intellectual Politics of the Late 1970s', *French Historical Studies* (Vol. 22, No. 4, 1999), pp. 421–47.

[9] Furet, 'La Révolution et ses fantômes'.

[10] François Furet, 'Raymond Aron, professeur d'une droite qui ne l'écoute pas', *Nouvel Observateur* (22 October 59).

[11] François Furet, 'Les intellectuels français et le structuralisme', *Preuves* (No. 92, February 1967) (reproduced in François Furet, *L'Atelier de l'Histoire* (Paris: Flammarion, 1982, p. 52).

liberal interpretation of Marxism. Liberalism and (reformed) Marxism were seen to go hand in hand – and Aron was used as the theoretical bridge between these two seemingly contradictory political traditions.

By the mid 1980s, the rehabilitation of Aron was complete. As we saw in the previous chapter, with the publication of his *Mémoires*, the erstwhile intellectual outcast had become the voice of twentieth-century France, and Furet's assessment fell in line with that of his peers. As he put it in a review of the *Mémoires*, 'there are few coincidences in a successful life and this one has hardly any'.[12] He continued the praise in his obituary of Aron, declaring that the shining star of post-war French liberalism had taken 'exceptional pleasure in the expression of the truth'.[13] Beyond the necessary eulogies, it is interesting that Furet picked out the *Opium of the Intellectuals* (1955) as the key text of Aron's life. He suggested that it was this book that facilitated his transition away from communism and made it possible for him to see beyond the doctrinaire Stalinism of the PCF.[14] We could follow Christofferson in arguing that this was simply another post hoc justification of the anti-totalitarian narrative, but the depth of Furet's debt and commitment to Aron suggests otherwise. Not only was he publicly endorsing Aron as early as 1959 (at which time Christofferson argues that he was still a card-carrying Communist), but Aron's interests left an important mark on much of Furet's work.

Furet's intellectual relationship to Aron provides an important indication as to the depth of his liberalism, but we can make an even stronger case for a nascent liberal sensibility by looking at the historical scholarship that ultimately made Furet a household name. It was Furet's reinterpretation of the French Revolution that laid the groundwork for a liberal reading of modern French history. It was already clear from the mid 1960s that he was breaking away from the Marxist and Jacobin orthodoxies that had defined the study of the Revolution in the post-war period. The publication of *La Révolution Française* (1965-6) with fellow historian Denis Richet, and especially his violently polemical attack on Marxist readings of the Revolution in an article entitled 'Le catéchisme révolutionnaire' published in *Annales* in 1971, marked him out as a dissident in the world of revolutionary studies. Some of this was

---

[12] François Furet, 'Quand Aron raconte notre histoire...', *Nouvel Observateur* (2 September 1983).

[13] François Furet, 'La rencontre d'une idée et d'une vie', *Commentaire* (No. 28-9, 1985). See also his eulogy of Aron on 21 October 1983 as president of the EHESS to the school's staff, republished in Prochasson, *François Furet*, pp. 532-5.

[14] He first makes this claim in Furet, 'Quand Aron raconte notre histoire ...' and reproduces it almost verbatim in his later obituary.

personal. The mutual animosity between Furet and the pre-eminent Marxist historians of the Revolution, Albert Soboul and Claude Mazauric, lay in their different trajectories.[15] Hard-working scholarship students, who had steadily climbed the academic ladder, Soboul and Mazauric resented Furet as an opportunist bourgeois, who not only had not completed his *doctorat d'État* but had chosen as his institutional home the Sixth Section of the EPHE, which at the time was presided over by the renegade Annalist Fernand Braudel. This lent a particularly acrimonious tone to the debate between the two sets of historians, with Soboul, for instance, famously remarking in 1970 that Furet and Richet were 'more publicists than historians'. But Furet's divergence from his peers was more than just a personal squabble, as he made plain in a now well-known set of essays entitled *Penser la Révolution Française* (1978).[16]

It was in this highly successful piece of historiography that Furet laid out most clearly both the significance of his reinterpretation of the Revolution and its political consequences. The volume was made up of one, long synoptic essay entitled 'La Révolution française est terminée', and three other articles: a reproduction of 'Le catéchisme révolutionnaire', and studies of Tocqueville and Cochin's interpretations of the Revolution. The opening essay provided the deepest insight into Furet's own ideas. It was here that he explored the problems of representation and political language, and the Jacobin fear of the plot, and made a powerful case for the view that the Terror emerged from and was inherent in the language of the Revolution from its inception. The result was a veritable historiographical masterpiece that succeeded in combining various developments in revolutionary scholarship with emerging French philosophical, intellectual and political currents of the 1970s.[17]

One of the key influences on Furet was the celebrated philosopher and political theorist Claude Lefort, whose work on political representation and totalitarianism was already well known by the mid 1970s.[18] It is with little difficulty that we can read Lefort's notion of a *lieu vide* into Furet's intepretation of the Revolution as a deadly battle to represent the

---

[15] On this, see Mona Ozouf, 'Préface', in François Furet, *La Révolution Française* (Paris: Gallimard, 2007), and Christofferson, 'An Antitotalitarian History of the French Revolution'.

[16] Prochasson traces some of the roots of Furet's divergence with his colleagues in Christophe Prochasson, 'François Furet, la révolution et le futur passé de la gauche française', unpublished conference paper, presented at the Colloquium in honour of Malcolm Crook, Oxford, 24 January 2010.

[17] François Furet, *Penser la Révolution Française* (Paris: Gallimard, 1978).

[18] Lefort was born in 1924; he died in 2010.

nation.[19] Indeed, the collapse of the Ancien Régime and the rapid pace of a 'democratic revolution' in 1789 left perhaps the quintessential example of the *lieu vide*.[20] At the same time, Lefort's critique of totalitarianism, which was to be vulgarised and distorted by the *nouveaux philosophes* in the late 1970s, provided Furet with another analytical tool with which to interpret the course of the Revolution.[21] Furet himself refers to this ideological shift in the text:

> I am writing these lines in late spring 1977, at a time when the critique of Soviet totalitarianism and, more generally, any movement that claims a Marxist heritage, is no longer the monopoly ... of the right, but has become a central point of reflection on the left ... The important thing is to reflect on the facts – in short, the disaster of the communist experience in the twentieth century – in the light of the values [of the left].[22]

The direct reference to anti-totalitarianism clearly situated Furet in the widespread critique of totalitarianism that, by the late 1970s, was common currency on the non-communist left.[23] While the *nouveaux philosophes* were railing against the totalitarianism of all grand ideologies, Furet was showing how totalitarianism could emerge from the process of revolution. By demonstrating (and criticising) the extent to which the French Revolution had been made into the precursor of the Russian Revolution of 1917 by twentieth-century Marxists, Furet was launching a powerful attack on a central historical narrative of the French left.[24]

The obvious influence of anti-totalitarianism on Furet's text has led scholars like Christofferson to argue that *Penser* was largely a political manifesto designed to discredit the PCF in advance of a possible victory of the Union de la Gauche in the 1978 legislative elections. But this reading of Furet as a by-product of the anti-totalitarian moment again

---

[19] On this, see Samuel Moyn, 'On the Intellectual Origins of François Furet's Masterpiece', *La Revue Tocqueville* (Vol. 29, No. 2, 2008). There is inadequate space here for a discussion of Lefort's notion of the *lieu vide*: see for instance Esteban Molina, *Le défi du politique: totalitarisme et démocratie chez Claude Lefort* (Paris: L'Harmattan, 2005), Hugues Poltier, *Passion du politique: la pensée de Claude Lefort* (Geneva: Labor et Fides, 1998), and Lefort's essays in Claude Lefort, *Essais sur le politique, XIXe – XXe siècles* (Paris: Seuil, 1986).

[20] Lefort himself wrote on the relationship between the Terror and the Revolution in 'La Terreur révolutionnaire' (1983), published in Lefort, *Essais sur le politique*.

[21] One of Lefort's most famous reflections on totalitarianism is Claude Lefort, *Un homme en trop: réflexions sur l'Archipel du Goulag* (Paris: Seuil, 1986 [1976]). Despite the influence of Lefort on the *nouveaux philosophes*, the former kept his distance from his disciples, whom he accused of a lack of intellectual rigour. On this see especially 'Préface' in Claude Lefort, *L'invention démocratique: les limites de la domination totalitaire* (Paris: Fayard, 1994), p. 6.

[22] Furet, *Penser la Révolution française*, pp. 24–5.   [23] Ibid., p. 18

[24] Prochasson, 'François Furet, la révolution et le futur passé de la gauche française'.

underplays a crucial part of Furet's project – namely, what I would call a liberal critique of modern French politics. Christofferson is right that Furet's purpose was 'as much political and institutional as intellectual', but this was not simply an anti-totalitarian project, designed to drive the final ideological nail into the coffin of the PCF.[25] Rather, Furet's desire to 'close' and 'cool down' the Revolution was part of a project to build a liberal political consensus around common institutions and a shared history. The clue is in the title of the synthetic essay with which the book opens: 'La Révolution Française est terminée'. This is a plea as much as a statement of fact. Furet *wants* the Revolution to be closed. He wishes the French to put behind them the divisions caused by the Revolution and, in particular, to interrogate themselves on its role as a modern political 'myth of origins'.[26] By recognising the extremely potent – but ultimately mythical – status of the French Revolution, the implication is that this will open the way for a different kind of politics.

By arguing that the French Revolution had within it totalitarian (and, by extension, 'illiberal') potential, Furet was laying the foundations for his liberal critique of contemporary France.[27] Only by 'closing' the French Revolution, and thereby putting to rest its illiberal elements, could the construction of any kind of liberal polity in France take place. He summarises this in an important passage:

For the most part, French thought rejects the idea of an overall harmony of interests and the common utility of specific conflicts; even when it turns towards liberal economics, as in the case of the physiocrats, there is a need to embody a unified image of the social that was expressed in the rational authority of legal despotism. [French thought] incessantly revolves around a political view of the social and it continuously interrogates the origins and legitimacy of the social pact ... [The question is] how can one balance simultaneously the free individual and the alienation of individual freedom in the state?[28]

---

[25] Christofferson, *French Intellectuals against the Left*, p. 255

[26] 'Or, la Révolution française n'est pas une transition, c'est une origine, et un fantasme d'origine. C'est ce qu'il y a d'unique en elle qui fait son intérêt historique, et c'est d'ailleurs cet "unique" qui est devenu universel: la première expérience de la démocratie.' Furet, *Penser la Révolution française*, p. 109.

[27] Isser Woloch, 'On the Latent Illiberalism of the French Revolution', *American Historical Review* (Vol. 95, No. 9, 1990), pp. 1452–70.

[28] Furet, *Penser la Révolution française*, p. 49. The original passage reads: 'La pensée française ignore pour l'essentiel le recours à l'harmonie finale des intérêts et à l'utilité commune des conflits particuliers; même quand elle est portée à l'économie libérale, comme dans le cas physiocratique, elle a besoin d'incarner le social dans une image unifiée, qui est l'autorité rationnelle du despotisme légal. C'est qu'elle ne cesse de tourner autour d'une vision politique du social, et de poser le problème des origines, et de la légitimité du pacte social ... Comment peut-on penser à la fois l'individu libre et l'aliénation de sa liberté dans l'Etat?'

For Furet, the tension between individualism and unity is the central paradox of post-revolutionary French politics, but his way of conceptualising it draws on a French liberal tradition that goes back to the early nineteenth century. His claim that French thought 'incessantly revolves around a political view of the social' directly reproduces a long-standing liberal critique of French politics.[29] In Furet's reading, the tragedy of the Revolution is that, despite its democratic claims, it fatally undermined the kind of 'harmony of interests' that might have laid the foundation for liberal politics in France. Aside from its value as a text of revolutionary historiography, then, *Penser* asks a fundamental question: how can one be a liberal in France? Or, to put it another way, how is it possible to imagine liberal politics in a France over-invested in its revolutionary heritage?

Furet's resounding answer to this problem is that the French must depoliticise the Revolution. In this way, he again builds on a nineteenth-century French liberal reading of the Revolution that rejected both the Jacobin celebration of revolutionary violence, and a counter-revolutionary vision of the Revolution as a sinful aberration. This liberal reading found renewed legitimacy in the late 1970s as communism – which, in Furet's eyes, was the heir to French Jacobinism – came under increasing attack in France.[30] Given the growing criticisms of the Soviet experiment and of Marxism in general, Furet suggested in *Penser* that all that was now needed in order to establish a liberal consensus was the closure of the Revolution, which naturally entails the dismantling of its Jacobin legacy. He reiterated this position in an interview in 1978; when asked if 'there are any more Bastilles to take', he replied 'no, and there haven't been for a long time'.[31] Furet's project, then, combined an interpretation of the Revolution that would have been familiar to – and was heavily inspired by – French liberal thinkers of the first half of the nineteenth century, alongside a contemporary project to reformulate French politics.

Nowhere is Furet's debt to nineteenth-century thinkers clearer than in his admiration for Tocqueville. In 1991, he credited him with providing the 'new perspective' on the Revolution that enabled him to write 'La Révolution Française est terminée'.[32] Furthermore, as the intellectual

---

[29] On this liberal interpretation of the Revolution and post-revolutionary French political culture, see Jeremy Jennings, *Revolution and the Republic: A History of Political Thought in France since the Eighteenth Century* (Oxford University Press, 2011), especially pp. 237–97, and Jaume, *L'individu éffacé*.

[30] François Furet, '1789–1917: aller et retour', *Le Débat* (No. 57, 1989).

[31] Furet, 'La Révolution et ses fantômes'.

[32] Furet includes a substantial article on Tocqueville, 'Tocqueville et le problème de la Révolution française, in his *Penser la Révolution française*. See also his acceptance speech for the Prix Tocqueville (11 June 1991) reproduced as François Furet, 'Ce que je dois à Tocqueville', *Commentaire* (No. 55, 1991).

historian Serge Audier has shown, Furet's reading of the nineteenth-century aristocrat drew heavily on that of Aron, in particular the tension between equality and democracy, which Aron considered central to Tocqueville's work.[33] It is here that we see the preoccupations of Aronian liberalism filter into the historical work of Furet, in this case, by means of Tocqueville. The conflict in the Revolution between the dangerous desire for complete equality of all citizens within the French nation and the liberal-democratic potential of 1789 become two of the central themes of *Penser* – and, by extension, of modern French politics. Furet maintains that closing the Revolution will make possible a reconciliation of these two conflicting tendencies and thereby allow for the construction of a liberal polity.

By 1990, it seemed as if Furet's call had been answered. Communism had definitively collapsed and the bicentennial seemed to have answered his call to end the Revolution once for all. Under the watchful gaze of a patriarchal Mitterrand, the celebrations brought together right and left around a 'soft' – and many claimed Furet-inspired – consensual view of the Revolution as the crucible of human rights.[34] Those still committed to the PCF denounced Furet's interpretation as nothing more than an argument to support the 'dominant ideology'. Nevertheless, it would be a mistake to suggest that Furet willingly endorsed the wave of liberal triumphalism that emerged from the United States in the late 1980s. On the contrary, unlike some of his American counterparts, who dreamed of a liberal democratic horizon stretching into the twenty-first century, Furet displayed one of the traits most commonly associated with French liberalism past and present: a gnawing pessimism about the future.[35]

It was in his non-academic writings – most notably his articles for *Nouvel Observateur* – that Furet discussed contemporary politics, and it is here we see most clearly the expressions of his pessimism. Furet did occasionally let himself be taken in by the spirit of the times. So, in 1991, he proclaimed boldly:

Two hundred years after the French Revolution, France and Europe have entered a new – and better – period in their history: fascism and communism have marked a century that ends as one of the most tragic and stupid in the realm

---

[33] Audier, *Tocqueville retrouvé*. For Aron on Tocqueville, see Aron, *Essai sur les libertés*.

[34] Christofferson is rather cynical about Furet's role in the bicentennial celebrations, and argues that 1989 saw Furet's interpretation rise to an untouchable hegemonic position that gave space to 'counter-revolutionary' histories such as Pierre Chaunu at the expense of alternative (non-Furetian) intepretations of the Revolution. This was, Christofferson argues, Furet's reward as a 'historian and political animal'. Christofferson, *French Intellectuals against the Left*, p. 256. For a similar perspective, see Kaplan, *Adieu 89*.

[35] In this regard, his scepticism towards Fukuyama's 'end of history' thesis is telling.

of the political passions. It is indisputable that, having just emerged from these nightmares, the peoples of Europe do not see any horizon other than that of liberal democracy.[36]

But Furet had already called into question this bold vision of a bright liberal future a few years earlier in his contribution to a highly influential collaboration with Pierre Rosanvallon and Jacques Julliard, entitled *La République du centre* (1988).[37] All three essays in the volume highlighted France's apparent drift into political centrism and the concomitant depoliticisation of the population. Even if centrism did not seem to be such a problem for Furet, he nevertheless cautioned that 'a profound political transformation is taking place, *which is not the end of ideology*, but, at the twilight of a France that has lasted for two hundred years, a reshaping and redeployment [of ideology]'.[38]

Warning had turned to sharp criticism by the mid 1990s. This new, more alarmist tone was evident in an article from 1995. What seven years previously had seemed to be a reformulating of ideologies in the wake of communism, had become a veritable 'democratic crisis':

[This crisis] relates to the an ever greater process of civic disengagement, connected to the extraordinary obsession with prosperity that seized European society after the end of the Second World War, the apogee of which was the end of communism ... [At this point] democracy buried the last of its crazy ideas. But, as a result, it is struggling to find any ideas at all.[39]

The possibility of soft, centrist politics no longer seemed as attractive as it had in *La République du centre*: the result of consensus politics had made public life in France 'a depressing spectacle'.[40] This perception of crisis was, of course, intimately tied to the fate of the non-communist left, which remained Furet's political home. Furet had never had particularly high regard for Mitterrand but, by 1995, his unease had turned to open disdain. Such was his hostility to the president that he explicitly argued that it was Mitterrand's tactics alone that had contributed to the decline in French politics.[41] Thus it was not only democracy that was 'struggling to find ideas', but also the PS, which seemed to reflect and magnify the crisis of democracy. As in the late 1970s, the contingencies of French politics provided the backdrop for Furet's arguments.

---

[36] François Furet, 'Un judoka nommé Mitterrand', *Nouvel Observateur* (2 May 1991).
[37] Furet, Julliard and Rosanvallon, *La République du Centre.*
[38] Furet, 'La France unie ...', in Furet, Julliard & Rosanvallon, *La République du Centre*, p. 66 (emphasis in original).
[39] François Furet, 'Chronique d'une décomposition', *Le Débat* (No. 83, 1995).
[40] Furet, 'Chronique d'une décomposition'.
[41] See the last part of Furet, 'Chronique d'une décomposition'.

Although France occupied a great deal of Furet's attention, it was not the only country where he saw democracy struggling to contain its 'passions'.[42] Furet had, for a long time, been interested in the United States. He had little time for misplaced expressions of French anti-Americanism and, as a director of the Committee on Social Thought at the University of Chicago, he had taught and lectured in the United States every year from 1985 until his death in 1997.[43] He was a careful observer of American politics and commented with some perspicacity on the challenges facing a number of American presidents, from Jimmy Carter to Bill Clinton.[44] It was not surprising, then, that his uneasiness about democracy in the 1990s should have found an echo on the other side of the Atlantic, specifically in the form of the movement for 'political correctness'. Diagnosing it as both a 'limited and deep' phenomenon in American politics, he expressed substantial reservations about the growing calls for 'minority rights'.[45] Though sensitive to the specific dimensions of the 'black problem', he called the minority rights movement among gays, feminists, Latinos and other minorities 'extravagant', 'ridiculous' and 'profound'.[46] The crisis of democracy, which in France took the form of depoliticisation and the atrophy of public life, in America took the shape of disproportionate calls for minority representation. In both cases, the future for liberal democracy appeared compromised by the continuing 'passions' of democratic citizens.

It is in this sense that Pierre Hassner's description of Furet as a 'melancholy liberal' is entirely appropriate, especially if we compare him to contemporaries such as Lefort. Where Lefort – whose work was a great influence on Furet – consistently remained cautiously optimistic about the consequences of the *lieu vide* at the heart of democratic politics, Furet was always more wary. In his interpretation of the Revolution,

---

[42] For a more extensive discussion of Furet's concept of the political 'passions', see Christophe Prochasson, 'The Melancholy of Post-communism: François Furet and the Passions', in Chabal, *France since the 1970s*.

[43] For an example of his impatience with French anti-Americanism, see his review of Claude Julien's book *Le Rêve et l'Histoire* in 1976. François Furet, 'Les deux cents bougies de l'Amérique', *Nouvel Observateur* (10 May 1976).

[44] For his analyses of the United States, see for instance, François Furet, 'Jimmy Carter, une révolution à l'américaine' (1977), in Furet, *L'Atelier de l'Histoire*, on the election of Carter; François Furet, 'Le paradoxe américain', *Nouvel Observateur* (15 December 80), on the presidential election victory of Ronald Reagan; François Furet, 'La grande bascule', *Nouvel Observateur* (26 October 84), on the success of Republican politics in the first half of the 1980s; and François Furet, 'L'Amérique de Clinton II', *Le Débat* (No. 94, 1997), on the challenges facing the second term of the Clinton presidency.

[45] Quotation drawn from an interview with Furet in 1992. François Furet, 'L'utopie démocratique à l'américaine', *le Débat* (No. 69, 1992).

[46] Furet, 'L'utopie démocratique à l'américaine'.

Furet showed the potentially deleterious consequences of the *lieu vide*
and how it had prevented France from achieving any kind of satisfactory
liberal consensus.[47] And, in his writings on contemporary politics, Furet
often worried about the implications of an 'apathetic' and 'depoliticised'
population. By contrast, Lefort had a more positive reading of contemporary political developments. In 1998 – a year after Furet's death – he
argued that 'The advent of a new style of intervention in political life, in
particular the Green Party, seems to give the lie to the notion of a
depoliticised society.' Although he admitted that an increasingly
detached 'technocracy' presented an important difficulty for a democratic political system, he nevertheless argued that this did not lead him
to 'conclude that democracy has deteriorated'. On the contrary, he
expressed surprise that 'discussions [surrounding the problems of dem-
ocracy] are multiplying: this suggests a renewed awareness of problems
[within democracies] that have existed for some time'.[48] Such optimism
was a far cry from Furet's warning of the pernicious consequences of
identity politics.

This contrast with Lefort highlights what was perhaps the central element of Furet's 'melancholy' liberalism: a certain unease with democracy.
Implicit in much of Furet's work was that democracy (or the democratic
idea, in the case of the French Revolution) cannot suffice to bring about
the ideological peace necessary for the foundation of a liberal politics of
consensus, despite the desirability of such a consensus in France. Furet's
journey away from communism no doubt explains some of this scepticism
with democracy. He had to construct an alternative philosophy on the
ruins of a Marxist worldview to which he had been attached in his youth.
Rather than letting himself be drawn into the orbit of structuralism or
confrontational post-1968 *gauchisme*, he used contemporary scholars
such as Aron and Lefort, and historical figures such as Quinet and
Tocqueville, in order to construct a new political and historical worldview. Nevertheless, his left-wing heritage defined his approach to liberalism. It meant, for instance, a resistance to the politics of 'human rights'
and 'anti-racism' in the 1980s, as empty rhetorical devices that were
inappropriate bases on which to build a political platform.[49] It also meant
a continuous commitment to the state as the arbiter of a liberal polity and a

---

[47] Claude Lefort, 'La Terreur révolutionnaire' (1983), in Lefort, *Essais sur le politique*.
[48] Claude Lefort, 'Reflexions sur la conjoncture actuelle (1998)', in Claude Lefort, *Le temps présent. Écrits 1945–2005* (Paris: Belin, 2007), pp. 938–40.
[49] On his criticisms of the politics of human rights, see Furet, 'La France unie …',
pp. 58–64; on his negative reaction to the 'anti-racism' movement, see an interview
with Furet in 1990: François Furet, 'Le drapeau de l'anti-racisme sur le désert des idées',
Commentaire (No. 51, 1990).

rejection of the more extreme forms of pluralism and multiculturalism, which came to the fore in the late-twentieth-century United States.[50] Finally, it meant the recognition that liberalism – and its corollary, liberal democracy – is weak and easily overrun by ideological 'passions'.[51]

Does such scepticism about democracy invalidate the claim that Furet was a key figure in the liberal revival of 1970s and 80s? I think not – and this for two important reasons. First, because Furet's work on the Revolution actively sought to contribute to a more consensual and ultimately more liberal reformulation of French politics. It is certainly true that, by breaking with the Labroussian socio-economic history of his youth, Furet's reinterpretation of the Revolution drew on the renewed interest in political history we analysed in the context of neo-republicanism. But unlike those historians who rehabilitated the Third Republic in an attempt to validate a new republican consensus, Furet's work instead sought to give legitimacy to a liberal narrative of French history.[52] Second, because an uneasiness with democracy has long been an integral component of French liberalism that can be traced back to the nineteenth century. Indeed, there is a foreshadowing of Furet's concerns in the writings of such complex nineteenth-century French thinkers as Tocqueville and Renan.[53] In this way, Furet was drawing on and bringing up to date a key component of the French liberal tradition. The very fact that Furet's liberal turn was mapped on to one of the most potent symbols of modern French history should remind us of the specificity of this French liberal tradition. Thus, while Furet's liberalism was influenced by developments outside France, it ultimately responded to a peculiarly Franco-French historiography. The combination of a seductive writing style and the polemics of the French Revolution gave Furet's liberal synthesis an extremely broad reach, and paved the way for other reinterpretations of modern French history that would be inspired by his 'liberal method'.[54]

---

[50] On this, see 'L'utopie démocratique à l'américaine'.

[51] On this, see in particular Furet's two most famous interpretative works: *Penser la Révolution française* and *Le passé d'une illusion*.

[52] In 1993, Furet discussed his reaction to the renewed interest in a 'représentation largement imaginaire... [et defensive] de la IIIème République' in an important passage in François Furet, 'Préface', in François Furet and Mona Ozouf (eds.), *Le siècle de l'avènement républicain* (Paris: Gallimard, 1993), p. 21–2.

[53] On the 'elitist' or 'pessimistic' aspects of French liberalism, and its commitment to the state rather than democracy, see Siedentop, 'Two Liberal Traditions'; Jaume, *L'individu efface*; George Armstrong Kelly, *The Humane Comedy: Constant, Tocqueville and French Liberalism* (Cambridge University Press, 1992); and Bernard Reardon, *Liberalism and Tradition: Aspects of Catholic Thought in Nineteenth-Century France* (Cambridge University Press, 1975).

[54] The expression is that of the historian Vincent Duclert. Ozouf, too, has stressed Furet's liberalism: when describing his work on the revolution, she says 'Lui était profondément

Solidarity and civil society: Pierre Rosanvallon and the construction of the liberal political space

One of Furet's most successful intellectual collaborators was Pierre Rosanvallon. The intimate intellectual relationship between the two men was a public affair almost from the moment they met, and it was Furet who invited Rosanvallon to participate in a number of seminars at the EHESS in the late 1970s.[55] The latter eventually joined the EHESS full-time with the creation of the Institut Raymond Aron in 1985, and, in 1992, was appointed Furet's successor as director of the newly rebaptised Centre de recherches politiques Raymond Aron.[56] Furet also worked with Rosanvallon to set up the Fondation Saint-Simon in 1982, a highly influential think tank dedicated to the study of contemporary politics.[57] It was disbanded in 1999, after a long period when its publications – among them *La République du Centre* – had had a significant impact on French politics.[58] In 2001, four years after Furet's death in 1997, Rosanvallon was elected to the Collège de France, but he did not forget the influence of his mentor. In his inaugural lecture in March 2002, he singled out his former colleague for special praise:

> François Furet ... helped me make the decisive jump [into academia] in the 1980s by inviting me to the EHESS when, as a young post-doc, I was in between two worlds, on the cusp of the academy as an intellectual free agent and in a rather precarious situation.[59]

This passage reveals not simply Rosanvallon's obvious intellectual and personal debt to Furet, but also his sense of marginalisation. Although

---

libéral ... Libéral, pourtant, il l'aurait dit de lui-meme'. Ozouf, 'Préface', in Furet, *La Révolution Française*, pp. xxvi–xxvii.

[55] For instance, when in 1980 Furet was asked to comment on responses by twenty-five French intellectuals to the question 'De quoi l'avenir intellectuel sera-t-il fait?', he had this to say: 'Les mœurs vont et viennent, la question seule est importante. Elle est très bien formulée par celui des auteurs qui m'a le plus intéressé, Pierre Rosanvallon. J'aurais aimé signer son texte.' François Furet, 'L'avenir est en retard', *Nouvel Observateur* (27 September 80).

[56] Rosanvallon discusses his move into academia in Pierre Rosanvallon, 'Sur quelques chemins de traverse de la pensée politique en France', *Raisons politiques* (No. 1, 2001), pp. 49–62.

[57] For a further discussion of the Fondation Saint-Simon, see chapter 9. See also Rosanvallon, 'Sur quelques chemins de traverse', p. 61.

[58] Rosanvallon outlined his reasons for stopping the Fondation Saint-Simon (one of which was Furet's death in 1997) in a public announcement published in *Le Monde*. Pierre Rosanvallon, 'La Fondation Saint-Simon, une histoire accomplie', *Le Monde* (23 June 1999).

[59] Rosanvallon, *Pour une histoire conceptuelle du politique*, p. 8.

Rosanvallon (like Furet) was eventually accepted by the French intellectual establishment, a feeling of precariousness has been an important aspect of modern French liberalism: one suspects that a vital source of French liberal 'melancholy' is this (partly cultivated) feeling that those who espouse any form of liberalism necessarily belong to a marginal group.[60]

Yet, as we saw in the previous chapter, the 1980s was a period of steady expansion of the liberal political space in France. For this, Rosanvallon can take a good deal of credit. His sophisticated, elegant and forceful attempts to write an alternative history of French democracy have given the liberal revival tremendous intellectual legitimacy. His work, always based on varying degrees of empirical investigation, is a powerful combination of history, political thought and political manifesto. It has proved invaluable in defining the contemporary liberal political space – a task which he has always seen as integral, rather than in opposition, to that of the historian. The ways in which Rosanvallon has emphasised the importance of the state, democratic pluralism and intermediate groups in civil society have given contemporary French liberalism a viable historical narrative that is distinct from that of the Anglo-American world. At the same time, his continuous concern with concrete social issues, such as unemployment or the welfare state, has encouraged him to make concrete proposals for reforms of the French state. Despite his marked reluctance to embrace the term 'liberal', Rosanvallon's oeuvre is perhaps the most wide-ranging effort to give historical depth and political potency to a critical liberal project in France.

Rosanvallon's unusual trajectory helps to explain his interest in the pragmatic reform of society. Two elements are important here: first, his training at a French business school and, second, his participation in one of France's most prominent trade unions, the CFDT.[61] This intellectual trajectory gave Rosanvallon a far greater awareness of economics than the majority of France's intellectual class. Moreover, by the time he became an academic in the 1980s, Rosanvallon had spent many years in a trade union movement that, as we shall see in chapter 10, was closely associated with the 'second left'. He ended his involvement with the CFDT after being editor of its journal *CFDT-Aujourd'hui* from 1973 to 1977, but these early years left a mark on him that is still

---

[60] This marginalisation has sometimes been real, but the fact that both Furet and Rosanvallon ultimately received the very highest accolades – Furet was elected to the Academie française in 1997, a few months before his death, and Rosanvallon was awarded a chair at the Collège de France – suggests that even the notoriously closed French intellectual space has slowly made room for liberals.

[61] He attended the Ecole des Hautes Etudes Commerciales.

visible.[62] From his interest in social issues to his emphasis on the importance of trade unions in the formation of civil society in the late nineteenth century, the traces of his intellectual heritage are easily discernible. Of particular relevance in this context are his espousal of *autogestion* and his elaboration of a notion of 'solidarity'.

The concept of *autogestion* grew from the French left's post-1968 critique of authority and the state.[63] Originally a term that referred specifically to the form of industrial management practised in Tito's Yugoslavia, it rapidly became a potent but short-lived intellectual fad in France. *Autogestion* was seen as a form of economic management that would encourage the autonomy of individual industrial units. It thus provided a way of conceptualising a socialist economic policy that did not rely on central planning – and, as Rosanvallon put it, offered a 'positive' programme for the non-communist left.[64] Such was the prevalence of the term that, after expressing much hostility, even the PCF felt the need to adopt it in the late 1970s. This, combined with the Socialist victory in 1981, precipitated the decline of *autogestion*. Delegitimised by its association with the PCF (when it had originally been designed as a conceptual tool with which to attack the party), and with the Socialists facing the complications of real governance, the concept of *autogestion* fell into disuse. Yet despite the almost complete disappearance of the idea by the mid 1980s, the zeal with which Rosanvallon defended it at the time tells us a great deal about his political priorities in the 1970s.[65] First and foremost, it placed him clearly on the second left. This political and intellectual current defined itself against Mitterrand's Common Programme, which, because of the need to gain the support of the PCF, relied to varying degrees on a combination of a traditional Marxist analysis and a statist model of French politics. By contrast, *autogestion* implied an anti-hierarchical and fundamentally more democratic approach to left-wing politics that would 'rehabilitate the individual by highlighting the idea of autonomy'.[66] *Autogestion* thus represented something of a liberal approach to left-wing politics. Already, at the beginning

---

[62] Andrew Jainchill and Samuel Moyn, 'French Democracy between Totalitarianism and Solidarity: Pierre Rosanvallon and Revisionist Historiography', *Journal of Modern History* (No. 76, 2004), pp. 110–12.

[63] I am grateful to Michael Behrent for sharing with me his work on these questions. Michael Behrent, 'Anti-statism in Theory and Practice: Foucault and the Second Left', unpublished ms. (2011).

[64] He assessed the rise and fall of *autogestion* in his article Pierre Rosanvallon, 'Mais où est donc passée l'autogestion?', *Passé Présent* (No. 4, 1984), pp. 186–95.

[65] His first major work was a defence of and manifesto for *autogestion*. Pierre Rosanvallon, *L'âge de l'autogestion, ou la politique au poste de commandement* (Paris: Seuil, 1976).

[66] Rosanvallon, 'Mais où est donc passée l'autogestion?', p. 188. See also Jainchill and Moyn, 'Pierre Rosanvallon and Revisionist Historiography', p. 113.

of his career, there were signs that Rosanvallon was committed to a rapprochement between liberalism and socialism.[67]

The second essential legacy of Rosanvallon's early years is the notion of 'solidarity'.[68] From his very earliest writings, he was interested in the 'crisis of the welfare state'. This referred to the tension between the rising costs of the welfare state and a shrinking tax base.[69] It was only by facing up to this problem directly, Rosanvallon argued, that the left could hope to preserve the positive aspects of the welfare state and rebuild 'solidarity' in the light of the 'individualisation of the social'.[70] In economic terms, this would mean making taxation, rather than direct contributions, the source of revenue for the social security system, thereby restoring a more 'progressive' character to the funding of welfare payments. At the same time, he argued that the state should scale back direct support to the unemployed in an effort to encourage employment; money originally used for unemployment benefit could thus be redirected into employment projects. For Rosanvallon, this twin approach represented – and continues to represent – the only way of adapting to changes in the nature of the welfare state. Unlike many Anglo-American liberals, then, Rosanvallon does not believe that reform of the welfare state entails a 'minimal state' – indeed, he has on numerous occasions been highly critical of the historical and philosophical foundations of an excessively market-oriented neo-liberalism.[71] Rather, Rosanvallon follows the overwhelming tradition of French political thought – whether liberal or not – in arguing that a strong state is needed in order to frame the nation and play a positive part in building solidarity.[72] The function of the state is, in his

---

[67] He developed this critique further with his colleague Patrick Viveret in Pierre Rosanvallon and P. Viveret, *Pour une nouvelle culture politique* (Paris: Seuil, 1977). This book argued for a reformation of politics that would to some extent disaggregate sovereignty from politics. This is in line with the kind of alternative liberal path Rosanvallon goes on to develop. A rather cynical perspective on the book can be found in Christofferson, *French Intellectuals Against the Left*, pp. 217–19.

[68] See, for instance, his collaboration with economist Jean-Paul Fitoussi on social inequalities: Jean-Pierre Fitoussi and Pierre Rosanvallon, *Le nouvel âge des inégalités* (Paris: Seuil, 1998).

[69] Pierre Rosanvallon, *La crise de l'État-providence* (Paris: Seuil, 1981) and a number of articles in Pierre Rosanvallon, *Misère de l'économie* (Paris: Seuil, 1983). He returned to the problems of the welfare state in Pierre Rosanvallon, *La nouvelle question sociale: repenser l'État providence* (Paris: Seuil, 1995).

[70] He refers specifically to France here, as he argues that France has one of the lowest proportions of direct taxation as a source of state income in the Western world. Rosanvallon, *La nouvelle question sociale*, pp. 81–90.

[71] Rosanvallon, *La crise de l'État-providence*, pp. 59–106, and Pierre Rosanvallon, *Le capitalisme utopique: critique de l'idéologie économique* (Paris: Seuil, 1979).

[72] See below for Rosanvallon's critique of the 'minimal state'. See also the illuminating Wim Weymans, 'Freedom through Political Representation: Lefort, Gauchet and

words, 'not simply to give power to the people but, more radically, to give it shape as a coherent collectivity'.[73] This does not, of course, mean that the state should not be reformed, but it does mean that Rosanvallon accepts the value and legitimacy of the state as a provider of social services.

Such a position is logical: even among those at the vanguard of France's liberal revival, few have been willing openly to endorse the dismantling of the state. Nevertheless, despite Rosanvallon's commitment to the state, his lengthy discussions of the tension between 'autonomy and solidarity' make it clear that he has assimilated one of the key elements of the liberal critique of contemporary France, namely the need for greater flexibility and the decentralisation of state institutions.[74] In 1981, he argued that France needed to develop

forms of horizontal solidarity that range from formal organisations to informal community support initiatives; these would allow solidarity to be resituated [réencastrer] at the heart of society ... This multi-socialisation, this pluralism in the forms of sociability, is not a constraint but rather the expansion of the freedom of each individual.[75]

In his later work *La nouvelle critique sociale* (1995), he extended this further:

The transformation of solidarity and the redefinition of rights imply a better articulation of the relationship between the theory of democracy and practice of democracy or, to put it another way, [a better articulation of the relationship between] the rules of living together and common justice, and the management of the social. It also encourages us to think differently about the very idea of social reform.[76]

The differences in emphasis are noticeable: the later quotation employs the language of 'civil society' more sparingly, but instead emphasises the need for a democratic system as the framework for any reform. However, in both cases, there is a clear call for a form of liberal democratic pluralism that is seen to underpin solidarity. In short, Rosanvallon uses the concept of solidarity as a bridge between ideas of liberal autonomy and the French tradition of statist centralisation that he had criticised in his earliest writings on *autogestion*. Even though the latter had

Rosanvallon on the Relationship between State and Society', *European Journal of Political Theory* (Vol. 4, No. 263, 2005), pp. 263–82.
[73] Pierre Rosanvallon, *La démocratie inachevée: histoire de la souveraineté du peuple en France* (Paris: Gallimard, 2000), p. 417. The state, as the embodiment of the nation, is the means to do this.
[74] Rosanvallon, *La nouvelle question sociale*, p. 183. See also chapter 10.
[75] Rosanvallon, *La crise de l'État-providence*, p. 122.
[76] Rosanvallon, *La nouvelle question sociale*, p. 12.

disappeared from French political discourse by the 1980s, Rosanvallon's work on the welfare state offered another forum in which he could develop a more decentralised, flexible vision of society. It also gave him the opportunity to develop a critique of the French state. For, even if he has always recognised the tremendous importance of the state in ensuring the solidaristic foundations of a liberal society, he has nevertheless repeatedly cast doubt on the strength and sustainability of the French statist tradition.[77]

This desire to develop new ways of imagining the state has, in the past twenty years, pushed Rosanvallon into the world of academic history. The majority of his more recent publications and lectures have tried to show both the limits of a 'Jacobin' reading of modern French history and the theoretical problems associated with the development of the state and democracy. Nevertheless, he still carries with him the spirit of activism: he has said himself that he sees the historian as both impartial analyst and active contributor to the political space.[78] It is entirely predictable therefore that Rosanvallon should have tried to develop a historical framework for his pluralist, liberal conception of 'solidarity'. He did this most consistently in his trilogy – *Le sacre du citoyen* (1990), *Le peuple introuvable* (1998) and *La démocratie inachevée* (2000) – but almost all his historical writings have contributed to his efforts 'to redraw the global framework that is used to understand the French [*hexagonal*] model'.[79] Rosanvallon's historical programme has been developed across a number of themes, four of which are of particular importance: the revisionist reference to the French Revolution, the rehabilitation of the 'Moment Guizot', the role of intermediary bodies in the consolidation of democracy and, finally, the 'crisis of representation' in the late twentieth century. Taken together, these build on Furet's innovations and give us an important insight into a contemporary interpretation of French history that acknowledges and celebrates France's liberal heritage.

Rosanvallon's vision of the French Revolution has been heavily influenced by that of Furet. He accepts unquestioningly the idea that any history of democracy in France begins with the symbolic moment of the Revolution. Furet's 'revisionist' interpretation of the Revolution appears as a necessary starting point, which makes sense given Rosanvallon's stated aim of unpacking the contradictions of the (French) democratic project. Without going as far as Furet in reading a proto-totalitarian

---

[77] Rosanvallon, *Le modèle politique français*
[78] Rosanvallon, *La démocratie inachevée*, p. 422. This, of course, is similar to Furet's project in *Penser la Révolution française*.
[79] Rosanvallon, *Le modèle politique français*, p. 19.

narrative into the Revolution, Rosanvallon nevertheless emphasises both its unifying and its individualising tendencies. 'The aspiration to unity' sets the tone for the period after 1789.[80] Rosanvallon calls this the theme of 'the utopian generality [*la généralité utopique*]' in modern French history. The desire for unity is interpreted as the principal legacy of the Revolution. Rosanvallon, who believes that intermediary bodies have been – and are – essential to the construction of a democratic polity, therefore emphasises on a number of occasions the attack on intermediary bodies in the Le Chapelier laws of 1791.[81] This 'war on corporate entities' is one aspect of a quasi-pathological yearning for a national unity that leaves a deep mark on French history.

However, there is another conflicting tendency at the heart of the democratic project: that of individualisation. The political equality implicit in the notion of democratic universal suffrage

can only be conceptualised within a framework of radical individualism, contrary to other forms of equality, which can perfectly well accommodate themselves to an organisational or differential hierarchy of the social.[82]

For Rosanvallon, the assumption at the heart of suffrage is a radical individualisation of the citizen. No longer perceived as a piece in a hierarchical whole, the revolutionary citizen is an individual in a direct and equal relationship with the nation.[83] This persistent attempt to highlight the importance of individualism in the development of democracy shows Rosanvallon's debt to another important French thinker of the post-war period, Louis Dumont. Audier has begun to document the influence of Dumont's interpretation of the connection between individualism and Western modernity – Furet, too, used Dumont's basic sociological framework in his reinterpretation of the Revolution.[84] Rosanvallon continues to invoke Dumont (quite explicitly in the footnotes) as he discusses the development of democracy. The Revolution is seen to sanctify the individual while simultaneously making unity the inalienable goal of the revolutionary project.

If Rosanvallon's interpretation of the Revolution departs only in a limited way from Furet's revisionism, his reading of the nineteenth century breaks with that of his mentor. In the first instance, he tried – in

---

[80] Ibid., p. 24.
[81] Rosanvallon, *La démocratie inachevée*, pp. 200–2, and Rosanvallon, *Le modèle politique français*, p. 27. A discussion of this can be found in Jainchill and Moyn, 'Pierre Rosanvallon and Revisionist Historiography', p. 131.
[82] Pierre Rosanvallon, *Le sacre du citoyen: histoire du suffrage universel en France* (Paris: Gallimard, 1992), p. 14.
[83] This theme is most fully developed in Rosanvallon, *Le sacre du citoyen.*
[84] Audier, *Tocqueville retrouvé*, especially pp. 234–47.

his influential doctoral thesis under the supervision of Lefort – to restore to prominence the period 1815–48. In the published version of his thesis, *Le Moment Guizot* (1985), he clearly reads present-day concerns into the Restoration period when he maintains:

> At the start of the nineteenth century, *the crucial question that a whole range of 'liberal' writers were trying to resolve was the relationship between liberalism and democracy.* Their aim was to understand the conditions in which the democratic ideal of civic participation violently turned against liberty.[85]

The reference to the economic reforms of the mid 1980s – another moment when the relationship between liberalism and democracy was called into question – is unambiguous. More than this, however, we see again how the tension between democratic participation and (national) unity lies at the heart of Rosanvallon's thought. It is present in equal measure in his analyses of the welfare state and his interpretation of the revolutionary period. By focusing on the period 1815–48 – when the potential of democracy was stifled by aristocratic liberalism – he can explore a historical moment in which the damaging consequences of an elitist liberalism imagined without its necessary democratic corollary were made manifest.

At the same time, his rehabilitation of the *moment Guizot* allowed Rosanvallon to modify Furet's conclusion that the Revolution 'came into port' in 1870.[86] On the contrary, Rosanvallon maintains that the roots of the Third Republic lie in the Restoration liberal thinker's specific notion of the enlightened citizen (*citoyen capacitaire*). This means that the 'underpinnings' of the French Republic lie in Guizot's conservatism rather than in the radicalism of the French Revolution – a historiographical inflection that has important political implications.[87] In particular, it distances Rosanvallon from the neo-republican consensus that was developing in the 1980s around the Third Republic.[88] By arguing that the Third Republic's roots are to be found in the Restoration, he cast doubt on its utility as a symbol of democratic, consensual republicanism; instead, his vision of the Republic placed the great founders of the Third

---

[85] Pierre Rosanvallon, *Le moment Guizot* (Paris: Gallimard, 1985), p. 13 (emphasis in original).

[86] The expression is from Furet, *La Révolution française*, p. 793.

[87] Rosanvallon, *Le moment Guizot*, p. 357.

[88] Rosanvallon denounces this tendency to 'canonise' the Third Republic on a number of occasions: 'Pour paraitre donner un sens à son lent enfoncement dans le pragmatisme, la classe politique presque unanime s'est drapée dans une double référence au gaullisme et à la IIIe République. La gauche tout particulièrement a restructuré sa mémoire sur cette base improbable et la vie politique a semblé aspirée vers un retour consensuel à l'origine.' Furet, Julliard and Rosanvallon, *La République du Centre*, p. 140.

Republic such as Ferry, Léon Gambetta and Littré alongside the openly elitist Guizot.[89] Although Rosanvallon paints a sympathetic portrait of Guizot, particularly emphasising the latter's concern with the business of politics, this interest in the Restoration marks an important break with Furet, who saw the foundation of the Third Republic as the closure of France's revolutionary passions.

Where, then, does Rosanvallon see French democracy as 'coming into port'? The answer is clear: it is the development of intermediary bodies, especially trade unions, that finally allows France to transcend its two original revolutionary pathologies. Rosanvallon develops this perspective in *Le peuple introuvable* (1998), in which he contends that the three most important modifications to France's political landscape in the late nineteenth century were the advent of political parties, the rise of the trade unions and the growth of a 'consultative state [*État consultatif*]'.[90] Instead of emphasising the centralising national project of republicanism, Rosanvallon's focus is firmly on the liberalisation of the French state in this period. The aim is to recover a history of France that makes spaces for its intermediary bodies. This makes for an alternative history that has a much greater liberal potential than that associated with a neo-republican or Jacobin teleology.[91] In *Le modèle politique français*, he makes explicit this new approach by arguing that there are two histories of France:

'Jacobinism' or the spectre of centralisation: this approach has been developed in every format – in essays, academic tomes and pamphlets, but also in electoral manifestos and political speeches ... But we cannot simply leave it at that. There is another history that must be taken into account in order to fill out this picture: that of the very strong resistance to this very same 'Jacobinism'. For this model has not stopped being overwhelmingly criticised and denounced even while it was generally held to be dominant ... One has to bear in mind this essential tension in order to appreciate fully the reality of [French political culture] [*la réalité hexagonale*].[92]

I have quoted this passage at length because it summarises the fundamental basis of Rosanvallon's historical framework. By giving French liberalism – understood here to be the opposite of 'Jacobinism' – a history, he legitimises the liberal political space in contemporary France. A project begun in the 1970s, with a commitment to *autogestion*, matured three decades later in the rehabilitation of an alternative French history.

[89] Rosanvallon, *Le moment Guizot*, p. 359–68.
[90] Pierre Rosanvallon, *Le peuple introuvable: histoire de la représentation démocratique en France* (Paris: Gallimard, 1998), esp. pp. 219–359.
[91] On this see Jean-Fabien Spitz, 'La culture politique républicaine en question: Pierre Rosanvallon et la critique du "jacobinisme" français', *Revues politiques* (No. 15, 2004), pp. 111–24.
[92] Rosanvallon, *Le modèle politique français*, pp. 10–11.

However, as with Furet, this attempt to 'find' a liberal narrative in French history has been compromised by a persistent pessimism about the potential of the democratic project.[93] Throughout Rosanvallon's more recent historical and theoretical work there is a continuous attempt to highlight the 'tensions' and 'ambiguities' at the heart of the democratic project. While Rosanvallon's form of liberal pessimism is not as pronounced as that of Furet, there is a clear sense that democracy is incomplete or imperfect. Rosanvallon's project is still open – and his conclusions therefore still provisional – but he remains fundamentally hostile to any kind of triumphalist 'liberal democratic horizon'. This quotation from *Le peuple introuvable* (1998) provides an excellent example of this unease:

The fiction of democracy contains within it a problem of figuration – namely, the tension between unity and equality ... With the rejection of an *organic* model of society, how then can a people be represented if it is composed of individuals? ... The idea of the people does not exist independently of attempts to invoke it and locate it: it has to be constructed. This contradiction is at the heart of modern politics.[94]

Here again we see the tension between a democratic society and a unified representation of the people. But there is a further paradox: Rosanvallon suggests that the only meaningful way in which modern France has been able to reconstitute the 'organic base' of society is through the nation state, and yet the nation state's attempts to construct the people have necessarily undermined the democratic autonomy of French society. French democracy is therefore continuously threatened by both a 'totalitarian' and a 'corporatist' reflex. As he puts it when discussing the democratic consolidation of the Third Republic,

[The Third Republic] was, by contrast, always 'precarious'. It does not represent the end of history or the ultimate realisation of a political system that has found its most appropriate form.[95]

Far from being a moment of political 'normalisation' in modern French history, the Third Republic reinforced the dichotomy between the (totalitarian) desire to represent all of society in one party or leader and the danger of fragmentation.[96] Now, in the twenty-first century, it is the latter that concerns Rosanvallon most:

[93] On this see, for instance, Geneviève Verdo, 'Pierre Rosanvallon, archéologue de la démocratie', *Revue historique* (No. 623, 2002–3), pp. 693–720.
[94] Rosanvallon, *Le peuple introuvable*, pp. 22, 23, 24.   [95] Ibid., p. 392.
[96] This reading of totalitarianism as a political system that seeks to represent all of society is strongly reminiscent of Lefort's definition of totalitarianism.

Society then becomes unrepresentable in another way; it is pulverised in a cacophonous juxtaposition of corporatist claims and clientelistic networks.[97]

This rather dramatic passage highlights what he sees as the primary danger to contemporary Western society: the prospect of its becoming atomised and fragmented.

Rosanvallon theorised this fragmentation in his concept of a *crise de la représentation*. There were hints of this in a 1982 article in *Libération*, when he warned:

France has become soft: political life has become dull, social mobilisation has been reduced to a few transitory skirmishes, and intellectual debate has reached a low-water mark. The passions are frustrated; imagination has gone into abeyance. Cinema, music and literature oscillate drearily between false intimacy [*intimisme*] and exoticism ... French society seems to have disenchantedly brought itself into the realm of hard facts[98]

By 1988, his prognosis had become gloomier. In his contribution to *La République du Centre*, he argued that

Democratic universalism is running on empty and the mechanisms of social integration no longer work as well as they did in the past. The result is a multi-faceted crisis of citizenship.[99]

As far as Rosanvallon was concerned, the specific crisis he had diagnosed in 1982 had, by 1988, become a crisis of the democratic system in general. Crucially, by the late 1980s it was the relation between state and citizen – expressed here in the term *intégration sociale* – that had been called into question. Here again we are confronted with the tension between French history's will to unity and the onward march of an egalitarian individualism: the latter was seen to be breaking the bonds of solidarity that, thus far, had been holding the nation together.

In his more recent work, Rosanvallon has continued to elaborate these concerns. In 1998, he claimed that democracy's 'founding contradictions' are still potent and that 'a new task of representation' is necessary in order, once again, to transcend the tensions that lie at the heart of the democratic project.[100] And in one of his most recent texts, he examined in some detail the fate of democracy in what he describes as 'the age of contestation'.[101] So, even at the high point of Rosanvallon's attempts to

---

[97] Rosanvallon, *Le peuple introuvable*, p. 394

[98] 'Le temps des paradoxes', reproduced in Rosanvallon, *Misère de l'économie*, p. 149.

[99] Pierre Rosanvallon, 'Malaise dans la représentation', in Furet, Julliard and Rosanvallon, *La République du Centre*, p. 155.

[100] On this see the final section of Rosanvallon, *Le peuple introuvable*, pp. 433–70.

[101] Pierre Rosanvallon, *La contre-démocratie: la politique à l'âge de la défiance* (Paris: Seuil, 2006).

construct a liberal political space in contemporary France, there remains a gnawing pessimism. Given Rosanvallon's focus on practical solutions, one could argue that his is a far more positive project than that of Furet. Yet the task always appears unfinished and imperfect. The potential for a deracination of the people from the democratic process continuously presents new challenges. Even if the perilous construction of a 'balanced democracy' at the start of the twentieth century brought France in line with its international peers, at the end of the century the need for an active political life remained as urgent as ever. Despite Rosanvallon's bold efforts to support a renewal of more liberal politics in France, one is left with the feeling that the solid base on which such a renewal must be built is still very much under construction.

The strange liberalism of François Furet and Pierre Rosanvallon

As I suggested at the start of this chapter, neither Furet nor Rosanvallon appear to fit comfortably into a generally accepted definition of 'liberal', especially when judged by the standards of their Anglo-American counterparts. They were both heavily involved with the left; they both explicitly rejected many of the fundamental tenets of Anglo-American neo-liberalism (the free market, identity politics …); and they were both sceptical of liberal democracy's potential to guarantee peace and stability. Even knowledgeable observers of French intellectual life have maintained that it would be a 'mistake' to read the anti-totalitarian moment from which both Furet and Rosanvallon emerged as a 'liberal' moment.[102] Why, then, have I argued here that they are crucial to an understanding of French liberalism since the late 1970s? It is primarily because they fit the contextual definition of liberalism that I outlined earlier: namely, that their work has contributed to a liberal critique of contemporary French intellectual and political life. Yes, it would be wrong simply to draw a line between anti-totalitarianism and liberalism – especially in the case of the anti-totalitarian moment's most polemical actors such as Lévy or Finkielkraut – but equally it would be reductive to ignore the wider effects of the anti-totalitarian moment. It did act as a catalyst for the revival of liberal approaches to history, politics and philosophy, if only because these could move under the 'cover' of the anti-totalitarian cacophony of the

---

[102] In his introduction to an English selection of Rosanvallon's texts, Moyn argues: 'Above all, it is a mistake to interpret the antitotalitarian moment as a "liberal" moment in French intellectual history'. Pierre Rosanvallon, *Democracy Past and Future*, ed. Samuel Moyn (London: Columbia University Press, 2006), p. 11.

late 1970s. This was certainly the case for Furet and Rosanvallon, who acknowledged their debt to anti-totalitarianism before moving away from it to create their own unique brand of historical liberalism that combined Tocqueville and Guizot, as well as Lefort and Dumont.

Among other things, this liberalism expressed itself in clear divergences with the neo-republican narratives that were the subject of the first part of the book. Unlike those who are the subject of the next chapter, neither Furet nor Rosanvallon have been outspoken critics of neo-republicanism, although Rosanvallon has been hostile to what he sees as a republican 'regression' since the 1980s.[103] But they have both attempted to nuance a neo-republican teleology that begins with the origin myth of the French Revolution, passes through the secular triumph of the Third Republic and the unifying spirit of Gaullist *grandeur*, and ends with a rejuvenated republican model in the 1990s. Thus Furet fought a pitched battle against a Jacobin-Marxist interpretation of the Revolution, while Rosanvallon set out to undermine the Jacobin-republican narrative of nineteenth-century French history. Both historians wanted, in their own ways, to open up a 'liberal horizon' in French politics that would be historically credible and politically feasible. And, through the EHESS, the Centre Raymond Aron and the Fondation Saint-Simon, they have cast a long shadow over contemporary French thought. Of course, this alone is unlikely to guarantee the successful spread of a liberal vision of history and politics, particularly on the left, where the legacy of Jacobin, Marxist and republican narratives is still extremely powerful. But Furet and Rosanvallon demonstrated that neo-republicanism was not the only response to the disintegration of the Marxist consensus in France in the 1980s.

---

[103] Rosanvallon, 'Malaise dans la représentation', p. 140.

8 Post-colonies II: the politics of multiculturalism and colonial memory

> Comme ça, vous m'avez trahi!/ ... Ala oujhi enkartouni, ou goltou étranger/Kont haseb fi bledi, ou hnaya enmout/Choftkom wellit ghrib la wal ou le hbib/Pourtant zeïd hna ou hadha echchay hram!
>
> (You betrayed me like this!/ ... Because of my appearance, you called me an 'étranger'/I thought I was at home and that here I would die/But I saw you and became a stranger, without mentor, without friend/ Knowing that I was born here, what you do is a sin!)
>
> Algerian rai singer Cheb Mami in his hit song *Parisien du Nord*[1]

In the first part of this book I discussed the extent to which France's post-colonial predicament gave a powerful impetus to the language of neo-republicanism. The rise of such defining concepts as *intégration* and *communautarisme* were intimately tied up with a growing awareness of the challenges posed by settled post-colonial immigration and the battle for France's colonial memory. However, my focus on the intellectual and political response to France's post-colonial predicament meant that I largely put to one side the political implications of this increasingly important counter-narrative. It is these implications that I intend to explore in this chapter. For if, as many have argued, the French academy has been slow to absorb the lessons of Anglo-American post-colonial theory, this does not mean that a French post-colonial critique has not emerged in the past three decades. On the contrary, it will be my contention that, even in comparison with the fundamental reinterpretation of modern French history that was the subject of the previous chapter, few counter-narratives have been as potent or as far-reaching.

The decision to include this chapter in a part devoted to liberal critics of contemporary France might appear unorthodox: at first glance,

---

[1] Cheb Mami, 'Parisien du Nord (Remix)' in *Meli Meli* (Virgin Music, 1998). This version of the song also features French lyrics from guest rapper Imhotep from the French rap supergroup IAM. My rendering of the North African Arabic is based on a translation by Professor Ted Swedenburg, who, in his blog, translated this song with the help of anthropologists Nadil Boudraa and David McMurray (http://swedenburg.blogspot.com/ 2005/11/parisien-du-nord-reprise.html, last accessed 30 January 2011).

we are far from the historiographical and intellectual concerns of anti-totalitarianism or even those of the *bande d'aroniens* who carried the liberal flame into the 1980s and 90s. Moreover, many of the actors discussed in this chapter have had extensive involvement with the left and even the far left. Nevertheless, the central themes of France's post-colonial critique – multiculturalism, colonial memory, 'ethnic' politics ... – fit perfectly with the contextual definition of liberalism which underpins Part II. Not only have the theoretical foundations of a good deal of French multicultural theory been influenced by an important pluralist strand in North American liberal thought, but the post-colonial critique discussed below provides possibly the most explicit recent challenge to a neo-republican national narrative.

This critique has employed three angles of attack. The first has condemned neo-republicanism for its lack of empirical sophistication: its normative prescriptions, it is argued, simply do not reflect the sociological realities in France. The second has accused neo-republicans of imposing a highly limiting, and quasi-colonial, notion of citizenship on post-colonial migrants; in particular, it is claimed that the neo-republican, colour-blind model of integration denies the racial and ethnic stigmatisation of minorities in France. The third has sought to delegitimise – or, at the very least, contextualise – a historical 'republican model' by exposing the extent to which it was implicated in France's colonial crimes. Together, these three approaches have constituted a formidable response to the basic assumptions of neo-republicanism. And, by explicitly targeting its 'rationalist' and 'universalist' pretensions, they offer an alternative vision of French history and society which belongs alongside other liberal attempts to reform the country's powerful statist and neo-republican traditions.

La France ethnique? Multiculturalism, *droit à la différence* and identity politics

Given the significance of the neo-republican resurgence in the 1980s, and its explicit criticism of multiculturalism and *communautarisme*, it is hard to believe that there could have been anything in France akin to the forms of ethnic 'identity politics' found in the United States or the United Kingdom. Nevertheless, as I suggested in my earlier analysis of *parité* and regional languages, there was a period in the mid 1980s when identity politics were an accepted part of the French political landscape. It was at this moment that a number of non- and semi-governmental organisations emerged, whose main aim was to combat racism and to defend the 'rights' of second- and third-generation migrant children, principally of North African origin. Their limited successes offer us a number of insights into France's complex negotiation of its colonial heritage, as well as providing a case study of how a liberal pluralist counter-narrative could develop in practice.

Two contexts are crucial to an understanding of how these organisations emerged: the change of government in 1981 and the appearance of the term *beur* in public discourse. As a number of scholars have persuasively argued, the electoral success of the Socialists marked a break in terms of cultural and political manifestations of 'diversity'.[2] Whether in terms of the state's stance on homosexuality, or of the efforts made to support the development of regional identities and language, the first years of the Socialist administration demonstrated a desire to dismantle those aspects of the Jacobin and Gaullist models considered most inimical to diversity. This was partly a belated recognition of important intellectual and political strands that had emerged on the left after 1968. It also reflected a shift away from Marxist economic orthodoxy to a more cultural approach to the question of inequality. Massive cultural events – such as the Fête de la Musique, set up by Culture Minister Jack Lang in 1981 – were designed to show that France could not only withstand the economic crises of the time, but also celebrate its diverse cultural heritage.[3] The concepts of 'difference' and 'identity', which had long been delegitimised by Gaullism's emphasis on national unity, began to make an appearance in political discussions. Within a year or two, this new trend had a name: *droit à la différence*, an idea that deftly combined the notion of difference with a (rather Jacobin-sounding) rights-based claim on the French state.

For a brief moment in the early 1980s, then, it was acceptable to articulate politically one's cultural, historical and linguistic diversity – and such expressions might receive significant state support. In this context, it is not surprising that second- and third-generation immigrant children found themselves at the heart of the debate surrounding *droit à la différence* and began to take on stronger, more militant identities. The most obvious manifestation of this was in the realm of language. It was in the early 1980s that the word *beur* – French *verlan* (reverse slang) for 'Arab' – emerged to describe what in an Anglo-American context would be called the North African 'ethnic minority'. For young North African immigrant children, the term gave them a distinct identity; and,

---

[2] William Safran, 'State, Nation, National Identity, and Citizenship: France as a Test Case', *International Political Science Review* (Vol. 12, No. 3, 1991), pp. 219–38.
[3] On Jack Lang's justification for a Fête de la Musique, see an interview in *Journal Télévisé 20h*, Antenne 2 (20 June 1982).

as France sought to understand the divided identities of its immigrant children, scholars, activists and journalists became increasingly interested in *beur* politics and literature.[4] The latter, embodied in the heavily-autobiographical early work of authors such as Leïla Sebbar and Azouz Bégag, provided an insight into the everyday contradictions of French republicanism and the predicaments of what commentators described as 'the Beur Generation'.[5] This literary consciousness was augmented by other cultural expressions of difference – such as the community radio 'Radio Beur' (later Beur FM), founded in 1981 and the contemporary dance troupe Black, Blanc, Beur, founded in 1984 – and above all a growing strand of political activism, which demanded that specific attention be paid to the problems of *beurs* and second-generation migrants.[6]

As the historian Daniel A. Gordon has argued in his work on immigrant activism during and after 1968, there was a wide range of immigrant politics before 1981 and immigrant groups were also mobilised by far-left trade union and activist organisations.[7] But the early 1980s marked a break as an older generation of activists – many of whom were left-leaning first-generation immigrants – gave way to a younger wave of second- and third-generation activists born in France.[8] These new forms of politicisation crystallised in the early years of the Socialist government, most notably in the Marche pour l'égalité et contre le racisme, more commonly known as the Marche des beurs, which reached Paris in December 1983.[9] Led by Père Christian Delorme

[4] Michel Laronde, 'La mouvance beur: une émergence médiatique', *French Review* (Vol. 61, No. 5, 1988), pp. 684–92.

[5] On this, see Alec Hargreaves, 'Beur Fiction: Voices from the Immigrant Community in France', *French Review* (Vol. 62, No. 4, 1989), pp. 661–8; Alec Hargreaves, 'Beurgeoisie: mediation or mirage', *Journal of European Studies* (Vol. 28, 1998), pp. 89–102; and Térrasse and Linhart, *Génération Beur*.

[6] Until its recognition by the state in 1983, Radio Beur was a pirate radio. Its founder Nacer Kettane would later participate in the Marche des beurs. Catherine Humblot, 'Beur FM, laïque d'abord', *Le Monde* (7 August 2005). On the foundation of 'Black, Blanc, Beur' see Térrasse and Linhart, *Génération Beur*, pp. 142–5 and www.blackblancbeur.fr.

[7] Daniel A. Gordon, *Immigrants and intellectuals: May '68 and the rise of anti-racism in France* (Pontypool: Merlin Press, 2012). See also Miriam Bouregba-Dichy, 'Des militants maghrébins de la deuxième génération en France', *Tiers-Monde* (Vol. 31, No. 123), pp. 623–36, and Didier Lapeyronnie, 'Assimilation, mobilisation et action collective chez les jeunes de la seconde génération de l'immigration maghrébine', *Revue française de sociologie* (Vol. 28, No. 2, 1987), pp. 287–318.

[8] Daniel A. Gordon, 'From militancy to history: Sans Frontière and immigrant memory at the dawn of the 1980s', in Chabal, *France since the 1970s*.

[9] Philippe Bernard, 'La longue marche des beurs', *Le Monde* (3 December 1983). The idea of a march was explicitly inspired by Gandhi and Martin Luther King's non-violent protests.

(a noted social activist in Lyon), the local branch of the Cimade (the Protestant assistance service) and a number of *beur* youths who had been the victims of urban violence in the Minguettes neighbourhood of Lyon, the marchers walked from Marseille to Paris, gathering support from local immigrant, anti-racist and left-wing groups as they went along.[10] The march gained significant media exposure and culminated in a meeting at the Elysée Palace between Mitterrand and the marchers, whose demands included, among other things, the granting of ten-year residency permits to migrants and the right to vote.[11] The national presence of the Marche des beurs encouraged similar initiatives in the following years, including a 'Marche des mobylettes' (scooter march) in 1984.[12] But the most powerful legacy of these early, ecumenical and media-friendly attempts to put forward the *beur* cause was the formation in 1985 of SOS Racisme.

This contested and sometimes controversial organisation perfectly embodied both the potential and the contradictions of 'ethnic politics' in France.[13] SOS Racisme was founded in late 1984 by a group of young former student radicals, of whom the most important were Harlem Désir and Julien Dray. As the sociologist Philippe Juhem has argued, the creation of a new anti-racist organisation was a way for Dray and Désir to develop their political careers on the left after their detachment from the world of far-left student politics.[14] At the same time, SOS Racisme's agenda explicitly endorsed a more 'modern', 'apolitical' form of activism. By founding an organisation that would revolve around anti-racism and provide a concrete response to the Front National's first electoral successes in 1984–5, Dray and Désir were deliberately canvassing a broad spectrum of opinion, particularly among a youth increasingly disillusioned with traditional party politics. It was this that led to SOS Racisme's extraordinary success. After a faltering start, a number of intellectuals and political leaders of the left and centre came out in support of the organisation, and intelligent public relations management on the part of its leaders

---

[10] The Marche des beurs was dramatised in Nabil ben Yadir's 2013 feature film *La Marche*. The film presents a rather romanticised and partisan account, which stresses the individual stories of the marchers over the political context.

[11] Mogniss Abdallah, '1983: la marche pour l'égalité', *Plein Droit* (No. 55, 2002). On the arrival of the Marche in Paris, see *Journal Télévisé 20h*, Antenne 2 (3 December 1983).

[12] On the arrival of the Marche des Mobylettes, otherwise known as Convergence 1984, see *Journal Télévisé 20h*, Antenne 2 (1 December 1984).

[13] I am grateful to Philippe Juhem for permission to consult his doctoral thesis on SOS Racisme; it is currently by far the most reliable account of the organisation's history.

[14] On this, see especially Philippe Juhem, 'Entreprendre en politique. De l'extrême gauche au PS: la professionnalisation politique des fondateurs de SOS Racisme', *Revue française de science politique* (Vol. 51, Nos. 1–2, 2001), pp. 131–45.

led to a deluge of positive press coverage.[15] With media success came the audience: the sale of its now-famous 'Touche pas à mon pote!' ('Hands off my pal!') badges took off in schools and *lycées* all over the country, and local offices were opened in numerous cities. By the end of 1985, SOS Racisme had overtaken the older Mouvement contre le racisme et pour l'amitié entre les peuples (MRAP) and the Ligue des droits de l'homme (LDH) as France's most important anti-racist organisation.

A clear indication of SOS Racisme's success was the enormous multicultural free concert it put together on 15 June 1985 in Paris, which gathered over 300,000 people and received substantial financial support from the Socialist government. Very much in the spirit of Lang's Fête de la Musique, this was the opportunity to put forward a political agenda using the language of cultural diversity and 'apolitical' anti-racism.[16] Inevitably, with the defeat of the Socialists in 1986, SOS Racisme lost much of its funding. It nevertheless continued to be active, organising large-scale public concerts every year and intervening frequently in public debates surrounding racism.[17] In the end, however, it was not the lack of financial support but the changing configuration of French politics that resulted in the organisation's demise. The rise of a strong neo-republican discourse severely delegitimised SOS Racisme. Already as early as 1985, a rival anti-racist organisation had been set up by Arezki Dahmani called France-Plus, which claimed that SOS Racisme's lukewarm endorsement of *droit à la différence* was inimical to the fight against racism.[18] A successful anti-racist movement, argued Dahmani, needed to promote republican integration rather than difference.[19] This became a familiar refrain, particularly after the *affaire du foulard* in 1989. At that point, intellectuals such as Taguieff, who had previously been strong supporters of the anti-racist movement, turned against 'antiracist ideology' on the grounds that it was the harbinger of divisive *communautarisme*.[20]

---

[15] See the quantitative analysis of the newspaper coverage of SOS Racisme in Philippe Juhem, 'La participation des médias à l'émergence des mouvements sociaux: le cas de SOS Racisme', *Réseaux* (Vol. 17, No. 98, 1999), p. 121–52.

[16] Philippe Juhem, 'SOS Racisme. Histoire d'une mobilisation "apolitique". Contribution à une analyse des transformations des représentations politiques après 1981', unpublished PhD thesis, Université de Nanterre: Faculté de Sciences Politiques (1998), esp pp. 613–30.

[17] For instance with respect to the reforms of the Code de la Nationalité in 1987.

[18] For a short history of France-Plus, see Hargreaves, 'Beurgeoisie', pp. 92–4.

[19] On France Plus's attitude towards integration, see for instance an interview with Dahmani and other members of France-Plus in 1990. *Du côté de chez Fred*, Antenne 2 (30 May 1990).

[20] See especially Taguieff, *Fins de l'antiracisme*. See also earlier publications such as Pierre-André Taguieff, 'Le néo-racisme différencialiste', *Langage et société* (No. 34, 1985),

SOS Racisme, which had become associated with the incipient multiculturalism of the *droit à la différence* movement, found itself in the firing line of this renewed neo-republican critique. By choosing not to support the banning of the headscarf in 1989, the organisation for the first time opened itself up to the hostility of the press, which followed Taguieff in condemning its potentially anti-republican position.[21] The widespread residual sympathy for SOS Racisme prevented it from falling apart altogether but, when Fodé Sylla took over as president in 1992, the organisation refocused its activities on local anti-racist campaigns rather than political pronouncements. Even so, it was not immune to the shifting ideological tides: the subsequent president, Malek Boutih (1999–2003), held a strongly neo-republican line on the integration of migrants, before resigning his post to join the higher levels of the PS.[22] At the time of writing, under the leadership of Dominique Sopo, SOS Racisme had a relatively low profile, although it still contributed to public debates.

This transformation of an organisation, whose commitment to *droit à la différence* was at best rather weak, into yet another vehicle for a neo-republican discourse of integration provides us with an important example of the limits of multicultural counter-narratives. For various political and conjectural reasons, the period from 1981 to 1989 was amenable to the celebrations of diversity that were implicit in much of what SOS Racisme did. But the return of neo-republicanism in the late 1980s damaged the legitimacy of this alternative voice. Moreover, the erstwhile extreme-left student activists who had given birth to the organisation were, by this stage, seeking respectability inside the PS, which was itself divided between those still committed to *droit à la différence* and those embracing the return to republicanism. Paradoxically, the external force that had given SOS Racisme such a push – the Front National – also acted as a powerful catalyst for the reformulation of the republican model. In the subsequent clash of ideologies, it was the latter that triumphed.

Yet, despite its failures, the *droit à la différence* moment in French politics has had a number of long-term effects. This is evident, for instance, in the success of less overtly political but still community-orientated projects such as Beur FM, which now has a wide listener base

---

pp. 69–98, and Pierre-André Taguieff, 'L'antiracisme en crise: élements d'une critique réformiste', in Michel Wieviorka (ed.), *Racisme et modernité* (Paris: La Découverte, 1992).

[21] Juhem, 'SOS Racisme. Histoire d'une mobilisation', pp. 44–62.

[22] Harlem Désir has followed a similar trajectory into mainstream politics, first as a Socialist and Green MEP for Paris in 1999–2012, then as first secretary of the PS and, most recently, as a minister in the Valls governments. On this metamorphosis see Christine Garin, 'Harlem Désir; au-delà des potes', *Le Monde* (4 June 2008).

across France; or in the creation of state anti-racism institutions such as the Haute autorité de lutte contre les discriminations et pour l'égalité (HALDE) in 2004.[23] We have also seen how the unexpected passing of the *loi pour la parité* was a legacy of this period. Perhaps most of all, the *droit à la différence* moment in the 1980s provided the necessary space for the development of a parallel movement in the academy, namely the development of a multicultural critique of French society and the creation of 'ethnic' histories. In Part I, devoted to neo-republicanism, we saw the sometimes violent polemics that have accompanied the emergence of these ideas in France, but here I should like to examine the debate as it was seen by those who were broadly supportive of a multicultural paradigm. This allows us to see more clearly the ways in which this counter-narrative sought to undermine an otherwise hegemonic language of neo-republican integration and citizenship.

If there is one person who can be credited with encouraging a positive debate around the merits of multiculturalism in the French academy, it is Michel Wieviorka. A student of the eminent sociologist Alain Touraine, with whom he published in the late 1970s and 1980s a number of collaborative volumes on social movements, Wieviorka has consistently sought to push a very broad multicultural agenda in his work and his public interventions since the 1980s.[24] Given his unusual and outspoken position, it would be fair to say that almost all the most significant sociological work on multiculturalism, diversity and difference in France has taken place under his supervision. Indeed, like Furet and Rosanvallon, he has sought to extend his intellectual reach by leading a research centre at the EHESS: the Centre d'analyses et d'interventions stratégiques (CADIS), originally founded in 1981 by Alain Touraine. By bringing together a number of specialists, and training a new generation of doctoral students, Wieviorka has been able to secure a (sometimes tenuous) place for empirical studies of multiculturalism and diversity.[25] His intellectual trajectory bears witness to the fact that the *droit à la différence* moment had a number of important consequences for the academic debate surrounding multiculturalism in France.[26]

---

[23] On Beur FM, see Nabil Echchaibi, 'Republican Betrayal: Beur FM and the Suburban Riots in France', *Journal of Intercultural Studies* (Vol. 28, No. 3, 2007), pp. 301–16.

[24] See for instance Alain Touraine, Michel Wieviorka and François Dubet, *Le mouvement ouvrier* (Paris: Fayard, 1984).

[25] A good example of such work by one of Wieviorka's doctoral students is N. Guénif-Souilamas, *Des 'Beurettes' aux descendants d'immigrants nord-africains* (Paris: Grasset, 2000).

[26] Wieviorka himself had good personal relations with the founders of SOS Racisme. Personal interview with the author (31 January 2011).

The first indication of Wieviorka's sustained interest in such questions was in the early 1990s, when he published a number of books on racism, anti-racism and the 'crisis of modernity'.[27] This culminated in a key collaborative text entitled *Une société fragmentée: le multiculturalisme en débat* (1996) that propelled Wieviorka and his colleagues at CADIS to the heart of an ongoing civic debate.[28] Almost all the essays in the volume agreed that the 'French model of integration' was outdated and struggling to keep pace with the transformation of post-industrial France. While a number of contributors warned that simply importing a vulgarised multicultural doctrine would do little to solve the problem, there was a general consensus that a much more serious debate on the tension between 'universal references ... and the respect for cultural particularisms' was long overdue.[29] In the intellectual climate of the time, this was a strong claim.

Of course, the emergence of the term *fracture sociale* in the mid 1990s put the problem of social 'fragmentation' centre stage, and it is hardly surprising that this apparently strong endorsement of multiculturalism would be controversial. To his detractors, Wieviorka became the embodiment of 'multicultural orthodoxy', and intellectuals such as Taguieff and Finkielkraut rushed to criticise him for his positions.[30] This has not deterred Wieviorka – who, on occasion, has chosen to reply in kind. Thus, in 2005, he memorably branded Finkielkraut a 'republican-communitarian ... [who] has gone off the rails', after the philosopher claimed that the riots that summer were provoked by an 'ethnic-religious revolt' on the part of Arabs and blacks, and more recently he has simply described Finkielkraut's ideas as 'unfounded and ignorant'.[31] More significantly, despite being highly contested, Wieviorka's ideas have gained ever greater exposure. In February 2008 he was called on by the Minister of Higher Education Valérie Pécresse to draft a report on 'diversity', which was published in paperback the same year as *La diversité: rapport à la ministre de l'Enseignement supérieur et de la Recherche*.[32] It is

---

[27] See especially Wieviorka, *Racisme et modernité*, and Michel Wieviorka, *L'espace du racisme* (Paris: Seuil, 1991).

[28] Thomas Ferenczi, 'Le refus du multiculturalisme se nourrit de peurs et de méconnaissance', *Le Monde* (8 October 1996).

[29] Michel Wieviorka, 'Introduction. Un débat nécessaire', in Michel Wieviorka (ed.), *Une société fragmentée: le multiculturalisme en débat* (Paris: La Découverte, 1996), p. 8.

[30] See for instance Taguieff, *La République enlisée*, p. 295.

[31] 'Interview avec Michel Wieviorka: l'affaire Finkielkraut', *Le Nouvel Observateur* (25 November 2005). Michel Wieviorka, *Neuf leçons de sociologie* (Paris: Pluriel, 2011), p. 174.

[32] Michel Wieviorka, *La diversité. Rapport à la ministre de l'Enseignement supérieur et de la Recherche* (Paris: Robert Laffont, 2008).

noteworthy that, of the team Wieviorka assembled to help him complete the report, half were members of CADIS, and the report's intellectual parameters were evidently set by Wieviorka himself.[33]

For this reason, it provides an excellent introduction to an alternative reading of the contemporary French national narrative. For, unlike neo-republicans who have continued to emphasise the primacy of a unified, political nation, the report makes an extended case for 'diversity'. The authors explicitly accuse neo-republicans of creating false dichotomies and polarising an otherwise delicate discussion surrounding the question of 'diversity' in France.[34] Instead of focusing obsessively on multiculturalism or *communautarisme*, the authors suggest that the term 'diversity' is more appropriate to contemporary French society.[35] 'Diversity' allows for the incorporation of 'difference', a key term in Wieviorka's sociology.[36] An appreciation of differences within a society is, the report argues, essential for an understanding of contemporary France. By minimising the importance of difference, neo-republicans limit their conceptual framework. Indeed, the report goes so far as to say that the 'framework of the nation state has been exhausted'.[37] Such a claim is an indication of the intellectual and political distance that separates Wieviorka from many of his peers: far from a neo-republican defence of the unified nation, here is an alternative reading of the nation as fragmented, stratified and differentiated. This vision supports the report's numerous proposals, which include recommendations that the European Charter for Regional or Minority Languages be ratified, and that French school and higher educational curricula pay more attention to the implications of cultural studies and anthropology in understanding France's post-colonial character.[38] These arguments are consistent with other positions Wieviorka has taken over the years, such as his open support for the collection of ethnic statistics.[39]

---

[33] The team consisted of the following members: Giulia Fabbiano, Yvon Le Bot, Jocelyne Ohana, Alexandra Poli (all at CADIS), Richard Beraha (president of the association Hui Ji), Hervé Le Bras (at the EHESS and the INED) and Catherine Wihtol de Wenden (at the CNRS and the CERI).

[34] The report launches a strong attack on neo-republicans: Wieviorka, *La diversité*, pp. 55–8.

[35] Ibid., pp. 23, 74–5.

[36] See especially Michel Wieviorka, *La différence. Identités culturelles: enjeux, débats et politiques* (Paris: Fayard, 2001).

[37] Wieviorka, *La diversité*, p. 43.   [38] Ibid., pp. 98–100.

[39] Michel Wieviorka and Patrick Lozès, 'Contre les discriminations, unissons-nous!', *Le Monde* (12 February 2008), or his critique of 'nationalist' and neo-republican interpretations of French national identity in Michel Wieviorka, 'La désacralisation de l'identité française', *Le Figaro* (11 June 2004).

This is not the only way in which Wieviorka has sought to undermine the hegemony of neo-republicanism: like many of the liberal intellectuals we have discussed so far, he has also been open to intellectual trends emanating from the English-speaking world. His work has shown a consistent engagement with figures such as Charles Taylor and Will Kymlicka – both of whom have been influential in theoretical elaborations of multiculturalism – and he was president of the International Sociology Association in 2006–10.[40] Indeed, as part of his efforts to force open the field of French sociology and politics, he has frequently argued that unreflexive anti-Americanism is, in his words, 'one of the most outdated expressions of the French intellectual'.[41] But, despite the fact that he has actively contributed to defining France's sociological image abroad, he has remained closely attached to political developments inside France, to the extent that one of his most recent works proposed a progressive programme for a Socialist government.[42] At the same time, he has explicitly supported those inside France who have worked on questions of identity, difference, migration and diversity. One of the results of this has been the very slow development of explicitly 'ethnic' or 'racial' histories in France.

Given the strong taboos attached in France to expressions of ethnic difference, there has been a good deal of reluctance towards the 'ethnicisation' of history. Nevertheless, there are a number of initiatives that suggest this attitude is changing. The best example is undoubtedly the controversial foundation in November 2005 of the Conseil représentatif des associations noires (CRAN), a lobbying organisation that focuses specifically on issues pertinent to the black community in France.[43] The CRAN has provided a framework for a form of black politics, and has encouraged work on race in France. So, for instance, they have supported scholars like Pap Ndiaye who have attempted to write a history of black people in France and explore the nature of the 'condition of black people' in contemporary French society.[44] However, this kind of

---

[40] For a recent theoretical discussion of multiculturalism, and the work of Taylor and Kymlicka, see Wieviorka, *Neuf leçons de sociologie*, pp. 143–85.

[41] Quoted in Thomas Ferenczi, 'Les impasses de l'antiaméricanisme', *Le Monde* (6 September 1999).

[42] Michel Wieviorka, *Pour la prochaine gauche. Le monde change; la gauche doit changer aussi* (Paris: Odile Jacob, 2011). See also Wieviorka's contribution to the PS's recent 'livre-programme' Martine Aubry (ed.), *Pour changer de civilisation* (Paris: Odile Jacob, 2011).

[43] For perspectives on the formation of the CRAN, see for instance Didier Arnaud, 'Si on est conscient de son passé, on devient sujet de son avenir', *Libération* (26 November 2005), Sylvie Kauffmann, 'Patrick Lozès', *Le Monde* (7 December 2005), and Benoît Hopquin, 'Colère noire', *Le Monde* (10 December 2005).

[44] Pap Ndiaye, *La condition noire: essai sur une minorité française* (Paris: Calmann-Lévy, 2008).

approach remains uncommon, and it is no coincidence that Ndiaye should be both a historian of the United States at the EHESS and a committee member of the CRAN. In his case, he has had significant exposure to American forms of identity politics that remain marginal in France.

Even so, it is clear that, in its broadest form, multiculturalism has made significant inroads into French academia. With the help of scholars like Wieviorka, it now has a guaranteed place at the heart of sociological enquiries dealing with society, migration and contemporary politics. Moreover, the growing support for initiatives that have sought to rehabilitate or write 'ethnic' histories has ensured that the nascent field of race and ethnicity studies in France has not gone unnoticed: if nothing else, Wieviorka's presidency of the CRAN's scientific advisory board will do much to guarantee the organisation's academic legitimacy.[45] Thus, despite the relative political failure of the *droit à la différence* movement, there has been a noticeable softening of France's attitude to such issues as diversity, race, multiculturalism, difference and ethnicity. The dominant presence of a neo-republican discourse has inevitably meant that it has faced strong opposition, but these issues are now being widely discussed.

La guerre des mémoires: colonial memory and the post-colonial challenge

Nowhere has this new consciousness been more evident than in the thorny arguments over France's colonial past. We saw in the first part of the book how France's post-colonial predicament helped to shape a neo-republican reading of France's national narrative and forge a consensus around the renewed value of *intégration républicaine* and *laïcité*. We did not, however, examine directly the development of France's post-colonial critique. In the second part of this chapter, I should like to show how the multifarious post-colonial 'memory wars' that have become an integral part of twenty-first-century French politics have come to constitute one of the most significant challenges to neo-republicanism. Unlike the development of 'ethnic politics' and 'ethnic histories', which have been continuously hampered by their supposedly anti-republican character, the post-colonial critique quite explicitly takes aim at historical and contemporary republicanism. By arguing that the legacies of imperialism

---

[45] Wieviorka supported the creation of the CRAN from its inception. Catherine Rotman, 'Michel Wieviorka, Sociologue, se félicite de la création du CRAN', *Libération* (29 April 2006).

and slavery must be incorporated into France's national narrative, it has undermined the universalist pretensions and progressive teleologies that were rehabilitated by scholars of the Republic and the nation in the 1980s.

Where advocates of *droit à la différence* in the 1980s – many of whom were ethnic minorities – continuously tried to find a middle ground between particularist representation and the desire to participate in a project of (national) integration, many of those who have campaigned for a greater appreciation of France's colonial past since the 1990s have publicly attacked what they see as a stultifying consensus surrounding the national narrative. Even if the *droit à la différence* movement had an important role to play in legitimising a multicultural discourse, it took the explosion of colonial memories in the late 1990s to bring the subject firmly into the public eye. In large part, this had to do with the fact that the post-colonial critique emerged first from the academy, unlike the *droit à la différence* movement, which was a political project built on the back of disparate local community organisations. But it also had to do with the fact that the post-colonial critique that has emerged in recent years, like anti-colonial movements in the past, has used the values of republicanism in order to build a critique of republicanism: by targeting the moral foundation of republicanism – that is, its historical narrative – it has ensured that colonial memories will continue to haunt France for years to come.

It has now become a truism to say that France was extremely resistant to the wave of post-colonial theory that shook the Anglo-American academy in the 1980s.[46] To the majority of French social scientists, literary scholars and historians, the influence of Edward Saïd's work on orientalism or the subaltern studies movement was negligible until the 1990s.[47] As the historian Catherine Coquery-Vidovitch put it in an article on the historiography of empire in 1987, 'the debate [over empire] ... seems today to be much more vibrant in the Anglo-Saxon world'.[48] Stranded between the collapse of a Marxist consensus that had emphasised above all the economic dimensions of the colonial project, and a renewed interest in the nation and the Republic, French imperial

---

[46] On this, see e.g. Charles Forsdick, 'Between "French" and "Francophone"': French Studies and the Postcolonial Turn', *French Studies* (Vol. 59, 2005), pp. 523–30, and Charles Forsdick and David Murphy (eds.), *Francophone Postcolonial Studies: A Critical Introduction* (London: Arnold, 2003).

[47] Marie-Claude Smouts (ed.), *La situation postcoloniale. Les postcolonial studies dans le débat français* (Paris: Presses de Sciences Po, 2007).

[48] Catherine Coquery-Vidovitch, 'Les débats actuels en histoire de la colonisation', *Tiers-Monde* (Vol. 28, No. 112, 1987), p. 777.

history in the 1980s appeared unusually detached from the innovations taking place outside France.[49] It was in this context that a number of individuals and research groups emerged, whose aim it was to re-energise the study of the French colonial empire and, above all, to introduce the questions of colonial memory and post-colonial identity that had transformed the study of imperial history in the English-speaking world.[50]

Foremost among these was the Association pour la connaissance de l'histoire de l'Afrique contemporaine (ACHAC), founded in 1989 by Pascal Blanchard, a scholar of the body and imperialism. Along with his colleagues Nicolas Bancel and Sandrine Lemaire, Blanchard built an organisation that has worked tirelessly to bring post-colonial studies to France. This has included frequent appearances in the print, radio and television media, and a number of exhibitions in Paris and elsewhere on subjects as varied as the presence of blacks in the French football team to the objectification of the exotic body in the colonial period.[51] Most importantly, ACHAC has supported a bewildering array of publications, which in a short space of time have come to constitute the most substantial corpus of explicitly 'post-colonial' scholarship in France. These have primarily turned around the four key research themes of the association: immigration from the south, stereotypes and images in colonial ethnography, the development of a colonial culture in France, and the post-colonial legacy of French imperialism. They have also almost always been vast transnational collaborative ventures, bringing together French and foreign scholars of empire – many of whom were involved in earlier attempts to rehabilitate multiculturalism.[52]

Many of ACHAC's publications have already left a lasting impression. For instance, *La Republique coloniale* (2003) dealt unambiguously with the troubled relationship between Republic and empire throughout its history.[53] Quite apart from the historiographical value of a post-colonial approach to republicanism, the authors use their arguments to build a

---

[49] For attempts to incorporate these Anglo-American methods, see for instance Vergès, *La mémoire enchaînée* or Ndiaye, *La condition noire*.

[50] Many of the actors involved in this renewed academic interest in colonial history and post-colonialism were represented at the Histoires coloniales conference, held at the Centre Pompidou, Paris, in November 2005. The proceedings were published as Benjamin Stora and Daniel Hémery (eds.), *Histoires coloniales. Héritages et transmissions* (Paris: Bibliothèque Centre Pompidou, 2007).

[51] For full details of ACHAC's activities, see www.achac.com/?P=10.

[52] For instance, in the ACHAC-sponsored volume entitled *La fracture coloniale* (2003), contributors included Wieviorka and Lapeyronnie, as well as Nacira Guénif-Souilamas, one of Wieviorka's students.

[53] Nicolas Bancel, Pascal Blanchard and Françoise Vergès, *La République coloniale* (Paris: Albin Michel, 2003).

critique of a contemporary republicanism that refuses to consider its colonial heritage. As they put it,

> Let us clearly state the paradox: [the French] Republic is born out of a revolution that brings to the world the ideals of the Enlightenment – against tyranny and exceptionalism, and for equality and liberty; this Republic takes shape over the course of centuries in its struggle against conservative political movements and advocates of social inequality; … yet, this same Republic builds a colonial empire where the rule is exceptionalism, inequality and arbitrary behaviour.[54]

The message is clear: by glorifying its 'rationalist', 'progressive' or 'revolutionary' credentials, neo-republicanism has deliberately contributed to France's colonial 'silence'. The authors extended this critique in a subsequent collaborative volume, entitled *La fracture coloniale* (2005), where they looked at the consequences of the colonial encounter for contemporary French society.[55] It was indicative of the changing attitudes towards post-colonialism in the mid 2000s that the notion of *la fracture coloniale* – like that of the *fracture sociale* which had inspired it – quickly passed into common usage.

More recently, another collaborative volume entitled *Les Guerres de Mémoires: La France et son histoire* (2008) has attempted to connect the current 'memory wars' with broader themes in French history.[56] While the contributions cover everything from slavery and immigration to the First World War and Internet 'memory wars', the underlying theme is that France has not resolved many of its *guerres de mémoires*. As the introduction makes clear, there is an ever growing number of claims for recognition.[57] Several other essays echo this sentiment; national memory has become 'fragmented' or 'confused'.[58] A purely national framework, it is argued, cannot integrate the many conflicting narratives that have emerged, say, from second-generation immigrant groups. In keeping with much of ACHAC's previous work, *Les Guerres de Mémoires* sets out to demonstrate that, in order to move beyond current disagreements, the French first have to develop a multilayered approach to memory. Any conception of the nation that endeavours to unite the French behind either a common secular culture or a common set of political and civic values is unlikely to

---

[54] Ibid., p. 16.   [55] Blanchard, Bancel and Lemaire, *La fracture coloniale.*
[56] Blanchard and Veyrat-Masson, *Les Guerres de Mémoires*, p. 32.
[57] Pascal Blanchard and Isabelle Veyrat-Masson, 'Les guerres de mémoires: un objet d'étude, au carrefour de l'histoire et des processus de médiatisation', in Blanchard and Veyrat-Masson, *Les Guerres de Mémoires*, p. 32.
[58] See Olivier Wieviorka, 'Francisque ou Croix de Lorraine: les années sombres entre histoire, mémoire et mythologie', and Françoise Vergès, 'Esclavage colonial: quelles mémoires? Quels héritages?', in Blanchard and Veyrat-Masson, *Les Guerres de Mémoires*.

be successful in resolving France's *guerres de mémoires* – at least not until the French pass through a thorough 'decolonisation' of the mind.[59]

Inevitably, ACHAC's wide-ranging and sustained attempt to raise the profile of post-colonial studies in France has met with opposition. Some, like Noiriel, have argued that ACHAC's post-colonial approach is deeply flawed and potentially dangerous on the grounds that it encourages today's generation to believe that their problems are all 'due' to France's colonial past, a position he obviously rejects, given his deep commitment to a French model of integration.[60] Likewise, scholars such as the African historian Jean-François Bayart and the venerable historian of French imperialism Claude Liauzu have been critical of the organisation, even though they remain broadly favourable to a reconsideration of France's colonial legacy.[61] The criticism of the latter – who died in 2007 – was a particularly good example of the kind ACHAC has faced from those who had always considered themselves to be engaged anti-colonial scholars. Despite the fact that Liauzu welcomed the opportunity to revisit France's colonial past, on several occasions he called into question ACHAC's tendency to 'polarise' colonial history and encourage 'divisions' in post-colonial memory.[62] In a revealing passage in an article published in 2005, he argued for the need to 'relativise the importance of colonialism in contemporary [social] problems' and work towards a 'recomposition' of the national community.[63] Such an argument reflected not just the generational differences between him and the ACHAC group of scholars, but also Liauzu's strong attachment to a republican narrative

[59] Pascal Blanchard, Sandrine Lemaire and Nicolas Bancel, 'Introduction. La fracture coloniale: une crise française', in Blanchard, Bancel and Lemaire, *La fracture coloniale*, pp. 18–30. See also Pascal Blanchard, Sandrine Lemaire and Nicolas Bancel (eds.), *Culture coloniale en France. De la Révolution française à nos jours* (Paris: Autrement, 2008), and Achille Mbembe et al., *Ruptures postcoloniales: les nouveaux visages de la société française* (Paris: La Découverte, 2010).

[60] Noiriel says that the notion of a 'fracture coloniale' is 'fausse et même injurieuse pour tous les collègues qui depuis trente ans (ou plus) ont travaillé sur cette question. De même, prétendre que les rapports entre immigration et colonisation n'ont jamais été étudiés est tout simplement risible ... Le faiblesse de ce type d'analyse fait le jeu de ceux qui, dans le camp d'en face, cherchent à réhabiliter la colonisation. Attribuer les problèmes sociaux qui touchent aujourd'hui les jeunes des quartiers populaires en invoquant rituellement "l'imaginaire colonial" interdit en effet de comprendre le fonctionnement *actuel* des relations de pouvoir, et le rôle que jouent les professionnels du discours public dans la construction des stéréotypes.' Noiriel, *Immigration, antisémitisme et racisme*, p. 681.

[61] See the radio debate between Blanchard and Bayart, on *Du grain à moudre*, France Culture (1 June 2010).

[62] Claude Liauzu, 'Pour une histoire critique de la colonisation. Pour un travail de mémoire', *Hommes et Migrations* (No. 1231, 2001), pp. 85–9.

[63] Claude Liauzu, 'Les historiens saisi par les guerres de mémoires coloniales', *Revue d'histoire moderne et contemporaine* (Vol. 52, No. 4, 2005), pp. 107–8.

of unity and progress, albeit one rooted in the communist anti-colonial engagement of his youth.[64]

Other scholars – many of whom have been closely associated with the neo-republican revival – have gone much further in their criticisms of ACHAC, by associating the attempt to examine critically France's colonial past with an outpouring of destructive 'colonial repentance'. To use the words of philosopher Henri Peña-Ruíz, '[Colonisation] was indeed terrible … But must we 'catch up' by prostrating ourselves in front of specific cultures, without any consideration of whether these deserve a critical approach or, on the contrary, targeted praise?'[65] In this (eminently neo-republican) line of reasoning, colonial guilt becomes the necessary prelude to 'dangerous' expressions of multiculturalism and religious pluralism. This is a claim we find repeated in other influential books that have appeared in recent years: it is one of many arguments mobilised by historian Daniel Lefeuvre in his *Pour en finir avec la répentance coloniale* (2006) and also, to some extent, in philosopher Pascal Bruckner's highly polemical diatribe, *La tyrannie de la pénitence: essai sur le masochisme occidental* (2006).[66] In each case, the threat of 'ethnic diversity' and a 'fragmentation' of memories lies at the heart of their arguments. Indeed, it is suggestive that Lefeuvre is a staunch opponent of the European Charter for Regional or Minority Languages and a supporter of the increasingly controversial notion of 'identité nationale'.[67] For him, to defend France's colonial past is also to defend the value and integrity of the French Republic.

This heated debate over colonial memory inside the academy has mirrored, refracted and pre-empted wider political divisions that, from the mid 1990s onwards, have helped push the post-colonial revival to centre stage. Many of these new developments have been related to the memory of the Algerian War – collective memories of which had been repressed since the 1970s.[68] However, in 1998, the trial of Maurice

---

[64] Laetitia van Eeckhout, 'Disparitions: Claude Liauzu', *Le Monde* (1 June 07).
[65] Henri Peña-Ruíz, 'Culture, cultures et laïcité', *Hommes et Migrations* (No. 1259, Jan-Feb 2006), 7.
[66] Daniel Lefeuvre, *Pour en finir avec une répentance coloniale* (Paris: Flammarion, 2006); Pascal Bruckner, *La tyrannie de la penitence: essai sur le masochisme occidental* (Paris: Grasset, 2006), esp. ch. 6. For some responses to Lefeuvre, see 'B. Stora: les faits ne sont pas suffisants pour répondre aux victimes', *Marianne* (30 September 2006), and Catherine Coquery-Vidovitch, 'Une critique du livre de Daniel Lefeuvre', available at http://cvuh.free.fr/spip.php?article73 (accessed 26 March 2011).
[67] Daniel Lefeuvre, 'L'identité nationale et la République', *Le Figaro Magazine* (30 June 2007). He also lays out his positions clearly on his blog: www.blog-lefeuvre.com.
[68] A point forcefully made in Benjamin Stora, *La gangrène et l'oubli* (Paris: La Découverte, 1991).

Papon for crimes against humanity during the Second World War brought the Algerian War to the attention of a wider public after a long period of silence.[69] The trial itself was supposed to focus only on Papon's actions during the Second World War. But, in addition to his role in the deportation of Jews during the Vichy period, Papon was also the police chief in Paris at the time of the repression of the Algerian pro-independence demonstration on 17 October 1961, in which many protestors were killed by police.[70] This meant that during the court proceedings Papon was repeatedly questioned about his role in policing Paris, notably by the historian Jean-Luc Einaudi, who had written extensively on the repression of 1961.[71] One of the results of this conflation of periods in the Papon trial was to create an association between Vichy and Algeria as 'dark' and 'silenced' moments in French history. It is hardly surprising, therefore, that many commentators compared the sudden outpouring of colonial memory in the late 1990s to the reassessment of Vichy that had taken place in the 1970s.[72] As an article in Le Monde put it starkly in 2002, 'Après Vichy, l'Algérie'.[73] Moreover, since Papon had always maintained that he had only ever acted as a loyal servant to the state, his trial raised a number of questions about the French state's responsibility to apologise for its actions. These concerns were central in subsequent attempts in the 2000s to manage France's colonial memory.

In a symbolic gesture to combat the 'amnesia' surrounding France's colonial past, the French state formally recognised in October 1999 that the Algerian conflict had been a 'war'.[74] Along with the

[69] Much has been written on the Papon trial. For some perspectives, see Nancy Wood, 'Memory on Trial in Contemporary France: The Case of Maurice Papon', History and Memory (Vol. 11, No. 1, 1999), pp. 41–76, and Richard Golsan, 'Papon: The Good, the Bad, the Ugly', SubStance (Vol. 29, No. 1, 2000), pp. 139–52.

[70] On this, see House and Macmaster, Paris 1961. On the subsequent controversy surrounding the number of deaths see J.-P. Brunet, 'Police violence in Paris, October 1961: historical sources, methods, and conclusions', Historical Journal (Vol. 51, No. 1, 2008), and the reply, Jim House and Neil Macmaster, 'Time to move on: a reply to Jean-Paul Brunet', Historical Journal (Vol. 51, No. 2, 2008), pp. 205–14.

[71] In 1999, Papon tried to sue Einaudi for defamation when the latter claimed in an editorial in Le Monde that he had been responsible for the deaths of protestors in 1961.

[72] Richard Golsan, 'Memory's Bombes à Retardement: Maurice Papon, Crimes against Humanity, and 17 October 1961', Journal of European Studies (Vol. 28, 1998), pp. 153–72.

[73] Philippe Bernard, 'Quarante ans après, les Français osent regarder en face la guerre d'Algérie', Le Monde (1 January 2002).

[74] Loi n°99–882 du 18 octobre 1999 relative à la substitution, à l'expression 'aux opérations effectuées en Afrique du Nord', de l'expression 'à la guerre d'Algérie ou aux combats en Tunisie et au Maroc', available at http://legifrance.gouv.fr/affichTexte.do?cidTexte=JORFTEXT000000578132, (accessed 22 March 2011). On recent

growing interest in post-colonial studies, this opened the door for a reassessment of France's colonial past and its responsibility for colonial violence. In some cases, the re-examination has been instigated by the actors themselves. This was evident in the widespread public debate in 2000–1 over the use of torture during the Algerian War, which saw conflicting testimonies from generals and victims come together with new historical work on the subject by younger scholars such as Sylvie Thénault and Raphaëlle Branche.[75] Likewise, the growing recognition of the *harkis* – those Algerians who fought for the French during the Algerian War – has stemmed from increasing activism within and outside the community by the *harkis* and their descendants.[76] In other cases, specific political causes or events have opened up questions of memory and responsibility. Thus Jacques Chirac claimed in 2006 that Rachid Bouchareb's film *Indigènes* (2006) – which vividly portrayed the difficult lives of colonial soldiers who fought for France during the Second World War – was a major factor in his pushing for the equalisation of pensions for French and foreign ex-servicemen.[77] Finally, attempts to resolve France's *guerres de mémoires* have also involved the passing of legislation on events of world-historical importance. The most famous of these so-called *lois mémorielles* (memory laws) are the Loi Taubira, recognising slavery as a 'crime against humanity', and the law recognising the 1915 Armenian genocide carried out by the Ottoman Empire, both of which were promulgated in 2001.[78]

memories of the Algerian conflict, see Sylvie Thénault, 'France-Algérie. Pour un traitement commun du passé de la guerre d'indépendance', *Vingtième Siècle* (No. 85, 2005), pp. 119–28.

[75] For instance, Branche's public viva examination was covered in *Le Monde* – one of only a very few vivas to receive this honour. Philippe Bernard, 'Guerre d'Algérie: une thèse souligne la généralisation de la torture', *Le Monde* (7 December 2000).

[76] Claire Eldridge, '"We've Never Had a Voice": Memory Construction and the Children of the *Harkis* (1962–1991)', *French History* (Vol. 23, No. 1, 2009), pp. 88–107.

[77] Chirac claimed that 'Il n'est pas inexact de dire qu'ayant eu le privilège de voir avant sa sortie le film "Indigènes", j'ai été particulièrement touché par ce qu'il exprimait . . . Cela m'a conduit à accélérer et à annoncer un certain nombre de mesures . . . notamment dans la communauté militaire et qui étaient à juste titre revendiquées par les anciens militaires qui avaient combattu à nos côtés pour le drapeau français.' 'Anciens combattants: le film "Indigènes" a accéléré la décision de Chirac', *Agence France-Presse* (27 September 2006).

[78] Loi n°2001–434 du 21 mai 2001 tendant à la reconnaissance de la traite et de l'esclavage en tant que crime contre l'humanité, available at www.legifrance.gouv.fr/affichTexte.do?cidTexte=JORFTEXT000000405369 (accessed 22 March 2011); Loi no 2001–70 du 29 janvier 2001 relative à la reconnaissance du génocide arménien de 1915, available at www.legifrance.gouv.fr/affichTexte.do?cidTexte=JORFTEXT000000403928 (accessed 22 March 2011).

In many ways, however, all this was a prelude to the events of 2005, which will almost certainly be to the post-colonial turn what 1989 was for the republican revival. It was in 2005 that the French *banlieues* were torn apart by riots and violence, which led to the declaration of the first state of emergency in metropolitan France since the Algerian War and immediately called into question France's model of integration.[79] And it was in 2005 that the French parliament, led by a right-wing majority and under pressure from years of lobbying by *pied-noir* groups, passed a highly contentious law which recognised France's 'debt' to all those who had participated in the colonisation of the French empire.[80] Article 4 of the legislation stipulated that the French school curriculum should recognise 'the positive role of the French presence overseas, notably in North Africa ... and the sacrifices of those combatants of the French army who came from these territories'.[81] No other former European colonial power had passed legislation that sought so explicitly to defend its imperial legacy in this way. Predictably, it drew widespread condemnation from historians: Liauzu repeatedly attacked the premises of the legislation, while a separate group of historians joined together to form Liberté pour l'histoire, an association to combat the 'politicisation' of history through *lois mémorielles*.[82] The outcry ultimately led to Chirac abrogating Article 4 of the law by presidential decree in 2006, but the rest of the law remained untouched.[83] The whole fiasco seemed to confirm what ACHAC had been arguing for over a decade – that, despite the

[79] For a history of the 'state of emergency' in France, see Sylvie Thénault, 'L'état d'urgence (1955–2005). De l'Algérie coloniale à la France contemporaine: destin d'une loi', *Le Mouvement Social* (No. 218, 2007), pp. 63–78.

[80] For the role of the *pieds-noirs* and their 'fight' for recognition, see Yann Scioldo-Zürcher, *Devenir métropolitain: Politique d'intégration et parcours de rapatriés d'Algérie en métropole (1954–2005)* (Paris: Editions de l'EHESS, 2010).

[81] The original wording of Article 4 of the law was: 'Les programmes scolaires reconnaissent en particulier le rôle positif de la présence française outre-mer, notamment en Afrique du Nord, et accordent à l'histoire et aux sacrifices des combattants de l'armée française issus de ces territoires la place éminente à laquelle ils ont droit.' Loi n° 2005–158 du 23 février 2005 portant reconnaissance de la Nation et contribution nationale en faveur des Français rapatriés, available at www.legifrance. gouv.fr/jopdf/common/jo_pdf.jsp?numJO=0anddateJO=20050224andnumTexte=2and pageDebut=03128andpageFin=03130 (accessed 23 March 2011).

[82] Claude Liauzu, 'Histoire et politique, le débat enfin ouvert: il faut refuser d'appliquer l'article 4 sur le rôle positif de la colonisation', *Libération* (3 January 2006). Founder members of Liberté pour l'histoire included Pierre Nora, Jean-Pierre Azéma, René Rémond, François Chandernagor and François Dosse. For the association's activities and selected public interventions in the press, see www.lph-asso.fr.

[83] 'Colonisation: l'Assemblée rejette la modification de la loi de février demandée par le PS', *Le Monde* (29 November 2005), and 'L'Algérie outrée par le vote sur la colonisation', *Le Monde* (30 November 2005). On Jacques Chirac's withdrawal of the law, 'Mémoire coloniale: Jacques Chirac temporise', *Le Monde* (10 December 2005).

outpouring of testimonies and the soul-searching since the mid 1990s, France had not yet dealt with its deafening 'colonial silence'.[84]

Yet, paradoxically, the law also acted as a catalyst for the emergence of new post-colonial movements: in the same way that the Marche des beurs in 1984 brought *beur* politics into the mainstream, the 2005 law seemed to open a space for more militant expressions of difference. It is in this light that we can interpret, for instance, the creation of the CRAN. But numerous other organisations and individuals have come to prominence since 2005. One of the best known of these is the association called Indigènes de la République, founded by a group that included the social activist Houria Bouteldja, the sociologist Saïd Bouamama and former members of the Ligue communiste révolutionnaire (LCR) and various pro-Palestinian groups.[85] Like the CRAN, the Indigènes movement has aimed to become an umbrella organisation, bringing together a number of 'anti-colonial' groups, many of whom had been associated with the far left. And, like almost all political movements in contemporary France, it began with a written call to arms.

Released on the Internet in January 2005, before the urban unrest but just as the press had begun to take note of the controversy surrounding the 2005 law, *L'appel des indigènes de la République* immediately made the headlines. Simply resurrecting the term *indigènes*, with its heavily colonial connotations, would have been enough to provoke controversy. But the foundational text of the movement went further, by claiming that 'France remains a colonial state', that the 'treatment of peoples of colonial origin [*issus de la colonisation*] is an extension of colonial policies', and that the 'decolonisation of the Republic is still a priority'. The *appel* also condemned the 2004 law banning the 'ostentatious religious symbols in schools' as a 'law ... with colonial overtones'.[86] Within a month the Indigènes claimed that over a thousand people had signed the petition based on their manifesto, and a march was organised on 8 May 2005 to commemorate the fiftieth anniversary of the Sétif massacre in Algeria in 1945. With press coverage of the movement growing, by mid 2005 the Indigènes had developed a strong media presence. Numerous articles discussed the implications of the movement, while figures such as

---

[84] See Sandrine Lemaire, 'Une loi qui vient de loin', *Le Monde Diplomatique* (January 2006), and the response by Claude Liauzu and Daniel Hémery in the letters page of *Le Monde Diplomatique* (February 2006).

[85] One of the few academic studies of the genesis of the Indigènes movement is Jérémy Robine, 'Les "indigènes de la République": nation et question postcoloniale', *Hérodote* (No. 120, 2006), pp. 118–48.

[86] 'Nous sommes les indigènes de la République', published online on 20 January 2005, at www.indigenes-republique.org/spip.php?article835 (accessed 23 March 2011).

Finkielkraut declared the *appel* to be 'a real declaration of war'.[87] In the ongoing battle for control over France's nascent post-colonial discourse, the Indigènes seemed to have stolen a march on their counterparts in the same way that SOS Racisme came to dominate the *droit à la différence* movement in the mid 1980s.

It is unclear whether the organisation will have a long-term impact. Since 2005 it has matured and developed a more openly political agenda. It is now called the Parti des Indigènes de la République, and has declared that it will put forward candidates in future elections.[88] The close relationship between the polemical philosopher Tariq Ramadan and the Indigènes, as well as their support for the Palestinian cause have further focused the movement's political message. But they nevertheless remain committed to a radical variant of the post-colonial critique, the virulence of which is both a cause and a consequence of the explosion of France's post-colonial memory after the controversy over the 2005 law. Even if the organisation has frequently been accused of promoting 'anti-white racism' and encouraging 'a hatred of France', it is more accurate to see in the Indigènes what one scholar describes as a movement 'about and to the nation'.[89] In the end, it is the Indigènes' desire to reform the conception of the French nation that has given rise to their peculiarly concentrated and politicised post-colonial critique.

Postcolonialism as liberalism: an impossible equation?

As I suggested at the start of the chapter, there are two key ways in which the politics of post-colonialism can be characterised as liberal. First, in its explicit attempts to absorb and adapt outside influences to reform French politics and society, in this case by drawing on elements of Anglo-American multicultural theory and ethnic politics. This has unsettled the resolutely French framework of neo-republicanism by validating expressions of ethnic difference and introducing 'culture' as a legitimate intermediary body between the French state and its citizens. The second way in which the politics of post-colonialism belongs alongside other liberal critiques of contemporary France lies in its sustained attack on the historical and moral assumptions of neo-republicanism. This is what

---

[87] Elisabeth Lévy, 'Débat François Gèze-Alain Finkielkraut; La France est-elle un état colonial?', *Le Point* (12 May 2005).

[88] See the movement's manifesto, 'Que voulons-nous?', available at www.indigenes-republique.fr/statique?id_article=189 (accessed 23 March 2011).

[89] On the question of 'shame', see e.g. Eric Conan, 'Faut-il avoir honte d'être français?', *L'Express* (21 September 2006). The quotation is from Robine, 'Les "indigènes de la République"', pp. 118–19.

has given the movement its potency. For, more than any other liberal critique discussed in this section, it has taken neo-republicanism as its target by repeatedly chipping away at the legitimacy of its historical teleologies. Seen in this light, the politics of post-colonialism actually bears a striking resemblance to Furet and Rosanvallon's projects, in that it, too, seeks to rewrite the narrative of modern French history. Furet and Rosanvallon would be hostile to the 'identity politics' implicit in the post-colonial project, but, just as they wanted to restore to prominence certain neglected ideas and personalities, so advocates of multiculturalism and post-colonialism have tried to do the same with France's colonial past and multi-ethnic present.

Of course, in their attempts to rewrite history, they have provoked extremely strong reactions from those who remain committed to a Jacobin and neo-republican narrative of modern French history. This has included a large number of people beyond the limited confines of the French elite. So, for instance, a survey in December 2005 found that 64 per cent of French people approved of Article 4 of the 2005 law.[90] Notwithstanding the difficulties of extrapolating 'public opinion' from isolated surveys, this meant that, even in the midst of a vigorous public debate, the majority of French citizens of all political tendencies supported legislation to 'remind' schoolchildren of a republican narrative of 'benevolent' and 'positive' colonisation – a narrative which, by 2005, was under sustained attack.[91] It was a salutary reminder that the debate over the way in which French history is written is far from being resolved, and that a post-colonial counter-narrative still remains a dominated rather than dominant discourse.

[90] Gilles Perrault, 'Deux Français sur trois saluent le "rôle positif" de la colonisation', Le Figaro (2 December 2005).
[91] Remarkably, the survey found no significant differences in opinion on either side of the political spectrum. The only noticeable difference was that the more affluent and educated the respondent, the more critical they were of Article 4.

9 Whither the Trente Glorieuses? The language of crisis and the reform of the state

[L]e drame de la société française dans les années à venir c'est qu'elle est menacée d'une succession de ruptures qui risquent d'avoir plutôt une signification régressive.   Michel Crozier, *La société bloquée* (1970)[1]

For the vast majority of scholars, commentators and critics of France, the focal point of the 'French model' is the state. Whatever the words used to describe France's dominant discourse – be it 'Jacobin', 'Bonapartist' or 'republican' – it is almost impossible to understand it without reference to the overwhelming symbolic role of the state. It is little wonder, then, that criticisms of the power, reach and efficacy of the state have usually been equated with a much wider project; in modern French history, it has frequently been the case that those attacking the state sought to undermine the legitimacy of the French political system as a whole. This was certainly true of left and far-left attacks on the 'bourgeois Republic' at the turn of the nineteenth century, and it was true – in a rather different way – of de Gaulle's disdain for the fragmented politics of the Third and Fourth Republics. Paradoxically, by the time de Gaulle had consolidated his power in the 1960s, his own vision of the state was itself under attack after the *évenements* of May 1968 had seen hundreds of thousands of students take to the streets to denounce the hierarchy and conservatism of the Gaullist state.

One of the peculiarities of the past thirty years, however, has been a growing sense of unease at the role of the state, not from the extremes of French politics, but from its consensual centre ground. It has become increasingly commonplace to talk of a 'French model' that is 'blocked', 'broken down' or simply 'falling'. The end of the Trente Glorieuses, the decline in French geopolitical power and increasingly fractious *guerres de mémoires* have all damaged the legacy of Gaullist *grandeur*. The French themselves seem to 'lack confidence' and suffer from 'anxiety', while, at a collective level, French society is divided by a *fracture sociale* that feeds

---

[1] Michel Crozier, *La société bloquée*, 3rd edn (Paris: Seuil, 1994 [1970]), p. 187.

off a growing sense of 'precariousness'. If such concerns are hardly unusual to France, the particular form they have taken has appeared to constitute a fundamental reassessment of the way in which the French see their relationship to the state: as the title of a recent book suggests, the last three decades have seen a France quite openly 'in crisis'.[2] While some have bemoaned this obsessive 'declinism', it is hard to avoid the conclusion that it has become an integral part of the French political landscape.[3]

In this chapter, I want to revisit this language of crisis, and show how it has coalesced into a powerful critique of contemporary French polit-ics. While it is easily dismissed as hyperbole or paranoia, I want to explore its genealogy, assumptions and metaphors.[4] I shall suggest that, far from an ephemeral discourse, the language of crisis in contemporary France has been a key catalyst for various ostensibly liberal reforms of the French state. By the same token, the claim that the 'French model' has expired represents another important challenge to a language of neo-republicanism that emphasises the primacy of politics, and the pre-eminence of the state. While the language of crisis has not focused on French history in the same way as, say, the post-colonial critique, it has contributed to a general re-evaluation of the functioning and pur-pose of the state. As a result, it has had a major impact on contemporary political discourse. Perhaps most importantly, it has pushed France's intellectual elite to focus more and more on questions of economic reform, a change of orientation that is likely to have significant long-term consequences for French politics.

La France bloquée: the critique of the bureaucracy and the crise de la représentation

One of the most powerful metaphors used to describe contemporary France is that of a 'blocked' society. The meaning of such a concept is usually fairly clear: France, it is argued, has been paralysed by its inability to reform; its elites have become conformist and unoriginal; and its

---

[2] Timothy Smith, *France in Crisis: Welfare, Inequality, and Globalisation since 1980* (Cambridge University Press, 2004).

[3] For instance, Michel Wieviorka, *Le printemps du politique: pour en finir avec le déclinisme* (Paris: Robert Laffont, 2007).

[4] There are very few sustained attempts to do this in the academic literature about France. One of the rare examples is a recent attempt to contextualise and analyse the notion of the 'modèle social français' in the period 2005–7. Frédéric Lebaron, Florence Gallemand and Carole Waldvogel, 'Le 'modèle social français' (est à bout de souffle): genèse d'une *doxa* – 2005–2007', *La Revue de l'IRES* (No. 61, Vol. 2, 2009), pp. 129–64.

education system has singularly failed to produce a new generation of leaders adapted to the exigencies of a changing world. One of the pre-eminent consequences of this 'blocked' society is a 'detachment' of the elites from the people, frequently referred to as a 'crisis of representa-tion', or simply a 'political crisis'. As the country's technocratic elite becomes increasingly separated from a changing society, it becomes prone to a lack of realism (at best) or straightforward corruption (at worst). In this dystopic vision of twenty-first-century France, the country is on the road to irrelevance and poor governance – something which seems only to be confirmed by the succession of political scandals that follow almost every major political figure before, during and after his or her time in office.[5] Yet, if the diagnosis of the problem seems self-evident, the genesis of this critical discourse is poorly understood. One might be tempted to ascribe it to a long-standing perceived division in French politics between 'the people [*le peuple*]' and 'the fat cats (*les gros*)'.[6] Or one might draw parallels with the critical attitude towards politicians and the elite under the Third and Fourth Republics. But, while these deeply ingrained perceptions help us to understand the historical struc-tures of French politics, they cannot explain the specific form that it has taken since the late 1970s. For this, we need to look to a number of developments in French sociology, above all the work of Michel Crozier, whose ideas had a profound influence on his field and subsequently the world of politics.

Like Rosanvallon, Crozier (who died in 2013) was trained at the Ecole des Hautes Etudes Commerciales de Paris (HEC). He went on to become a sociologist of systems and organisation but, unlike the majority of his peers, he divided his professional life between France and the United States, where he taught at Stanford and Harvard at various points in the 1960s and 70s.[7] Once he returned definitively to France in the early 1970s, he helped found the Centre de Sociologie des Organisations and was, for a long time, the head of the sociology department at Sciences Po. Eventually, in 1999, he was made a member of the Académie des sciences

---

[5] During his period in office from 2007 to 2012, Sarkozy alone managed to become implicated in numerous scandals (l'Affaire Clearstream, l'Affaire Karachi, l'Affaire Bettencourt), while former president Jacques Chirac was found guilty in 2011 of massive political corruption during his time as mayor of Paris.

[6] Pierre Birnbaum, *Le peuple et les gros: histoire d'un mythe* (Paris: Grasset, 1979); Gérard Fritz, *L'idée du peuple en France du XVIIe au XIXe siècle* (Strasbourg: Presses Universitaires de Strasbourg, 1988).

[7] He was Fellow at the Center for Advanced Studies in the Behavioural Sciences at Stanford in 1959–60 and 1973–4. He taught sociology at Harvard in 1966–7, 1968–70 and 1980.

morales et politiques.[8] As with Rosanvallon, Crozier's trajectory via a French business school is important to understanding his critical position. Like his younger counterpart, Crozier emerged from the left. But he rapidly moved to the centre ground, in particular through his involvement with the influential Club Jean Moulin, which was founded in 1958 and whose members included Michel Rocard and Jacques Delors.[9] Profoundly affected by and ambivalent towards the *évenements* of 1968 – he had been elected in 1967 to a chair at Nanterre, where the student protests began – he began shortly afterwards to develop a critique of contemporary France based on his interest in organisational sociology.[10] The result of this reflection was the widely read and much discussed essay entitled *La société bloquée* (1970).

The notion of a *société bloquée* was quite explicitly drawn from the work of the international relations expert Stanley Hoffmann, who had used the idea of a 'stalemate society' to characterise inter-war France. Crozier's innovation was to take this idea, translate it into French and use it to describe the country's contemporary ills.[11] Thus, in his 1970 essay, Crozier set out explicitly what we now recognise as the central themes of the contemporary language of crisis, starting from the premise that France's bureaucratic and organisational structure had become 'blocked'. Crozier argued that old forms of participation were falling apart and France had to take 'the risk of freedom' through a reform of its bureaucracy and its university system. It needed to create 'new collective capacities' by grappling with the paradox of individualism in contemporary society.[12] As he put it, there was an urgent need to do away with

the passion for leadership, control and the logic that motivates the executives, business leaders, engineers and mandarins who govern us, all of whom are too

---

[8] Crozier has written a two-volume memoir (in a similar style to Aron), which traces both these biographical details and his reactions to events at various moments in his life. Michel Crozier, *Ma belle époque: mémoires 1947–1969* (Paris: Fayard, 2002), and Michel Crozier, *À contre-courant: mémoires 1969–2000* (Paris: Fayard, 2004).

[9] Michel Crozier, *La crise de l'intelligence: essai sur l'impuissance des élites à se réformer* (Paris: InterEditions, 1995), pp. 17–18.

[10] Crozier has summarised the paradox of 1968 as the fact that '68 fut une explosion de paroles mais personne n'écoutait personne'. At the time of the protests, he was, unsurprisingly, branded a 'reactionary'. Crozier, *Ma belle époque*, p. 316 (and on 1968 in general, pp. 305–50). Coincidentally, the following year Crozier was at Harvard during the student protests – giving him an interesting comparative perspective.

[11] On the relationship between Crozier and Hoffmann, see Stanley Hoffmann, 'Être ou ne pas être français (I)', *Commentaire* (Vol. 18, No. 70, 1995), pp. 313–24, and Stanley Hoffmann, 'Être ou ne pas être français (II)', *Commentaire* (Vol. 18, No. 71, 1995), pp. 571–82.

[12] This is a highly schematic summary of Crozier, *La société bloquée*.

brilliant, too competent and, simultaneously, too easily overtaken by the demands of economic and social development.[13]

This reform was to come in three principal domains: the administration, the school system and the political system – and much of Crozier's work from the 1970s was devoted to these three key elements of the *société bloquée*. More surprising, perhaps, is the fact that he hardly changed his attitude from the 1970s until his death. When discussing the passage quoted above in the preface to a new 1994 edition of his seminal essay he declared emphatically (and with a 'certain sadness') that 'I do not think I should change a single line'.[14]

This recognition that little had changed did not stop Crozier from restating his case on numerous occasions. In *État moderne, État modeste* (1987) he argued for a profound reform of France's centralising, bureaucratic and statist tradition to make way for a more 'modest' and flexible vision of the state.[15] His focus was much the same in *La crise de l'intelligence* (1995), although he limited his lines of attack by arguing that 'it is not society that is blocked … it is the political-administrative system or, rather, the system of elites'[16] No doubt this was a way of distancing himself from the 'declinism' that was becoming more and more prevalent by the mid 1990s: certainly, in his later works, Crozier went to greater lengths to show France's 'potential' for adaptation. Nevertheless, his *Quand la France s'ouvrira* (2000) and to some extent his memoirs (2002–4), betrayed a deep frustration with France's inability to confront 'reality' and its continued attachment to a statist 'French exception'.[17] He acknowledged in an interview in 2007 that 'we have slowly begun to accept, if only in theory, the idea of a modest state', but it seems clear that, for Crozier, there was much more to be done before France could truly reform its institutions.[18]

Crozier's acknowledgement that the French had begun to take note of his ideas was a rather modest claim. In fact, the main elements of his critique of the French state in *La société bloquée* have today become widely understood and accepted far beyond the confines of the academy.[19]

---

[13] Crozier, *La société bloquée*, p. 7.   [14] Ibid.

[15] Michel Crozier, *État moderne, état modeste. Stratégies pour un autre changement* (Paris: Fayard, 1987).

[16] Crozier, *Essai sur l'intelligence*, p. 12.

[17] Michel Crozier and B. Tilliette, *Quand la France s'ouvrira* (Paris: Fayard, 2000).

[18] Michel Crozier (interviewed by B. Tilliette), *Nouveau regard sur la société française* (Paris: Odile Jacob, 2007), p. 212.

[19] On this, see, for instance, Isabelle Berrebi-Hoffmann and Pierre Grémion, 'Elites intellectuelles et réforme de l'Etat. Esquisse en trois temps d'un déplacement d'expertise', *Cahiers internationaux de sociologie* (Vol. CXXVI, 2009), pp. 39–59. For a perspective that emphasises the extent to which managerial ideas became 'hegemonic' in

This is true, most of all, of the world of business, where Crozier's explicit efforts in the 1980s to reform French managerialism, and in the 1990s to demonstrate the importance of an 'economy of innovation', provided valuable alternative models for French business.[20] In politics, too, the concept has become familiar. The term *société bloquée* was frequently invoked by Jacques Chaban-Delmas during his term as Prime Minister (1969–74), while Crozier's personal influence on such influential figures as Jean-Jacques Servan-Schreiber and Michel Rocard played a key role in the dissemination of his ideas on both the right and the left of the political spectrum.[21] At the same time, the *société bloquée* received significant attention in journals such as *Commentaire* and *Esprit*, both of which also published articles by Hoffmann in the 1970s, 80s and 90s that reinforced Crozier's central ideas.[22] Above all, however, Crozier's analysis found a large audience in the 1980s and 90s when the detachment of the elite and the depoliticisation of the masses seemed to have become the reality of French politics.

This growing pessimism made Crozier's predictions more urgent and we begin to find his message – sometimes unwittingly – filtering into general public discourse in the early 1980s. A good example of this was a television programme provocatively entitled *Vive la crise!* Aired on France 2 at prime time on 22 February 1984, and led by the singer Yves Montand, its purpose was to 'educate' the French about the possible consequences of the economic crisis. Through a series of fictitious and bizarrely apocalyptic vignettes, it attempted to show that only full-scale (neo-liberal) reform of the French economy and society could halt the impending crisis.[23] Significantly, it used one of Crozier's formulations to describe how traditional legislative solutions to the crisis would be ineffective.[24]

France in the 1980s, Luc Boltanski and Ève Chiapello, *Le nouvel ésprit du capitalisme* (Paris: Gallimard, 1999).

[20] On Crozier's influence in business and management, see Francis Pavé (ed.), *L'analyse stratégique: sa genèse, ses application et ses problems actuels. Autour de Michel Crozier* (Paris: Seuil, 1993), and Matthias Finger and Bérangère Ruchat (eds.), *Pour une nouvelle approche du management public. Réflexions autour de Michel Crozier* (Paris: Editions Seli Arslan, 1997).

[21] See the following chapter for a discussion of this. Crozier writes an eloquent eulogy to Rocard at the end of his term as Prime Minister in 1994 in Crozier, *La crise de l'intelligence*, pp. 15–7.

[22] For instance, Stanley Hoffmann, 'Un état sans frein et une société rétive', *Esprit* (May 1974), pp. 782–800, and Stanley Hoffmann, 'Quand la France tient la bride à ses vieux démons', *Esprit* (June 1994), pp. 109–24.

[23] *Vive la crise!*, France 2 (first broadcast 22 February 1984).

[24] For instance, part of the programme showed that simple solutions ('Il n'y a qu'à [all we have to do] …') would result in economic disaster. Crozier, too, was using the expression 'il n'y a qu'à' to describe the simplistic, bureaucratic and legislative

Although more focused on economic than bureaucratic reform, the programme – which received widespread praise from the press and recorded high viewer numbers – indicated that Crozier's ideas were slowly becoming 'vulgarised'.[25]

The programme also revealed some of the intellectual networks that were being influenced by this emerging language of crisis. Two of the key 'consultants' for *Vive la crise!* were the economists and *haut fonctionnaires* Alain Minc and Michel Albert. Both had already published and would continue to publish on the pressing need for France and the French state to reform itself. Minc, in particular, has retained a high profile: his numerous essays and articles in the daily press have cemented his reputation as a sometimes acerbic critic of France's many pathologies.[26] He has repeatedly bemoaned 'France's incurable inability to reform itself', and urged the French state to streamline and modernise itself.[27] By his own admission a 'liberal of the left', Minc was a prominent member of the Fondation Saint-Simon until it was disbanded in 1999. This, and the fact that he headed a government commission on state reform in 1994, meant that by the mid 1990s he was frequently referred to as one of the *chefs de file* of *la pensée unique* in France alongside Pierre Rosanvallon.[28] Unlike Rosanvallon, however, the turn of the century saw Minc turn away from the left. He supported Edouard Balladur in the late 1990s and, more recently, endorsed Sarkozy, whom he described in 2001 as a 'liberal Bonapartist'.[29] His political commitments aside, what is significant is that Minc has become one of the best-known intellectuals consistently to endorse a liberal programme of economic and state reform over the past thirty years.

Another example of the growing appeal of a language of crisis can be found in the essays of the journalist François de Closets. Closely involved with television, radio and print media, de Closets has, since the late 1970s, written regularly about France's *blocages* and its 'taboos' in a series

---

solutions proposed to solve the crisis in the early 1980s. See Georges Santoni, 'Trois sociologues parle de la France', *French Review* (Vol. 56, No. 5, 1983), p. 729 ('[L]a gauche ... [prend la décentralisation] de façon tout à fait théorique, dans une perspective trop intellectuelle, un peu trop juridique, un peu comme si c'était "il n'y a qu'à": "il n'y a qu'à" passer des lois ou des décrets ... et tout marchera bien').

[25] For a rather cynical retrospective view on the programme, see Pierre Rimbert, 'Il y a quinze ans, vive la crise!', *Le Monde Diplomatique* (February 1999).

[26] See especially his collections of articles: Alain Minc, *Contrepoints* (Paris: Grasset, 1992), and Alain Minc, *Contrepoints II: Je persiste et signe* (Paris: Grasset, 2002).

[27] Alain Minc, *Français, si vous osiez ...* (Paris: Grasset, 1991), p. 12.

[28] The report of the commission was published as Alain Minc, *La France de l'an 2000* (Paris: Odile Jacob, 1994). Rosanvallon was a member of the commission.

[29] Alain Minc, 'Un libéral bonapartiste (2001)', *Contrepoints II*, pp. 368–71.

of books, many of which became best-sellers.[30] Starting with *La France et ses mensonges* (1977) and *Toujours Plus!* (1986), through to more recent works such as *Le Compte à rebours* (1998) and *Plus encore!* (2006), he has incessantly condemned the country's love affair with *étatisme* and the 'administration'.[31] Even though he was not an *haut fonctionnaire* or an established academic, he was sufficiently prominent to be chosen in 1988 to head a government commission, L'efficacité de l'Etat, at the Commissariat Général du Plan. Again, the message was that the state needed to become more streamlined and efficient. Inevitably, the journalistic nature of de Closets's writing has often led him to exaggeration and hyperbole. But, given the unity at the heart of his writings and public interventions, it is hard not to see the influence of Crozier's ideas – and, indeed, he recognised the importance of the sociologist's thinking at a colloquium in 1990.[32]

It is clear, then, that the key elements of the concept of the *société bloquée* were being widely disseminated in France by 1990. At the same time, this language of crisis was beginning to find its way beyond the realm of economic and bureaucratic reform. The end of Mitterrand's reign was marked by deep cynicism and the persistent threat of an extreme-right protest vote. It was in this context that scholars began to elaborate the notion of a *crise de la représentation* that extended the idea of a *société bloquée* into politics. As we have already seen, one of the earliest to develop this idea was Rosanvallon, whose contribution to *La République du centre* (1988) was tellingly entitled 'Malaise dans la représentation'. In keeping with the long-standing tradition of French 'liberal pessimism' discussed above, Rosanvallon bemoaned both the 'slow descent' into bland, consensual republicanism, and the growing depoliticisation of the French.[33] The massive public-sector strikes in 1995 seemed to confirm Rosanvallon's diagnosis.[34] The prospect of a deep-seated 'rejection' of the political elite was elaborated in such books as the collaborative volume *Le Grand Refus* (1995), edited by Crozier's contemporary and friendly 'enemy' Alain Touraine, and featuring contributions by Wieviorka and

---

[30] Not surprisingly, Minc has written favourably of de Closets's work. See Alain Minc, 'L'état, c'est toi . . .' (1992), in Minc, *Contrepoints*, pp. 238–41.

[31] François de Closets, *La France et ses mensonges* (Paris: Denoël, 1977); F de. Closets, *Toujours Plus* (Paris: Grasset, 1984); François de Closets, *Plus encore* (Paris: Fayard, 2006).

[32] François de Closets, 'La réforme modeste', in Pavé, *L'analyse stratégique*, pp. 265–71.

[33] Rosanvallon, 'Malaise dans la représentation', in Furet, Julliard and Rosanvallon, *La République du centre*.

[34] On Rosanvallon's attitude to the *crise de la représentation* in early 1995, see Thomas Ferenczi, 'La politique et le conflit: Un dialogue entre Alain Duhamel et Pierre Rosanvallon', *Le Monde* (16 January 1995).

his colleagues.[35] In his introduction, Touraine distances himself from Crozier's analysis, claiming that the state alone is not to blame for the growing crisis of representation. Nevertheless, he does question the way in which France imagines the relationship between politics, economics and society:

France has almost never represented itself as a society that has had to manage change with reference to external constraints and internal social needs, but instead as an entity [*état*] charged with an exceptional mission, well above any social or economic problems.[36]

For Touraine, the French state's inability to adapt to outside pressures in a realistic and coherent way puts it at risk of the kind of generalised resentment that characterised the strikes of 1995.

Predictably, Jean-Marie Le Pen's success in 2002 fanned a debate that was still very much alive.[37] The questions of where France was going and the virtues of its 'model' once again appeared as major public issues. Perhaps the most emblematic standard-bearer of this new wave of 'declinism' has been Baverez. We already know him as one of the *bande d'aroniens*, closely involved with *Commentaire* and a member of the executive board of the Club Le Siècle, an exclusive organisation that brings together France's most prominent social, cultural and political figures.[38] However, in 2003, he came to wider prominence with the publication of his pamphlet, *La France qui tombe*, in which he denounced political 'immobilism', the absence of realism among the elites, a poorly adapted economic model and the inability to get beyond a 'frozen' nostalgia for the Trente Glorieuses.[39] The book was an enormous popular success and, like *La société bloquée*, became one of the most talked-about books of the year.

One of the best ways to judge the varying reactions it provoked is by looking at *Commentaire*, where he first presented a condensed version of his essay in summer 2003.[40] Over three issues, a substantial section of *Commentaire* was devoted to the long list of eminent personalities who felt moved to comment on Baverez's argument. Many agreed with his general conclusions, choosing only to augment or nuance it according to

[35] Touraine, *Le Grand Refus*.
[36] Alain Touraine, 'L'ombre d'un mouvement', in Touraine, *Le Grand Refus*, p. 33.
[37] See, for instance, Colette Ysmal, 'Le symptôme d'une crise de la représentation', *Le Figaro* (20 March 2002).
[38] On the Club Le Siècle see their official website www.lesiecle.asso.fr/. Lists of attendees have been published (illegally) on the Internet by protest groups: the guestlist is a veritable who's who of French politics, culture, business, finance and industry.
[39] Baverez, *La France qui tombe*.
[40] Nicolas Baverez, 'Le déclin français', *Commentaire* (Vol. 26, No. 102, 2003), pp. 299–316.

218 The language of crisis and the reform of the state

their particular interests. Some like Alain Besançon, Pascal Bruckner and Max Gallo felt that Baverez had underplayed the 'moral', 'societal' or even 'religious' elements of the crisis; others – like the journalist Patrick Jarreau – focused on French anti-Americanism as a vehicle for decline; still others emphasised the disabling of 'civil society' as an additional factor in Baverez's unremittingly gloomy picture of France.[41] Those who were more critical often objected to the negative 'tenor' of the original essay, suggesting that France had a great deal of potential and had changed profoundly since the early 1980s. The former right-wing Prime Minister Alain Juppé took Baverez to task for criticising Chirac and de Villepin's anti-Iraq stance, arguing that it had not been a fiasco, but that it was actually to France's credit that it had had the courage to stand its ground over Saddam Hussein.[42] Only a few of those who were sceptical tried to take a step back and examine whether France was actually in decline or simply drowning in what the editor of *Esprit* Olivier Mongin described as a powerful 'feeling of decline'.[43]

Nevertheless, there was an awareness on the part of both his supporters and his critics that Baverez was part of a much longer tradition of liberal criticism of the French state in being since the 1970s. In many of the responses to his essay there were references to France as a 'blocked' country, while the scholar of Franco-American relations Sophie Meunier made an explicit reference to Crozier when she perceptively noted that 'even during the Trente Glorieuses . . . naysayers were already denouncing the "French sickness [*mal français*]" and the "société bloquée"'.[44] It was evident, then, that Baverez's diagnosis belonged to a powerful language of crisis that had its roots in the 1970s. However, by 2003 this language encompassed a much wider range of ills: the decline of French geopolitical power after 1989 and the relative success of its neighbours Germany and the United Kingdom seemed to confirm the persistence not just of an 'economic' crisis, but also of a 'moral and intellectual' crisis. Symptomatic of this extension of the language of crisis were the growing calls for a reform of what had become known by the 1990s as the 'French model'.

---

[41] Alain Besançon, 'Réponse à Nicolas Baverez', *Commentaire* (Vol. 26, No. 103, 2003), pp. 579–87; Pascal Bruckner, 'Remarques sur le déclin français', ibid., pp. 587–90; Max Gallo, 'Une crise morale', ibid., pp. 591–5; P. Jarreau, 'La société fermée et la fonction de l'antiaméricanisme', ibid., pp. 596–8.
[42] Alain Juppé, 'L'insoutenable légèreté du "déclinisme"', *Commentaire* (Vol. 26, No. 104, 2003), pp. 789–95.
[43] Olivier Mongin, 'Déclin ou sentiment de déclin', ibid., pp. 837–40.
[44] Sophie Meunier, 'La France qui se mondialise', *Commentaire* (Vol. 27, No. 105, 2004), p. 120.

La France malade: reforming the 'French model'

Thus far we have focused our attention primarily on criticisms of the French state as a bureaucratic and administrative entity. Yet many of those who have bemoaned the organisation of the state have also argued that the ways in which it intervenes in society are no longer effective. Critics have focused their attention on three areas in particular: the provision of health care, the school system and higher education. By looking briefly at these three challenges facing the French state, we can see more clearly how the language of crisis has expanded beyond the meanings given to it by Crozier and others – and how it has begun to shape social policy in France.

It has become increasingly evident that the French welfare state – like that of its European neighbours – has struggled to cope with the demographic and social changes of the past three decades. As a result, it has become one of the most important elements of the language of crisis, particularly for those on the centre-left who are not as committed to the kind of 'neo-liberal' reforms of the state that have been advanced by people like Baverez. This difference is reflected in the genesis of this critique of the welfare state and the French model of state intervention. Much of it can be traced to Rosanvallon, who, as we saw above, has maintained a consistent interest in the reform of the welfare state. In works such as *La crise de l'État providence* (1981) and *La nouvelle critique sociale* (1995), he developed a model that stresses both the importance of solidarity and the need to introduce greater flexibility in welfare provision. But Rosanvallon has not limited his contributions to his own written work; he has also encouraged others to investigate the same questions.

This meant that the welfare state and the 'French social model' featured prominently among the interests of the Fondation Saint-Simon, especially after 1990. Rosanvallon himself published a synthesis of his own position in 1993 under the title *La nouvelle crise de l'État providence*,[45] and this was followed in the next twelve months by contributions to the debate by two senior civil servants, François Stasse and Nicolas Dufourcq. Both agreed that the welfare state in France was in crisis, locked into an unsustainable pattern of funding that risked imminent bankruptcy. Following Rosanvallon's example, they each argued – in different ways – for the importance of greater selectivity in welfare provision and the need to change the way the system is funded (without falling

---

[45] Pierre Rosanvallon, *La nouvelle crise de l'État providence* (Paris: Notes de la Fondation Saint-Simon, September 1993).

into what Stasse described as a neo-liberal 'American temptation').[46] A few years later, in 1998, another senior civil servant who had collaborated with Baverez in the late 1980s, Denis Olivennes, pushed the rhetoric a little further by announcing that the French social model was little more than a 'Malthusian compromise'. Economically inefficient, weakly redistributive and unable to tackle chronic high unemployment, the French social model was described by Olivennes as the finest example of France's 'backwardness' that had left the country increasingly detached from changes that were taking place elsewhere in Europe.[47] Olivennes was already well known for coining the expression 'the French preference for unemployment', and his critique of the French model showed distinct parallels with the critique elaborated by Baverez.[48]

The Fondation Saint-Simon's activities came to an end in 1999, but Rosanvallon quickly found another outlet for his ideas in the world of publishing. Since 2002, he has edited a series for Seuil entitled 'La République des idées', which publishes short essays (about 100 pages) on topics of contemporary social significance. In addition to volumes on France's intellectual and economic life, the series has contributed to the continuing debate over the future of the welfare state. Once again, Rosanvallon outlined his own position in 2006 in a collaborative volume with sociologists Thierry Pech and Eric Maurin.[49] More recently, the work by Danish sociologist Gøsta Esping-Andersen on different welfare models in Europe appeared in translation,[50] while the series has also published essays on social exclusion, the negative effects of globalisation and fiscal reform. In much the same way as the Fondation Saint-Simon, 'La République des idées' has sought to contribute to civic and political life in France – and, like its predecessor, it has been relatively successful.

---

[46] François Stasse, *L'économie de la santé en France: l'heure des choix* (Paris: Notes de la Fondation Saint-Simon, November 1993); Nicolas Dufourcq, *L'État providence sélectif* (Paris: Notes de la Fondation Saint-Simon, April 1994).

[47] Denis Olivennes, *Le modèle social français: un compromis malthusien* (Paris: Notes de la Fondation Saint-Simon, January 1998). See also Denis Olivennes, 'Modèle français: l'age des arrogances', *Le Débat* (No. 134, 2005), pp. 149–54. Olivennes's collaboration with Baverez was published as Denis Olivennes and Nicolas Baverez, *L'impuissance publique: l'État c'est nous* (Paris: Seuil, 1989).

[48] Olivennes had already published in 1994 a noted essay on 'la préférence française pour le chômage' for the Fondation Saint-Simon. In it, he argued that after the Trente Glorieuses, the French 'chose' unemployment over a more redistributive and competitive welfare state. The essay – and Olivennes's expression – were widely commented on by the media. 'La préférence française pour le chômage' (1994), in Denis Olivennes, *Les Notes de la Fondation Saint-Simon: Une expérience intellectuelle (1983–1999)* (Paris: Calmann-Lévy, 1999).

[49] Rosanvallon, Pech and Maurin, *La nouvelle critique sociale*.

[50] Gøsta Esping-Andersen, *Trois leçons sur l'État-providence* (Paris: Seuil, 2008).

For instance, we find many of the proposals outlined by a group of three French economists in a recent essay published by the 'République des idées' reproduced in the Socialist manifesto for the 2012 elections.[51] In this way, Rosanvallon and his collaborators have continued to extend his indirect influence over public debate.

An indication of the extent to which the ideas first presented by the Fondation Saint-Simon and 'La République des idées' have begun to permeate the wider political space is the vigorous discussions around the notion of the 'French model', increasingly seen as an unusual and pathological exception in Europe. The situation was well summarised in a substantial article published in *Le Monde* in June 2005, shortly after France's rejection of the European Constitution. Citing research by Olivennes and Maurin on unemployment and urban segregation respectively, the author synthesised the language of crisis into one devastating paragraph:

By what criteria should we measure the collapse of the French social model? By the repeated eruption of urban violence? By the rate of unemployment – up to four in ten in certain neighbourhoods? By the social and territorial segregation that the sociologist Eric Maurin has dubbed the 'French ghetto'? By the professional frustrations of over-qualified civil servants? By the statutory rigidities and what Denis Olivennes had already called in 1996 'the French preference for unemployment'? By the thousand and one blocks within a pessimistic society that cannot imagine a future for its children? By the inability of the political and economic elites to give direction to reform and change?[52]

As if this clinical deconstruction of France's ills were not enough, it was becoming increasingly clear by the 2000s that the language of crisis was not confined simply to the country's elite. Numerous opinion polls appeared to confirm a generalised penchant for 'declinism' and 'depression'. The French were mistrustful of each other, lacking in confidence in their own welfare system and unconvinced of France's place in the world.[53] While the *modèle français* seemed to regain some of its legitimacy in the financial crisis of 2008–9, there nevertheless remained ample

---

[51] Camille Landais, Thomas Piketty and Emmanuel Saez, *Pour une révolution fiscale: un impôt sur le revenu pour le XXIe siècle* (Paris: Seuil/La République des Idées, 2011).

[52] Claire Guélaud, 'Le modèle social français est à bout de souffle', *Le Monde* (2 June 2005).

[53] Ariane Chemin, 'Liberté, égalité, morosité', *Le Monde* (30 June 2013). See also the IPSOS report 'France 2013: les nouvelles fractures' (www.ipsos.fr/ipsos-public-affairs/actualites/2013-01-24-france-2013-nouvelles-fractures, last accessed 13 April 2014), and Claudia Senik, 'The French Unhappiness Puzzle: The Cultural Dimension of Happiness', Paris School of Economics Working Papers 34 (November 2013), available at http://halshs.archives-ouvertes.fr/halshs-00628837 (last accessed 13 April 2014).

222 The language of crisis and the reform of the state

evidence of a strongly negative public mood, a feeling well summarised in the title of a short pamphlet written by two economists in 2007: *La société de la défiance: comment le modèle sociale français s'autodétruit.*[54]

Perhaps one of the clearest signs of France's self-perception – and the relationship between the language of crisis and the welfare state – is in the metaphors and tropes used to describe the country in the past two decades. It is hard not to be struck by the relentless characterisations of the French state as 'sick' and the French as 'depressed'. For some, this has become the unambiguous reality of contemporary France. As the former senior civil servant Jacques Lesourne put it bluntly in an article in *Commentaire* in 1998, 'France is sick.'[55] Taking a slightly different view, the historian, journalist and former editor of *Le Nouvel Observateur*, Jacques Julliard, argued in a memorable passage in his *Le malheur français* (2005) that 'the French are the schizophrenics of the West'.[56] In a similar vein, in a pamphlet written in 2006 by the former president of the Sorbonne, Jean-Robert Pitte, on the inability to reform higher education, the French were described as 'anxious and unhappy'.[57] In *La France qui tombe* (2003), Baverez took another approach, claiming that Jean-Marie Le Pen's success in 2002 marked the beginning of a 'civic crash', while in his indictment of *Les illusions gauloises* (2005) the prominent right-wing politician Pierre Lellouche maintained that 'today, unfortunately, we are forced to contemplate a weakened France, losing influence and consumed by self-doubt'.[58]

Quite apart from the striking convergence of vivid, health-related metaphors, this proliferation of the language of crisis suggests that the French people have internalised what they perceive to be the ailments of the body politic; their 'depression' is the logical corollary to the sustained criticism of the state that has been growing since the late 1970s.[59] While it would be easy to dismiss such language as mere hyperbole, its recurrence – at the hands of France's most influential intellectual and political

---

[54] Yann Algan and Pierre Cahuc, *La société de la défiance: comment le modèle français s'autodétruit* (Paris: Editions de la Rue d'Ulm, 2007).

[55] Jacques Lesourne, 'La maladie française', *Commentaire* (Vol. 28, No. 81, 1998), p. 89.

[56] Jacques Julliard, *Le malheur français* (Paris: Flammarion, 2005), p. 139.

[57] Jean-Robert Pitte, *Jeunes, on vous ment! Reconstruire l'université* (Paris: Fayard, 2006), p. 7.

[58] Baverez, *La France qui tombe*, p. 19; P. Lellouche, *Illusions gauloises* (Paris: Grasset, 2005), p. 19

[59] Sadly, there is almost no discussion of the range of literary devices, images and tropes that have dominated the language of crisis in France. One of the few articles on the subject is Edward Knox, 'Regarder la France: une réflexion bibliographique', *French Review* (Vol. 72, No. 1, 1998), pp. 91–101. Further research would no doubt tell us much about the power of the language of crisis.

figures – is a striking example of the extent to which the French still see their fate as intimately tied to that of the state. Nowhere has this been more evident than in recent discussions over the reform of the French education system. In the same way that it was a defence of *l'école républicaine* that helped to crystallise a neo-republican consensus, criticisms of the school system have acted as a focal point for the language of crisis. The vast majority of those who have denounced French 'immobilism' in the past three decades have also called for reforms in the French education system.

These calls for reform have focused on three areas in particular: reform of the pedagogical philosophy and assessment structures of French schools; the need for greater selection and orientation in higher education; and the dismantling of the symbolic and status distinctions between the broad-based *universités* and the elite *grandes écoles*. Of course, these criticisms are not new – indeed, Aron repeatedly raised the issue of selection and reform of the *grandes écoles* in the 1960s and 70s – but they have taken on a new urgency with the emergence of the language of crisis.[60] This being the case, we should not be surprised to find Crozier leading the attack on French education: from his earliest work on the *société bloquée* to his more recent interventions, he repeatedly condemned the way in which higher education is organised and administered – especially in the *écoles de commerce* (business schools) and the Ecole Nationale d'Administration. One of the most important reasons for institutional paralysis has been the French elites' inability to think 'innovatively' or 'out of the box' and, for this, Crozier laid the blame firmly at the door of the French classroom.[61]

Rosanvallon has been less ruthless in his assessment of the French education system – perhaps because, unlike Crozier, he has not spent significant parts of his career teaching abroad – but the Fondation Saint-Simon and 'La République des idées' have nonetheless given a voice to such criticisms.[62] An essay published in 2009 by the sociologists Christian Baudelot and Roger Establet examined the failures of the French school system in comparison to those in other countries. Rather tellingly, the authors chose the title *L'élitisme républicain*. Not only did this reflect their argument that, while in theory highly meritocratic, French schools have actually reproduced status and class distinctions, it also presented a

---

[60] See, for instance, 'Sélection clandestine' (11–17 September 1978), in Raymond Aron, *De Giscard à Mitterrand, 1977–1983* (Paris: Editions de Fallois, 2006).
[61] On this see, for instance, Crozier, *La crise de l'intelligence*.
[62] For example, Joël Roman, *Propositions pour l'école* (Paris: Notes de la Fondation Saint-Simon, February 1998).

critique of a neo-republican conception of the French school.[63] Another essay, published a few years earlier in 2004, pushed this critique further. Written by François Dubet, a sociologist and colleague of Wieviorka at the CADIS, it was entitled *Une école juste* (2004). While its aim was to rethink the concept of equality in education, Dubet could not resist attacking the 'fundamentalists of republican meritocracy' who glorified *l'école républicaine* and remained in thrall to classical pedagogy. As with Wieviorka's defence of multiculturalism, Dubet was suggesting that neo-republicanism fails to provide a realistic account of French society and appropriate solutions to its current dilemmas.[64]

These disputes were more than just academic squabbles; they reflected political fault lines. This was made plain in the Commission Thélot formed by the French government in 2004 in order to devise a strategy for school reform.[65] The commission was widely perceived as a power struggle between neo-republican 'partisans of the traditional school' – such as Chevènement, Finkielkraut and Elisabeth Altschull – and proponents of newer pedagogical methods – such as Dubet. But, where the Commission Stasi the previous year had seen the triumph of the neo-republican bloc to the exclusion of all others, on this occasion the partisans of change were victorious, and all three prominent neo-republicans resigned before the Commission Thélot had finished its work. Interestingly, the silencing of the neo-republican voice did not ultimately lead to noticeably more radical conclusions: the report produced by the commission simply recommended a number of reforms to make schools more 'open' and 'diverse'.[66] Nevertheless, the Commission Thélot showed that the liberal critique of French education was being heard.

There had been a similar momentum in 1998 when Jacques Attali, the well-known economist and former adviser to Mitterrand, released his government report on the state of French higher education. The only difference was that, in this instance, there were few opposing voices on the commission itself since it was composed of senior academics and business leaders sympathetic to Attali's reformist agenda. This relative consensus resulted in a more strongly worded document than the Rapport Thélot: in the introduction, Attali decried French higher education

[63] Christian Baudelot and Roger Establet, *L'élitisme républicain: l'école française à l'épreuve des comparaisons internationales* (Paris: Seuil/République des Idées, 2009).
[64] François Dubet, *L'école juste* (Paris: Seuil/République des Idées, 2004), p. 2.
[65] Claude Thélot, *Pour la réussite de tous les élèves: Rapport de la Commission du débat national sur l'avenir de l'Ecole* (Paris: La Documentation Française, 2004).
[66] Luc Bronner, 'Commission Thélot: la défaite des partisans de la vieille école', *Le Monde* (11 October 2004).

as 'confused, bureaucratic and unequal'.[67] Although the report did not go so far as to suggest the abolition of the *grandes écoles*, its direct criticisms of French higher education and its proposals to increase adult education provision and reinforce the orientation of students towards appropriate subjects of study were rightly interpreted as a 'damning indictment' in the French press.[68] Of course, as we have seen, the Attali Commission has hardly been alone in pointing out these deficiencies. The most prestigious *grandes écoles* in France (the ENA, the Ecole normale supérieure, the Ecole polytechnique, HEC ...) have frequently been accused by critics of manufacturing and recycling elites, not least by sociologist Pierre Bourdieu, who famously described these elites as a 'noblesse d'Etat' in his magisterial study of higher education in France, published in 1989.[69] Even those who have not been as critical as Bourdieu – himself a graduate of the Ecole Normale Supérieure – have argued that the *grandes écoles* need to be more research-intensive and open to the outside world.[70]

A good indicator of the extent to which these criticisms of French higher education have begun to have an impact on the younger generation has been the increasing numbers of students applying to the Instituts d'Etudes Politiques (IEP), the most famous of which is Sciences Po, Paris. While the latter has long had a privileged position as the proving ground for the country's future political, economic and intellectual elite, the growing popularity of other IEP campuses – especially in cities such as Bordeaux, Lille and Grenoble – can in part be attributed to the more 'globalised' curriculum, which comprises an obligatory year abroad and classes taught in English.[71] Moreover, as we saw earlier, they have been the first to put in place a limited 'affirmative action' policy in the form of a special entrance examination for those from underprivileged urban areas. Clearly, this willingness to reform and adapt is consistent with the history of an institution that has long seen itself as more open than

---

[67] Jacques Attali, *Pour un modèle européen de l'enseignement supérieur* (Paris: La Documentation Française, 1998), p. 5.

[68] Michel Delberghe, 'La commission Attali préconise de moderniser l'enseignement supérieur', *Le Monde* (6 May 1998).

[69] Bourdieu's widely read volume on French higher education without a doubt helped to crystallise opposition to the *grandes écoles*, especially on the left. Pierre Bourdieu, *La noblesse d'État: grandes écoles et esprit de corps* (Paris: Editions de Minuit, 1989).

[70] See, for instance, the controversy over the relocation of the ENA from Paris to Strasbourg, first announced in 1991 by Edith Cresson, but only completed in the early 2000s after sustained opposition from faculty members and *haut fonctionnaires*. Laetitia Van Eeckhout, 'Il aura fallu treize ans pour délocaliser l'ENA à Strasbourg', *Le Monde* (17 January 2005).

[71] 'La ruée vers les Instituts d'études politiques', *Le Monde* (9 March 11).

other *grandes écoles*. But it also reflects a more generalised trend, which has become central to the language of crisis in contemporary France: the need to learn from and copy foreign models.

La France ouverte? Looking beyond the Hexagon

In chapter 5, I showed how the world beyond the Hexagon provided an enduring set of images, stereotypes and models against which neo-republicans built a rejuvenated French national narrative. European integration, British multiculturalism, 'Anglo-Saxon capitalism'... – these constructs served as negative reference points for all those who believed in the historical, moral and political value of a 'French model'. Logically, then, these same constructs were likely to reappear in the work of those who have attacked various aspects of the 'French model' since the late 1970s. Except that, on this occasion, they have carried positive connotations: Europe, the United Kingdom and the United States are not ugly dystopias to be avoided at all costs, but rather models to be admired and (where possible) emulated. This is not the first time in modern French history that an acute sense of comparative decline has taken hold. I made reference earlier to the construction of the Anglo-Saxon as a positive model for French liberal reformists in the period after 1870.[72] The same was true after the Second World War when, as Kuisel has persuasively argued, it was the recognition of France's chronic economic 'backwardness' compared with its neighbours that acted as the catalyst for the construction of the large, technocratic state that became synonymous with the France of the Trente Glorieuses.[73] Today, as liberal critics attack the legacies of this post-war 'French model', they, too, have turned to foreign models for inspiration.

We need look no further than higher education for emphatic confirmation of this trend. In recent years, a renewed sense of 'declinism' has accompanied the annual publication of both the Shanghai and the *Times Higher Education* rankings of world universities. French higher educational institutions have consistently been much further down the table than their British and American counterparts. Despite the obvious difficulty in making useful comparisons across different systems, these classifications have reinforced a trenchant critique of French higher education of the kind expressed by Crozier almost four decades ago and extended by prominent scholars in the sciences and the social

---

[72] Pitt, 'A Changing Anglo-Saxon Myth'. See also chapter 5 of this volume.
[73] Richard Kuisel, *Le capitalisme et l'État en France: modernization et dirigisme au XXe siècle* (Paris: Gallimard, 1984).

sciences who have left French academia in search of a more propitious intellectual environment abroad. There have been numerous suggestions as to how France's poor showing might be remedied – but the vast majority have involved emulating foreign models. One suggestion was that France should create *pôles d'excellence* of the kind that have been set up in Germany (and are soon to become a reality in France).[74] Others have proposed some kind of tuition fee along the lines of the English model.[75] Still others have argued that French *universités* must break one of the most important republican 'taboos' and institute some form of selection at entry to correct the extremely low degree completion rate.[76] There is a consensus that, for French universities to compete with their foreign counterparts, they must improve their 'competitivity' and their 'branding', even if this means simply setting up an American-style university shop where students and alumni can purchase T-shirts and hoodies.[77] Indeed, so complete is the sense of inadequacy today that, unlike the school system, very few public figures are willing to defend the structure and values of French higher education, despite its successes.[78] Many will continue to resist the idea of selection, an issue that was at the heart of the enormous student protests against the failed 1986 Loi Devaquet, which proposed to introduce pre-selection of students and competition between universities. And students and teachers' unions remain strongly opposed to any perceived 'marketisation' of higher education. But few students would contest the fact that the language of crisis has had a powerful negative effect on their perception of French universities. This in turn has led to an intense interest in – and often admiration for – foreign universities such as Oxford or Harvard, with increasing numbers of students wishing to go abroad, especially in science subjects.

[74] On this see, for instance, editorials by the president of the ENS-Ulm, Monique Canto-Sperber, and the *haut fonctionnaire*, Christian Saint Etienne. Monique Canto-Sperber, 'Des établissements français parmi les premiers mondiaux?', *Le Monde* (29 January 2010); Christian Saint-Etienne, 'Pour des universités de rang mondial', *Le Monde* (13 March 2007).
[75] Compagnon mentions Tony Blair's introduction of tuition fees as a model in Antoine Compagnon, 'Sauver les universités: Une priorité nationale', *Le Figaro* (6 February 2004), and Antoine Compagnon, P. Schapira and P. Merlin, 'Comment revaloriser l'enseignement supérieur', *Le Monde* (14 June 2007).
[76] On this debate see, for instance, a recent interview with the former president of the Sorbonne, Jean-Robert Pitte, and the former president of one of France's largest student unions (UNEF), Bruno Julliard. Stéphane Marchand, 'Pitte–Julliard: l'université française peut-elle survivre au XXIe siècle?', *Le Figaro* (5 October 2007).
[77] This is what Paris-Dauphine and Lyon-I have tried to do. Marie-Estelle Pech, 'L'enseignement supérieur français mal coté à l'étranger', *Le Figaro* (11 March 11).
[78] A typical plea for reform is an editorial from 2007 in *Le Monde* by the then president of the European University Institute in Florence, Yves Mény. Yves Mény, 'Universités ou naufrage', *Le Monde* (29 June 2007).

It is not only in higher education that there has been a move towards learning from foreign models. The same has also been true of welfare reform. Here, predictably, the American model remains the worst possible option, but other European models appear to offer more potential for emulation. In a study provocatively entitled *Faut-il brûler le modèle social français?* (2006), two sociologists suggested that the 'Nordic model' of welfare provision could serve as a template for France and the rest of Europe.[79] They were not alone. In a recent paper, the economists Jean-Paul Fitoussi and Eloi Laurent claimed that France was in thrall to a 'Nordic mania' in 'parliamentary reports, academic papers, [and] press articles'. In contrast to France, 'the Nordic paradise' was presented as one of 'openness, efficiency and equality' that should become France's 'new frontier'. While the authors cautioned against this idealised view of a mythical 'Nordic model', they did recognise that this turn to outside models was intimately tied up with France's 'crisis of confidence'.[80]

But, if Eloi and Fitoussi were clear that simply importing foreign models cannot solve the crisis, they have nonetheless stressed the importance of France's integration into the world economy and the need to learn positively from its neighbours. For example, in a 2008 collaborative volume entitled *La nouvelle écologie politique* published in the 'La République des Idées' series, they argued for the need to work towards a concept of 'ecological equality' by taking into account global environmental factors in economic forecasts.[81] Elsewhere, Fitoussi – who had a prominent role as president of the Observatoire Français des Conjonctures Economiques at Sciences Po from 1990 to 2010 – has argued for the importance of developing and deepening the European project, while maintaining the commitment to equality and democratic principles.[82] He has even defended 'affirmative action' policies at Sciences Po, where he teaches economics.[83] Thus, despite the fact that Fitoussi has repeatedly distanced himself from the notion of a *société bloquée* and the language of crisis, he has embodied the kind of outward-looking intellectual who has sought to temper neo-republicans' enthusiastic celebration of 'l'exception

---

[79] Alain Lefebvre and Dominique Méda, *Faut-il brûler le modèle social français?* (Paris: Seuil, 2006).

[80] Jean-Pierre Fitoussi and Eloi Laurent, 'Hawks and Handsaws: What Can France Learn from the "Nordic Model"?', Center for European Studies Working Paper Series, No. 168 (2008).

[81] Jean-Pierre Fitoussi and Eloi Laurent, *La nouvelle écologie politique: économie et développement durable* (Paris: République des Idées/Seuil, 2008).

[82] Jean-Pierre Fitoussi, *La règle et le choix: de la souveraineté économique en Europe* (Paris: République des Idées/Seuil, 2002).

[83] Jean-Pierre Fitoussi, 'Politiques d'égalité: pour les discriminations positives', *La revue de l'association des anciens élèves de Sciences Po* (No. 135, 2004).

française' by situating France's economic development alongside those of other European countries.[84] In this sense, his is the economic counterpart to Rosanvallon's historical project that aimed to show how modern French history was comparable to that of its European neighbours.

Other commentators have been more unequivocal in their judgement of France's ills and the need to learn from foreign models. For Minc, twenty-first-century France resembles Astérix's village in its incessant navel-gazing. He maintains that escaping this parochialism 'has now become a matter of life or death' and that the French need to recognise that they have become a 'province' of Europe, and a mere 'canton' of the planet. Consequently, France must accept a more modest role in the new world order and be willing to learn from others, for instance in higher education or models of competitivity.[85] We find a similar argument in an essay by the senior civil servant and former Fondation Saint-Simon member Jean Peyrelevade. In his short book on the perils of global capitalism published in Rosanvallon's series in 2005, he claimed that 'we [the French] will not progress as long as our own intellectuals have not globalised themselves and continue to take their village for the centre of the world'.[86] The message was clear: if pure Anglo-American predatory capitalism carries with it many dangers, the French must at all costs avoid their tendency towards parochialism if they are to survive.

This plea for greater openness was echoed in almost all of Crozier's work on France. In the 2000s, he defended the value of the United States' 'entrepreneurial model' in the same way that he championed efficient 'managerial' techniques in the 1970s and 80s.[87] His call to arms has not gone unnoticed. As a number of scholars have argued, the push to 'import' Anglo-American business concepts, above all into the French public sector, had a profound effect on the values and aims of the country's administrative elites (*grand corps*). The development of large American consultancy firms such as McKinsey in the 1990s, their aggressive recruitment in the *grandes écoles* and their growing presence in debates over reform of the French state all suggest the penetration of Anglo-Saxon methods.[88] Given Baverez's enthusiasm for exactly these kinds of reform, it makes sense that he, too, should have celebrated the power of American business practices. In *La France qui tombe*, he maintained that 'in contrast to the United States, France has chosen the status

[84] Fitoussi argued against the notion of the *société bloquée*, in his 1996 collaboration with Rosanvallon: Fitoussi and Rosanvallon, *Le nouvel âge des inégalités*.
[85] Alain Minc, *Ce monde qui vient* (Paris: Grasset, 2004), p. 144–5.
[86] Jean Peyrelevade, *Le capitalisme total* (Paris: Seuil/La République des idées, 2005), p. 85.
[87] See, for instance, Crozier and Tilliette, *Quand la France s'ouvrira*, pp. 15–25.
[88] Berrebi-Hoffmann and Grémion, 'Elites intellectuelles'.

quo and rigidity'. The result is that France is 'swimming against the tide'.[89] In order to halt the country's decline, the French need to look at previous experiences – especially the *réformes liberales* of the Reagan–Thatcher era, the modernisation of the UK left under Tony Blair, or the mixed economies of New Zealand, Australia or Spain under Aznar.[90] Of course, Baverez's choice of examples is highly suggestive: the only way forward seems to be to adopt a (neo-) liberal reformist agenda – a far cry from neo-republicanism's reflexive hostility towards the outside world and those who attack the 'French model'.

Another example of an endorsement of certain aspects of the Anglo-Saxon model could be found in a 2005 essay by one of the economics editors at *Le Monde*, Eric Le Boucher. He went so far as to write a 'eulogy to Tony Blair', whose reformism he suggested might offer a way to combine high employment with open markets.[91] This was not without qualification – he still argued that Britain's lack of commitment to Europe was counterproductive – but with France in the throes of what many at the time called *immobilisme*, Blair's Britain seemed to offer a new approach to Europe's economic predicaments. This view was no doubt helped by the steady stream of French people migrating to the United Kingdom and the rising profile of the United Kingdom in French eyes in the 1990s. The result has been a growing desire – especially on the part of right-wing politicians – to lure migrants back to France with promises of a more flexible labour market and reduced red tape, especially given that the majority of them living in Britain are under the age of 30.[92] Sarkozy's courting of the expatriate community in London during his presidential election campaign in 2007 was an indication of the importance of this more outward-looking perspective: his campaign strategists had clearly decided that demonstrating his fondness for the Anglo-American world would more than compensate for the derision that greeted his Atlanticist pretensions in France, where he was rapidly dubbed 'Sarkozy l'Américain'.[93]

One might be tempted to attribute Sarkozy's Atlanticism to an insincere attempt at image management. But – as many of the US diplomatic cables released by WikiLeaks subsequently confirmed – he was genuinely fond of the United States.[94] This was all the more unusual in a country

---

[89] Baverez, *La France qui tombe*, p. 42.   [90] Ibid., p. 110.

[91] Eric Le Boucher, *Economiquement incorrect* (Paris: Grasset, 2005), p. 132.

[92] See, for instance, Angélique Chrisafis, 'Sarkozy's London mission', *Guardian* (30 January 2007).

[93] 'Les attaques du PS contre Sarkozy "l'Américain" sont "xénophobes" dit l'UMP', *Le Monde* (10 January 2007).

[94] Rémy Ourdan, 'Nicolas Sarkozy, "l'Américain"', *Le Monde* (2 December 2010).

where anti-Americanism has a long history, and where only a few years before Sarkozy's Gaullist predecessor had embodied worldwide opposition to the US-led invasion of Iraq.[95] In this context, it seems reasonable to suggest that Sarkozy's unusual enthusiasm for the Anglo-Saxon world was, in part, due to the widespread prevalence of a language of crisis that stressed the need to look beyond the Hexagon for solutions to its predicament. As awareness of France's deficiencies and its apparently 'unreformable' social model has grown, more and more voters have been convinced by the need to learn from foreign models. While neo-republicans have been fighting to preserve the integrity of the nation state from the ravages of globalisation and Anglo-Saxon Europeanism, the language of crisis has made a reform of the state seem not only desirable but inevitable.

La France économique? A changing language of politics

Far from being simply a political epiphenomenon, the language of crisis has become an essential part of the French political space. The critique of the French 'model' and calls for greater openness to foreign influences have profoundly shaped the priorities of contemporary French politics and undermined some of the symbols that are dearest to neo-republicans (the state, the nation ...). What began as a relatively marginal movement for bureaucratic reform led by Crozier in the 1970s had, by the 1990s, metamorphosed into a language of crisis familiar to large swathes of France's middle and working classes. As Touraine put it in 1995, 'where outside France has one heard crisis talk so regularly in the past twenty years?'.[96] Two years later, in an article in the *New York Review of Books*, Hoffmann argued that the mood of 'national dissatisfaction and self-doubt' that hung over France was comparable to that of the 'last years of the Fourth Republic, before de Gaulle returned to power'.[97] Whether the historical comparison is a valid one remains a subject of debate, but it was more than a little ironic that one of the intellectual figures who provided the ideas used to conceptualise the *société bloquée* should, almost three decades later, find himself assessing its impact.

There is another reason to pay close attention to the language of crisis. Clearly, it has undermined neo-republican symbols, ideas and narratives, but it has also weakened the *form* of neo-republicanism. As I suggested

---

[95] Tony Judt, 'A New Master Narrative', in Tony Judt and Denis Lacorne (eds.), *With Us or Against Us: Studies in Global Anti-Americanism* (London: Palgrave, 2004).
[96] Touraine, 'L'ombre d'un mouvement', in Touraine, *Le Grand Refus*, p. 70.
[97] Stanley Hoffmann, 'Look Back in Anger', *New York Review of Books* (17 July 1997).

earlier, one of neo-republicanism's most powerful assets is that it has focused incessantly on the political, thereby reproducing a major characteristic of French political culture. By emphasising concepts such as citizenship and the nation, it has been able to dominate debates that deal with these subjects. By contrast, the language of crisis has tried to restore to prominence the importance of economics as an explanatory factor in French politics. The vast majority of the authors discussed in this chapter marshal large numbers of graphs, statistics and 'empirical' data in order to make their arguments. In a distant echo of Aron's defence against his detractors in the 1940s and 50s, they often see themselves as more 'realistic' and 'pragmatic' than neo-republicans, who are cast as 'nostalgic' and 'idealistic'.[98]

To invoke the empirical legitimacy of economics is, therefore, not simply an intellectual strategy; it is also a political gesture. The deployment of a more 'rigorous' and 'economistic' language has directly challenged the forms of debate and reference points of neo-republicanism and, more generally, the French elite's perceived obsession with all things political. This does not, of course, mean that the authors discussed in this chapter avoid politics. Quite the opposite: they often see their projects as profoundly political. Nevertheless, the ways in which they justify their positions using empirical data suggests a very different approach to contemporary issues, in which economic 'facts' are given at least as much prominence as political 'values'. Given French political culture's deep attachment to the primacy of politics and tendency to abstract theorising, this change in direction could have significant consequences. It is likely to pose a further threat to the French intellectual who, traditionally, has built his or her arguments on the basis of normative outrage and critique. In a parallel development, it is likely to give further legitimacy to French economists: already, in recent years, the most prominent French intellectuals at a global level have been economists such as Thomas Piketty and Philippe Aghion, whose ideas are far more widely discussed than those of, say, Pierre Rosanvallon.[99] And, above all, it is likely to strengthen those voices calling for more liberal reforms of the French state – and make their claims seem increasingly urgent.

---

[98] For example, it is no coincidence that Baverez should have chosen *Commentaire* as the forum for his critique of France: it was precisely the journal's commitment to 'empiricism' that made it the perfect outlet for his ideas.

[99] Take, for instance, the international success and controversy surrounding Piketty, *Capital in the Twenty-First Century*.

10   Liberal politics in France: a story of failure?

The previous four chapters have sought to build a credible narrative for contemporary French liberalism. From *Commentaire* and the *société bloquée* to the Institut Raymond Aron and les Indigènes de la République, I have tried to show that a more contextual definition of French liberalism is possible. I have also suggested that, despite its apparent marginalisation, it has had an impact on policy and legislation in the form of, say, social welfare reform or the reassessment of France's colonial past. In this final chapter, I explore in greater detail the explicitly political consequences of the French liberal revival. In the same way that I looked earlier at the instrumentalisation of neo-republicanism by the left and the right, I want here to examine the various ways in which an emerging liberal discourse has shaped party political affiliations. Once again, the intention is not to write an exhaustive political history; rather, the aim is to situate contemporary French liberalism in its political and historical context.

This kind of contextualisation is particularly important given the two prevalent interpretations surrounding the development of liberalism in late-twentieth-century France. The first, as I mentioned earlier, sees the French liberal tradition as fundamentally 'disabled': even as communism lost ground and the legacy of Gaullism waned in the 1980s, the French political elite remained resolutely hostile to liberalism and preferred to avoid being associated with it in any form.[1] The second interpretation – dear to the left and extreme left – is that since the 1980s (neo-)liberalism has become an overwhelming hegemonic discourse. In this view, the socialists' about-turn in the early 1980s and the subsequent push for increasingly 'liberal' economic reform went hand in hand with the rise of a consensual *pensée unique*. This left French politics unable to resist the onslaught of Anglo-American neo-liberal thinking, which has since

---

[1] On this see, for instance, Judt, *Past Imperfect*; Hazareesingh, *Political Traditions in Modern France*; and Jack Hayward, 'La persistance de l'antilibéralisme: rhétorique et réalité', *Pouvoirs* (No. 126, 2008), pp. 115–32.

become the stultifying orthodoxy of an elite detached from the concerns of ordinary Frenchmen.[2]

That two such sharply opposing visions of the same phenomenon can coexist is a testimony to the fact that there is an enormous amount of confusion over the definition of liberalism in France. Many of those who hold to the first interpretation are foreign scholars, quite legitimately surprised at the remarkable stigmatisation of the word liberal in everyday politics. They conclude that the absence of any 'liberal' political movement in France must mean the relative absence of liberalism altogether. By contrast, those who see liberalism everywhere take it to refer to the wave of so-called 'neo-liberalism' that swept across the world in the 1980s and 90s; for them it is precisely France's *failure* to stand up to this global trend that merits attention. Of course, neither of these simplistic interpretations provides an adequate account of the impact of the French liberal revival. As I have already suggested, we need to start with a contextual redefinition of the term. Thus, while the French political elite was indeed influenced by the international rehabilitation of liberalism in the 1980s, there have also been internal intellectual and political dynamics at play. I shall argue that these have allowed the liberal revival to penetrate French party politics. The strength of other languages of politics – not least neo-republicanism – has prevented any kind of liberalism from becoming dominant. Nevertheless, it has provided an influential counter-narrative that has been put to various political uses in the struggle against the legacy of Marxism on the left and that of Gaullism on the right.

Liberalism and the left: the legacies of the *deuxième gauche*

Where the relationship between republicanism and the French left has a well-established historiography, the same cannot be said of liberalism. If anything, it is the opposite: in most accounts, the French left has failed to incorporate any form of liberalism over the course of the twentieth century. In part, this view stems from the heavy stigmatisation of the term 'liberal' that reached its apogee with the pre-eminence of the PCF in the decades following the Second World War. But even among the post-war non-communist left, liberalism was kept at arm's length. On the one

---

[2] For example, Pierre Larrouturou, *Le livre noir du libéralisme* (Paris: Editions du Rocher, 2007). Tellingly, Larrouturou does not belong to the extreme left; he considers himself a 'Rocardien' and his critique of contemporary economic (neo-)liberalism is followed by a plea for a modernisation of the PS.

hand, there were the strongly anti-liberal roots of left-wing Christian personalism; on the other, there was the absence of a meaningful 'social-liberal' or 'social democratic' tradition of the type that existed at various moments in Italy or the United Kingdom.[3] As the PS unified itself in the early 1970s and stumbled towards electoral success in 1981, it seemed to have done so by renewing itself, not with any putative liberal elements, but by promising an updated, socially responsible Jacobin state under Mitterrand.

This interpretation has much to commend it, particularly if we accept doctrinal definitions of liberalism imported from the Anglo-American world. But, by following a more specifically French story and exploring the interplay between the non-communist left and the intellectual currents described in the previous four chapters, we can see that it is also a very one-sided interpretation. Despite the apparent electoral failure of the liberal strand within the non-communist left – widely known as the *deuxième gauche* (second left) – I argue that it had a significant impact on the shape of the PS and its policies. Above all, this was expressed through various key figures whose presence cast a long shadow over the party in the latter decades of the twentieth century. Perhaps the most famous of these was Michel Rocard, who, from the mid 1970s to the mid 1990s came to embody many of the qualities of the *deuxième gauche*.

Since Rocard's political activities date back to the 1950s, a complete biography would be well beyond the chronological scope of this chapter.[4] Nevertheless, it is important to sketch some of the key influences that had made him, by 1981, one of the few viable alternatives to Mitterrand as a Socialist presidential candidate. A graduate of Sciences Po and the ENA, Rocard's most important formative engagement was in the anti-colonial struggle of the late 1950s. A passionate defender of Algerian self-determination as a student, he left the youth section of the Section française de l'internationale ouvrière (SFIO) in 1958 in protest at the party's support for the escalation of the conflict in Algeria. He remained outside the 'official' Socialist fold for almost a decade and a half, first in the Parti socialiste autonome (PSA) and subsequently in the dissident Parti socialiste unifié (PSU) from 1960. He was the PSU's presidential candidate in 1969 – gaining 3.6 per cent of votes in the first round – before finally joining the reformed PS under Mitterrand in 1974.

---

[3] Serge Audier, *Le socialisme libéral* (Paris: La Découverte, 2006).
[4] On Rocard's rise to prominence see Robert Schneider, *Michel Rocard* (Paris: Stock, 1987), Hervé Hamon and Patrick Rotman, *L'effet Rocard* (Paris: Stock, 1980), and Vincent Duclert, 'La deuxième gauche', in Jean-Jacques Becker and Gilles Candar (eds.), *L'histoire des gauches en France, Volume 2. XXe siècle: à l'épreuve de l'histoire* (Paris: La Découverte, 2004).

Between 1974 and 1981, Rocard emerged as a major player in the PS, developing his networks of contacts inside and outside the party to pave the way for his bid to be president. Ultimately, he was defeated by Mitterrand, who succeeded in winning the support of the party and went on to win the election.

Despite his failure to impose himself in 1981, by this time Rocard had become the standard-bearer of a political current on the non-communist left that would come to be known as the *deuxième gauche*. In a book that became something of an 'official history' of the movement, the journalists Hervé Hamon and Patrick Rotman outlined in 1982 what constituted this new movement.[5] Above all, they emphasised the importance of the CFDT trade union, which had its roots in anti-communism and social Catholicism. Many of those who became the vanguard of the *deuxième gauche* were intimately connected with the CFDT. This included people who would become prominent Socialist politicians in the 1980s – such as Rocard and Delors – and intellectuals like Julliard and Rosanvallon.[6] All these figures – as well as many others within the union, such as the secretary-general Edmond Maire – were drawn to the idea of *autogestion*.[7] As we have already seen, this provided the ideal ideological framework for the development of a decentralised non-communist socialism and it was enthusiastically endorsed by those – like Rocard – who were fighting to make this the dominant force on the left.[8] At the same time, its status as the ideology of choice for the pre-eminent non-communist trade union in France gave the *deuxième gauche* a connection to the workers' movement.

In addition to the CFDT, many have argued that the highly charged political environment of the late 1970s was the unavoidable context for the *deuxième gauche*. The priority for non-communists was to limit the power and influence of the PCF, especially during the period of the Union de la gauche in 1972–7 and the Programme commun in 1981–4. In common with other anti-totalitarians, Rocard naturally gravitated towards the most powerful non-communist political currents of the time in his attempts to outmanoeuvre and discredit Mitterrand, who was the architect of both the major power-sharing agreements with the PCF. But while the anti-communism of Rocard and the *deuxième gauche* was never in doubt, such a reading risks reducing it to a by-product of

---

[5] Benoît Hamon and Patrick Rotman, *La deuxième gauche. Histoire intellectuelle et politique de la CFDT* (Paris: Seuil, 2002 [1982]).

[6] Ibid., pp. 344–5.   [7] Maire was secretary-general of the CFDT in 1971–88.

[8] See for instance the strongly *autogestionnaire* 1972 manifesto of the PSU, drafted by Rocard. 'Pour l'autogestion' (1972), in Michel Rocard, *Parler vrai. Textes politiques précédés d'un entretien avec Jacques Julliard* (Paris: Points, 1979), pp. 102–3.

a party-political battle for electoral control. This would be to ignore the ways in which the *deuxième gauche* attempted to renew a much longer non-Marxist and liberal tradition of French socialism, which had its roots in the politics of Jean Jaurès and Pierre Mendès-France.[9] Rocard himself was well aware of this distinct genealogy. Indeed, one could argue that since the late 1970s he has been largely responsible for popularising it, by repeatedly stressing the conflict between 'the two cultures of the left'. He outlined what exactly this meant in a now famous speech to the PS congress in Nantes in April 1977.

There are two political cultures on the French left ... The most typical – and the one which was dominant for a long time – is Jacobin, centralising, statist, nationalist and protectionist ... the other culture that is reappearing within the French left today ... is decentralising, whether this refers to dependent majority groups like women, or minorities who have not been adequately integrated into society [*mal accueillis dans le corps social*]: young people, immigrants, disabled people. It is wary of regulation and administration, and prefers the autonomy of local collectivities and experimentation.[10]

The consequences of this speech were immense, both for Rocard – who was henceforth cast as the voice of a 'Jaurèsian' *deuxième gauche* against Mitterrand's 'Guesdist' *première gauche* – and for the PS as a whole. Yet, despite its obviously anti-totalitarian overtones, this was one of the clearest conceptual presentations of the distinct genealogies within the French left and it was one that Rocard would never disown. On the contrary, the passing of time made him more convinced than ever of the longevity of the 'two cultures' and the perils of what his supporters called 'Jacobin socialism'.[11] In large part, this had to do with Rocard's marginalisation inside the PS, where his motions rarely carried more than 25 per cent of party members in the 1980s and 90s.[12] Moreover, his poor relations with Mitterrand – who systematically sidelined him in favour of exponents of the *première gauche* (Laurent Fabius, Henri Emmanuelli, Edith Cresson ...) – did little to convince him that the two cultures could be reconciled.[13] In economic policy, too, he failed to impose himself: the

[9] On Mendès-France's legacy for the *deuxième gauche*, see the summary by V. Duclert, 'Mendès, l'oublié de la gauche', *Le Monde* (16 January 2007).
[10] 'Les deux cultures politiques' (1977), in Rocard, *Parler vrai*, pp. 76–7.
[11] The expression 'socialiste jacobin' is taken from Jacques Julliard, *La faute à Rousseau* (Paris: Seuil, 1985), especially pp. 59–80. On the different cultures of the left see also Christophe Prochasson, *Les intellectuels et le socialisme* (Paris: Plon, 1997).
[12] A. Bergounioux and G. Grunberg, 'L'union de la gauche et l'ère Mitterrand', in Becker and Candar, *L'histoire des gauches en France, Volume 2*.
[13] Rocard deals with Mitterrand's betrayals at length in Michel Rocard, *Si la gauche savait. Entretiens avec Georges-Marc Benamou* (Paris: Points, 2007).

full nationalisations against which he had vigorously campaigned in the late 1970s were implemented immediately in 1981, resulting in a series of debilitating devaluations. The PS's economic about-turn in 1982–3 restored some credibility to the 'Rocard approach' through austerity and budget control, but only at the cost of humiliation and, ultimately, defeat at the polls in 1986. This less favourable political climate may well have played a part in Mitterrand choosing to appoint Rocard as Prime Minister after his re-election in 1988. Rocard himself remains puzzled by Mitterrand's decision, but admits that it could have been part of a strategy of 'opening [*ouverture*]'.[14] It was almost certainly also an attempt by Mitterrand to find a plausible bridge between the avowedly neo-liberal Chirac administration of 1986–8 and his own *première gauche* inclinations. Seen this way, the choice of Rocard was a good one, particularly as he remained very popular in the polls. Whatever Mitterrand's exact motivations, the partnership was only to last three years before Rocard was replaced by Cresson. After a brief stint as head of the PS in 1993, Rocard increasingly withdrew from French politics, and was elected to the European Parliament from 1994 to 2009.

Nevertheless, with a prominent role in government, first as Minister for Economic Planning (1981–3) and subsequently as Minister for Agriculture (1983–5) and Prime Minister (1988–91), one is tempted to say that Rocard suffered less from actual marginalisation than from the kind of 'liberal pessimism' that we saw earlier in the case of Raymond Aron.[15] While he scarcely concealed his desire to run for the presidency, and repeatedly bemoaned his frosty relationship with Mitterrand, Rocard left an important imprint on the non-communist left. This goes back to his conceptualisation of the 'two cultures', which prefigured the transformations in French politics that have been the subject of the previous nine chapters. In fact, it is without much difficulty that we can map the characteristics of the *deuxième gauche* on to the definition of French liberalism I have proposed thus far, and those of the *première gauche* on to neo-republicanism. This parallel is more than just an example of analytical ingenuity. It had its real-life expression in the clash between two key currents at the heart of the PS in the late 1970s and early 1980s: the CERES think tank, led by Chevènement, and the journal *Faire*, led by Rosanvallon.

---

[14] Rocard gives his interpretation in Rocard, *Si la gauche savait*, pp. 323–35.
[15] Some ideas in this chapter, in particular on Rocard's 'marginality', were inspired by papers presented at a colloquium organized by Sylvie Guillaume and Jean-François Sirinelli entitled 'Les marges en politique: le rocardisme', held at the Centre d'histoire de Sciences Po on 14 December 2010.

Both at the time and in retrospect, the CERES was seen as the vanguard of the *première gauche*, pushing the PS towards its Marxist, Jacobin and, what Rocard called, its 'Guesdist' roots. By contrast, the journal *Faire* sought to renew socialist thinking by introducing new ideas. Although still within a fairly orthodox Marxist and socialist framework, it incorporated the ideas of *autogestion* in an effort to give intellectual depth to the *deuxième gauche* and create what the historian Christophe Prochasson describes as 'a liberal axiom ... of a new intellectual practice'.[16] However, these two diverging currents within the PS soon came to embody bigger fault lines in French politics. In 1986, the CERES changed its name to Socialisme et République and, in 1991, after the first Gulf War and shortly before the referendum on the Maastricht Treaty, broke away from the PS altogether. By this time, Chevènement had become the leading light of neo-republican politics, defending the virtues of a neo-republican national narrative as fiercely as he once defended Marxism. This trajectory could scarcely have been more different from that of Rosanvallon who, while never renouncing his socialist roots, became a key figure in the liberal revival and has actively contributed to the modernisation of the left through his work and his intellectual networks.

There can be few better examples of the importance of the 'two cultures' – not just for the left but for French politics as a whole. Little wonder, then, that Rocard has continued to claim the heritage of the *deuxième gauche* as his own: he reproduced almost verbatim his definition of the 'two cultures' in lengthy interviews with François Furet in 1986 and Georges-Marc Benamou in 2005.[17] But Rocard's contribution has not been limited solely to repackaging a historical dichotomy in French politics; he also tried to implement the project of the *deuxième gauche*. This was evident, for example, in the 1982 Defferre laws on decentralisation that gave greater powers to regions, and the renegotiation of the status of Nouvelle-Calédonie that resulted in the Nouméa Accords of 1988.[18] In the long term, the movement for *parité* – which Rocard had long supported – was directly inspired by the concerns of the *deuxième gauche*.[19] And, while he said relatively little on the question of

---

[16] Prochasson, *Les intellectuels et le socialisme*, p. 209.
[17] Michel Rocard, 'Entretien avec François Furet', *Le Débat* (No. 38, Vol. 1, 1986), pp. 4–50. Rocard, *Si la gauche savait*.
[18] For a selection of speeches by Rocard on the question of Nouvelle-Calédonie, see Michel Rocard, *Un pays comme le nôtre. Textes politiques 1986–9* (Paris: Seuil, 1989), pp. 63–90.
[19] Already in 1988 Rocard was arguing for a woman's quota (albeit only at 25 per cent). 'Les droits des femmes' (1988), in Rocard, *Un pays comme le nôtre*, p. 214.

integration and multiculturalism, his repeated denunciations of France's *chauvinisme xénophobe* and explicit support for 'civil society' gave important legitimacy to celebrations of diversity, multiculturalism and regionalism that developed in the early 1980s.[20]

In a more general sense, Rocard brought the language of crisis and the critique of the state to the heart of the French left. This had much to do with his participation in the Club Jean Moulin in the 1950s and his close relationship with Michel Crozier.[21] As one of the founders of the Club put it in 1977, '[Rocard] seems to me to be ten times more marked by Crozier than Marx, Jules Guesde or even Jaurès'.[22] This bold claim was borne out by Rocard's stance on a number of key issues. In the late 1970s and early 1980s, his attacks on proposals to nationalise major industries was underpinned by a critique of the state which reflected that of Crozier. During a speech to the PS in Metz in 1979, Rocard adapted the title of Crozier's most recent book – *On ne change pas la société par décret* – to the more targeted 'l'économie ne se change par décret'.[23] The implication was clear both to the audience and to his followers: using Crozier as his alibi, Rocard intended to cast himself as the leader of the 'reformists' whose aim it was to limit nationalisation. It is true that, by the late 1980s, the compromises of power and the rising tide of neo-liberalism had made Rocard more cautious. In a speech in 1987, he responded to another Crozier title by arguing that 'the modern state is not a "modest" state, but an "efficient" state'.[24] Nevertheless, the sociologist's ideas were central to Rocard's attempts to implement administrative reform during his time as Prime Minister.[25] One might even go so far as to say that Rocard single-handedly made Crozier's ideas acceptable to parts of the left – a remarkable achievement, given that the latter has usually been associated with the right.[26]

---

[20] Rocard interviewed in 1978. Quoted in Hamon and Rotman, *L'effet Rocard*, p. 189.
[21] In addition, Rocard's second wife – Michèle Legendre – worked in Crozier's research group.
[22] Olivier Chevrillon, interviewed in 1978. Quoted in Hamon and Rotman, *L'effet Rocard*.
[23] 'L'économie ne se change pas par décret' (1979), in Michel Rocard, *A l'épreuve des faits. Textes politiques 1979–1985* (Paris: Seuil, 1986), p. 20.
[24] 'L'Etat moderne, c'est l'Etat éfficace' (1988), in Rocard, *Un pays comme le nôtre*, p. 164.
[25] Florence Gallemand, 'La politique rocardienne de modernisation administrative', in Eric Derras et al., *La gouvernabilité* (Paris: Presses Universitaires de France, 1996).
[26] As he put it in 2008, 'Oui, j'ai lu et relu avec une grande joie intellectuelle Le phénomène bureaucratique de Crozier. Et, en effet, je crois être l'un des rares hommes politiques à prendre très au sérieux la sociologie et à essayer de me comporter en fonction des enseignements que cette discipline nous apporte.' Serge Guérin, 'Entretien avec Michel Rocard', *Revue Civique* (Spring 2008), available at www.revuecivique.eu/index.php?option=com_contentandtask=viewandid=28andItemid=9 (accessed 12 June 2011).

It was not only the critique of the state that Rocard brought to the PS; it was also a firm commitment to Europe. Here, Rocard and his followers were in good company. Not only was Mitterrand himself deeply committed to Europe; so too was Delors, whom Rocard described as a member of the *deuxième gauche* 'to the core' even though he never formally belonged to the *rocardien* current inside the PS.[27] But, where a large swathe of the PS supported the European project in the 1980s, this began to fade in the early 1990s with the referendum on the Maastricht Treaty exposing the party's latent Euroscepticism. By the time of the 2005 referendum, this became an open schism. Rocard's arch-enemy Fabius led a heterogeneous socialist 'no' camp that brought together Chevènement's neo-republicans and a conglomerate of anti-globalisation and anti-capitalist movements. Drawing on the widespread popular resentment towards Europe, particularly among left-leaning public-sector workers, this growing Euroscepticism was instrumental in the victory of the 'no' camp.

Predictably, Rocard felt that the 'no' movement was little more than a repackaged *première gauche*, minus Mitterrand: by opposing the European Constitution, the left was once again choosing Guesde over Jaurès.[28] Since Rocard had been 'retired' to the European Parliament in 1994, he could no longer play as direct a role in orientating Socialist policy as he had in the 1980s. But he did intend to shape the European orientation of the next generation of Socialist leaders. Already in 1996, his 'kindred spirit' Delors had founded the pro-European think tank Notre Europe to support greater European integration and continue his legacy.[29] Rocard did the same shortly after the disastrous electoral defeat in 2002 by inaugurating with the well-known *rocardiens* Pierre Moscovici and Dominique Strauss-Kahn the think tank A gauche, en Europe.[30] Unlike Delors's think tank, which focused squarely on European policy, Rocard and Strauss-Kahn's initiative was much more actively committed to reforming the PS. It built on existing networks of reformists who had been part of the 'Alternative pour un renouveau' and 'Socialisme et Démocratie' groups inside the PS in the late 1990s and early 2000s. By bringing together intellectuals – some of whom had been part of Rosanvallon's projects – A gauche, en Europe became a means to further

---

[27] On Rocard's attitudes towards and relationship to Delors, see Rocard, *Si la gauche savait*, pp. 281, 287, 298
[28] Rocard, *Si la gauche savait*, pp. 417–18.
[29] Details of the club's activities are available at www.notre-europe.eu.
[30] Isabelle Mandraud, 'Au parti socialiste, les clubs de réflexion se multiplient aussi', *Le Monde* (6 November 2002).

a recognisably *rocardien* agenda within the party (reform of welfare provision and taxation, greater European integration . . .).[31] At the same time, Rocard's choice to align himself with Strauss-Kahn and Moscovici made clear from where he thought a twenty-first-century *rocardisme* might emerge.[32] Indeed, it almost appeared as if Rocard had made a winning choice: Moscovici and Strauss-Kahn wielded considerable influence in the party after 2000, with the latter repeatedly tipped as Sarkozy's only credible successor after 2007.

Another indication that the concerns of the *deuxième gauche* were being heard was the tentative attempts by some socialists to reclaim the word 'liberal'. In the early 2000s, there was even for the first time a current in the PS that openly declared itself *social-libéral*, led by a deputy from Mulhouse, Jean-Marie Bockel, an erstwhile fellow traveller of Chevènement and the CERES.[33] Inspired by New Labour and the German Sozialdemokratische Partei Deutschlands (SPD), Bockel's goal was to push the PS to embrace a reformist 'third way'.[34] But, despite its *deuxième gauche* overtones, his motion received a mere 0.6 per cent of the vote at the PS party conference in Le Mans in 2005, and after Sarkozy was elected in 2007 Bockel broke away from the PS to create his own party – La Gauche Moderne – and become a minister in the Fillon administration.[35] However, Bockel was not the only one to raise the question of the left's relationship to liberalism.[36] In 2008, the issue surfaced again in a lengthy interview with the prominent Socialist and mayor of Paris from 2001 to 2014, Bertrand Delanoë. While rejecting Bockel's *social-libéralisme*, Delanoë argued that it was time to reclaim liberalism for the left:

---

[31] For instance, the economist Thomas Piketty. I. Mandraud, 'Sans courant au PS, Dominique Strauss-Kahn préfère tisser un réseau à l'échelle européene', *Le Monde* (24 November 2003).

[32] It could be argued that Strauss-Kahn's *La Flamme et le Cendre* (2002) was in both style and substance one of the most *rocardien* manifestos of recent years. Among many things, Strauss-Kahn came out in support of greater decentralisation, a more effective managerial state and deeper European integration. Dominique Strauss-Kahn, *La Flamme et le Cendre* (Paris: Hachette, 2003 [2002]). He also defended a 'yes' to the European Constitution in D. Strauss-Kahn, *Oui! Lettre ouverte aux enfants d'Europe* (Paris: Grasset, 2004).

[33] Michel Noblecourt, 'M. Bockel (PS) crée un club pour moderniser la gauche', *Le Monde* (15 December 2001).

[34] Jean-Marie Bockel, *La 3ème gauche. Petit manifeste social-libéral* (Paris: L'Archer, 1999).

[35] Marion Van Renterghem, 'Jean-Marie Bockel. Fidèle à lui-même', *Le Monde* (10 July 2007). See also the website of La Gauche Moderne at www.lagauchemoderne.org. In 2011, La Gauche Moderne joined a larger centrist coalition led by the leader of the Parti radical, Jean-Louis Borloo.

[36] Even outside party politics, there were signs that this was the case – for instance, in the work of Monique Canto-Sperber. See Canto-Sperber, *Le libéralisme et la gauche*.

I do not automatically reject the term 'liberal'. And, when it is applied to a political doctrine in the broadest sense, I even think that any Socialist activist should claim it ... It is therefore time for us to stop getting fixated on this word; we need to put behind us those sad days of our collective history when a large part of the French left rejected a European constitution on the grounds that it was 'liberal'. This is all the more absurd ... since the left that I advocate is, by its very nature, liberal.[37]

This bold statement of intent was entirely in keeping with the spirit of the *deuxième gauche*. By rejecting free-market neo-liberalism but rehabilitating the principles of political liberalism, Delanoë's argument echoed that of Rocard in the late 1970s and 80s.[38] But, where few left-wing figures of the late 1970s (even those drawn to the *deuxième gauche*) were willing openly to endorse the term 'liberal', Delanoë's statement was immediately given an enthusiastic public endorsement by Rocard.[39] Moreover, with the mayor of Paris poised to make a bid for the leadership of the PS in 2008, it seemed as if the party was on the point of reconciling itself, in some form or another, with its liberal heritage.

The enthusiasm was short-lived. Almost immediately, the left-wing press and a majority of Socialist politicians denounced Delanoë's claim that he could be 'liberal and socialist'.[40] In much the same way as Rocard had been dismissed as an exponent of a rightist 'American left' in the 1970s, Delanoë found himself very much a minority on the left. This was confirmed at the 2008 party conference where his motion carried only 25 per cent of a bitterly divided party vote – almost identical to the support achieved by Rocard and his followers in previous decades. Delanoë subsequently withdrew his leadership bid and supported the majority candidate Martine Aubry. This withdrawal seemed to sound the death knell of a new *rocardien* revival, not least because Strauss-Kahn failed to secure the Socialist presidential nomination in 2006 (he received 20.7 per cent of the party vote). Worse was to come a few years later in 2011, as Strauss-Kahn was forced to resign as Managing Director of the International Monetary Fund (IMF) and abandon a further campaign for the Socialist presidential nomination amid allegations of serious sexual misconduct.

---

[37] Bertrand Delanoë, *De l'audace. Entretiens avec Laurent Joffrin* (Paris: Robert Laffont, 2008), pp. 43–5.

[38] See for instance Rosanvallon, *Le capitalisme utopique*.

[39] 'Rocard le libéral', *L'Express* (19 June 2008); 'Michel Rocard et ses proches s'engagent en faveur de Bertrand Delanoë', *Le Monde* (10 September 2008).

[40] On the reactions to Delanoë, see for instance, 'Delanoë se définit comme 'socialiste et liberal', *Libération* (21 May 2008), and Xavier Barotte and François Xavier Bourmaud, 'Le credo libéral de Delanoë trouble le PS', *Le Figaro* (23 May 2008).

Even outside the world of party politics, the *deuxième gauche* looked to be in trouble. In a symbolic gesture, one of the longest-standing supporters of the *deuxième gauche* – the historian and journalist Jacques Julliard – left the magazine *Nouvel Observateur* in 2010 and joined its rival publication *Marianne*. Since the early 1970s, Julliard had been instrumental in bringing the ideas of the *deuxième gauche* to the French intelligentsia with a wide network of contacts and a regular column in an influential left-leaning weekly magazine.[41] This made his departure all the more surprising, particularly as he chose a publication that has tended to endorse a more neo-republican line. But his justification was unambiguous:

> I belong to the *deuxième gauche*. For a long time, I thought that a compromise with capitalism was possible. The financial crisis revealed that capitalism was out of control. The conclusion is that we must react more decisively and accept confrontation.[42]

Julliard's 'conversion' was a reminder that the legacy of the *deuxième gauche* is an uncertain one. Like most of the variants of 'liberalism' I have examined in the previous four chapters, it is shot through, not simply with a deep pessimism about the potential for change, but also an acute sense of its own marginality.

Does this mean that the legacy of the *deuxième gauche* is a story of failure – another example of France's 'disabled' liberal tradition?[43] There is certainly plenty of evidence to support this argument. More than many other social-democratic parties in Europe since 1980, the PS has been uniquely hostile to its more liberal tendencies. Thus, successive generations of *rocardiens* have failed to gather more than 30 per cent of the party vote, and no leader of the *deuxième gauche* has been able to win the Socialist presidential nomination. Rocard was outmanoeuvred by Mitterrand, Delors refused to stand in 1995, and Strauss-Kahn's presidential bid ended in ignominy in 2011. In all three cases, opinion polls were extremely favourable but a combination of personal and political factors prevented any of them from standing. There is a further paradox, which has often contributed to the apparent marginalisation of the *deuxième gauche*, namely the fact that some of its most eloquent exponents were seen to be more successful in international affairs than domestic politics.

---

[41] On Julliard's influential network, and his relationship to the *deuxième gauche*, see Jean-Claude Casanova, Robert Chapuis, Jean Daniel et al., *Pour une histoire de la Deuxième Gauche. Hommage à Jacques Julliard* (Paris: Editions BNF, 2008).

[42] Xavier Ternisien, 'Marianne prend à l'Obs le chroniqueur Jacques Julliard', *Le Monde* (19 November 2010).

[43] Gilles Martinet, 'Les malheurs de la deuxième gauche', *Le Monde* (23 December 1994).

This was certainly true of Delors, who remains a vital figure in the history of European integration, and Strauss-Kahn, who was widely credited with having given the IMF a more 'social' inflection. More adept at seducing an international community that admired them, these leading lights of the *deuxième gauche* struggled when it came to taming 'Jacobin socialism' at home.

Yet these strategic failures may not offer the best way of judging the legacy of the *deuxième gauche*. While it has undoubtedly struggled to gain a foothold inside the PS, its emergence reflected and amplified the progression of liberalism in the French political space. Seen this way, its most powerful legacy has been to provide a language that a unified non-communist left could use to negotiate a rapidly changing ideological landscape. From the anti-totalitarian and anti-communist moment of the late 1970s and 80s, to the debates surrounding 'social-liberalism' in the mid 2000s, it has offered left-wing 'liberals', 'social-democrats' and 'social-liberals' a positive identity. This has largely consisted in a commitment to pragmatism and realism – Rocard's famous 'straight talking [*parler vrai*]' – alongside a firm belief in the need for state reform, greater European integration and innovative approaches to social exclusion. Most of these have today been absorbed into the PS's broad ideological framework. Indeed, I would argue that Ségolène Royal's unexpected nomination as the Socialist presidential candidate in 2007 reflected the style – if not always the substance – of the *deuxième gauche*. Her emphasis on 'participatory democracy' and especially her success among the party's youth wing suggested that what might formerly have been described as 'the Rocard method' could succeed among the party faithful. Her subsequent failure to sell this vision to French voters beyond her party was a sign not so much that her unusual synthesis was insufficiently liberal but that her opponent had been more effective in instrumentalising the language of pragmatic, outward-looking and reformist liberalism.

Liberalism and the right: from neo-liberalism to declinism

At first glance, it is easier to write a recent history of the French right's relationship to liberalism than it is for the left. This is because the stigma attached to the word 'liberal' among right-wing politicians has not been nearly as pronounced as for their left-wing counterparts. Where it took until the turn of the twentieth century for some members of the PS to reclaim the term 'liberal', this process had been taking place on the right at least since de Gaulle's resignation in 1969. Indeed, one could argue that there is an even longer history of liberalism on the French right.

This was certainly the view of the most famous contemporary historian of the French right, René Rémond. As early as 1954, Rémond identified 'three cultures' of the modern French right: the first extreme and 'counter-revolutionary', the second 'Orleanist', liberal and conservative, and the third 'Bonapartist', authoritarian and nationalist.[44] In a more recent work, published two years before his death, Rémond argued that, under the Fifth Republic, these three cultures have been reflected in the extreme right and the rise of the Front National, the non-Gaullist right (primarily the UDF), and the neo-Gaullist right respectively.[45]

There are few compelling reasons to contest the broad outline of Rémond's classificatory framework. There is, however, an urgent need to tell the story of the French right since 1981. Other than Rémond's overview – and a vast literature on the extreme right in the form of the Front National – there are still relatively few systematic analyses of the ideological and party-political developments of the contemporary French right.[46] Hence the importance of the second part of this chapter, the aim of which is to present a chronology of liberalism's interaction with the non-Gaullist culture of the right in the past three decades. Given their respective genealogies, it is not surprising that it has been the non-Gaullist right that has been most susceptible to liberalism. Much like the *deuxième gauche* – which it has, in some ways, mirrored – it has often appeared to be marginalised and dominated by its (neo-) Gaullist brother. Sometimes it has even sought to cast itself as a 'non-partisan' centre. Nevertheless, it is clear that the slow penetration of a liberal sensibility on the non-Gaullist right has gradually effected a change on the French right as a whole. Inevitably, the contours of this revival have been marked by the concerns of the right: where the *deuxième gauche* sought to mobilise civil society and 'liberalise' socialism, the liberal right has focused much more on entrepreneurialism, deregulation and the free market. Yet, despite these differences, the right's instrumentalisation of liberalism ensured that by the first decade of the twenty-first century the liberal revival had spread to almost every corner of the political space.

---

[44] My references are to the 1982 revised edition of Rémond's book. René Rémond, *Les droites en France* (Paris: L'Audibert, 1982), p. 37.

[45] René Rémond, *Les droites aujourd'hui* (Paris: L'Audibert, 2005).

[46] This is no doubt a consequence of the strongly left-leaning bias of French academia. Apart from Rémond, the only other major studies of the post-war right in France are Andrew Knapp, *Gaullism since de Gaulle* (London: Dartmouth, 1994), and the extensive Jean-François Sirinelli (ed.), *Histoire des droites en France*, 3 vols. (Paris: Gallimard, 1992). The contributions by Marc Sadoun, Jean-Marie Donegani and François Bourricaud look at the period 1945–1992.

Any discussion of the relationship between liberalism and the right since 1980 must look briefly at what came before, in large part because it was between 1974 and 1981 that the non-Gaullist right can legitimately claim to have been dominant. This was the period of the presidency of Valéry Giscard d'Estaing, who quite explicitly sought to break with both the style and substance of the de Gaulle and Pompidou years.[47] In an effort to draw a line under the politics of *dirigisme* and *grandeur*, the new president proposed to make France into an 'advanced liberal society' that would be pluralist, open and forward-thinking. By positioning himself at the centre of the political spectrum and offering 'pragmatic' solutions to the pressing problems facing the country – not least the consequences of the oil shocks of the 1970s – he sought to transcend the traditional clash between Gaullists and communists that had defined French politics since 1945. Even if most commentators agree that the Giscard presidency became increasingly conservative as the threat of a Socialist victory became likely from 1978 onwards, few doubted his desire to give a more liberal shape to French politics.

The president outlined this new vision most clearly in his manifesto *La démocratie française* (1976).[48] He argued that France had been transformed by the Trente Glorieuses and that 'there is today no other legitimate conception of power other than a liberal one'. Traditional ideologies – by which he meant Marxism and 'classical liberalism' – were no longer satisfactory; what was needed instead was a society in which there was greater 'liberty' and 'pluralism'.[49] Among other things, this required a 'normalised' political system in which opposition and government could peacefully coexist, as well as a free economy to promote growth. The aim was to build a society 'that resists immobilism and makes revolution useless'.[50] This plea for a specifically French brand of consensual liberalism helps to explain why Rémond described *La démocratie française* as one of the key texts in the elaboration of a 'French neo-liberalism'.[51] But this new approach was also backed by liberal policies and legislation: the Giscard years were characterised by economic rigour and budgetary control, alongside social legislation such as the lowering of the voting age to 18, the legalisation of abortion and

---

[47] Jean-Pierre Dubuis, 'La conception de la présidence de Valéry Giscard d'Estaing', in Serge Berstein, René Rémond and Jean-François Sirinelli (eds.), *Les années Giscard. Institutions et pratiques politiques 1974–1981* (Paris: Fayard, 2003).
[48] On this text and its precedents, see the overview in Mathias Bernard, 'Le projet giscardien face aux contraintes du pouvoir', in Serge Berstein and Jean-François Sirinelli (eds.), *Les années Giscard. Les réformes de société* (Paris: Armand Colin, 2007).
[49] Valéry Giscard d'Estaing, *La démocratie française* (Paris: Fayard, 1976), pp. 39, 95.
[50] Ibid., p. 172.   [51] Rémond, *Les droites en France*, pp. 290–305.

divorce, and the end of state control over the audiovisual media. At the same time, there was a clear break with a Gaullist vision of Europe as Giscard d'Estaing became personally involved with European administrative reform and enlargement of the European Community.[52] Whether at home or abroad, the president hoped that the measures he enacted – often in the face of considerable hostility from Gaullists like Chirac – would provide the blueprint for a pragmatic, modernising and pro-European brand of French liberalism.

The implosion of the right in 1981 put an end to this moderate liberalism. Both the strident rhetoric of the *première gauche*'s 'rupture' with capitalism in 1981 and the right's attempt to realign itself after its defeat led to a radicalisation of right-wing liberal discourse. But the trauma of being consigned to the opposition for the first time since the foundation of the Fifth Republic in 1958 was not the only reason for a rising tide of 'neo-liberal' thought that was committed above all to the promotion of free enterprise and the market. Already during the Giscard years there were signs that a much more strident liberalism was threatening to undermine the president's moderate, consensual project. During this period, a new generation of right-wing politicians, technocrats and *haut fonctionnaires* – many of whom had graduated from Sciences Po and the ENA in the late 1960s – began to coalesce in a number of think tanks. As Denord has suggested, these newer groups were built in the shadow of older organisations, such as the Association pour la liberté économique et le progrès social (ALEPS), founded in 1966.[53] Participants at ALEPS's regular events included many of the most famous French liberal intellectuals and economists of the post-war period (Raymond Aron, Maurice Allais, Jacques Rueff ...), as well as younger figures such as the neo-liberal economist, Pascal Salin, who contributed to popularising the work of Friedrich von Hayek in France in the 1960s and became the president of Hayek's Mont Pelerin Society in 1994–6. In this way, ALEPS acted as a key conduit for liberal thinking during the high period of Gaullism in the 1960s and laid the foundation for more militant liberal organisations of the late 1970s and 80s.[54]

---

[52] Serge Berstein and Jean-François Sirinelli (eds.), *Les années Giscard: Valéry Giscard d'Estaing et l'Europe* (Paris: Armand Colin, 2006).

[53] François Denord, 'La conversion au néo-libéralisme. Droite et liberalisme économique dans les années 1980', *Mouvements* (Vol. 5, No. 35, 2004), p. 18. Denord is one of the few scholars to have made a sustained attempt to examine the changes in economic thought in France in the past three decades.

[54] On this see especially Michael Behrent, 'Justifying Capitalism in an Age of Uncertainty: L'Association pour la Liberté Economique et le Progrès Social, 1969–1973', in Chabal, *France since the 1970s*.

One of these new groupings was the team that founded *Commentaire* in 1978. As we have seen, their aim was to create a viable forum for the development of liberal thought in an increasingly unfavourable political climate. The journal's longevity and ecumenism prevented it from becoming solely a platform for aggressive neo-liberalism, but it nevertheless counted among its regular contributors many enthusiastic right-leaning liberals such as Salin – who made no secret of his admiration for Hayek and his distaste for 'totalitarian' social democracy – and the sociologist Raymond Boudon, whose sociology of the individual provided an important intellectual context for the emergence of neo-liberal thought.[55] By giving a voice in particular to more 'moderate' forms of liberalism, it paved the way for the rehabilitation of liberalism across the centre-right.

Equally focused on the elite, but more radical and more obviously polemical than *Commentaire*, was the Club de l'Horloge. Founded in 1974 by a group of five ENA graduates, it would be best remembered for publishing a book in 1985 defending the notion of a 'national preference' in French immigration and subsequently supporting a 'union of the right' that would incorporate the Front National.[56] However, this relationship with the extreme right has partly obscured the origins of the Club. While the problem of 'national identity' was always central to its activities, many of the Club's early meetings and publications in the 1970s focused as much on the need to combat Crozier's 'bureaucratic peril' and build an entrepreneurial free-market economy as on questions of national sovereignty.[57] In 1979, we even find Crozier participating in one of the Club's conferences on the reform of the state and the administration.[58] After the left's victory in 1981, the Club's publications took on an increasingly neo-liberal – and virulent – tone. In 1984, in a preface to a new edition of one of the Club's first books – *Les racines du futur* (1977) – Jean-Yves Le Gallou vigorously denounced the 'egalitarian' and 'totalitarian' character of Mitterrand's 'hard socialism', while simultaneously claiming that he and other founding members of the Club had been the 'first' to see the imminent bankruptcy of

[55] See for instance Pascal Salin, 'Le piège de la social-démocratie', *Commentaire* (Vol. 5, No. 20, 1982), pp. 597–601, and Pascal Salin, 'Démocratie et liberté', *Commentaire* (Vol. 8, No. 36, 1986), pp. 673–7.
[56] Jean-Yves Le Gallou and Club de l'Horloge, *La Préférence nationale: Réponse à l'immigration* (Paris: Albin Michel, 1985). For an overview see C. Chombeau, 'La droite de la droite tente de s'organiser', *Le Monde* (21 October 1997).
[57] See for instance Philippe Baccou and Club de l'Horloge, *Le Grand Tabou. L'économie et le mirage égalitaire* (Paris: Albin Michel, 1980).
[58] Michel Crozier, 'Y a-t-il une fatalité bureaucratique?', in Club de l'Horloge, *Le péril bureaucratique* (Paris: Le Club de l'Horloge, 1980).

socialism.[59] A year later, Le Gallou would join the FN (along with another founding member of the Club, Bruno Mégret), but this growing co-operation with a burgeoning extreme right did not stop the Club from seeking to influence the centre right as well. Regular meetings in the late 1980s and early 1990s with prominent members of Chirac's RPR ensured that the Club's 'liberal-national' message remained high on the agenda both during and after the right's brief return to power in 1986–8.[60]

This strategy of influence was reinforced by the Club de l'Horloge's connections with another think tank, the Club 89. Set up in 1981, this was a more decentralised and less elitist organisation, with branches across the country. Its goal was, in the words of its founders, to bring together those on the right who wanted to 'express their desire for a society of freedom and progress'.[61] This essentially resulted in a set of policy proposals very similar to those of the Club de l'Horloge – liberalisation of the economy, privatisation, a defence of national identity . . . – but presented in a consensual language more appropriate to everyday party politics than that of the Club de l'Horloge.[62] Their different styles notwithstanding, the proximity between the two organisations was confirmed by a number of collaborative projects, including a joint publication in 1989, the aim of which was to defend a 'liberal Europe' in the face of Delors's bureaucratic, statist and socialist 'social Europe'.[63] Operating in a new space opened by the right's defeat in 1981, both clubs acted as ideological melting pots in which neo-liberal ideas that were attractive to the centre right could be developed alongside 'nationalist' themes that appealed to a resurgent FN.

Of course, the renewed enthusiasm for economic liberalism among various right-wing think tanks in the 1980s was not simply a result of political transformations inside France; even at the time, the international context was seen to be crucial.[64] If in the mid 1970s there was

---

[59] 'Préface pour la nouvelle edition: la revolution républicaine', in Jean-Yves Le Gallou and Club de l'Horloge, Les racines du futur: demain la France (Paris: Editions Albatros, 1984), pp. 1–8.

[60] 'Pour récupérer le pouvoir Le Club de l'Horloge incite la droite et le FN à affirmer leurs "valeurs communes"', Le Monde (18 June 88). Bertrand Le Gendre, 'A l'écoute de la droite qui pense', Le Monde (22 November 1989).

[61] Michel Aurillac and Nicole Catala, Pour une société de progrès et de liberté (Paris: Editions Albatros, 1988), p. 7. On the differences between the Club de l'Horloge and Club 89, see Denord, 'La conversion au néo-libéralisme', p. 22.

[62] See Aurillac and Catala, Pour une société de progrès et de liberté.

[63] 'Le Club 89 et le Club de l'Horloge publient un rapport commun sur l'Europe sociale', Le Monde (2 May 1989).

[64] On the wider international context for the rise of neo-liberalism, see François Denord, 'Le Prophéte, le Pélerin et le Missionnaire. La circulation internationale du

concern about 'American cultural imperialism' among some members of the Club de l'Horloge, by the 1980s there was open admiration for the liberalising reforms of Thatcher and Reagan. In the triumphal words of Le Gallou in 1984: 'the West is being won over every day by the renewal of nationalist and liberal ideas'[65] Members of the Club 89 and the Club de l'Horloge were inspired by Thatcher's strident defence of national sovereignty during the Falklands War (1982) and, later, her famous Bruges speech (1988) on Europe.

They were not alone. In 1983, another graduate of the ENA and economics lecturer at Sciences Po – Guy Sorman – published an essay in which he announced the advent of an American 'neo-conservative revolution' that would transform Western politics. He wrote admiringly of what he described as the first 'anti-statist revolution' of the twentieth century, and suggested that the principles which underpinned Reagan's neo-liberalism could usefully be imported into France.[66] The book was a huge success. It received widespread coverage in the press – much of it favourable – and Sorman was promptly invited in June 1983 to speak to the Club de l'Horloge.[67] This moment of celebrity marked the start of Sorman's career as one of France's foremost neo-liberal ideologues: in the following years, he published numerous books and articles in defence of the 'small state', 'decentralisation' and 'real liberal solutions' to France's problems.[68] In this quest for 'liberal solutions', Sorman and other neo-liberal fellow travellers of the 1980s hoped that Thatcher and Reagan's seductive mix of economic liberalism and defensive national-ism would offer a means for the French right to move beyond its Gaullist heritage and embrace modernity. As a former secretary-general of the Club de l'Horloge put it in 1988, 'a nationalist, liberal and democratic

néo-libéralisme et ses acteurs', *Actes de la recherche en sciences sociales* (No. 145, 2002), pp. 9–20.

[65] Le Gallou and Club de l'Horloge, *Les racines du futur: demain la France*, p. 1. On the threat of American cultural imperialism, see pp. 87–92.

[66] Guy Sorman, *La révolution conservatrice américaine* (Paris: Pluriel, 1985).

[67] The 1985 edition of Sorman's essay features a *revue de presse* that includes a wide selection of reviews (pp. 259–95). Among the favourable reviews was one by the former minister and close adviser to Giscard d'Estaing, Michel Poniatowski ('A lire, si vous voulez en sortir...', *Le Figaro Magazine* (23 April 1983)). The Club de l'Horloge maintains a historic list of events and speakers on its website: www.clubdelhorloge.fr/liste_chronologique.php (last accessed 20 June 2011).

[68] See especially Guy Sorman, *La solution libérale* (Paris: Fayard, 1986 [1985]). This edition also includes a *revue de presse* (pp. 271–307), which again shows favourable reviews in the right-wing press (*Le Figaro*, *Le Point* ...) and more critical perspectives in the left-wing press (in particular, a negative review by Rosanvallon: 'Le petit Hayek illustré', *L'Expansion* (2 November 1984)).

synthesis will allow the right to reconstruct a popular base, just like Gaullism in the past'.[69]

But, beyond the restrictive world of clubs, what were the consequences of this radical programme for the centre right once it returned to power – briefly in 1986–8 and more substantially after 1995? While Le Gallou's 'union of the right' including the FN remained a minority position, there is ample evidence to suggest that the neo-liberal and free-market vision of this right-wing vanguard was being heard at the very highest level of government.[70] We can trace the complex interaction between party politics and the right-wing liberal revival by looking at two prominent figures of the French right since 1980: Alain Madelin and Jean-Pierre Raffarin. Despite their differences, their shared trajectories and political commitments make them exemplary case studies of the diverse ways in which the language of liberalism has penetrated the centre right.

Since 1986, when he first became a minister in the Chirac government, Madelin has been one of the best-known political exponents of economic liberalism in France. He began his political life in 1964 as a founding member of the extreme-right-wing organisation Occident. Fiercely anti-communist and pro-colonial, Occident was a mirror image of its dissident left-wing Trotskyist and Maoist counterparts. During its four years of existence, it was frequently involved in violent clashes with *gauchistes*, which earned Madelin numerous arrests. Eventually, in October 1968, the organisation was dissolved, in part because some of its members – including future ministers Gérard Longuet and Patrick Devedjian – wanted to leave the restrictive orbit of the extreme right.[71] For Madelin, this meant becoming involved with ALEPS and then choosing to join Giscard d'Estaing's centrist Républicains indépendants (RI) in 1968.[72] First elected as a young deputy for Ille-et-Vilaine in 1978, he immediately caused a stir with his bold commitment to liberalism and his controversial decision not to wear a tie in the Assemblée Nationale.[73]

---

[69] Michel Leroy, 'Une stratégie d'union, pour un libéralisme national et démocratique', in Club de l'Horloge, *L'Union de la droite est-elle possible?* (Paris: Club de l'Horloge, 1989), p. 40.

[70] On the influence of 'neo-liberal' thought on the right, see J. Baudoin, 'Le "moment néo-libéral" du RPR: essai d'interprétation', *Revue française de science politique* (Vol. 40, No. 6, 1990), pp. 830–44.

[71] On Occident and its influence see Frédéric Charpier, *Génération Occident. De l'extrême droite à la droite* (Paris: Seuil, 2005). See also Gérard Davet and Philippe Ridet, 'Quarante ans après, les anciens d'Occident revisitent leur passé', *Le Monde* (13 February 2005).

[72] According to Charpier, Madelin was in charge of preparing meetings and editing the ALEPS newsletter. Charpier, *Génération Occident*, pp. 187–8.

[73] Philippe Benassaya, *Les hussards perdus de la République* (Paris: Bourrin Editeur, 2007), p. 12.

He also became a regular attendee and occasional contributor at the Club de l'Horloge, and soon formed a small neo-liberal group inside the RI with Longuet and former PSU activist François Léotard, both of whom had been elected deputies in 1978 and had joined Giscard's government at the same time as Madelin.[74]

Consigned to the opposition benches after 1981, this so-called 'bande de Léo' exploited the ideological space opened up by a Socialist victory to push their neo-liberal and anti-communist agenda. It was a successful strategy. When the RPR–UDF coalition won the legislative elections in 1986, Chirac chose Madelin as Minister of Industry, Posts and Telecommunications and Tourism, and Longuet as his assistant secretary. This gave Madelin the opportunity finally to put into practice a 'truly liberal' agenda, which included extensive tax breaks for entrepreneurs and small businesses, as well as the privatisation or closure of large industries. The most famous example of this reforming zeal was the closure in 1987 of the loss-making ship-building company NorMed in La Ciotat (although, as commentators noted at the time, the generous severance package negotiated by the state was more in keeping with a left-wing interventionist tradition than the strident neo-liberalism championed by the young minister). There were other signs that bureaucratic and political considerations were getting in the way of Madelin's vision: his enthusiastic endorsement of liberal reformism was popular among small business owners but hard to swallow for the heads of France's large industries. After a year on the job, a lengthy profile in *Le Monde* gave a picturesque description of Madelin's ministry as 'an island of liberalism amidst an ocean of *colbertisme*'.[75] In the same way that Rocard had struggled to tame the statism of the *première gauche*, so the Industry Minister found it difficult not to bow to the needs of France's industrial 'champions'. It almost seemed as if the terms in which Madelin described his opponent's policies in 1989 – '*rocardisme* starts well and ends badly' – could have been applied retrospectively to his own period in office.[76]

With the right's defeat in 1988, Madelin once again found himself in the opposition. But he was determined to continue playing a role in political debate. He did so by following almost all of his contemporaries in creating a think tank, the Institut Euro 92, which built on the network of major business leaders and political sympathisers he had developed

---

[74] On Madelin's relationship with the Club de l'Horloge, see Charpier, *Génération Occident*, pp. 340–1.

[75] Claire Blandin, 'Alain Madelin, le liberal piégé', *Le Monde* (25 April 1987).

[76] 'M. Madelin (PR): le rocardisme commence bien et finit mal', *Le Monde* (10 February 1989).

since 1986.[77] Committed to the European project, the Institut organised conferences and publications that defended the values of the free market and the contemporary relevance of liberalism.[78] This reflected the development of Madelin's own positions. During the 1990s, he regularly reiterated his support for a 'deeper' and 'wider' Europe, and distanced himself from the growing Euroscepticism on both the right and the left.[79] At the same time, he maintained his presence in politics and, in 1995, chose to support Chirac's bid for the presidency.[80] Once again, he was rewarded for his loyalty. He had already been Minister of Small and Medium-sized Enterprises under the Balladur government in 1993–5; the new president gave him a promotion by appointing him Minister of the Economy and Finance, presumably in the hope that the new minister's enthusiasm for reform would help heal the *fracture sociale*. Unfortunately, only three months into his term, Madelin was forced to resign after he undermined delicate negotiations with unions by claiming that public-sector pensions needed to be reformed and that the minimum wage was 'too high'.[81] By the time large-scale strikes erupted at the end of that year, Madelin no longer held any position of responsibility in the government. But the public-sector pension reforms that resulted in the strike action were broadly similar to positions he himself had defended over the previous decade.

In the wake of the left's success in the 1997 legislative election, and increasingly dissatisfied with the party to which he belonged – the Parti républicain – Madelin decided to found a new party, Démocratie libérale (DL). Initially part of the UDF, it brought together many of Madelin's supporters, including a number who had been members of extreme-right organisations in their youth.[82] The party also acted as a platform for Madelin's presidential bid in 2002. With a score of 3.9 per cent in the first round, it was clear that his 'neo-liberal' platform was even less appealing than the neo-republican platform of Chevènement (5.3 per cent). He did, however, come ahead of the PCF candidate, Robert Hue (3.3 per cent),

---

[77] 'Les europatrons de Madelin', *Le Monde* (21 May 88). Benassaya, *Les hussards perdus*, p. 311.

[78] See especially the Institut's website: www.euro92.com. Speakers have included Nicolas Baverez, Florien Aftalion and Pascal Salin.

[79] For instance Alain Madelin, *Quand les autruches relèveront la tête* (Paris: Robert Laffont, 1995), pp. 172–205.

[80] For an outline of his policy proposals before the election, see Alain Madelin and Cercle Idées-Action, *Chers compatriotes . . .* (Paris: Editions Jean-Claude Lattès, 1994).

[81] Thierry Brehier, 'Jean Arthuis remplace Alain Madelin au ministère des Finances', *Le Monde* (27 August 1995).

[82] The party was excluded from the UDF in 1998 when it supported UDF candidates who were elected with Front National votes.

a sign perhaps that his long battle against communism had been won. Either way, shortly after Chirac's victory, he disbanded Démocratie libérale and joined the newly founded UMP. The latter was yet another attempt to unify the different cultures of the right behind one programme and it provided Chirac with a relatively cohesive presidential majority. At the same time, the new party laid the foundation for Sarkozy's successful presidential bid in 2007 and, with Madelin now in the same party, he was able to extend his influence over the future candidate. As early as 1998–9, commentators had noticed the apparent convergence between the two politicians in terms of economic policy.[83] This tendency was reinforced by the appointment of Longuet as adviser to Sarkozy in 2005–7. It came as little surprise, therefore, that Sarkozy's campaign rhetoric of 'rupture' emphasised repeatedly both the language of crisis and the need for (liberal) economic reform. With Sarkozy's victory, it seemed as if many of the themes and ideas that Madelin and his fellow neo-liberals had defended for two decades now belonged to the political mainstream. While Madelin ruefully acknowledged before the elections that 'circumstances mean that it is almost certainly impossible to get a liberal candidate elected in 2007', this was perhaps because Sarkozy had already stolen the liberal vote.[84]

Raffarin's political origins were less controversial than those of Madelin. He, too, came to politics through the youth movements supporting Giscard d'Estaing in the 1960s, but he had no connection with the extreme right. His roots were to be found instead in local politics: Raffarin always saw himself first and foremost as a regional politician from the Poitou-Charentes. This regionalist perspective made him a fervent partisan of greater decentralisation once in power. But, even before fully embarking on a political career, he claims to have recognised the need for greater regional autonomy. Thus, in an interview in 2003, he argued that decentralisation was 'the main lesson of 1968'.[85] Even if such a bold statement suggests that he was attempting to justify his forthcoming legislative proposals for further decentralisation in 2004, there can be little doubt that Raffarin was drawn to the principles of Giscard's 'advanced liberal society' as a student. Friends remember him as one of the most active members of the Giscardian youth organisation Génération sociale

---

[83] Laurent Mauduit, 'Nicolas Sarkozy et Alain Madelin, le tandem libéralo-libéral', *Le Monde* (23 April 1999).

[84] Quoted in Benassaya, *Les hussards perdus de la République*, p. 317.

[85] He also says that he lived in May 1968 'comme Jean-Jacques Servan-Schreiber et Pierre Mendès-France. Pas tout à fait comme les gaullistes; pas du tout comme Daniel Cohn-Bendit.' Jean-Pierre Raffarin, *La France de mai. Entretiens avec Eric Mandonnet* (Paris: Grasset, 2003), p. 51.

et libérale (GSL) in the early 1970s, and he confirmed his commitment by joining the newly founded PR in 1977.[86]

Unlike Madelin, however, Raffarin held no national elected office in the 1970s and 80s; during the 'dark years' of the 1980s, he focused his efforts on his region, holding a series of local posts on the *conseil régional.* During the same period, he also continued his close involvement with the private sector. His long-standing association with the public relations firm Bernard Krief Communications in the 1980s earned Raffarin a place in Madelin's Institut Euro 92. He was a regular attendee at meetings, contributing to the elaboration of a positive, business-friendly and pro-European neo-liberalism that would set the tone for his return to politics after Chirac's victory. The proximity between the controversial Madelin and the more austere Raffarin was cemented in 1995 when the latter was appointed Minister of Small and Medium-Size Enterprises. This had been Madelin's post between 1993 and 1995, and his successor adopted an equally pro-business stance. Already in 1992, Raffarin had indicated that there was a great deal that the public sector could learn from business techniques; he even suggested that it was possible to 'manage a region like a business'.[87] But, where Madelin had come to similar conclusions about the value of business in the course of his journey away from the extreme right, Raffarin's position represented what the historian Sylvie Guillaume has termed the politics of the post-war 'small and medium-sized manager class'.[88] Focused on regional job creation, and committed to the liberalisation of bureaucratic controls, this insufficiently studied political movement became increasingly visible with the rehabilitation of small business during the liberal revival. As faith in France's state-driven heavy industry faltered in the 1980s, successive governments sought to mobilise the 'potential' of small business.[89] A product of exactly this milieu, Raffarin had the ideal profile to fit this new orientation and as a minister he was committed to encouraging small business and local entrepreneurs.[90]

Shortly before the 1997 legislative elections, Raffarin publicly asked Chirac to bring Madelin and Léotard back into the government in order

---

[86] On the Jeunes giscardiens movement, see a number of testimonies in Berstein and Sirinelli, *Les années Giscard. Les réformes de société.*

[87] Jean-Pierre Raffarin, *Pour une morale de l'action* (Paris: Editions Hermé, 1992), p. 49.

[88] Sylvie Guillaume, *Le petit et moyen patronat dans la nation française, de Pinay à Raffarin* (Bordeaux: Presses Universitaires de Bordeaux, 2005).

[89] On the changing economic policy of the 1980s and 90s, see J. D. Levy, *Tocqueville's revenge: state, society and economy in contemporary France* (London: Harvard University Press, 1999).

[90] See for instance, 'Le gouvernement veut réduire de moitié, en trois ans, la mortalité des jeunes entreprises', *Les Echos* (14 November 1996).

to ensure centrist support for the governing coalition.[91] But it was to be of no avail: the right were defeated and Raffarin retreated again to local politics, successfully winning the presidency of the Poitou-Charentes region from 1998 to 2002. However, he clearly intended to remain present at the national level. In 1997, he joined Madelin in forming Démocratie libérale, and he quickly became the new party's vice-president. This national orientation became clearer still when he published a manifesto entitled *Pour une nouvelle gouvernance* (2002) shortly before the 2002 elections. Where many of his previous publications had focused on the management of his region, this essay went much further, suggesting that France needed a new form of government.[92] In a style that seemed to be a mix of *rocardisme* and *giscardisme*, and with references to commentators like Crozier and Minc, it argued for a 'humanist' conception of the state that would be a 'Republic of proximity rather than an "all-encompassing" state'.[93] Decentralisation remained at the heart of Raffarin's vision, but he now had wider aims that drew on the language of crisis and the liberal critique of the state.

It is almost certainly this moderate liberalism that made Raffarin an attractive – if unexpected – choice for prime minister after Chirac's landslide victory of 2002. With Le Pen an unexpected presence in the second round of the presidential elections, a concession to the centre seemed a reasonable gesture in favour of cross-party consensus. But it was also an opportunity for the marginalised liberal current of the right to impose its platform under Raffarin's tutelage. This was obvious in the two reforms most strongly associated with the Raffarin government. The first was further decentralisation. In a landmark bill passed in 2003, financial autonomy was granted to French regions, local referendums were authorised and, in a highly symbolic change, the terms 'region' and 'decentralisation' were included in the French Constitution for the first time. Such measures matched the new Prime Minister's long-standing commitment to decentralisation and marked the return of an issue that had previously been prominent at the time of the Defferre laws in 1982.

The second major reform of the Raffarin government was in the realm of pensions and social security. Here, there was a long tradition of liberal solutions; the previous major reform, in 1993, had been completed by

---

[91] 'Jean-Pierre Raffarin plaide pour le retour au gouvernement d'Alain Madelin et l'entrée de François Léotard', *Le Monde* (10 February 1997).

[92] Earlier publications by Raffarin – all focused on the management of regional affairs – included Jean-Pierre Raffarin, *92 Nous sommes tous des régionaux* (Paris: Projets Editions, 1992), and, in the same year, Raffarin, *Pour une morale de l'action*.

[93] Jean-Pierre Raffarin, *Pour une nouvelle gouvernance* (Paris: L'Archipel, 2002), p. 116. There are references to Crozier on p. 124 and Minc on p. 18.

the then Prime Minister Edouard Balladur. His project was based almost entirely on a report previously commissioned by Rocard. Likewise, the 'Loi Fillon' of 2003 built on the so-called 'Loi Madelin' of 1994 – that encouraged the expansion of private pensions – and the abortive 'Loi Juppé' of 1995, which had sought to decrease the value of state pensions and increase required contributions. Predictably, Fillon's reforms were deeply unpopular on the left but, unlike in 1995, they passed through parliament. By 2003, the electorate was finally ready to accept significant changes to one of the most cherished pillars of the French social security system. The fact that Sarkozy was able to continue these reforms in 2010 only confirmed that the message of the liberal right has succeeded in imposing itself, despite widespread contestation.

The 'no' vote in the referendum of 2005 put an abrupt end to Raffarin's term as Prime Minister: he resigned three days after the result. As a fervent pro-European, he had campaigned for the European Constitution and, although he claimed in an interview that his departure was not 'painful', the result was clearly a bitter blow.[94] It also marked the end of his period at the highest levels of government. By this time, DL had been absorbed into the newly founded UMP in 2002, which meant that, after his resignation, Raffarin rejoined the ranks of the right-wing majority party in the Sénat. Like Madelin, he threw his weight behind Sarkozy in 2007 in a lengthy 'letter' to the presidential candidate, but he has mostly kept a low profile.[95] He has been an active member of the Sénat – and was chosen as one of its vice-presidents in 2008 – but he decided not to associate himself with the attempts of the liberal right to regroup under the banner of Les Réformateurs. Set up in 2002 by figures such as Devedjian, Longuet, Madelin and Hervé Novelli, this group of politicians tried to push a liberal agenda within the UMP in much the same way as Club 89 a decade earlier. Sarkozy's victory vindicated this approach as the new president took up a number of causes – especially reform of the public sector and pension reform – that had been part of the heritage of the liberal right for three decades. Swept to victory on a theme of 'rupture', Sarkozy successfully combined the reforming zeal and pro-Americanism that has characterised the liberal right, with the statist and security-orientated reflexes of the Gaullist right. His rival might have been a young female who had risen to prominence on the basis of her model of 'participatory democracy', but it was Sarkozy who most effectively absorbed the lessons of French liberalism and packaged these for a French public notoriously hostile to liberalism.

[94] Gérard Davet, 'Ses 1123 jours à Matignon', *Le Monde* (2 June 2005).
[95] Jean-Pierre Raffarin, *La dernière marche: lettre à Nicolas Sarkozy* (Paris: Grasset, 2007).

Liberal politics: defeated or defeatist?

I have suggested in this chapter that liberal politics – whether on the right or left – has found it difficult to impose itself on French politics. Since the early 1980s, emblematic figures of right- and left-wing liberalism have encountered resistance to their attempts to 'reclaim' liberalism (often without explicitly using the term) both among their own parties and the French electorate.[96] This relative failure has contributed to the deep feeling of pessimism that has been a consistent theme of contemporary French liberalism. It is a feeling perfectly summarised in the personality of Rocard, whose most recent interviews are filled with the same sense of melancholy that was present in Aron's memoirs.[97] For those of a liberal sensibility, French politics appears to be a deeply frustrating place, paralysed by grand ideologies and anti-reformism. Moreover, the French public's continued hostility to the term 'liberal' makes it difficult for politicians to endorse liberal reforms. If there was something of a thaw in the 1990s and 2000s, there has been a noticeable hardening of attitudes towards liberalism again since the financial crisis of 2008–9. Sarkozy himself quickly backtracked from his pro-liberal positions in the wake of the global downturn, but he could not save himself from defeat in the presidential elections of 2012. Sarkozy's peculiar brand of statist liberalism only lasted for one term. Indeed, it is more than a little ironic that the only other one-term president under the Fifth Republic was Giscard d'Estaing, whose liberal reforms also failed to halt the expansion of the state apparatus in the 1980s. Little wonder, then, that French liberals like Baverez remain fearful that the country is 'falling' inexorably towards a stagnant future.

However, this defeatist view of liberalism does not tell the whole story. As we have seen, the language of crisis has now become a common reference point for most politicians of the centre left and the centre right. Even more importantly, it is widely accepted among senior civil servants and business leaders. These are the groups within the French elite that are most likely to have read Aron, Crozier or *Commentaire* and, even if they seldom express their political opinions in public, their political orientations have had a powerful effect on economic and administrative policy. If some areas have proved resistant to reform – such as schools and higher education – this chapter shows that there have been a number

---

[96] This failure is examined in the context of 'centrist' politics in Sylvie Guillaume (ed.), *Le centrisme en France aux XIXème et XXè siècles: un échec?* (Paris: Maison des Sciences de l'Homme Aquitaine, 2005).
[97] See especially Rocard, *Si la gauche savait…*.

of attempts to impose an agenda heavily defined by the liberal critique. For instance, attempts at decentralisation have almost always been underpinned by a critique of the Jacobin state, while the centre right (and centre left)'s numerous proposals to reduce the number of civil servants have followed directly from Crozier's repeated appeals for a 'modest state'.[98]

Liberalism, then, has penetrated deeply into France's state apparatus and, with the gradual weakening of Gaullism and Marxism, there has been a renewed interest in a peculiarly French mix of state-driven, anti-Jacobin and Aronian liberalisms. Rocard, Strauss-Kahn, Madelin, Raffarin and a number of others have amplified this new liberalism and brought it to a wide audience. This means that the idea of a 'French model' of integration or state intervention – which neo-republicans have worked so hard to defend – no longer appears an incontrovertible part of French political culture. In discussions surrounding subjects as varied as ethnic minority politics, pension reform or American culture, a liberal view has become, if not dominant, certainly a prominent part of the debate. There are, of course, many dissenting voices: the Front National and the parties of the far left still decry France's subservience to a global liberal orthodoxy. But these anti-liberal perspectives are themselves fiercely contested by a large swathe of the French electorate which believes that the country must 'adapt' if it is to remain relevant to the modern world. In this sense – and for all its subsequent contradictions – Sarkozy's election in 2007 showed that a liberal discourse of crisis, 'rupture' and reform could not only galvanise a small intellectual elite but also win votes among France's vast middle class.

---

[98] As Raffarin put it in 2003, 'Il y a un refus jacobin à s'intéresser à la décentralisation'. Raffarin, *La France de mai*, p. 111.

Conclusion: the search for consensus in twenty-first-century France

The notion of political consensus generally implies a broad agreement on the values that underpin a given political system. With the advent of the Fifth Republic, the appeasement of the extremes and successful cohabitation, France has appeared to conform to the basic conditions of consensus. Few now contest the French state's right to act on behalf of its citizens, and fewer still contest the legitimacy of the ballot box as a means to choose elected representatives. France seems to have closed its *guerres franco-françaises* and become a mature democratic polity.[1] Yet the French have been unusually unwilling to accept this emerging 'consensus à la française'.[2] As we have seen, few were taken in by the promise of a liberal democratic horizon after the fall of the Berlin Wall and the penetration of a language of crisis in the 1990s damaged whatever was left of France's sense of superiority. Even outside the vibrant political extremes, there is still a potency to French political language that is striking by west European standards: when, in 1989, a motley group of neo-republicans claimed that allowing headscarves in schools was the 'Munich of the republican school', all but the most sympathetic observers were taken aback by the combination of political polemic and historical hyperbole. French politics, it seemed, was far from consensus.

How to explain this tension between an increasingly peaceful political landscape and a still violent polemical language of politics? One explanation is that French politics is simply in denial. For a long time, foreign commentators have analysed contemporary French politics, at best, in terms of its flagrant 'contradictions' and, at worst, as straightforward 'hypocrisy'.[3] Most often, this critique has centred on the wide – sometimes

---

[1] On this, see some of the illuminating essays in Tony Chafer and Emmanuel Godin (eds.), *The End of the French Exception: Decline and Revival of the 'French Model'* (London: Palgrave, 2010).

[2] Sylvie Guillaume, *Consensus à la française* (Paris: Belin, 2002).

[3] Some examples are the strong criticisms formulated by Smith, *France in Crisis*; or the conclusion to Hayward, *Fragmented France*, where he argues that 'the [French] political system operates as an organised hypocrisy' (p. 372). And, as we saw earlier, in the 1960s

261

yawning – gap between France's elevated political rhetoric and its messier, more compromised practice. So, we are often told (not without reason) that sophisticated justifications of *intégration* simply conceal a reality of racism and chronic ethnic inequality. Or that the much discussed idea of 'the French exception' obscures the fact that the French have accepted globalisation as much as any other west European nation in the past three decades. In this view, the inability of the French to adapt to the exigencies of postmodern politics rests on the persistence of anachronistic languages of protest, legislative inertia and a collective unwillingness to respond productively to a new age of political uncertainty. Somehow, French political culture always seems to be out of touch with empirical reality.

There is a certain logic to this argument – and it is one that French liberal critics like Rosanvallon or Wieviorka would recognise. But I believe that it also rests on implicit and long-standing images of the French as an argumentative, politicised, tempestuous people, more given to abstract theory than to the world of everyday affairs. These preconceptions supplement an interpretation of French political culture that emphasises its obvious inability to match up to its high-minded rhetoric. However, as the historian Theodore Zeldin pointed out several decades ago in his masterful studies of the Third Republic, continuous attempts to unearth the hypocrisies of French politics risk distorting the reality of political life in France.[4] Over the course of this book, I have tried to show that one of the reasons that scholars have failed to understand the perennial contradiction between the practice of consensus and the violence of political language in France is that they have consistently underestimated the importance of French liberalism. This critical political language has always been in dialogue with republican, socialist and counter-revolutionary languages – and it has often found itself completely marginalised by its more polemical and abstract competitors. Yet it is French liberalism that has translated France's high ideals into everyday practice. It has acted as a bridge – a language of pragmatism that has allowed administrators and politicians to justify what they do.

---

and 70s, some of Stanley Hoffmann's work was deeply critical of France's 'stalemate society'.

[4] 'The history of French politics is usually presented as a record of failure. That is why French politics is confusing. But to present it as a failure is to misunderstand the significance of politics in French life ... To understand French politics, one must first get rid of the Anglo-Saxon model on which so much criticism of them is based, not least by Frenchmen ... France has indeed borrowed ideas and labels from abroad but it has assimilated them very thoroughly into its own tradition.' Theodore Zeldin, *France 1848–1945: Politics and Anger* (Oxford University Press, 1973), p. 1.

If the Fifth Republic has been a period of relative stability and compromise, it is because this unusual – and uniquely French – brand of liberalism
has finally begun to take shape.

What is important for our purposes is that the regeneration of French
liberalism has brought with it an alternative way of imagining the relationship between nation, state and citizen. Put very schematically, we
might describe this as a still unified, but open, conception of the nation,
embodied in a streamlined and reformed state that relies heavily on a
'civil society' of autonomous but politically engaged citizens. While this
might not appear to be an especially controversial model, it is noticeably
different from its neo-republican counterpart, which continues to
emphasise the primacy of the nation, the importance of state-led national
integration and the long-standing notion of the citizen as a secular and
rational actor in the public sphere. The latter remains more familiar
abroad and has been the primary focus of attention for foreign scholars;
it is the 'strange' attachment to the vigorously articulated language of
republicanism that has attracted widespread criticism (and occasional
praise). But, while neo-republicanism is obviously crucial, I would argue
that it is above all the creative interaction between a resurgent republican
language and a powerful liberal critique of this language that has structured contemporary French politics. It is around these two poles that the
search for political consensus in twenty-first-century France has been
articulated.

This leads us to an important point, namely that French politics has
not simply become a bland, apolitical and post-ideological affair. Rather,
it has been driven by a series of lively debates about the meaning of the
nation, the terms of citizenship and the role of the state. Furet,
Rosanvallon and Julliard were correct when they analysed the emergence
of a consensual 'République du centre' in the late 1980s, but their
influential formulation obscured as much as it illuminated. For a start,
they underestimated the longevity of the Front National as a party of
protest, resistance and anger. They also failed to recognise how decentralisation and the flourishing of civil society might create effective new
kinds of activism. Most of all, their conclusions encouraged a subsequent
generation of commentators to fall into the trap of imagining that centre
left, centrist and centre right parties in France largely think the same way
and that political actors are all but indistinguishable (unless they obviously inhabit the political extremes). This has no doubt been fuelled by a
growing sense among the French population that politics is little more
than an insider's game, played by over-privileged Parisian elites. Yet
scholars must resist the temptation to proclaim another 'end of ideology'
and instead look for the key questions that continue to motivate political

action.[5] Whether we like it or not, politics will not go away, nor will the ideas and debates that underpin it. And this is especially true in France, which has a highly developed and vigorously articulated political culture.

Such a conclusion has wider implications for European history after the fall of communism and in the light of the devastating financial crisis of 2008. If we reject the idea that Europe has entered a period in which key concepts such as the state or the nation have fallen into terminal decline, we can see more clearly that the new contours of politics do not always conform to our models of right and left. Instead, they focus on issues that cross traditional party lines. Who can be a citizen and under what conditions? How far must the state intervene in society? What is the appropriate response to the fragmentation of post-industrial society? How should political actors persuade a sceptical and fickle electorate of their manifestos? These are the questions that form the core of many civic debates. By looking at France – a country in which politics is taken very seriously – we have an excellent case study of a declining European power and its attempts to negotiate the end of the grand ideologies that defined its history from the 1780s to the 1970s. The intensity of its republican narrative – and the peculiar contours of its liberal critique – makes France an unusual example among European countries. But these very specificities hint at the new directions that European politics might take in future. If France is anything to go by, the advent of political consensus is not a sign of decadence; it is an urgent call to scholars to rethink the categories they use to study politics. By looking at the tension between two languages of politics in France, we have not exhausted the new possibilities for the study of political consensus. But this framework does allow us to appreciate more clearly the richness and texture of political life in France. This in turn can help us to understand the changes that are taking place and, ultimately, make French politics appear a little less contradictory.

---

[5] Daniel Bell, *The End of Ideology: On the Exhaustion of Political Ideas in the Fifties* (London: Collier-Macmillan, 1960).

Bibliography

Archives and libraries consulted

- Bibliothèque Nationale de France, site François Mitterrand, Paris
- Institut National de l'Audiovisuel (INA), Paris
- Bibliothèque de l'Ecole Normale Supérieure (Ulm et Jourdan), Paris
- La Documentation Française, Paris

Interviews

- Jean Baubérot, chaire de laïcité at l'Ecole Pratiques des Hautes Etudes, Paris-Sorbonne, and a member of the Commission Stasi. Interviewed in Paris on 13 February 2007.
- Jean-Robert Pitte, president of l'Université Paris-Sorbonne and professeur de géographie. Interviewed in Paris on 14 February 2007.
- Dominique Schnapper, professor of sociology at the Ecole des hautes études en sciences sociales, Paris. Interviewed in Paris on 27 June 2011.
- Patrick Weil, senior researcher CNRS, member of the Commission Stasi and the Commission pour la Nationalité in 1993. Interviewed in Cambridge on 1 March 2007.
- Michel Wieviorka, professor of sociology at the Ecole des hautes études en sciences sociales, Paris. Interviewed in Paris on 31 January 2011.

I was also grateful for the opportunity to talk to a number of the key political and academic actors of my work at a major conference entitled 'La République sort ses griffes: origine et modernité des valeurs républicaines', held in Belfort on 12–13 October 2010.

Published material

Newspapers and magazines

I have not listed individual newspaper articles here: these can be found in the footnotes. I have limited this list to publications and, where appropriate, the online database of these newspapers and/or the

LexisNexis Academic online world newspaper database. Issues were consulted for the period 1980–2011 inclusive. References from learned journals (such as *Commentaire, Esprit* and *Le Débat*) are listed by individual article in the 'Books and journal articles' section of the bibliography.

France
- Agence France-Presse (bulletins accessible via LexisNexis)
- *Le Figaro*
- *Le Monde*
- *Le Monde Diplomatique*
- *Le Nouvel Observateur*
- *Le Point*
- *Les Echos*
- *L'Express*
- *L'Humanité*
- *Libération*
- *Marianne*

United Kingdom and United States
- *The Economist*
- *The Guardian*
- *London Review of Books*
- *New York Review of Books*
- *The New York Times*
- *Time*

I also used the following CD-ROMs, which included text-searchable databases:

- *Commentaire, 1978–2009*
- *Esprit, Collection Intégrale 1932–2006*
- *Le Monde: l'histoire au quotidien* (released in 2005)
- *Le Monde Diplomatique 1978–2004*

Government publications and reports

Attali, Jacques, *Pour un modèle européen de l'enseignement supérieur* (Paris: La Documentation Française, 1998)
Centre d'analyse stratégique, *Colloque sur les statistiques ethniques* (Paris: Centre d'analyse stratégique, 2006)
Comité de reflexion sur le préambule de la Constitution, *Redécouvrir le préambule à la Constitution: rapport de la commission présidé par Simone Veil* (Paris: La Documentation Française, 2008)

Commission de la Nationalité, *Rapport: Etre français aujourd'hui et demain* (Paris: La Documentation Française, 1987)

Commission de reflexion sur l'application du principe de la laïcité dans la République, *Rapport au Président de la République* (Paris: La Documentation Française, 2003)

Cour des Comptes, *L'accueil des immigrants et l'intégration populations issues de l'immigration* (Paris: La Documentation Française, 2004)

Debray, Régis, *L'enseignement du fait religieux dans l'école laïque* (Paris: La Documentation Française, 2002)

Giordan, Henri, *Démocratie culturelle et droit à la difference: Rapport au ministère de la culture* (Paris: Documentation Française, 1982)

Haut Conseil à l'intégration, *Études et intégration: faire connaître les valeurs de la République* (Paris: La Documentation Française, 2009)

L'affaiblissement du lien social (Paris: La Documentation Française, 1997)

Le bilan de l'intégration (Paris: La Documentation Française, 2005)

Le contrat et l'intégration (Paris: La Documentation Française, 2003)

Les Indicateurs de l'intégration: statistiques ethniques, enquêtes sur les patronymes, mesure de la diversité, baromètre de l'intégration (Paris: La Documentation Française, 2007)

Les parcours de l'intégration (Paris: La Documentation Française, 2001)

Liens culturels et l'intégration (Paris: La Documentation Française, 1995)

L'islam et la République (Paris: La Documentation Française, 2000)

Projet de charte de la laïcité dans les services publics (Paris: La Documentation Française, 2007)

La Documentation Française, *Les Cahiers Français, no. 336: Les valeurs de la République* (Paris: La Documentation Française, 2007)

Ministère de l'Emploi, de la cohésion sociale et du logement, *Célébrer la bienvenue dans la République Française: rapport sur les cérémonies célébrant l'acquisition de la nationalité française* (Paris: La Documentation Française, 2006)

Observatoire de la Parité, *Effets directs et indirects de la loi du 6 juin 2000* (Paris: La Documentation Française, 2005)

Queyranne, Jean-Jacques, *Les régions et la décentralisation: Rapport au ministère de la culture* (Paris: Documentation Française, 1982)

Raoult, Eric, *Rapport d'information fait en application de l'article 145 du Règlement: Au nom de la mission d'information sur la pratique du port du voile intégral sur le territoire national* (Paris: La Documentation Française, 2010)

Thélot, Claude, *Pour la réussite de tous les élèves: Rapport de la Commission du débat national sur l'avenir de l'Ecole* (Paris: La Documentation Française, 2004)

Books and journal articles

Abdallah, Mogniss, '1983: la marche pour l'égalité', *Plein Droit* (No. 55, 2002)

Agulhon, Maurice, *Histoire vagabonde II: Idéologies et politique dans la France du XIXème siècle* (Paris: Gallimard, 1988)

Histoire vagabonde III: La politique en France d'hier et d'aujourd'hui (Paris: Gallimard, 1996)

Les métamorphoses de Marianne: l'imagerie et la symbolique républicaines de 1914 à nos jours (Paris: Flammarion, 2001)

Marianne au combat: l'imagerie et la symbolique républicaines de 1789 à 1880 (Paris: Flammarion, 1979)

Marianne au pouvoir: l'imagerie et la symbolique républicaines de 1880–1914 (Paris: Flammarion, 1989)

République, Tome 1: 1880–1914 (Paris: Hachette, 1990)

République, Tome 2: 1914 à nos jours (Paris: Hachette, 1990)

Agulhon, Maurice, Becker, Annette and Cohen, Evelyne (eds.), *La République en Représentations: autour de l'œuvre de Maurice Agulhon* (Paris: Publications de la Sorbonne, 2006)

Algan, Yann and Cahuc, Pierre, *La société de la défiance: comment le modèle français s'autodétruit* (Paris: Editions de la Rue d'Ulm, 2007)

Amar, Micheline (ed.), *Le piège de la parité: textes pour un débat* (Paris: Hachette Littératures, 1999)

Anderson, Benedict, *Imagined Communities* (London: Verso, 1991)

Anderson, Perry, *La pensée tiède: un regard critique sur la culture française* (Paris: Seuil 2005)

Ardagh, John, *France in the New Century: Portrait of a Changing Society* (London: Viking, 1999)

Armenteros, Carolina, DiVanna, Isabel, Blanning, Tim and Dodds, Dawn (eds.), *Historicising the French Revolution* (Newcastle: Cambridge Scholars, 2008)

Aron, Raymond, *De Giscard à Mitterrand, 1977–1983* (Paris: Editions de Fallois, 2006)

Démocratie et totalitarisme (Paris: Folio, 1965)

Essai sur les libertés (Paris: Calmann-Lévy, 1973)

'Incertitudes françaises', *Commentaire* (Vol. 1, No. 1, 1978)

Introduction à la philosophie politique: démocratie et révolution (Paris: Editions de Fallois, 1997 [1952])

Les articles de politique internationale dans Le Figaro de 1947 à 1977, 2 vols. (Paris: Editions du Fallois, 1997)

Le spectateur engagé: entretiens avec Jean-Louis Missika et Dominique Wolton (Paris: Livre de Poche, 2005 [1981])

Mémoires (Paris: Julliard, 1983)

The Opium of the Intellectuals, trans. D. J. Mahoney and B. C. Anderson (London: Transaction, 2001)

Plaidoyer pour l'Europe décadente (Paris: Editions Robert Laffont, 1977)

Révolution Introuvable (Paris: Fayard, 1968)

Artus, Patrick, 'Capitalisme anglo-saxon et capitalisme européen continental: une question d'aversion au risque', *Revue d'économie politique* (Vol. 112, No. 4, 2002)

Aubry, Martine (ed.), *Pour changer de civilisation* (Paris: Odile Jacob, 2011)

Audier, Serge, *La pensée anti-68: essai sur une restauration intellectuelle* (Paris: La Découverte, 2008)

Le socialisme libéral (Paris: La Découverte, 2006)

Néolibéralismes: une archéologie intellectuelle (Paris: Grasset, 2012)

Théories de la République (Paris: La Découverte, 1994)

Tocqueville retrouvé: genèse et enjeux du renouveau tocquevillien français (Paris: Editions EHESS/Vrin, 2004)

Aurillac, Michel and Catala, Nicole, *Pour une société de progrès et de liberté* (Paris: Editions Albatros, 1988)

Baccou, Philippe and Club de l'Horloge, *Le Grand Tabou. L'économie et le mirage égalitaire* (Paris: Albin Michel, 1980)

Baechler, Jean, 'Maître et disciple', *Commentaire* (Vol. 8, No. 28–9, 1985)

Baker, Keith Michael, 'Transformations of Classical Republicanism in Eighteenth-Century France', *Journal of Modern History* (Vol. 73, No. 1, 2001)

Balassa, Béla, 'Après cinq ans. Bilan de la politique économique socialiste', *Commentaire* (Vol. 8, No. 33, 1986)

'L'économie française à l'aube du nouveau septennat', *Commentaire* (Vol. 10, No. 42, 1988)

'L'économie politique de Rocard', *Commentaire* (Vol. 13, No. 54, 1991)

Bancel, Nicolas, Blanchard, Pascal and Vergès, Françoise, *La République coloniale* (Paris: Albin Michel, 2003)

Baring, Edward, *The Young Derrida and French Philosophy, 1945–1968* (Cambridge University Press, 2010)

Basso, Keith and Selby, Henry (eds.), *Meaning in Anthropology* (Albuquerque, NM: University of New Mexico Press, 1977)

Baubérot, Jean, *L'intégrisme républicain contre la laïcité* (Paris: Editions de l'Aube 2006)

Laïcité 1905–2005, entre passion et raison (Paris: Editions du Seuil, 2005)

Baubérot, Jean and Wieviorka, Michel (eds.), *De la séparation des Eglises et de l'Etat à l'avenir de la laïcité* (Paris: L'Aube, 2005)

Baubérot, Jean, Houziaux, Alain, Bouzar, Dounia and Costa-Lascoux, Jacqueline, *Le voile, que cache-t-il?* (Paris: Les Editions Ouvrières, 2004

Baudelot, Christian and Establet, Roger, *L'élitisme républicain: l'école française à l'épreuve des comparaisons internationales* (Paris: Seuil/République des Idées, 2009)

Baudoin, Jean, 'Le "moment néo-libéral" du RPR: essai d'interprétation', *Revue française de science politique* (Vol. 40, No. 6, 1990)

Baudouin, Jean and Hourmant, François (ed.), *Les revues et la dynamique des ruptures* (Rennes: Presses Universitaires de Rennes, 2007)

Bauman, Zygmunt, *Liquid Times: Living in an Age of Uncertainty* (London: Polity, 2007)

Baverez, Nicolas, *La France qui tombe* (Paris: Perrin, 2003)

'L'année du réveil français', *Commentaire* (Vol. 29, No. 119, 2007)

'Le déclin français', *Commentaire* (Vol. 26, No. 102, 2003)

Raymond Aron: un moraliste au temps des idéologues (Paris: Flammarion, 1993)

Becker, Jean-Jacques and Candar, Gilles (eds.), *L'histoire des gauches en France, Volume 2. XXe siècle: à l'épreuve de l'histoire* (Paris: La Découverte, 2004)

Bell, Daniel, *The End of Ideology: On the Exhaustion of Political Ideas in the Fifties* (London: Collier-Macmillan, 1960)

Bell, David A., *The Cult of the Nation in France: Inventing Nationalism, 1680–1900* (London: Harvard University Press, 2001)

Benassaya, Philippe, *Les hussards perdus de la République* (Paris: Bourrin Editeur, 2007)

Benoist, Alain de, 'Jacobinisme of federalisme. Beschouwingen over Frankrijk, *Europa en de regio's*', *TeKos* (No. 108, 2002)

Berlin, Isaiah, *Four Essays on Liberty* (Oxford University Press, 1979)

Berrebi-Hoffmann, Isabelle and Grémion, Pierre, 'Elites intellectuelles et réforme de l'Etat. Esquisse en trois temps d'un déplacement d'expertise', *Cahiers internationaux de sociologie* (Vol. CXXVI, 2009)

Berstein, Serge (ed.), *Les Cultures Politiques en France* (Paris: Seuil, 1999)

Berstein, Serge and Milza, P., *Histoire du XXe siècle: Tome 3, de 1973 à nos jours: vers la mondialisation et le XXIe siècle* (Paris: Hatier, 2006)

Berstein, Serge and Rudelle, Odile (eds.), *Le modèle républicain* (Paris: Presses Universitaires de France, 1992)

Berstein, Serge and Sirinelli, Jean-François (eds.), *Les années Giscard: Valéry Giscard d'Estaing et l'Europe* (Paris: Armand Colin, 2006)

Berstein, Serge and Sirinelli, Jean-François (eds.), *Les années Giscard. Les réformes de société* (Paris: Armand Colin, 2007)

Berstein, Serge, Rémond, René and Sirinelli, Jean-François (eds.), *Les années Giscard. Institutions et pratiques politiques 1974–1978* (Paris: Fayard, 2003)

Bertaux, Pierre, 'Amitiés normaliennes', *Commentaire* (Vol. 8, No. 28–9, 1985)

Besançon, Alain, 'Pourquoi nous aimions tant Raymond Aron', *Commentaire* (Vol. 28, No. 110, 2005)

'Raymond Aron à l'oral', *Commentaire* (Vol. 8, No. 28–9, 1985)

'Réponse à Nicolas Baverez', *Commentaire* (Vol. 26, No. 103, 2003)

Birnbaum, Pierre, *Jewish Destinies: Citizenship, State and Community in Modern France* (New York: Hill & Wang, 2000)

La France imaginée: Déclin des rêves unitaires? (Paris: Fayard, 1998)

Le peuple et les gros: histoire d'un mythe (Paris: Grasset, 1979)

Les fous de la République: histoire politique des juifs d'État de Gambetta à Vichy (Paris: Fayard, 1992)

Blanchard, Pascal and Veyrat-Masson, Isabelle (eds.), *Les Guerres de Mémoires: La France et son histoire* (Paris: La Découverte 2008)

Blanchard, Pascal, Bancel, Nicolas and Lemaire, Sandrine (eds.), *La fracture coloniale: la France au prisme de l'héritage colonial* (Paris: La Découverte, 2006)

Bancel, Nicolas and Lemaire, Sandrine (eds.), *Culture coloniale en France. De la Révolution française à nos jours* (Paris: Autrement, 2008)

Blanning, T. C. W., *The Rise and the Fall of the French Revolution* (London: University of Chicago Press, 1996)

Bockel, Jean-Marie, *La 3ème gauche. Petit manifeste social-libéral* (Paris: L'Archer, 1999)

Bodnar, John, 'Pierre Nora, National Memory and Democracy: A Review', *Journal of American History* (Vol. 87, No. 3, 2000)

Boltanski, Luc and Chiapello, Ève, *Le nouvel ésprit du capitalisme* (Paris: Gallimard, 1999)

Boudic, Goulven, *Esprit, 1944–1982: les métamorphoses d'une revue* (Paris: Editions de l'IMHC, 2005)

Boudon, Raymond, 'Pourquoi les intellectuels n'aiment pas le libéralisme', *Commentaire* (Vol. 26, No. 104, 2003)

'Raymond Aron et la pensée sociologique: le non-dit des *Etapes*', *Commentaire* (Vol. 8, No. 28–9, 1985)

Bourdieu, Pierre, *Distinction: Critique social du jugement* (Paris: Editions de Minuit, 1979)

La noblesse d'État: grandes écoles et esprit de corps (Paris: Editions de Minuit, 1989)

Bouregba-Dichy, Miriam, 'Des militants maghrébins de la deuxième génération en France', *Tiers-Monde* (Vol. 31, No. 123)

Bourg, Julian, *From Revolution to Ethics: May 1968 and Contemporary French Thought* (London: McGill-Queen's University Press, 2007)

Bourg, Julian (ed.), *After the Deluge: New Perspectives on the Intellectual and Cultural History of Postwar France* (Lanham, MD: Lexington Books, 2004)

Bourricaud, François, 'Entre 1947 et 1950', *Commentaire* (Vol. 8, No. 28–9, 1985)

Bourseiller, Christophe, *Les maoïstes: La folle histoire des gardes rouges français* (Paris: Points, 2008)

Boutih, Malek and Lévy, Elisabeth, *La France au français? Chiche!* (Paris: Mille et une nuits, 2001)

Bowen, John, *Why the French Don't Like Headscarves: Islam, the State and the Public Space* (Princeton University Press, 2007)

Bozo, Frédéric, *Mitterrand, la fin de la guerre froide et l'unification allemande: de Yalta à Maastricht* (Paris: Odile Jacob, 2005)

Brubaker, Rogers, *Citizenship and Nationhood in France and Germany* (London: Harvard University Press, 1999)

Bruckner, Pascal, *La tyrannie de la pénitence: essai sur le masochisme occidental* (Paris: Grasset, 2006)

'Remarques sur le déclin français', *Commentaire* (Vol. 26, No. 103, 2003)

Brunet, Jean-Paul, 'Police Violence in Paris, October 1961: Historical Sources, Methods, and Conclusions', *Historical Journal* (Vol. 51, No. 1, 2008)

Burke, Peter, *What is Cultural History?* (Cambridge: Polity Press, 2004)

Cabrera, Manuel, *Postsocial History: An Introduction* (Oxford: Lexington, 2004)

Canto-Sperber, Monique, *Le libéralisme et la gauche* (Paris: Hachette, 2008)

Casanova, Jean-Claude, 'Pour Raymond Aron', *Commentaire* (Vol. 6, No. 24, 1983)

Casanova, Jean-Claude (ed.), *Raymond Aron et la démocratie au XXIe siècle* (Paris: Editions de Fallois, 2007)

Casanova, Jean-Claude, Chapuis, Robert, Daniel, Jean et al., *Pour une histoire de la Deuxième Gauche. Hommage à Jacques Julliard* (Paris: Editions BNF, 2008)

Caute, David, *Communism and the French Intellectuals, 1914–1960* (London: Macmillan, 1964)

Cerny, Philip, *The politics of grandeur: ideological aspects of de Gaulle's foreign policy* (Cambridge University Press, 2008 [1980])

Chabal, Emile, 'Managing the Postcolony: Minority Politics in Montpellier, c.1960–c.2010', *Contemporary European History* (Vol. 23, No. 2, 2014)

'The Rise of the Anglo-Saxon: French Perceptions of the Anglo-American World in the Long Twentieth Century', *French Politics, Culture and Society* (Vol. 31, No. 1, 2013)

'Writing the French National Narrative in the 21st Century', *Historical Journal* (Vol. 53, No. 2, June 2010)

Chabal, Emile (ed.), *France since the 1970s: History, Politics and Memory in an Age of Uncertainty* (London: Bloomsbury Academic, 2014)

Chafer, Tony, *The End of Empire in French West Africa* (Oxford: Berg, 2002)

Chafer, Tony and Godin, Emmanuel (eds.), *The End of the French Exception: Decline and Revival of the 'French Model'* (London: Palgrave, 2010).

Charpier, Frédéric, *Génération Occident. De l'extrême droite à la droite* (Paris: Seuil, 2005)

Chevènement, Jean-Pierre, *La République prend le maquis* (Paris: Fondation du 2 Mars, 2001)

Une certaine idée de la République m'amène à . . . (Paris: Albin Michel, 1992)

Christofferson, Michael Scott, 'An Antitotalitarian History of the French Revolution: Francois Furet's "Penser la Revolution française" in the Intellectual Politics of the Late 1970s', *French Historical Studies* (Vol. 22, No. 4, 1999)

French Intellectuals against the Left (Oxford: Berghahn, 2004)

Clark, Christopher and Kaiser, Wolfram (eds.), *Culture Wars: Secular–Catholic Conflict in Nineteenth-Century Europe* (Cambridge University Press, 2003)

Closets, François de, *La France et ses mensonges* (Paris: Denoël, 1977)

Plus encore (Paris: Fayard, 2006)

Toujours Plus (Paris: Grasset, 1984)

Club de l'Horloge, *Le péril bureaucratique* (Paris: Club de l'Horloge, 1980)

L'Union de la droite est-elle possible? (Paris: Club de l'Horloge, 1989)

Cohen, Samy (ed.), *Mitterrand et la sortie de la guerre froide* (Paris: Presses universitaires de France, 1998)

Cohn-Bendit, Daniel and Guiano, Henri, *La France est-elle soluble dans l'Europe?* (Paris: Albin Michel/Fondation Marc Bloch, 1999)

Cole, Alastair, *François Mitterrand: A Study in Political Leadership* (London: Macmillan, 1997)

Cole, Alastair and Raymond, Gino (eds.), *Redefining the French Republic* (Manchester University Press, 2006)

Collin, Denis, *Revive la République!* (Paris: Armand Colin, 2005)

Collini, Stefan, *Absent Minds: Intellectuals in Britain* (Oxford University Press, 2006)

Compagnon, Antoine, *Les antimodernes: De Joseph de Maistre à Roland Barthes* (Paris: Gallimard, 2005)

Conklin, Alice, *A Mission to Civilise: The Republican Idea of Empire in France and West Africa, 1895–1930* (Stanford University Press, 1997)

Coquery-Vidovitch, Catherine, 'Les débats actuels en histoire de la colonisation', *Tiers-Monde* (Vol. 28, No. 112, 1987)

Crick, Malcolm, *Explorations in Language and Meaning: Towards a Semantic Anthropology* (New York: Wiley, 1976)

Cross, Gary, *Immigrant Workers in Industrial France: The Making of a New Laboring Class* (Philadelphia: Temple University Press, 1983)

Crozier, Michel, *À contre-courant: mémoires 1969–2000* (Paris: Fayard, 2004)

État moderne, état modeste. Stratégies pour un autre changement (Paris: Fayard, 1987)

La crise de l'intelligence: essai sur l'impuissance des élites à se reformer (Paris: InterEditions, 1995)

La société bloquée, 3rd edn (Paris: Editions du Seuil, 1994 [1970])

Ma belle époque: mémoires 1947–1969 (Paris: Fayard, 2002)

Nouveau regard sur la société française (Paris: Odile Jacob, 2007)

Crozier, Michel and Tilliette, Bruno, *Quand la France s'ouvrira* (Paris: Fayard, 2000)

Daileader, Philip and Whalen, Philip (eds.), *French Historians 1900–2000: New Historical Writing in Twentieth-Century France* (London: Blackwell, 2010)

Darriulat, Philippe, *Les Patriotes: la gauche républicaine et la nation, 1830–1870* (Paris: Seuil, 2001)

Debord, Guy, *La Société du Spectacle* (Paris: Folio, 2000)

Debray, Régis, *A demain de Gaulle* (Paris: Le Débat, 1990)

Ce que nous voile le voile: la République et le sacré (Paris: Folio, 2004)

Contretemps: éloges des idéaux perdues (Paris: Folio, 1992)

La République expliquée à ma fille (Paris: Editions du Seuil, 1998)

Le moment fraternité (Paris: Gallimard, 2009)

Le Pouvoir Intellectuel en France (Paris: Editions Ramsey, 1979)

L'obscénité démocratique (Paris: Flammarion, 2008)

Mai 68, une contre-révolution réussie (Paris: Mille et une nuits, 2008)

Que vive la République! (Paris: Editions Odile Jacob, 1989)

Delanoë, Bertrand, *De l'audace. Entretiens avec Laurent Joffrin* (Paris: Robert Laffont, 2008)

Delors, Jacques, *Le nouveau concert européen* (Paris: Odile Jacob, 1992)

Mémoires (Paris: Plon, 2004)

Demolins, Edmond, *À quoi tient la supériorité des Anglo-Saxons* (Paris: Firmin-Didot, 1898)

Denord, François, 'La conversion au néo-libéralisme. Droite et libéralisme économique dans les années 1980', *Mouvements* (Vol. 5, No. 35, 2004)

'Le Prophéte, le Pélerin et le Missionnaire. La circulation internationale du néo-libéralisme et ses acteurs', *Actes de la recherche en sciences sociales* (No. 145, 2002)

Descombes, Vincent, *Le même et l'autre: Quarante-cinq ans de philosophie française (1933–1978)* (Paris: Editions de Minuit, 1979)

D'Iribarne, Philippe, 'L'intégration des immigrés: modèle français et modèle anglo-saxon', *Cahiers Français* (No. 352, 2009)

Drake, David, *Intellectuals and Politics in Post-War France* (London: Palgrave, 2002)

Drake, Helen (ed.), *French Relations with the European Union* (London: Routledge, 2005)

Dubet, François, *L'école juste* (Paris: Seuil/République des Idées, 2004)

Dubois, Laurent, 'La République Métissée: Citizenship, Colonialism, and the Borders of French History', *Cultural Studies* (Vol. 14, No. 1, 2000)

Duclert, Vincent and Prochasson, Christophe (eds.), *Dictionnaire Critique de la République* (Paris: Flammarion, 2002)

Dufourcq, Nicolas, *L'État providence sélectif* (Paris: Notes de la Fondation Saint-Simon, April 1994)

Duhamel, Eric, *François Mitterrand: l'unité d'un homme* (Paris: Flammarion, 1998)

Dutartre, Elisabeth (ed.), *Fonds Raymond Aron: Inventaire* (Paris: Editions BNF, 2007)

Echchaibi, Nabil, 'Republican Betrayal: Beur FM and the Suburban Riots in France', *Journal of Intercultural Studies* (Vol. 28, No. 3, 2007)

Eldridge, Claire, '"We've Never Had a Voice": Memory Construction and the Children of the Harkis (1962–1991)', *French History* (Vol. 23, No. 1, 2009)

Engerman, David (ed.), *Staging Growth: Modernization, Development and the Global Cold War* (Boston, MA: University of Massachusetts Press, 2003)

Englund, Steven, 'The Ghost of Nation Past', *Journal of Modern History* (Vol. 64, No. 2, 1992)

Derras, Eric et al. (eds.), *La gouvernabilité* (Paris: Presses Universitaires de France, 1996)

Esping-Andersen, Gøsta, *Trois leçons sur l'État-providence* (Paris: Seuil, 2008)

Fabre-Luce, Alfred, 'Benjamin Constant et ses partenaires', *Commentaire* (Vol. 1, No. 2, 1978)

Farnetti, Richard and Warde, Ibrahim, *Le modèle anglo-saxon en question* (Paris: Economica, 1997)

Favell, Adrian, *Eurostars and Eurocities* (Oxford: Wiley, 2008)

Philosophies of Integration (London: Macmillan 1998)

Finger, Matthias and Ruchat, Bérangère (eds.), *Pour une nouvelle approche du management public. Réflexions autour de Michel Crozier* (Paris: Editions Seli Arslan, 1997)

Finkielkraut, Alain, *Au nom de l'autre: réflexions sur l'antisémitisme qui vient* (Paris: Gallimard, 2003)

La défaite de la pensée (Paris: Gallimard, 1987)

Le Juif imaginaire (Paris: Seuil, 1980)

L'imparfait du présent: pièces brèves (Paris: Gallimard, 2002)

The Undoing of Thought (London: Claridge Press, 1988)

Finkielkraut Alain (ed.), *Où va la France?* (Paris: Stock, 2007)

Finkielkraut, Alain and Bruckner, Pascal, *Le nouveau désordre amoureux* (Paris: Seuil, 1977)

Finkielkraut, Alain and Lévy, B., *Le Livre et les livres: entretiens sur la laïcité* (Paris: Editions Verdier, 2006)

Fitoussi, Jean-Pierre, *La règle et le choix: de la souveraineté économique en Europe* (Paris: République des Idées/Seuil, 2002)

'Politiques d'égalité: pour les discriminations positives', *La revue de l'association des anciens élèves de Sciences Po* (No. 135, 2004)

Fitoussi, Jean-Pierre and Laurent, E., *Hawks and Handsaws: What Can France Learn from the 'Nordic Model'?* (Center for European Studies Working Paper Series, No. 168, 2008)

Fitoussi, Jean-Pierre and Laurent, E., *La nouvelle écologie politique: économie et développement durable* (Paris: République des Idées/Seuil, 2008)

Fitoussi, Jean-Pierre and Rosanvallon, Pierre, *Le nouvel âge des inégalités* (Paris: Editions du Seuil, 1998)

Flood, Christopher, 'National Republican Politics, Intellectuals and the Case of Pierre-André Taguieff', *Modern and Contemporary France* (Vol. 12, No. 2, 2004)

Flynn, Gregory (ed.), *Remaking the Hexagon: The New France in the New France* (London: Westview Press, 1995)

Forsdick, Charles and Murphy, David (eds.), *Francophone Postcolonial Studies: A Critical Introduction*, (London: Arnold, 2003)

Forsdick, Charles, 'Between "French" and "Francophone": French Studies and the Postcolonial Turn', *French Studies* (Vol. 59, 2005)

Fourastié, Jean, *Les Trente Glorieuses ou la Révolution invisible de 1946 à 1975* (Paris: Fayard, 1979)

Freund, Julien, 'Raymond Aron: Directeur de thèse', *Commentaire* (Vol. 8, No. 28–9, 1985)

Friedlander, Judith, *Vilna on the Seine: Jewish Intellectuals in France since 1968* (London: Yale University Press, 1990)

Fritz, Gérard, *L'idée du peuple en France du XVIIe au XIXe siècle* (Strasbourg: Presses Universitaires de Strasbourg, 1988)

Fukuyama, Francis, 'La fin de l'histoire', *Commentaire* (Vol. 22, No. 50, 1989)

The End of History and the Last Man (London: Harper Perennial, 1993)

Furet, François, '1789–1917: aller et retour', *Le Débat* (No. 57, Nov-Dec 1989)

'Ce que je dois à Tocqueville', *Commentaire* (No. 55, Autumn 1991)

'Chronique d'une décomposition', *Le Débat* (No. 83, Jan-Feb 1995)

Interpreting the French Revolution (Cambridge University Press, 1981)

'Interview (8 juin 1995)', *Derrière Le Mur. Revue universitaire de sciences sociales* (Spring 1996)

'L'Amérique de Clinton II', *Le Débat* (No. 94, 1997)

'La rencontre d'une idée et d'une vie', *Commentaire* (Vol. 8, No. 28–9, 1985)

La Révolution Française (Paris: Gallimard, 2007)

L'Atelier de l'Histoire (Paris: Flammarion, 1982)

'Le drapeau de l'anti-racisme sur le désert des idées', *Commentaire* (No. 51, 1990)

'Le système conceptuel de la Démocratie en Amérique', *Commentaire* (Vol. 3, No. 12, 1980)

'L'institut Raymond Aron', *Les Cahiers du Centre de Recherches Historiques* (No. 2, 1988)

'L'utopie démocratique à l'américaine', *le Débat* (No. 69, 1992)

Penser la Révolution Française (Paris: Gallimard, 1978)

Penser le XXème siècle (Paris: Robert Laffont, 2007)

'Quinet et Tocqueville: un dialogue posthume à propos de l'Ancien Régime', *Commentaire* (Vol. 7, No. 26, 1984)

Furet, François and Ozouf, Mona (eds.), *Le siècle de l'avènement républicain* (Paris: Gallimard, 1993)

Furet, François, Julliard, Jacques and Rosanvallon, Pierre, *La République du Centre: la fin de l'exception française* (Paris: Calmann-Lévy, 1988)

Gadrey, J., 'Modèle nordique vs. Modèle anglo-saxon', *L'Economie politique* (No. 19, 2003)

Gallo, Max, *L'amour de la France expliqué à mon fils* (Paris: Seuil, 1999)

'Une crise morale', *Commentaire* (Vol. 26, No. 103, 2003)

Gauchet, Marcel, *La condition historique* (Paris: Gallimard, 2003)

La condition politique (Paris: Gallimard, 2005)

La démocratie contre elle-même (Paris: Gallimard, 2002)

Geertz, Clifford, *The Interpretation of Cultures* (New York: Basic Books, 1977)

Gellner, Ernest, *Nations and Nationalism* (Oxford: Blackwell, 1996)

George, François, 'Un trop bref dialogue', *Commentaire* (Vol. 8, No. 28–9, 1985)

Geuss, Raymond, *History and Illusion in Politics* (Cambridge University Press, 2001)

Gibson, Ralph, *A Social History of French Catholicism* (London: Routledge, 1989)

Gildea, Robert, *Children of the Revolution: The French, 1799–1914* (London: Harvard University Press, 2008)

Gilroy, Paul, *There Ain't No Black in the Union Jack: The Cultural Politics of Race and Nation* (London: Hutchinson, 1987)

Girardet, Raoul, *Mythes et mythologies politiques* (Paris: Le Seuil, 1990)

Giscard d'Estaing, Valéry, *La démocratie française* (Paris: Fayard, 1976)

Godin, Emmanuel and Chafer, Tony (eds.), *The French Exception* (London: Berghahn, 2004)

Goldstein, Claudine, *République et républicains en France de 1848 à nos jours* (Paris: Ellipses, 2000)

Golsan, Richard, 'Memory's *Bombes à Retardement*: Maurice Papon, Crimes against Humanity, and 17 October 1961', *Journal of European Studies* (Vol. 28, 1998)

'Papon: The Good, the Bad, the Ugly', *SubStance* (Vol. 29, No. 1, 2000)

Gordon, Daniel A., *Immigrants and Intellectuals: May '68 and the Rise of Anti-racism in France* (Pontypool: Merlin Press, 2012)

Gorz, André, *Adieux aux prolétariat: au-delà du socialisme* (Paris: Galilée, 1980)

Métamorphoses du travail (Paris: Galilée, 1988)

Misères du présent, richesses du possible (Paris: Galilée, 1997)

Goulemot, Jean-Marie and Ory, Pascal, *Dernières questions aux intellectuels* (Paris: Olivier Orban, 1990)

Goux, Dominique and Maurin, Eric, '1992–2005: la décomposition du oui' (CEPREMAP Working Papers, 2005)

Guénif-Souilamas, Nacira, *Des 'Beurettes' aux descendants d'immigrants nord-africains* (Paris: Grasset, 2000)

Guérin, Serge, 'Entretien avec Michel Rocard', *Revue Civique* (Spring 2008)

Guillaume, Sylvie, *Consensus à la française* (Paris: Belin, 2002)

Le petit et moyen patronat dans la nation française, de Pinay à Raffarin (Bordeaux: Presses Universitaires de Bordeaux, 2005)

Guillaume, Sylvie (ed.), *Le centrisme en France aux XIXème et XXè siècles: un échec?* (Paris: Maison des Sciences de l'Homme Aquitaine, 2005)

Halévi, Ran, *L'experience du passé: François Furet dans l'atelier de l'histoire* (Paris: Gallimard, 2007)

Hammerschlag, Sarah, 'Reading May '68 through a Levinasian Lens: Alain Finkielkraut, Maurice Blanchot, and the Politics of Identity', *Jewish Quarterly Review* (Vol. 98, No. 4, 2008)

Hamon, Benoît and Rotman, Patrick, *La deuxième gauche. Histoire intellectuelle et politique de la CFDT* (Paris: Seuil, 2002 [1982])

Hamon, Hervé and Rotman, Patrick, *L'effet Rocard* (Paris: Stock, 1980)

Hargreaves, Alec, 'Beur Fiction: Voices from the Immigrant Community in France', *French Review* (Vol. 62, No. 4, 1989)

'Beurgeoisie: mediation or mirage', *Journal of European Studies* (Vol. 28, 1998)

Immigration, 'Race' and Ethnicity in Contemporary France (London: Routledge, 1995)

Harris, Ruth, 'Letters to Lucie: Spirituality, Friendship, and Politics During the Dreyfus Affair', *Past and Present* (Vol. 1, 2006)

Lourdes: Body and Spirit in a Secular Age (London: Penguin, 1999)

The Man on Devil's Island: Alfred Dreyfus and the Affair that Divided France (London: Penguin, 2011)

Hassner, Pierre, 'Aron et l'histoire du XXème siècle', *Commentaire* (Vol. 8, No. 28–9, 1985)

'Fin de l'histoire ou fin d'un cycle?', *Commentaire* (Vol. 21, No. 47, 1989)

'Raymond Aron et la philosophie des relations internationales', *Commentaire* (Vol. 31, No. 122, 2008)

Hatier, Cécile, 'The Liberal Message of Raymond Aron: A Substantial Legacy', *European Journal of Political Theory* (Vol. 2, No. 5, 2003)

Hayward, Jack, *Fragmented France: Two Centuries of Disputed Identity* (Oxford University Press, 2007)

'La persistance de l'antilibéralisme: rhétorique et réalité', *Pouvoirs* (No. 126, 2008)

Hazareesingh, Sudhir, *Intellectual Founders of the Republic: Five Studies in Nineteenth-Century French Political Thought* (Oxford University Press, 2001)

Intellectuals and the French Communist Party: Disillusion and Decline (Oxford: Clarendon Press, 1991)

Le mythe gaullien (Paris: Gallimard, 2010)

Political Traditions in Modern France (Oxford University Press, 1994)

Hazareesingh, Sudhir (ed.), *The Jacobin Legacy in Modern France* (Oxford University Press, 2002)

Herzfeld, Michael, *Cultural Intimacy: Social Poetics in the Nation-State* (London: Routledge, 2005)

Hewlett, Nicholas, *The Sarkozy Phenomenon* (London: Imprint Academic, 2011)

Ho Tai, Hue-Tam, 'Remembered Realms: Pierre Nora and French National Memory', *American Historical Review* (No. 106, 2001)

Hobsbawm, Eric, *Nations and Nationalism since 1780* (Cambridge University Press, 1990)

Hobsbawm, Eric and Ranger, Terence (eds.), *The Invention of Tradition* (Cambridge University Press, 1983)

Hoffmann, Stanley, *Chaos and Violence: What Globalisation, Failed States and Terrorism Mean for US Foreign Policy* (Lanham, MD: Rowman & Littlefield, 2006)

Decline or Renewal? France since the 1930s (New York: Viking Press, 1974)

'Être ou ne pas être français (I)', *Commentaire* (Vol. 18, No. 70, 1995)

'Être ou ne pas être français (II)', *Commentaire* (Vol. 18, No. 71, 1995)

The European Sisyphus: Essays on Europe, 1964–1994 (Oxford: Westview Press, 1995)

'Gaullism by any other name', *Foreign Policy* (No. 57, Winter 1984)

'Quand la France tient la bride à ses vieux démons', *Esprit* (June 1994)

'Raymond Aron and the Theory of International Relations', *International Studies Quarterly* (Vol. 29, No. 1, 1985)

'Un état sans frein et une société rétive', *Esprit* (May 1974)

House, Jim and Macmaster, Neil, *Paris 1961: Algerians, State Terror and Memory* (Oxford University Press, 2006)

'Time to Move On: A Reply to Jean-Paul Brunet', *Historical Journal* (Vol. 51, No. 2, 2008)

Howarth, David and Varouxakis, Giorgios, *Contemporary France* (London: Arnold, 2003)

Howarth, Jolyon and Cerny, Philip (eds.), *Elites in France: Origins, Reproduction and Power* (London: Frances Pinter, 1981)

Hunt, Lynn, *Politics, Culture and Class in the French Revolution* (London: Methuen, 1986)

Jackson, Julian, *France: The Dark Years, 1940–44* (Oxford University Press, 2001)

Jaffré, Philippe and Riès, Philippe, *Le jour où la France a fait faillite* (Paris: Editions Grasset, 2006)

Jainchill, Andrew, *Reimagining Politics after the Terror: The Republican Origins of French Liberalism* (London: Cornell University Press, 2008)

Jainchill, Andrew and Moyn, Samuel, 'French Democracy between Totalitarianism and Solidarity: Pierre Rosanvallon and Revisionist Historiography', *Journal of Modern History* (No. 76, 2004)

Jallon, Hugues and Mounier, Pierre, *Les enragés de la République* (Paris: Editions La Découverte, 1999)

Jarreau, Philippe, 'La société fermée et la fonction de l'antiaméricanisme', *Commentaire* (Vol. 26, No. 103, 2003)

Jaume, Lucien, *L'individu effacé, ou le paradoxe du libéralisme français* (Paris: Fayard, 1997)

Jay, Martin, *Marxism and Totality: The Adventures of a Concept from Lukács to Habermas* (Berkeley, CA: University of California Press, 1984)

Jelen, Christian, *Les casseurs de la République* (Paris: Plon, 1997)

Jennings, Jeremy, 'Citizenship, Republicanism and Multiculturalism in Contemporary France', *British Journal of Political Science* (Vol. 30, No. 4, 2000)

'Conceptions of England and its Constitution in Nineteenth-Century Political Thought', *Historical Journal* (Vol. 29, No. 1, 1986)

'France and the Anglo-Saxon Model: Contemporary and Historical Perspectives', *European Review* (Vol. 14, No. 4, 2006)

'Raymond Aron and the Fate of European Liberalism', *European Journal of Political Theory* (Vol. 2, 2003)

Revolution and the Republic: A History of Political Thought in France since the Eighteenth Century (Oxford University Press, 2011)

Jennings, Jeremy (ed.), *Intellectuals in Twentieth-Century France: Mandarins and Samurais* (New York: St Martin's Press, 1993)

Judaken, Jonathan, 'Alain Finkielkraut and the Nouveaux Philosophes: French-Jewish Intellectuals, the Afterlives of May '68 and the Rebirth of the National Icon', *Historical Reflections/Réflexions historiques* (Vol. 32, No. 1, 2006)

Judt, Tony, *The Burden of Responsibility: Blum, Camus, Aron and the French Twentieth Century* (London: University of Chicago Press, 1998)
Marxism and the French Left: Studies on Labour and Politics in France 1830–1981 (Oxford: Clarendon Press, 1986)
Past Imperfect: French Intellectuals, 1944–1956 (Oxford: Clarendon Press, 1992)
Reappraisals (London: Penguin, 2008)

Judt, Tony and Lacorne, Denis (eds.), *With Us or Against Us: Studies in Global Anti-Americanism* (London: Palgrave, 2004)

Juhem, Philippe, 'Entreprendre en politique. De l'extrême gauche au PS: la professionnalisation politique des fondateurs de SOS Racisme', *Revue française de science politique* (Vol. 51, Nos. 1–2, 2001)
'La participation des médias à l'émergence des mouvements sociaux: le cas de SOS Racisme', in *Réseaux* (Vol. 17, No. 98, 1999)

Julliard, Jacques, *La faute à Rousseau* (Paris: Seuil, 1985)
Le malheur français (Paris: Flammarion, 2005)
Les gauches françaises. 1762–2012: Histoire, politique et imaginaire (Paris: Flammarion, 2012)

Juppé, Alain, 'L'insoutenable légèreté du "déclinisme"', *Commentaire* (Vol. 26, No. 104, 2003)

Kaci, Rachid, *La République des lâches* (Paris: Editions des Syrtes, 2003)

Kaplan, Steven, *Adieu 89* (Paris: Fayard, 1993)

Kastoryano, Riva, *Negotiating Identities: States and Immigrants in France and Germany* (Princeton University Press, 2002)

Kelly, George Armstrong, *The Humane Comedy: Constant, Tocqueville and French Liberalism* (Cambridge University Press, 1992)

Kennedy, Sean, 'The End of Immunity? Recent Work on the Far Right in Interwar France', *Historical Reflections* (Vol. 34, No. 2, 2008)

Khilnani, Sunil, *Arguing Revolution: The Intellectual Left in Postwar France* (London: Yale University Press, 1993)

Kissinger, Henry, 'My Teacher', *Commentaire* (Vol. 8, No. 28–9, 1985)

Knapp, Andrew, *Gaullism since de Gaulle* (London: Dartmouth, 1994)

Knox, Edward, 'Regarder la France: une réflexion bibliographique', *French Review* (Vol. 72, No. 1, 1998)

Kojève, Alexandre, *Introduction to the Reading of Hegel: Lectures on the Phenomenology of Spirit*, ed. Allan Bloom (New York: Basic Books, 1969)

Kritzmann, Lawrence (ed.), *The Columbia History of Twentieth-Century French Thought*, (New York: Columbia University Press, 2006).

Kuisel, Richard, *Le capitalisme et l'État en France: modernisation et dirigisme au XXe siècle* (Paris: Gallimard, 1984)
Seducing the French: The Dilemma of Americanization (Berkeley: University of California Press, 1993)

Laborde, Cécile, *Critical Republicanism: The Hijab Controversy and Political Philosophy* (Oxford University Press, 2008)

'The Culture(s) of the Republic: Nationalism and Multiculturalism in French Republican Thought', *Political Theory* (Vol. 29, No. 5, 2001)

Français, encore un effort pour être républicains! (Paris: Seuil, 2010)

Lacorne, Denis (ed.), *The Rise and Fall of Anti-Americanism: A Century of French Perception* (Basingstoke: Macmillan, 1990)

Lacorne, Denis, Rupnik, J. and Toinet, M.-F., *L'Amérique dans les têtes: un siècle de fascinations et d'aversions* (Paris: Hachette, 1986)

Lacouture, Jean, *De Gaulle* (Paris: Seuil, 1986)

Lacroix, Justine, 'Le national-souverainisme en France et en Grande Bretagne', *Revue Internationale de Politique Comparée* (Vol. 9, No. 3, 2002)

Laloy, Jean, 'Un libéral passionné', *Commentaire* (Vol. 8, No. 28–9, 1985)

Lamberti, Jean-Claude, 'Tocqueville et la constitution de 1848', *Commentaire* (Vol. 7, No. 25, 1984)

'Tocqueville et les deux démocraties', *Commentaire* (Vol. 5, No. 19, 1982)

Landais, Camille, Piketty, Thomas and Saez, Emmanuel, *Pour une révolution fiscale: un impôt sur le revenu pour le XXIe siècle* (Paris: Seuil/La République des Idées, 2011)

Landfried, Julien, *Contre le communautarisme* (Paris: Armand Colin, 2007)

Lapeyronnie, Didier, 'Assimilation, mobilisation et action collective chez les jeunes de la seconde génération de l'immigration maghrébine', *Revue française de sociologie* (Vol. 28, No. 2, 1987)

Larkin, Maurice, *Church and State after the Dreyfus Affair* (London: Macmillan, 1974)

Laronde, Michel, 'La mouvance beur: une émergence médiatique', *French Review* (Vol. 61, No. 5, 1988)

Larrouturou, Pierre, *Le livre noir du libéralisme* (Paris: Editions du Rocher, 2007)

Laurence, John and Vaïsse, Justin, *Integrating Islam: Political and Religious Challenges in Contemporary France* (Washington, DC: Brookings Institution, 2006)

Lebaron, Frédéric, Gallemand, Florence and Waldvogel, Carole, 'Le 'modèle social français' (est à bout de souffle): genèse d'une *doxa* – 2005–2007', *La Revue de l'IRES* (No. 61, Vol. 2, 2009)

Le Boucher, Eric, *Economiquement incorrect* (Paris: Grasset, 2005)

Le Bras, Hervé, *Le démon des origines: la démographie et l'extrême droite* (Paris: Editions de l'Aube, 1998)

Le Bras, Hervé and Badinter, Elisabeth, *Retour de la race* (Paris: La Découverte, 2008)

Lefebvre, Alain and Méda, Dominique, *Faut-il brûler le modèle social français?* (Paris: Seuil, 2006)

Lefeuvre, Daniel, *Pour en finir avec une repentance coloniale* (Paris: Flammarion, 2006)

Lefort, Claude, *Essais sur le politique, XIXe – XXe siècles* (Paris: Editions du Seuil, 1986)

Le temps présent. Écrits 1945–2005 (Paris: Belin, 2007)

L'invention démocratique: les limites de la domination totalitaire (Paris: Fayard, 1994)

Un homme en trop: réflexions sur l'Archipel du Goulag (Paris: Editions du Seuil, 1986 [1976])

Le Gallou, Jean-Yves and Club de l'Horloge, *La Préférence nationale: Réponse à l'immigration* (Paris: Albin Michel, 1985)
Les racines du futur: demain la France (Paris: Editions Albatros, 1984)
Le Goff, Jean-Pierre and Nora, Pierre (eds.), *Constructing the Past: Essays in Historical Method* (Cambridge University Press, 1985 [1974])
Lellouche, Pierre, *Illusions gauloises* (Paris: Grasset, 2005)
Lesourne, Jacques, 'La maladie française', *Commentaire* (Vol. 28, No. 81, 1998)
'Les Rencontres de Pétrarque', *Commentaire* (Vol. 8, No. 34, 1986)
Lévi-Strauss, Claide, 'Aron était un esprit droit', *Commentaire* (Vol. 8, No. 28–9, 1985)
Lévy, Bernard-Henri, *American Vertigo: Travelling America in the Footsteps of Tocqueville* (London: Random House, 2006)
Levy, Jonah, *Tocqueville's Revenge: State, Society and Economy in Contemporary France* (London: Harvard University Press, 1999)
Lévy-Willard, Annette, 'Paris, le 11 septembre', *South Central Review* (Vol. 19, No. 2, 2002)
Lewis, Mary Dewhurst, *Boundaries of the Republic: Migrant Rights and the Limits of Universalism, 1918–1940* (London: Stanford University Press, 2007)
Liauzu, Claude, 'Les historiens saisi par les guerres de mémoires coloniales', *Revue d'histoire moderne et contemporaine* (Vol. 52, No. 4, 2005)
'Pour une histoire critique de la colonisation. Pour un travail de mémoire', *Hommes et Migrations* (No. 1231, 2001)
Liauzu, Claude and Manceron, Gilles (eds.), *La colonisation, la loi et l'histoire* (Paris: Editions Syllepse, 2006)
Lilla, Mark (ed.), *New French Thought: Political Philosophy* (London: Princeton University Press, 1994)
Lindenberg, Daniel, *Le rappel à l'ordre, Enquête sur les nouveaux réactionnaires* (Paris: Seuil, 2002)
Lindenberg, Daniel et al., *Esprit, 1932–2002: une revue dans l'histoire* (Paris: Editions Esprit, 2002)
Littré, Emile, *Dictionnaire de la langue française, Tome I* (Paris: Hachette, 1877)
Macé-Scaron, Joseph, *La tentation communautaire* (Paris: Plon, 2001)
Maclean, Máiri (ed.), *The Mitterrand Years: Legacy and Evaluation* (London: Macmillan, 1998)
Macmaster, Neil, *Colonial Migrants and Racism* (London: Macmillan, 1997)
Madelin, Alain, *Quand les autruches relèveront la tête* (Paris: Robert Laffont, 1995)
Madelin, Alain and Cercle Idées-Action, *Chers compatriotes . . .* (Paris: Editions Jean-Claude Lattès, 1994)
Mahoney, Daniel J., 'The Politic Liberal Rationalism of Raymond Aron', *Polity* (Vol. 24, No. 4, 1992)
Manent, Pierre, 'Aux origines du libéralisme: Benjamin Constant', *Commentaire* (Vol. 3, No. 11, 1980)
'La démocratie sans la nation', *Commentaire* (Vol. 19, No. 75, Autumn 1996)
'Le philosophe et l'Etat', *Commentaire* (Vol. 31, No. 121, 2008)
'Raymond Aron, éducateur', *Commentaire* (Vol. 8, No. 28–9, 1985)
'Situations du libéralisme', *Commentaire* (Vol. 8, No. 35, Autumn 1986)
Manent, Pierre, *Histoire intellectuelle du libéralisme* (Paris: Calmann-Lévy, 1987)

Les libéraux (Paris: Hachette, 1986)

Manent, Pierre, Hausheer, R., Karpinski, W. and Kaiser, W., *European Liberty: Four Essays on the Occasion of the 25th Anniversary of the Erasmus Prize Foundation* (Berlin: Springer, 1983)

Marseille, Jacques, *Empire colonial et capitalisme français: histoire d'un divorce* (Paris: Albin Michel, 1984)

La guerre des deux Frances (Paris: Editions Perrin, 2005)

Mathy, Jean-Philippe, *Extrême Occident: French Intellectuals and America* (London: University of Chicago Press, 1993)

French Resistance: The French-American Culture Wars (Minneapolis, MN: University of Minnesota Press, 2000)

Mbembe, Achille et al., *Ruptures postcoloniales: les nouveaux visages de la société française* (Paris: La Découverte, 2010)

Mentré, Paul, *Gulliver enchaîné, ou Comment dérèglementer l'économie* (Paris: Table Ronde, 1982)

'La politique économique du gouvernement Raffarin', *Commentaire* (Vol. 24, No. 99, 2002)

'Les politiques économiques libérales: bilan d'une décennie', *Commentaire* (Vol. 9, No. 41, 1988)

'Les privatisations. Bilan et perspectives', *Commentaire* (Vol. 14, No. 60, 1992)

'Les trois corbeaux ou le dilemme de l'économie française', *Commentaire* (Vol. 4, No. 19, 1982)

Merleau-Ponty, Maurice, *Humanism and Terror* (Boston, MA: Beacon Press, 1969)

Meunier, Sophie, 'La France qui se mondialise', *Commentaire* (Vol. 27, No. 105, 2004)

Minc, Alain, *Ce monde qui vient* (Paris: Grasset, 2004)

Contrepoints (Paris: Grasset, 1992)

Contrepoints II: Je persiste et signe (Paris: Grasset, 2002)

Français, si vous osiez . . . (Paris: Grasset, 1991)

La France de l'an 2000 (Paris: Odile Jacob, 1994)

Minogue, Keith, *Nationalism* (London: Batsford, 1967)

Mitterrand, François, *Coup d'état permanent* (Paris: Plon, 1964)

Molina, Esteban, *Le défi du politique: totalitarisme et démocratie chez Claude Lefort* (Paris: L'Harmattan, 2005)

Mongin, Olivier, 'Commentaire et le libéral catholicisme', *Esprit* (9/88)

'Déclin ou sentiment de déclin', *Commentaire* (Vol. 26, No. 104, 2003)

'L'été corse: Matignon et la réforme', *Esprit* (10/00)

'Nicolas Baverez: A consommer avec modération', *Esprit* (11/03)

Montbrial, Thierry de, 'Aron et l'action politique', *Commentaire* (Vol. 8, No. 28–9, 1985)

'La géopolitique entre guerre et paix', *Commentaire* (Vol. 33, No. 131, 2010)

Moruzzi, Norma Claire, 'A Problem with Headscarves: Contemporary Complexities of Political and Social Identity', *Political Theory* (Vol. 22, No. 4, 1994)

Moyn, Samuel, 'On the Intellectual Origins of François Furet's Masterpiece', *La Revue Tocqueville* (Vol. 29, No. 2, 2008)

Moyn, Samuel, *Origins of the Other: Emmanuel Levinas between Revelation and Ethics* (London: Cornell University Press, 2005)

Mulholland, Jon and Ryan, Louise, 'Trading Places: French Highly Skilled Migrants Negotiating Mobility and Emplacement in London', *Journal of Ethnic and Migration Studies* (Vol. 40, No. 4, 2014)

Ndiaye, Pap, *La condition noire: essai sur une minorité française* (Paris: Calmann-Lévy, 2008)

Nicolet, Claude, *L'idée républicaine en France: essai d'histoire critique* (Paris: Gallimard, 1982)

La République en France: état des lieux (Paris: Seuil, 1992)

Noiriel, Gérard, *État, nation, immigration* (Paris: Editions Bélin/Folio, 2001)

Immigration, antisémitisme et racisme en France (XIXe-XXe siècle): Discours publics, humiliations privées (Paris: Fayard, 2007)

Le Creuset Français (Paris: Edition du Seuil, 1988)

Les origines républicaines de Vichy (Paris: Hachette, 1999)

Longwy: immigrés et prolétaires (Paris: Presses Universitaires de France, 1984)

Penser avec, penser contre: itinéraire d'un historien (Paris: Belin, 2003)

Sur la crise de l'histoire (Paris: Belin, 1996)

Nora, Pierre, 'Le Débat', *Le Débat* (No. 1, May 1980)

Nora, Pierre (ed.), *Les Lieux de mémoire*, 7 vols. (Paris: Gallimard, 1984–1992)

Realms of Memory: Rethinking the French Past, trans. A. Goldhammer, 3 vols (London: Columbia University Press, 1996)

Nord, Philip, *The Republican Moment: Struggles for Democracy in Nineteenth-Century France* (London: Harvard University Press, 1995)

Northcutt, Wayne, 'François Mitterrand and the Political Use of Symbols: The Construction of a Centrist Republic', *French Historical Studies* (Vol. 17, No. 1, 1991)

Mitterrand (London: Holmes & Meier, 1992)

Olivennes, Denis, *Le modèle social français: un compromis malthusien* (Paris: Notes de la Fondation Saint-Simon, Jan 1998)

Les Notes de la Fondation Saint-Simon: Une expérience intellectuelle (1983–1999) (Paris: Calmann-Lévy, 1999)

'Modèle français: l'âge des arrogances', *Le Débat* (No. 134, 2005)

Olivennes, Denis and Baverez, Nicolas, *L'impuissance publique: l'État c'est nous* (Paris: Seuil, 1989)

Ozouf, Mona, *L'école, l'église et la République* (Paris: Editions Cana, 1982)

'L'idée républicaine et l'interprétation du passé national', *Annales* (Vol. 53, No. 6, 1998)

Paligot, Carole, *La République Raciale: paradigme racial et idéologie républicaine* (Paris: PUF, 2006)

Pavé, Francis (ed.), *L'analyse stratégique: sa genèse, ses application et ses problems actuels. Autour de Michel Crozier* (Paris: Seuil, 1993)

Paxton, Robert, *Vichy France: Old Guard and New Order, 1940–44* (London: Barrie & Jenkins, 1972)

Péan, Pierre, *Une jeunesse française. François Mitterrand, 1934–1947* (Paris: Fayard, 1994)

Peña-Ruiz, Henri, 'Culture, cultures et laïcité', *Hommes et Migrations* (No. 1259, Jan-Feb 2006)

La laïcite pour l'égalité (Paris: Fondation du 2 Mars, 2001)

Perreau-Saussine, Emile, *Alasdair Macintyre: une biographie intellectuelle: introduction aux critiques contemporaines du libéralisme* (Paris: Presses Universitaires de France, 2005)

Perreau-Saussine, Emile, *Catholicism and Democracy: An Essay in the History of Political Thought* (London: Princeton University Press, 2012)

Perrineau, Pascal, *Le choix de Marianne: pourquoi, pour qui votons-nous?* (Paris: Fayard, 2012)

Pettit, Philipp, *Republicanism: A Theory of Freedom and Government* (Oxford: Clarendon Press, 1997)

Peyrelevade, Jean, *Le capitalisme total* (Paris: Seuil/La République des idées, 2005)

Piketty, Thomas, *Capital in the Twenty-First Century* (London: Harvard University Press, 2014)

Pitt, Alan, 'A Changing Anglo-Saxon Myth: Its Development and Function in French Political Thought, 1860–1914', *French History* (Vol. 14, No. 2, 2000)

Pitte, Jean-Robert, *Jeunes, on vous ment! Reconstruire l'université* (Paris: Fayard, 2006)

Pitts, Jennifer, *A Turn To Empire: The Rise of Imperial Liberalism in Britain and France* (Oxford: Princeton University Press, 2005)

Podhoretz, Norman, 'Combattre pour la liberté', *Commentaire* (Vol. 8, No. 28–9, 1985)

Poltier, Hugues, *Passion du politique: la pensée de Claude Lefort* (Geneva: Labor et Fides, 1998)

Priestland, David, *Merchant, Soldier, Sage: A New History of Power* (London: Penguin, 2013)

Prochasson, Christophe, *François Furet: les chemins de la mélancolie* (Paris: Stock, 2013)

'Introuvable modèle républicain', *Cahiers Français: Les valeurs de la République* (No. 336, 2007)

Les intellectuels et le socialisme (Paris: Plon, 1997)

Rachlin, Nicole, 'Alain Finkielkraut and the Politics of Cultural Identity', *Substance* (No. 76–77, 1995)

Raffarin, Jean-Pierre, *92 Nous sommes tous des régionaux* (Paris: Projets Editions, 1992)

La dernière marche: lettre à Nicolas Sarkozy (Paris: Grasset, 2007)

La France de mai. Entretiens avec Eric Mandonnet (Paris: Grasset, 2003)

Pour une morale de l'action (Paris: Editions Hermé, 1992)

Pour une nouvelle gouvernance (Paris: L'Archipel, 2002)

Rapport, Michael, *Nationality and Citizenship in Revolutionary France: The Treatment of Foreigners 1789–99* (Oxford: Clarendon Press, 2000)

Raynaud, Philippe, 'La mort de Raymond Aron', *Esprit* (May 1984)

'Qu'est-ce que le libéralisme', *Commentaire* (Vol. 30, No. 118, 2007)

'Raymond Aron et Max Weber'. Epistémologie des sciences sociales et rationalisme critique', *Commentaire* (Vol. 8, No. 28–9, 1985)

Reader, Keith, *Intellectuals and the Left in France since 1968* (London: Macmillan, 1987)

Régis Debray: A Critical Introduction (London: Pluto Press, 1995)

'Three Post-1968 Itineraries: Régis Debray, Daniel Cohn-Bendit, Marin Karmitz', *South Central Review* (Vol. 16, No. 4, 1999)

Reardon, Bernard, *Liberalism and Tradition: Aspects of Catholic Thought in Nineteenth-Century France* (Cambridge University Press, 1975)

Rémond, René, *Les droites aujourd'hui* (Paris: L'Audibert, 2005)

Les droites en France (Paris: L'Audibert, 1982)

Renaut, Alain and Touraine, Alain, *Un débat sur la laïcité* (Paris: Stock, 2005)

Revel, Jean-François, *L'obsession anti-américaine: son fonctionnement, ses causes, ses inconséquences* (Paris: Plon, 2002)

'Raison pure et raison pratique', *Commentaire* (Vol. 21, No. 48, 1989)

Reynolds, Chris, *Memories of May'68: France's Convenient Consensus* (Cardiff: University of Wales Press, 2011)

Rieffel, Rémy, *La Tribu des clercs: Les intellectuels sous la Vème République (1958–1990)* (Paris: Editions Calmann-Lévy, 1993)

Rigaud, Jacques, *L'exception culturelle: culture et pouvoirs sous la Ve République* (Paris: Editions Grasset, 2001)

Robcis, Camille, '"China in Our Heads": Althusser, Maoism, and Structuralism', *Social Text* (Vol. 30, No. 1, 2012)

The Law of Kinship: Anthropology, Psychoanalysis, and the Family in France (London: Cornell University Press, 2013)

Robine, Jérémy, 'Les "indigènes de la République": nation et question postcoloniale', *Hérodote* (No. 120, 2006)

Rocard, Michel, *A l'épreuve des faits. Textes politiques 1979–1985* (Paris: Seuil, 1986)

'Entretien avec François Furet', *Le Débat* (No. 38, Vol. 1, 1986)

Parler vrai. Textes politiques précédés d'un entretien avec Jacques Julliard (Paris: Points, 1979)

Si la gauche savait. Entretiens avec Georges-Marc Benamou (Paris: Points, 2007)

Un pays comme le nôtre. Textes politiques 1986–9 (Paris: Seuil, 1989)

Rochefort, Florence, 'Foulard, genre et laïcité en 1989', *Vingtième siècle* (No. 75, 2002–3)

Rodgers, Daniel T., *Age of Fracture* (London: Harvard University Press, 2011).

Rogachevsky, Neil, 'Are Plebiscites Constitutional? A Disputed Question in the Plebiscite Campaign of 1870', *French History* (Vol. 27, No. 2, 2013)

Roger, Philippe, *L'ennemi américain: généalogie de l'antiaméricanisme français* (Paris: Seuil, 2002)

Rolland, Patrice, 'Equivoques du libéralisme: à propos de Benjamin Constant', *Commentaire* (Vol. 4, No. 15, 1981)

Roman, Joël, *Propositions pour l'école* (Paris: Notes de la Fondation Saint-Simon, 1998)

Roman, Joël and Donzelot, Jacques, '1972–1998: les nouvelles donnes du social', *Esprit* (March–April 1998)

Rosanvallon, Pierre, *Democracy Past and Future*, ed. S. Moyn (London: Columbia University Press, 2006)

L'âge de l'autogestion, ou la politique au poste de commandement (Paris: Editions du Seuil, 1976)

La contre-démocratie: la politique à l'âge de la defiance (Paris: Seuil, 2006)

La crise de l'État-providence (Paris: Editions Le Seuil, 1981)

La démocratie inachevée: histoire de la souveraineté du peuple en France (Paris: Gallimard, 2000)

La nouvelle crise de l'État providence (Paris: Notes de la Fondation Saint-Simon, Sept 1993)

La nouvelle question sociale: repenser l'État providence (Paris: Seuil, 1995)

Le capitalisme utopique: critique de l'idéologie économique (Paris: Editions du Seuil, 1979)

Le moment Guizot (Paris: Gallimard, 1985)

Le peuple introuvable: histoire de la représentation démocratique en France (Paris: Gallimard, 1998)

Le sacre du citoyen: histoire du suffrage universel en France (Paris: Gallimard, 1992)

'Mais où est donc passée l'autogestion?', *Passé Présent* (No. 4, 1984)

Misère de l'économie (Paris: Editions du Seuil, 1983)

Pour une histoire conceptuelle du politique. Leçon inaugurale au Collège de France faite le jeudi 28 mars 2002 (Paris: Editions du Seuil, 2004)

'Sur quelques chemins de traverse de la pensée politique en France', *Raisons politiques* (No. 1, 2001)

Rosanvallon, Pierre and Pech, Thierry (eds.), *La nouvelle critique sociale* (Paris: Seuil, 2006)

Rosanvallon, Pierre and Viveret, P., *Pour une nouvelle culture politique* (Paris: Editions du Seuil, 1977)

Ross, George, *Jacques Delors and European Integration* (Cambridge: Polity, 1995)

Roy, Olivier, 'Les immigrés dans la ville: peut-on parler de tension "ethniques"?', *Esprit* (May 93)

Rubel, Paula and Rosman, Abraham (eds.), *Translating Cultures: Perspective on Translation and Anthropology* (Oxford: Berg, 2003)

Ryan, Alan (ed.), *The Idea of Freedom: Essays in Honour of Isaiah Berlin* (Oxford University Press, 1979)

Safran, William, 'The Mitterrand Regime and its Policies of Ethnocultural Accommodation', *Comparative Politics* (Vol. 18, No. 1, 1985)

'Politics and Language in Contemporary France: Facing Supranational and Infranational Challenges', *International Journal of the Sociology of Language* (Vol. 137, 1999)

'State, Nation, National Identity, and Citizenship: France as a Test Case', *International Political Science Review* (Vol. 12, No. 3, 1991)

Sahlins, Marshall, *Culture in Practice* (New York: Zone Books, 2000)

How Natives Think: about Captain Cook, For Example (London: University of Chicago Press, 1995)

Said, Edward, *Orientalism* (London: Penguin, 1995)

Salin, Pascal, 'Démocratie et liberté', *Commentaire* (Vol. 8, No. 36, 1986)

'Le piège de la social-démocratie', *Commentaire* (Vol. 5, No. 20, 1982)

Santoni, Georges, 'Trois sociologues parlent de la France I', *French Review* (Vol. 56, No. 5, 1983)

Sayad, Abelmalek, *La double absence: des illusions de l'émigré aux souffrances de l'immigré* (Paris: Seuil, 1999)

Schnapper, Dominique, *La communauté des citoyens: sur l'idée moderne de nation* (Paris: Seuil, 1994)

La France de l'Intégration (Paris: Gallimard, 1991)

La relation a l'autre: au cœur de la pensée sociologique (Paris: Seuil, 1998)

'La République face aux communautarismes', *Études* (Vol. 2, 2004)

'Les enjeux démocratiques de la statistique ethnique', *Revue française de sociologie* (Vol. 49, No. 1, 2008)

Qu'est-ce que l'intégration? (Paris: Folio, 2005)

'Unité nationale et particularismes culturels', *Commentaire* (Vol. 10, No. 38, 1987)

Schneider, Robert, *Michel Rocard* (Paris: Stock, 1987)

Schor, Ralph, *Opinion Française et les Etrangers (1919–1939)* (Paris: Publications de la Sorbonne, 1985)

Scioldo-Zürcher, Yann, *Devenir métropolitain: Politique d'intégration et parcours de rapatriés d'Algérie en métropole (1954–2005)* (Paris: Editions de l'EHESS, 2010)

Scott, Joan Wallach, *Parité! L'universel et la différence des sexes* (Paris: Albin Michel, 2005)

The Politics of the Veil (London: Princeton University Press, 2007)

'Symptomatic Politics: The Banning of Islamic Head Scarves in French Public Schools', *French Politics, Culture and Society* (Vol. 23, No. 3, 2005)

Shepard, Todd, *Invention of Decolonization: The Algerian War and the Remaking of France* (London: Cornell University Press, 2008)

Shields, Jim, *The Extreme Right in France, from Pétain to Le Pen* (London: Routledge, 2007)

'Marine Le Pen and the "New" FN: A Change of Style or of Substance?', *Parliamentary Affairs* (Vol. 66, No. 1, 2013)

Silverman, Max, *Deconstructing the Nation: Immigration, Racism and Citizenship in Modern France* (London: Routledge, 1992)

Simon, P., 'Raymond Aron dans l'histoire du siècle', *Vingtième Siècle* (No. 9, 1986)

Sirinelli, Jean-François, *Comprendre le XXe siècle français* (Paris: Fayard, 2005)

Sirinelli, Jean-François, *Les intellectuels en France, de l'affaire Dreyfus à nos jours* (Paris: Armand Colin, 1986)

Sirinelli, Jean-François (ed.), *Histoire des droites en France, 3 vols.* (Paris: Gallimard, 1992)

Skinner, Quentin, 'Meaning and Understanding in the History of Ideas', *History and Theory* (Vol. 8, No. 1, 1969)

Slama, Alain-Gérard, 'Le triomphe de l'idée', *Commentaire* (Vol. 22, No. 49, 1990)

Smith, Timothy, *France in Crisis: Welfare, inequality and globalisation since 1980* (Cambridge University Press, 2004)

Smouts, Marie-Claude (ed.), *La situation postcoloniale. Les postcolonial studies dans le débat français* (Paris: Presses de Sciences Po, 2007)

Société des amis de Raymond Aron, *Bulletins d'information, 1985–2010* (Paris: Société des amis de Raymond Aron, 1985–2010)

'Société des amis de Raymond Aron', *Commentaire* (Vol. 8, No. 31, 1985)

Sorman, Guy, *La révolution conservatrice américaine* (Paris: Pluriel, 1985)

La solution libérale (Paris: Fayard, 1986 [1985])

Spitz, Jean-Fabien, 'La culture politique républicaine en question: Pierre Rosanvallon et la critique du "jacobinisme" français', *Revues politiques* (No. 15, 2004)

Stasse, François, *L'économie de la santé en France: l'heure des choix* (Paris: Notes de la Fondation Saint-Simon, Nov 1993)

Stedman Jones, Gareth, *Languages of Class: Studies in English Working-Class History, 1932–1982* (Cambridge University Press, 1983)

Sternhell, Zeev, *Ni droite ni gauche: l'idéologie fasciste en France* (Paris: Fayard, 2000)

Stoffaës, Christian, 'Apprivoiser le libéralisme', *Commentaire* (Vol. 10, No. 41, 1988)

Stoffaës, Christian et al. (eds.), *Psychanalyse de l'antilibéralisme: les Française ont-ils raison d'avoir peur?* (Paris: Saint-Simon, 2006)

Stora, Benjamin, *La gangrène et l'oubli* (Paris: La Découverte, 1991)

Stora, Benjamin and Hémery, Daniel (eds.), *Histoires coloniales. Héritages et transmissions* (Paris: Bibliothèque Centre Pompidou, 2007)

Strauss, David, *Menace in the West: The Rise of French Anti-Americanism in Modern Times* (London: Greenwood Press, 1978)

Strauss-Kahn, Dominique, *La Flamme et le Cendre* (Paris: Hachette, 2003 [2002])

Oui! Lettre ouverte aux enfants d'Europe (Paris: Grasset, 2004)

Sudlow, Brian J. (ed.), *National Identities in France* (London: Transaction Press, 2011)

Taguieff, Pierre-André, *Les fins de l'antiracisme* (Paris: Editions Michalon, 1995)

La force du préjugé: essai sur le racisme et ses doubles (Paris, 1987)

La République enlisée: pluralisme, communautarisme et citoyenneté (Paris: Editions des Syrtes, 2005)

La République menacée: entretien avec Philippe Petit (Paris: Textuel, 1996)

'Le néo-racisme différencialiste', *Langage et société* (No. 34, 1985)

Les contre-réactionnaires: le progressisme entre illusion et imposture (Paris: Denoel, 2007)

Résister au bougisme (Paris: Fondation du 2 Mars, 2001)

Sur la Nouvelle Droite: jalons d'une analyse critique (Paris: Descartes, 1994)

Taithe, Bertrand, 'Should the Third Republic Divide Us the Least?', *French History* (Vol. 18, No. 2, 2004)

Taylor, Charles, *Philosophy and the Human Sciences*, Philosophical Papers 2 (Cambridge University Press, 1985)

Térrasse, Jean-Marie and Linhart, Virginie, *Génération Beur* (Paris: Plon, 1989)

Tévanian, Pierre and Tissot, Sylvie, *Mots à Maux: le dictionnaire du lepénisation de l'esprit* (Paris: Dagorno, 1998)

Thatcher, Margaret, *The Collected Speeches of Margaret Thatcher* (London: HarperCollins, 1997)

Thénault, Sylvie, 'France–Algérie. Pour un traitement commun du passé de la guerre d'indépendance', *Vingtième Siècle* (No. 85, 2005)

'L'état d'urgence (1955–2005). De *l'Algérie coloniale à la France contemporaine: destin d'une loi*', *Le Mouvement Social* (No. 218, 2007)

Thibaud, Paul, 'L'oeil du cyclone: Raymond Aron', *Esprit* (May 84)

'Rendre plus sobre', *Commentaire* (Vol. 10, No. 41, Spring 1988)

Thier, Maike, 'The View from Paris: "Latinity", "Anglo-Saxonism", and the Americas, as Discussed in the *Revue des Races Latines*, 1857–1864', *International History Review* (Vol. 3, No. 2, 2011)

Todd, Emmanuel, *After the Empire: The Breakdown of the American Order* (New York: Columbia University Press, 2003)

Illusion économique. Essai sur la stagnation des sociétés développées (Paris: Folio, 1999)

Toinet, Marie-France, 'French Pique and Piques Françaises', *Annals of the American Academy of Political and Social Science* (Vol. 497, 1988)

Tombs, Robert, *France 1814–1914* (London: Longman, 1996)

Tombs, Robert (ed.), *Nationhood and Nationalism in France* (London: HarperCollins, 1991)

Tombs, Robert and Tombs, Isabelle, *That Sweet Enemy* (London: Heinemann, 2006)

Toulemonde, Bernard, 'La discrimination positive dans l'éducation: des ZEP à Sciences-Po', *Pouvoirs* (No. 111, 2004)

Touraine, Alain (ed.), *Le Grand Refus* (Paris: Fayard, 1996)

Touraine, Alain, Wieviorka, Michel and Dubet, F., *Le mouvement ouvrier* (Paris: Fayard, 1984)

van Gelderen, Martin and Skinner, Quentin (eds.), *Republicanism: A Shared European Heritage*, 2 vols. (Cambridge University Press, 2005)

Verdo, Geneviève, 'Pierre Rosanvallon, archéologue de la démocratie', *Revue historique* (No. 623, 2002–3)

Vergès, Françoise, *La mémoire enchaînée* (Paris: Albin Michel, 2006)

Vinen, Richard, *Bourgeois Politics in France, 1945–1951* (Cambridge University Press, 2002)

Vries, Hent de (ed.), *Political Theologies* (New York: Fordham University Press, 2006)

Wahrman, Dror, *Imagining the Middle Class: The Political Representation of Class in Britain, c. 1780–1840* (Cambridge University Press, 1995)

Wall, Irwin, 'From Anti-Americanism to Francophobia: The Saga of French and American Intellectuals', *French Historical Studies* (Vol. 18, No. 4, 1994)

Weber, Eugen, *Peasants into Frenchmen: The Modernization of Rural France, 1870–1914* (Stanford, CA: Stanford University Press, 1977)

Weil, Patrick, *La France et ses étrangers* (Paris: Folio, 1991)

La République et sa diversité (Paris: Seuil, 2005)

Weymans, Wim, 'Freedom through Political Representation: Lefort, Gauchet and Rosanvallon on the Relationship between State and Society', *European Journal of Political Theory* (No. 263, Vol. 4, 2005)

Wieviorka, Michel, *La différence. Identités culturelles: enjeux, débats et politiques* (Paris: Fayard, 2001)

La diversité. Rapport à la ministre de l'Enseignement supérieur et de la Recherche (Paris: Robert Laffont, 2008)

Le printemps du politique: pour en finir avec le déclinisme (Paris: Robert Laffont, 2007)

L'espace du racisme (Paris: Seuil, 1991)

Neuf leçons de sociologie (Paris: Pluriel, 2011)

Pour la prochaine gauche. Le monde change; la gauche doit changer aussi (Paris: Odile Jacob, 2011)

L'espace du racisme (Paris: Seuil, 1991)

Wieviorka, Michel (ed.), *Racisme et modernité* (Paris: La Découverte, 1992)

Une société fragmentée: le multiculturalisme en débat (Paris: La Découverte, 1996)

Wilcox, Lynne, '*Coup de Langue*: The Amendment to Article 2 of the Constitution: An Equivocal Interpretation of Linguistic Pluralism?', *Modern and Contemporary France* (Vol. 2, No. 3, 1994)

Wilkes, George (ed.), *Britain's Failure to Enter the European Community, 1961–63* (London: Frank Cass, 1997)

Winock, Michel, *Histoire politique de la revue Esprit* (Paris: Seuil, 1975)

La Fièvre Hexagonale: les grandes crises politiques 1871–1969 (Paris: Calmann-Lévy, 1986)

Winter, Bronwyn, *Hijab and the Republic: Uncovering the French Headscarf Debate* (Syracuse, NY: Syracuse University Press, 2008)

Wolin, Richard, *The Wind from the East: French Intellectuals, the Cultural Revolution and the Legacy of the 1960s* (Princeton University Press, 2010)

Woloch, Isser, 'On The Latent Illiberalism of the French Revolution', *American Historical Review* (Vol. 95, No. 9, 1990)

Wolton, Dominique, '"Je ne suis pas la conscience universelle . . ."', *Commentaire* (Vol. 8, No. 28–9, 1984)

Wood, Nancy, 'Memory on Trial in Contemporary France: The Case of Maurice Papon', *History and Memory* (Vol. 11, No. 1, 1999)

Zeldin, Theodore, *France 1848–1945: Politics and Anger* (Oxford University Press, 1973)

Unpublished material

Behrent, Michael, 'Anti-Statism in Theory and Practice: Foucault and the Second Left', unpublished ms. (2011)

Berstein, Serge, 'La gauche française entre marxisme et République', paper presented at the conference 'Origine et modernité des valeurs républicaines', Belfort, France (12–13 November 2010)

Châton, Gwendal, 'La Libertée Retrouvée: Une histoire du libéralisme politique en France à travers les revues aroniennes "Contrepoint" et "Commentaire"', PhD thesis, Université de Rennes-I, Faculté de Droit et de Sciences Politiques (2006)

Guillaume, Sylvie and Sirinelli, Jean-François, 'Les marges en politique: le rocardisme', series of papers presented at the Centre d'histoire de Sciences Po (14 December 2010).

Jones, Colin, 'Les Anglo-Saxons in French Culture', paper presented at
    Cambridge University (2005)
Juhem, Philippe, 'SOS Racisme. Histoire d'une mobilisation "apolitique".
    Contribution à une analyse des transformations des représentations
    politiques après 1981', PhD thesis, Université de Nanterre: Faculté de
    Sciences Politiques (1998)
Prochasson, Christophe, 'François Furet, la révolution et le futur passé de la
    gauche française', paper presented at the Colloquium in honour of Malcolm
    Crook, Oxford (24 November 2010)
Stewart, Iain, 'Raymond Aron and the French Liberal Renaissance', PhD thesis,
    University of Manchester, Department of History (2011)

Audiovisual sources

Audiovisual sources were consulted for the period 1980–2011 inclusive.
I have included here only programmes that repeat on a weekly or
monthly basis. Details of specific broadcasts are given in the footnotes.

Radio

- France Culture, *Du grain à moudre*
- France Culture, *Répliques*
- France Culture, *Rumeur du Monde*
- France Culture, *Radio Libre*

Television

- Antenne 2, *Du côté de chez Fred*
- Antenne 2, *Journal télévisé, 20h*
- France 2, *Mots croisés*
- France 2, *À vous de juger*
- France 5/La Cinquième, *C dans l'air*
- France 5/La Cinquième, *Ripostes*
- France 5/La Cinquième, *On aura tout lu!*

I also made use of interviews, debates and discussions posted on *You-
Tube* and *Dailymotion* (for instance, by the French news agency
Mediapart).

Music/Audio/Film

- Cheb Mami, *Meli Meli* (Virgin Music, 1998)
- *Anthologie Sonore des discours de François Mitterrand* (1981–95) (France
  Inter/Editions Frémeaux)
- *La Marche* (dir. Nabil ben Yadir, 2013)

Internet resources and websites

The internet is a rich but fallible resource. Websites disappear; links fail; scholarly reference apparatus mysteriously goes missing. Nevertheless, it has become an invaluable tool and a forum for political debate at least as vibrant as pamphlets and political tracts in earlier periods. I frequently made use of activist websites, government portals, search engines and blogs as part of my research. Those which I found particularly useful or relevant are listed individually in the footnotes.

Index

20337574R00174

Printed in Great Britain
by Amazon